Doing Research in Political Science

Doing Research in Political Science

second edition

**Paul Pennings, Hans Keman
and Jan Kleinnijenhuis**

SAGE Publications
London • Thousand Oaks • New Delhi

SAGE Publications Ltd
1 Oliver's Yard
55 City Road
London EC1Y 1SP

SAGE Publications Inc.
2455 Teller Road
Thousand Oaks, California 91320

SAGE Publications India Pvt Ltd
B-42, Panchsheel Enclave
Post Box 4109
New Delhi 110 017

British Library Cataloguing in Publication data

A catalogue record for this book is available
from the British Library

ISBN 978-1-4129-0377-6

Library of Congress Control Number Available

Typeset by C&M Digitals (P) Ltd., Chennai, India

Contents

Preface

This second edition of *Doing Research in Political Science* is a thoroughly revised and updated version of the book that was originally published in 1999. In revising this edition we have benefited from several constructive and positive reviews and personal communications. One comment in particular made us reconsider the target readership for which this textbook is intended. Apparently – so some of the critics maintained – the level of information makes the book especially suitable for *advanced* students (e.g. in the final year of BA training, during MA studies and in the preliminary stages of a PhD). With this caveat in mind we have rewritten parts of the book and attempted to improve the presentation.

The book maintains its original structure consisting of three parts representing in our view the basic stages of any theory-driven empirical-analytical research in the social and, in particular, the political sciences. In each chapter there is an introduction to its contents, and at the end there is a list of the main topics covered, which may help both teacher and student to find the information she or he needs. In addition, each chapter contains examples that are taken from existing comparative research and are partially based on data made accessible by us via the World Wide Web (http://research.fsw.vu.nl/DoingResearch).

In Part 1 we present our own arguments concerning the comparative approach in the social sciences: namely, that any empirical research ought to be theory-driven and must be formulated in a well-elaborated research design. Part 2 is essential reading for those who wish to understand the use of (advanced) statistics in order to be able to conduct an explanatory analysis (including its caveats and pitfalls!). Part 3 can be seen as an attempt to pull together the threads of our way of doing comparative research and will be of interest to any reader, whether a freshman or an advanced student of comparative politics and social sciences at large.

Without claiming that this approach is the one and only way to teach comparative methods and statistics in political science, we are certain that it offers a valuable 'springboard' to judging the comparative information with which most, if not all, students are confronted. It will help the student to shape a theory-inspired research design in such a way that it leads to plausible and adequate results. These are valuable skills that are lacking in too many textbooks that focus on methodology.

During the process of writing this book, we have benefited from contributions many institutions, scholars and students, to whom we wish to express our thanks. First of all, the Essex Summer School in Social Science Data Analysis and Collection gave us the chance to test the draft version of the book on an international group of graduate students. We thank a number of colleagues for their detailed and helpful corrections to the manuscript. Linde Wolters, an assistant in our department, carefully organized the references and bibliography. Sabine Luursema has been helpful in producing the manuscript. Klaus Armingeon, Ian Budge, Kaare Strøm, Ross Burkhart, Michael S. Lewis-Beck and Alan Siaroff kindly permitted us to use their data in this book. Valuable advice on the whole or parts of the manuscript have been given by Klaus Armingeon (Berne), Francis G. Castles (Edinburgh), Jan-Erik Lane (Geneva and Singapore), Arend Lijphart (San Diego), Peter Mair (Leiden), Michael McDonald (Binghamton), Lawrence LeDuc (Toronto), Guy Whitten (Texas) and Ekhart Zimmerman (Dresden).

Finally, we wish to note that this book has been a genuine example of 'collective action'. At the same time the 'order of appearance' of the authors indicates the relative input given by each author.

Class material is available at http://research.fsw.vu.nl/DoingResearch

Paul Pennings
Hans Keman
Jan Kleinnijenhuis
Amsterdam, Summer 2005

Part 1

Comparative Methodology

Comparative methodology and statistics in political science

1.1 Introduction

Almost everyone watches daily TV, regularly reads a daily newspaper and often discusses what goes on in the world. These activities shape our views on society and, in particular, influence our views on and perspective of the role and impact of politics on societal developments. In this era of easy access to electronic communication (e.g. Internet), worldwide TV coverage of events (e.g. CNN) and rapid changes in the political mapping of the world (globalization), one is confronted not only with a multitude of bits and pieces of information, but also with various and often conflicting opinionated views what events may mean and what consequences they may have for our lives and the society we are part of and live in.

Although we do not realize it all the time (or at all) we use this information in its multifarious forms in a comparative way. Both the 'messengers' (e.g. journalists, political spokesmen and so-called opinion leaders) and the 'receivers' (readers, TV watchers, person-to-person communicators) are, more or less consciously, using the 'art' of comparing in order to come to a more or less well-founded interpretation of what goes on in public life.

The *first* point of departure of this book is therefore not only that students of social and political sciences are in fact comparing information to form an opinion, but that everyone is doing this in assessing the facts of life around him or her. For instance, how often do you use the words 'more' and 'less' or 'bigger' and 'smaller', and this is 'different' from or 'similar' to that, and so on? All these expressions, used by everyone in their daily conversation, basically imply that you (seem to) have a comparative idea about what occurs in reality. And not only that – most of the time, if not always, you do deliver a statement about, for instance, politics and society that is, more or less, implicitly of an evaluating nature. To give an example: in New Zealand in 1996 the first elections were held under a new system (it used to be 'First Past the Post' and it is now a variation of a proportional representation electoral system). The electoral outcome necessitated the formation of a coalition government instead of a one-party government. Apart from the fact that this type of government and the related procedure of government formation were new to both the public and the politicians, everyone could now compare the actual result of changing the electoral system and what it implies in reality. Hence, one could now evaluate what goes on by means of comparing the old with the new situation.

The 'art of comparing' is thus one of the most important cornerstones to develop knowledge about society and politics and insights into what is going on, how things develop and, more often than not, the formulation of statements about why this is the case and what it may mean to all of us. To take another example: in a number of Western European democracies one can witness recently a rise of so-called 'populist' parties (e.g. in Austria, Belgium, France, Italy, and the Netherlands; see Mair, 2002). The problem that emerged was *how* to define 'populism' as such in order to indicate which party was more (or less) populist, or – for instance – extreme right-wing or not, and therefore a threat to the existing party system (Mény and Surel, 2002). Hence, the problem was *less* to observe the phenomenon, and more *how* to measure it properly from a comparative point of view.

Yet, and this is our *second* point of departure, the use and application of the *comparative method* is often not systematic, nor is it applied rigorously in most cases. This may result not only in unfounded opinions or flawed conclusions, but also in biased views of reality as well as in inappropriate generalizations about what goes on in society. In this book we wish to introduce you to the comparative method and related statistical tools in order to help you to reduce these hazards and to develop standards for you and others to gain a more sustainable view on the world. In addition, we shall provide you with a clear schedule to develop an adequate research design that helps to avoid the mistakes and biases. This is the assignment of Part I.

In this chapter we shall therefore discuss how to do research in 'comparative politics'. This means that the focus is on the development of a proper research design that enables one to translate questions about real-world events into observations, which allow for drawing systematically conclusions that can be generalized. For instance: is there a relationship between the (electoral) rise of populist parties and a growing dissatisfaction of the public with the working of parliamentary democracy? This type of Research Question can and should be elaborated in a proper Research Design. This crucial step in doing research in political science is the subject of the next chapter. It requires the *elaboration* of the phenomenon under review (e.g. what is populism, and which parties can be viewed as 'populist' or 'right wing'?), the *mode of analysis* that makes a comparison useful and meaningful (e.g. relating the emergence of populist parties to subsequent events such as elections and stable government), and – in addition – the *empirical* investigation of *all* relevant cases (in comparing political systems that allow for corroborating hypotheses). Hence, instead of focusing on 'events' or isolated developments, the point of departure of our approach is:

- developing systematic knowledge that transcends mere description and allows for generalizations (i.e. external validity);
- deriving answers to questions on the basis of existing *theory* or, if possible, plausible hypotheses (i.e. theory guidance);
- striving for exact information and comparable indicators that are *reliable* and open to replication (i.e. internal validity).

In summary: without a proper research question and research design, the 'art of comparing' becomes meaningless and – which is worse – may lead to dubious evidence and conclusions that affect many in society. Max Weber – the famous German sociologist – warned against these practices in 1918 in his major work *Economy and Society* (Weber, 1972), by discussing value-free science *vis-à-vis* ideologically driven analysis, which would not only harm scientific progress, but also jeopardize the correct use and application of social scientific results in practice (see Bendix, 1977; Giddens, 1971).

From this follows, as the *third* point of our presentation, that it is crucial to know from the beginning *what, when* and *how* to compare. Seemingly this triad goes almost without saying. Yet, it is vital for any comparative analysis to ask him or she whether or not there is indeed a proper answer to these methodological questions. If not, the chances to come up with valid and reliable answers will be reduced and the quality of knowledge advanced will be less. Hence, you must know beforehand what the phenomenon is that you wish to research, when – or at what point of time or period under review – the phenomenon can be best studied, and how to do this.

This highlights perhaps the most important message we wish to emphasize. We view the 'art of comparing', or what is generally called the 'comparative approach' to political and social science, *not* as an 'art' in itself (or a method *per se*), but as one of the most adequate ways to connect ideas (theory) about society and politics with what is actually going on in the world we live in (i.e. empirically founded facts). In short, we wish to introduce you to the comparative approach in such a way that one can explain convincingly and plausibly what is going on in the real world of politics and society.

Box 1.1   Comparing as a basic tool of the social sciences

The British poet Rudyard Kipling (1865–1936) wrote: 'And what should they know of England who only England know?' He meant to say that without comparing there is little to gain from a description only. Therefore the 'art of comparing' is a basic tool for linking ideas and, eventually, theory to evidence. Conversely, without theory a comparison remains meaningless. Our view is thus that 'doing research' in the social sciences always implies – be it implicitly or explicitly – the application of the comparative approach to gain knowledge of politics and society and to assess its plausibility.

1.2 The Comparative Approach to Political and Social Science: Theory and Method

We contend that the comparative approach and its methodological application must be conducted by means of theory-driven research questions. This is to say: a research question must be formulated as a point of departure of comparative investigation, which enables the student to reflect on what, when and how to compare and for what purpose. If not, the comparison becomes a recording instrument only. This, however, is not our goal, nor is it in our view scientific. Scientific activities always imply the quest for explanations, which are not only empirically based and yield systematic results, but also lead to results which are plausible. It is vital to realize that throughout this book we shall contend that empirical-analytical analysis is an instrument to develop social and political knowledge that is both scientifically valid and plausible for a wider audience.

Valid means here not only whether or not it is devoid of mistakes of the 'Third Order' (Blalock, 1979), i.e. avoiding wrong operationalizations, incorrect indicators and inadequate levels of measurement and inferring false causal conclusions – these matters will be dealt with in Part II of this book – but primarily whether or not the research design is indeed adequately derived from the research question which underlies the comparative research. Validity in comparative (and other types of) research is a very central concept. However, more often than not, it is used in different ways and its use may well confuse the student. Throughout this book we shall employ the concept as follows:

- *Internal validity* concerns the question whether or not the measurements used in a given research are properly, i.e. correctly, operationalized in view of the theoretical concept as intended. For instance: in a research project on political parties, can *all* the parties under review be considered to be identical in terms of their properties (e.g. participating in elections by putting forward candidates for office), and can they be seen as unique entities and not be confused with other types of social and political movements (like interest groups or new social movements)? Hence research results are internally valid if and when they are *truly* comparative, i.e. yield the *same* results for all cases under review (if not, then a case is 'deviant').

- *External validity* presupposes that the concepts used in a given piece of research, and the related outcomes, apply not only to the cases under review but to *all similar* cases that satisfy the conditions set out in the research question and related research design. Similarity implies here comparability through space or time. For example, the factors found to explain the variations in government formation in terms of the resulting types of government (e.g. majority or minority and one-party versus multi-party governments) should also apply to those cases that were not included or in periods that were not covered in the original analysis. Another example would be the study of populism, right-wing parties and party system development (see, for instance, Kitschelt, 2002; Pennings and Keman, 2003). Obviously this requires careful and qualified arguments and spills over into the quality of operationalization and measurement (i.e. internal validity!). Hence research results are viewed as externally valid if they yield *truly* comparable results for *similar* cases that have *not* yet been under review. This implies that one would expect that a replication of such a research should produce by and large the same results (King et al., 1994: 100).

It should be realized that the concepts of internal and external validity are of an *ideal-typical* nature: in a perfect world with complete information the standards of validity may well be met, but in practice this is not a realistic goal. Yet, and this is what we put forward, one should try to get as close as feasible to these standards (see Mayer, 1989: 55; King et al., 1994). Only by keeping these standards is it possible to strive for *positive* theory development, that is, systematically relating extant theory to evidence and so improving the theory.

To enhance this process of theory development we argue throughout this book that one needs to formulate a Research Question (*RQ*) first, in order to be able to decide what, how and when to compare. This leads in turn to the development of a Research Design (*RD*) in which these matters are addressed and elaborated in such a way that the research results will be valid, reliable and plausible. It is also important to note that the comparative approach allows for two types of analysis: one is the explorative type that aims at identifying relationships which may be conducive to theory *formation*; the other is driven by theory and aims at *testing* causal relationships, which is necessary to corroborate extant theory and to develop these further. Only then it is possible to decide which data must be collected to carry out the empirical and statistical analysis for a meaningful comparison that may produce substantial explanations of *why* societal and political events and developments have taken place. In short: substance comes before method, questions come before answers, and theory always precedes comparative analysis.

The issue at stake is therefore what, when and how to compare. As the relation between politics and society is not only dynamic but also obviously a process, we need a clear and systemic *model* that can be applied to various situations and related questions that cry out for explanatory analysis by means of the 'art of comparing' (see, for example, Lane and Ersson, 1994; Keman, 1993c; Schmidt, 1995). Hence, we are interested in how to consciously make correct choices to allow for proper answers to the question(s) asked in a systematic fashion; this is conducive to furthering theory as well as valid answers and plausible results. We shall demonstrate that on the basis of a research question it is possible (and sometimes inevitable) to develop a research design (RD) that allows for different answers which can be considered as equally plausible. In Chapter 3 we shall elaborate on this by introducing the central concepts of any political analysis – actors, institutions and performances – that will figure eventually in Part III of this book (for this kind of approach to the political process, see Hague and Harrop, 2004; Almond et al., 1993).

However, before jumping to matters of measuring and modelling politics in relation to society and discussing related matters such as the use of statistics, we must and shall discuss how to organize matters related to collecting data. Data, in general, are the information we wish to gather with a view to supplying a research answer. This can be quantitative or qualitative information (i.e. numbers or descriptions related to various events). These terms are often considered as mutually exclusive. We do not think this to be the case: all information used in social science, if used comparatively, needs to be subject to the rule of reliability, validity and replicability (see also King et al., 1994; Burnham et al., 2004: 140). Hence, data – quantitative and qualitative – can be considered as equivalent, if and only if they are correctly organized. We need therefore to develop a collection of data in order to carry out a systematic comparison.

1.3 Comparing Data: Selecting Cases and Variables

The term 'cases' is often used in the comparative literature in various ways. On the one hand, cases may simply refer to the units of observation in a data matrix. This is the general meaning of the term and will be found in most textbooks on methodology. On the other hand, the comparative approach generally uses the term 'cases' to refer to the combination of the level of measurement employed (e.g. individuals, parties, or government) and the units of variation or variables employed (e.g. electoral attitudes, party programmes, or government policies). The problem which arises from this kind of formulation boils down to the difference between seeing cases as an *empirical* entity (fixed in time and space – see Ragin and Becker, 1992: 4–5; Lijphart, 1975: 160) and as a *theoretical* construct or convention. An example of the first kind are representatives of any type of system, such as countries, parties, voters, years or decades. This type of case defines the boundaries of investigation. The second type refers to theoretical properties from which the researcher derives the units of observation, i.e. cases.

Welfare states, left-wing parties or coalition governments are examples. Whatever way one argues, however, we feel that cases should always be defined as empirical entities in relation to the research question asked. We shall therefore define cases as those *units of observation* that are:

- identically defined by time and place; and
- logically connected to the research question under review.

Cases are then 'carriers of information' which must and can be collected by means of translating concepts into empirical indicators, such as having a written constitution or not, having a certain type of multi-party system, the size of the electorate, and so on.

In comparative research the term 'cases' is reserved for the units of observation that are compared, be it voters in different countries or regions, parties in various political systems, or welfare states across nations. The information in each row of the data matrix is two-dimensional: it concerns the voter in country A, B or C or it refers to a party family X, Y or Z (if we wish to compare differences between party families and/or within party families). Or, for example, the row displays information on welfare states as a whole (equals one country). In the same vein, variables may well represent conceptual information *over time* (e.g. years), and the number of cases is still the number of variables times the number of units of observation. Hence the term 'case' basically refers to the units of observation that are compared. The following rule of thumb may be of help to the reader: if the research question is elaborated in terms of an *inter*national comparison, the number of cases is identical to the number of nations included; if the research question is said to be *cross*-national, the number of cases is defined by the units of observation, such as parties or governments, regardless the number of nations or systems; finally, if the research question focuses on change over time (i.e. *inter*-temporal) then the time units included indicate the number of cases. In summary: what is compared determines the number of cases rather than the total number of cells in a data matrix. In other words, a 'case' carries vital information that varies according to a theoretical concept (e.g. type of welfare state) and this concept is usually operationalized by means of quantified indicators (e.g. public expenditure on social security as a percentage of GDP). Together this leads to unique information that is comparable between cases and variables across cases (number of variables × number of values). That outcome (denoted N) is used in statistical procedures, in particular for tests of significance, and refers to the total number of observations or *values* under scrutiny (see Figure 1.1).

- *Units of variation*   ⇒ *Variables* = columns of data matrix indicating the *variation* across the units of observation according to empirical features derived from theoretical concepts.
- *Units of observation*   ⇒ *Cases* = objects of comparison with *separate* values for each variable along the row of the matrix representing the universe of discourse.

- *Units of measurement* ⟹ *Values* = operational *features* (i.e. scores) of each separate case on each variable presented in the cells in the matrix. The total number of values or the cells is represented by the N.

Another important matter with regard to the number of cases is thus the question to what extent the cases under review indeed represent the so-called *universe of discourse*. As we shall elaborate in Chapter 2, there is quite some variation in various research designs as to how many relevant cases can or should be involved. This depends not only on the research question under review, but also on the mode of analysis which is considered to be proper for answering it. For example, if we study the development of welfare states, we may opt to compare them all, or a number of them. This choice, i.e. of the number of (relevant) cases involved, is related to the dichotomy – proposed by Przeworski and Teune (1970) – between a 'most similar' and a 'most different' design. In the former instance we seek to analyse a causal relationship by collecting data for all the cases that can be assumed to be similar in terms of their contextual features. In the latter case it is assumed that the causal relation under review remains identical notwithstanding systemic differences. Francis Castles has put the difference between the two approaches succinctly as follows:

> A most similar approach implies that … the more circumstances the selected cases have in common, the easier it is to locate the variables that do differ and which may thus be considered as the first candidates for investigation as causal or explanatory variables. A most different approach involves … a comparison on the basis of dissimilarity in as many respects as possible in the hope that after all the differing circumstances have been discounted as explanations, there will remain one alone in which all the instances agree. (quoted in Keman, 1993: 37)

Hence, the issue is how to control for contextual or exogenous variation given the Research Question. For instance, if we wish to analyse the role of parties in government with regard to welfare statism, we could decide – on the basis of the research question – to restrict ourselves to a certain type of party or government. In this case not the system as such, nor its features are decisive with respect to the research design, but the actual unit of variation that is central in the theory underlying the research question (i.e. how do parties matter in or out of government?).

Another issue is then that the research question – which forms the starting point for the research design – informs us on the implicit or explicit causality by means of a controlled comparison. In the example we use in this section the comparative issue is the explanation of the degree of 'welfare statism' as a result of the behaviour and actions of parties in government (see Castles, 1982; Keman, 1988; Janoski and Hicks, 1994; Swank, 2002). Hence, it is expected that party

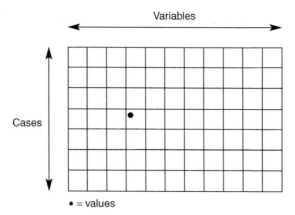

Variables

Cases

• = values

Figure 1.1   *Units of variation, observation and measurement (NB: cases × variables = total N of values). Unit of variation = variable; unit of observation = case; unit of measurement = value*

differences matter with respect to the level and type of welfare services organized and supplied in a country. Obviously, political parties are considered to be effect-producing for welfare statism. The latter is then the *dependent* variable, whereas parties in government are seen as the *independent* variable. This distinction is not only crucial as regards the organization of the units of variation – observation – measurement (see Figure 1.1), but also with respect to the determination of the 'universe of discourse' and whether we must employ a 'most similar' or 'most different' research design. Obviously, in this example, we must exclude political systems without parties (the effect-producing variable). Secondly, we can opt for systems where either welfare state development is (more or less) comparable or include all systems with an established practice of party government. The first option allows the researcher to explore variation that is truly comparative and enables the inclusion of many variables. The second option makes it possible to include all relevant systems (i.e. democracies) in order to test the hypothesized causality of the argument. Whatever the options, it is clear that the choices made on the basis of the research question will direct the research design and the problems (and caveats) that must be overcome. These have been listed in Table 1.1. The four clusters in Table 1.1 represent choices as regards relating the research question to an adequate research design. Secondly, the clusters are steps the researcher must take in order to establish a comprehensive and feasible research design.

So, the first step is to assess whether or not we try to find answers to a specific question or a general one. For instance, Lijphart's analysis of the Dutch system (Lijphart, 1975) was based on the explanation of a *deviant* case (i.e. consociation-alism) within a general theory (of stable democracy). The problem he was confronted with was whether or not his comparative case study allowed for external valid conclusions. Later on he has remedied this problem by using

Table 1.1 *Summary of choices that link the research question to the research design*

	Research question	Research design	Problem or caveat
1	General Or Specific	Most similar Or Most different	Internal validity and External validity
2	Descriptive Explorative Testing	Truly comparing Selecting cases Causality	Many Variables Comparability Ecological fallacy
3	Units of variation Units of measurement Units of observation	Variables Indicators Cases	External validity Internal validity Proper selection
4	Qualitative Quantitative	Equivalent information Reliable data	Systematic comparison Parsimony

more comparable cases to corroborate his ideas (Lijphart, 1977). Hence, although the research question remained the same, a different research design was developed to improve the generalizing capacity of his conclusions regarding the occurrence and working of consociationalism as a subtype of stable democracy. This example of Lijphart's work also can serve to illustrate the second step: from a descriptive study the research design was changed in the direction of consciously selecting a number of cases to explore the original explanation in order to study its occurrence and working elsewhere. The problem for Lijphart was, however, to enhance the comparability, since the cases selected had less in common than seems admissible. To remedy this apparently valid criticism, Lijphart revised and extended his analysis of consensus democracies (originally published in 1984) by including more variables and concomitant indicators (e.g. on policy performance) as well as the number of observations from 21 to 36 cases in all (Lijphart, 1999). This example on the basis of Lijphart's work only shows how important the third step is as well, for critics of Lijphart pointed out that the internal validity was insufficient due to the fact that the indicators used as units of measurement were not comparable for the cases involved. In fact, the critics claimed that a qualitative approach should have been pursued rather than a quantitative one.

Step four rests on this choice. For some time a debate has raged around this topic, but it remains difficult to say which direction, qualitative or quantitative, should be preferred. In fact, this again is a choice the researcher ought to make him/herself depending on the research question. Yet, each direction has its hazards, and the problem of data availability *and* its comparability should not be underestimated regardless what direction is chosen. Hence, it is not only crucial to establish a proper relation between the research question and research design, but also to employ the correct methodology, the proper data, and the adequate statistical tools. And that is what this book is about.

Box 1.2 Comparing without theory and method is useless

Lord Bryce was one of the first political scientists who attempted to systematically compare political systems. In his two volumes on *Modern Democracies* (Bryce, 1921) he compared the institutional organization of democracy. His point of departure was that what was needed is 'Facts, facts, facts': if you knew how political systems are institutionalized, you would know how they operated. Yet, as history has proven, pure description was not good enough to understand the actual working of many a democracy before the Second World War. In fact, a theory of the democratic process, including its pitfalls and vulnerabilities, was absent. The lesson that was derived from this is that without theory-guided research the comparative method cannot provide adequate answers or give a proper explanation for actual developments.

1.4 Developing Empirical-Analytical Comparative Analysis

In Part II of the book we shall introduce and elaborate the tools of comparative *statistical* analysis. Also, in Chapter 4 the issue of organizing data is taken up in conjunction with problems of measurement. In other words, how to transform the proposed theoretical relations as derived from the research question into testable propositions. 'Testable' means first of all the elaboration of the research question in terms of relations between independent (X) and dependent (Y) variables. This important step means the transformation of the research question into an empirical investigation by means of the process of operationalization and by means of developing empirical indicators which allows us to start the – often difficult and seemingly tedious – task of collecting the proper data for analysis.

In Part III of this book we shall demonstrate that there is more than one way to develop variables and indicators of politics. To give an example: political parties perform various functions at the same time, and thus the study of their behaviour should be analysed according to these functions or roles. On the one hand a party is, for instance, striving for maximum influence by acquiring as many offices as possible (such as representatives in parliament or ministers in a coalition government). On the other hand, a party is more often than not the bearer of an ideology by means of a programme, which is conducive to its policy-making behaviour. In this way it is possible not only to compare parties in performing their different functions, but also analyse to what extent parties *per se* behave differently within a system as well as across systems. Other examples can be given (and will be elaborated in Part III) of party behaviour in differently organized democratic systems, such as has been distinguished by Lijphart (1999), or the behaviour of organized interests, as Siaroff (1999) has done.

Another type of comparative investigation in which the importance of a proper operationalization of the research question will be highlighted is that in which one shows how existing variables representing public policies and related performances can be developed into proxies and composite indicators (examples of this practice are the Misery Index and fiscal and monetary policy instruments as well as functional expenditures by state agencies: Keman, 2000a; Lane and Ersson, 1999; Swank, 2002). These procedures are vital in order to be able to construct a proper data set on the basis of the empirical model representing the relation between research question and research design. In Part II we will present the statistical techniques available to describe the model in empirical terms (Chapter 5) and how to find out which answers appear statistically valid with regard to the research question posed (in Chapter 6).

Finally, we shall discuss in Part III the topic of a 'truly' comparative analysis: instead of endeavouring to explain the 'universe of discourse' *per se*, the mode of explanation is directed to test the theoretical relations as such. In other words, how to develop and test a theory empirically rather than to confirm or falsify a theory as applied to reality. Przeworski and Teune (1970) attempt to make this difference clear by suggesting that 'variables replace proper names' and are meant to explain empirical phenomena by concepts independent of their empirical origins.

Yet, one should be aware of the caveats present and the pitfalls lurking as we are dealing with social reality and related political action. This implies that the relationship between theory (Research Question) and empirical analysis (Research Design) not is only dynamic, but also can only produce 'middle-range' theories. The term *middle-range* indicates here the situation that only in a perfect world could the results of comparative inquiry be considered as an absolute truth for all times and situations. Of course, this cannot be the case. However, one should always aim at comprehensively analysed results, which allow for valid and plausible research answers (RA). Hence, the bottom line is and ought to be that a research question is translated into a proper research design leading to plausible research answers.

In Part III of this book we also turn to what partially could be labelled as the manual for doing your own research. We shall then be applying what has been put forward in Parts I and II. To this end we take as a point of departure one of the best-known (and often disputed on various grounds) comparative models used in political science: the input–throughput–output model, or the empirical elaboration of the political systems approach (Powell, 1982; Almond et al., 1993; Lane and Errson, 1994; Keman, 1997; Hix, 1999).

This general model, introduced by Easton (1965), places the *polity* (the political-institutional framework of any society) in a dynamic context. The political system receives 'inputs' from its environment (i.e. society) in the form of demands (e.g. issues and conditions that are considered to influence societal development) or support (e.g. allegiance to leaders, and acceptance of the existing rules of the game by the population). These inputs are subsequently handled by means of the conversion process of the system (e.g. decision-making by means of democratic procedures or binding regulation through a political elite or bureaucracy), resulting in 'outputs' (public actions and expenditures). Eventually, so the argument goes, the *performances* or, effects of the outputs, are monitored back by an information feedback loop, affecting the ensuing societal demands and support for the political system that is conducive to a 'stable equilibrium'. It is obvious that this model of politics and society can be formulated in terms of *politics* (issue competition and choosing preferences for action = input), *polity* (relating inputs to outputs by means of rules that direct decision-making = throughput) and *policy* (public action by means of regulation and provisions = output).

In Part III of this book we focus explicitly on comparing democratic systems by means of the 'democratic chain of popular control and political command' (Keman, 1997). Yet, it should be noted that the principal aim of these exercises is not to confirm or disprove the empirical quality of systems theory, but rather to make the student familiar with doing comparative research in practice. This means that the world must be decomposed first, before we can start – on the basis of valid and plausible findings – to *integrate* the various answers to research questions posed into genuine models that are based on 'truly' comparative knowledge. Such knowledge can be acquired by any student of social and political sciences and can be applied by her or him if, and only if, he or she is conscious of the steps to be taken in the process of developing the relationship between question and answer on the basis of an adequate research design and employing the correct statistical tools and methods.

1.5 How to Use This Book

This book consists of three parts which represent in our view the basic stages of any empirical-analytical research driven by theory in political and social sciences. As the aim of the book is to serve as a coursebook, we feel that students should go through the whole text, chapter by chapter. In each chapter there is an introduction to its contents, and where necessary there is a glossary of the core terms used, to help both teacher and student to find information she or he needs (e.g. whilst doing research). In addition, each chapter contains examples which are taken from existing comparative research that has been published elsewhere and is partially based on data that are accessible (provided by us, or we specify where to obtain them). Finally, some texts are mentioned for further reading on the topics discussed in the chapter.

In Part I we present our own arguments concerning the comparative approach: namely, that any empirical research needs to be theory-driven and must be formulated in a well-elaborated research design. Chapter 6 is essential reading for anyone wishing to understand the use of advanced statistics in order to be able to conduct explanatory analysis (including its caveats and pitfalls!). The final part can be seen as our attempt to pull together the threads of our way of doing comparative research and will be of interest to any reader, whether a freshman or an advanced student of comparative politics and sociology.

Part II can also be used independently by anyone who wishes to 'catch up' with the statistical techniques whilst conducting research. Part III may also be used separately and will be very useful for those who are investigating the dynamic and interactive processes of politics and society. Without claiming that this approach and its elaboration is the one and only way to do it, we feel that it offers a valuable 'springboard' to judge comparative information confronting you or to shape your own theory-inspired research design in such a way that it leads to positive theory development. This is the subject of Chapter 2.

1.6 Endmatter

Topics highlighted

- The 'art of comparing' as a theory-driven method for empirical analytical research.
- The types of explanation that can be developed from research questions into research designs.
- The meaning of cases, variables and measurement in comparative empirical research.
- System theory as a descriptive analytical model of politics in society.
- How to use this book for different types of students.

Questions

- Why is the 'art of comparing' not only useful but rather a *necessary* part of the toolkit of any social scientist? Give an example.
- Try to elaborate whether or not the rules of *internal* or *external* validity are violated in the following statements:

  1 Political parties and social movements are functional equivalents and can therefore be compared throughout the whole world.
  2 The study of government as a system must be researched cross-nationally.
  3 Party government in whatever political system provides a representative basis for analysing the process of government formation.

- Is there a difference between a theoretical proposition and posing a research question? Whatever your answer is, give an example of a proposition and a question to support your view.

Exercises

If you look up Volume 31: 1–2 (1997) of the *European Journal of Political Research* in your library, you can try to answer the following questions:

1 Reproduce by means of a 'diagram' the research design as described by Geoffrey Roberts on pp. 100–1. What are the *units of variation* and what are the *units of*

observation (for this, see also Castles and McKinley: pp. 102–6 in the same volume).

2 Ask the same question by using pp. 159–66 of the same volume. However, focus now on the *units of measurement*.

3 Now turn to pp. 83–93 of the same volume and describe the *unit of observation*, which is central here and is related to a crucial *unit of variation*. To what is it crucial? (Explain)

Further reading

Key texts: Landman (2003), Peters (1998), Lane (1997).
Advanced texts: Kamrava (1996), Stepan (2001), Lichbach and Zuckerman (1997).

The comparative approach: theory and method

2.1 Introduction

In this chapter we shall elaborate on the essentials of the 'art of comparing' by discussing the relation between theory and method in the comparative approach. In order to clarify this point of view, we shall first discuss some of the existing ideas about what the comparative approach is in terms of a scientific undertaking. In addition, we shall argue in Section 2.2 that one can distinguish in comparative politics a 'core subject' that enables us to study the relationship between 'politics and society' in a fruitful and viable way. In Section 2.3 we shall enter into the important topic of the comparative approach, i.e. the comparative method and its implications for a 'proper' research design. The central argument will be that a coherent framework of theoretical references and a corresponding logic of inquiry are required. If it is not possible to do this, the comparative approach will still remain a valuable asset to political and social science, yet any claim of being a 'scientific' approach should then be put to rest (Mayer, 1989; Keman, 1993a; Lane and Ersson, 1994; Lichbach and Zuckermann, 1997).

A final concern involves scrutinizing existing logics of comparative inquiry to account for the observed variation by means of testing empirical hypotheses, thereby either corroborating or falsifying them (Lijphart, 1975: 159; Przeworski and Teune, 1970; Peters, 1998). Hence we explicitly aim at the relation between proposition and empirical evidence and consider that as the cornerstone of social science. This implies the use of *positive theory development* as a stepping stone to advancing our knowledge of politics and society. The central feature of this approach to social science is embedded throughout this book by the relationship between research question, research design and empirical data analysis on the basis of (statistical) methods.

All these concerns are in themselves worthy of serious discussion and deliberation, and the main issue at hand is that the comparative approach often lacks coherence in terms of a set of theoretical references and related logics of inquiry. Therefore this chapter must be seen as an attempt to relate theory and method in order to gain a viable and feasible approach to explaining political and social processes. To this end we propose the following guidelines to define the comparative approach as a distinctive way of analysing and explaining social and political developments. The guidelines can be considered as 'flags' that mark the process of doing research by means of the comparative method:

1 Describe the core subject of comparative inquiry. In other words, formulate the question of what exactly is to be explained and how we recognize a need for comparison – i.e. what are the essential *systemic* features?
2 Develop a view on the theoretical concepts that can 'travel' comparatively as well as measuring what is intended (internal validity) as well as possessing a unifying capacity for explaining political and social processes in general (external validity).
3 Discuss the logic of the comparative method as a *means* to an end, rather than as an end in itself. In other words, which instrument fits the research questions to be answered best by means of what type of research design?

We therefore now turn to the next point on the agenda: the comparative approach as an important instrument of researching the relationship between politics and society.

2.2 Comparative Research and Case Selection

Comparative political and social research is generally defined in two ways: either on the basis of its supposed core subject, which is almost always defined at the level of political and social *systems* (Lane and Ersson, 1994; Dogan and Pelassy, 1990; Keman, 1997), or by means of descriptive features that claim to enhance knowledge about politics and society as a *process* (e.g. Roberts, 1978;

Macridis and Burg, 1991; Almond et al., 1993). These descriptions are generally considered to differentiate the comparative approach from other approaches within political and social science. Although it is a useful starting point, it is not sufficient. The comparative approach must be elaborated in terms of its theoretical design and its research strategy on the basis of a goal-oriented point of reference, i.e. what exactly is to be explained.

A way of accomplishing this is to argue for a more refined concept of 'politics and society' and develop concepts that 'travel' – i.e. are truly comparative – and can thus be related to the political process in various societies (Collier, 1993; Landman, 2003). In addition, a set of rules must be developed that direct the research strategy, aiming at explanations rather than at a more or less complete description of political phenomena by comparing them across systems, through time, or cross-nationally. At this point most comparativists stop elaborating their approach and start investigating – often, however, without realizing that theory and method are mutually interdependent (Keman, 1993c; Stepan, 2001). For the goal of comparative analysis is to explain those 'puzzles' which cannot be studied without comparing *and* which are derived from logical reasoning. Hence, there can be no comparative research without an extensive theoretical argument underlying it, or without a methodologically adequate research design to undertake it. A first and vital step in the process is to ponder the relationship between the cases under review and the variables employed in the analysis (Landman, 2003; Peters, 1998; Keman, 1993c). There is a trade-off between the two: in general, the more cases one compares, the fewer variables are often available and vice versa (Przeworski, 1987; Ragin, 1987). In Chapter 3 we shall elaborate this problem in full; for now it suffices to suggest that the conversion of research question into a viable research design is confronting the researcher with this inevitable problem. To complicate things even more, one has also to consider whether or not 'time' is a relevant factor to be taken into account (Bartolini, 1993). This problem of choice is illustrated in Figure 2.1. Figure 2.1 shows that there are five options available:

1   The *single* case study (either a country, an event or systemic feature)
2   The single case study *over time* (i.e. a historical study or time series analysis)
3   *Two or more* cases at a *few time* intervals (i.e. closed universe of discourse)
4   *All* cases that are relevant regarding the research question under review
5   *All* relevant cases across time and space (e.g. pooled time series analysis).

Obviously a single case study (see Yin, 1996; Peters, 1998) cannot be considered as genuinely comparative. Implicitly it is, but in terms of external validity it is not. Nevertheless, it is used for developing hypotheses and reasons of validation *post hoc* to inspect whether or not the general results of a comparative analysis hold up in a more detailed analysis (see, for instance, Castles, 1993; Vergunst, 2004) or to study a *deviant* case for theory generation (i.e. a case that is seemingly an 'exception to the rule'; see Lijphart, 1968). A single case study has the advantage that it allows for the inclusion of many variables. This method is often referred to as 'thick description' (Landman, 2003: Chapter 2).

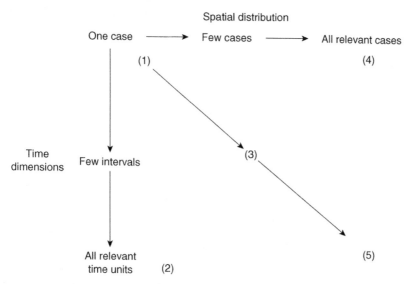

Figure 2.1   *Selecting the number of comparable cases and variables with respect to the research question: (1) case study (at one time point); (2) time series (one case over time); (3) closed universe (relevant cases in relevant periods); (4) cross-section (all cases at one time point); (5) pooled analysis (maximizing cases across time and space). NB: these terms are explained in depth in the following chapters*

A single case study over time is often used as a theory confirming or contesting analysis based on a country's history with a specific focus derived from the research question in use (Lijphart, 1971: 692). Examples of such studies can be found in the analysis of consolidation of democracy (Stepan, 2001). This type of case analysis can be performed qualitatively or quantitatively. In the latter case it is often applying econometric models over a set of many time points (Beck and Katz, 1995).

The third option in Figure 2.1 concerns the 'few' cases alternative, and more often than not takes time into account (be it before/after an event – like war or economic crisis – or certain periods that are seen as crucial for the cases involved; Berg-Schlosser and Mitchell, 2002). A few(er) cases research design is seen as a 'focused comparison' which is directly derived from the research question under review (Ragin, 1991). Here the specific features of core subject under study explicitly direct the inclusion of relevant cases, more or less forming a 'closed shop'. A good example of this is the qualitative study of revolutions by Theda Skocpol (1979), on the one hand, and the quantitative analysis on the same topic by Gurr (1970), on the other hand.

Option 4 is the most prevalent one in comparative research: it concerns those cases that have more in common that they differ from each other, *depending* on the research question (Collier, 1993). The advantage is that the universe of discourse is limited on the basis of the 'most similar systems design' and therefore that *both* internal and external validity are considered to be enhanced. Examples of this approach are the numerous analyses of industrial democracies (Bryce, 1921; Almond and Verba, 1965; Lipset and Rokkan, 1967; Powell, 1982; Hibbs, 1987; Keman, 1997; Lane and Ersson, 1999; Gallagher et al., 2001).

The fifth and final option is the subject of fierce debate among comparativists. On the one hand, the number of cases is indeed maximized, but, on the other hand, there is the pitfall that time is considered to be constant across all cases – or, at least, that change is consistent within the cases (see Janoski Hicks, 1994; see also Chapter 6 in this book, where the statistical problems related to pooled time series are discussed). Yet, the obvious advantage is that the universe of discourse can be extended and thus the scope of comparison widened across time and space (Stimson, 1985). If one went through the literature or a major political science journal (such as the *American Political Science Review, Comparative Studies,* or the *European Journal of Political Research*), one would find numerous examples of how a research question is indeed translated into a research design in which each of the possibilities has been chosen. For instance, the study of Dutch consociationalism is a one case/time series research design (no. 2 in Figure 2.1) whereas Lijphart's study of consensus democracies (Lijphart, 1999) is a cross-sectional analysis of *all* relevant cases (no. 4). Many studies on welfare states more often than not use a research design in which *all* relevant cases are included and studied over time, albeit for a few points in time only (no. 3; see Castles, 1993; Esping-Andersen, 1999). The analysis of the working of coalition governments (see Laver and Schofield, 1990; Budge and Keman, 1990) is often done in combination with as many relevant cases as possible and for as many points in time as feasible. This is what is often called a pooled time series research design (no. 5). In fact, the last example also demonstrates that we are interested not only in countries as cases, but also – depending on the research question – in elements central to the political system such as governments, parties, interest groups, voters and institutions. In these instances the number of cases will often be much larger, if and when all relevant cases are included. Yet – and this is an important point – the options for choice as depicted here are not free.

However, in most discussions of the comparative approach, it appears that both theoretical and methodological aspects of case selection are divorced, or at least treated separately. For example, Ragin (1987) and Przeworski (1987) emphasize predominantly the methodological aspects of the art of comparison as a 'logic of inquiry', which is often underdeveloped or incompletely elaborated. At the same time these authors argue their case by means of examples that are seemingly picked at random. Theoretical progress and explanatory results appear then to emanate from their 'logic' (see Przeworski, 1987: 45ff.; Ragin, 1987: 125ff.). Yet, the comparative analysis of the political process must be instead founded a priori in theory and then related to the best-fitting 'logic of inquiry' or, in our terms: a proper research design.

The principal message is that much of the research that is labelled as comparative either lacks theoretical foundation of why mechanisms in various systems have much in common or not, or is based on a research design that is not comparative but is rather a collection of bits of information about a number of systems. The main lesson that can be drawn from the examples listed here as an elaboration of Figure 2.1 is that the research question *per se* directs the research design in terms of the central units of variation (governments, elections, welfare state, etc.) which imply the theoretical relations under review and also direct the units of observation (e.g. years if change is focused upon or all parliamentary governments across the whole universe of discourse). These choices or decisions – made by the researcher – also dictate, then, the units of measurement (or values) that make up the total number of cases. Given this line of reasoning, which is essential to our approach to comparative research, it is crucial, therefore, to develop a theoretical perspective in order systematically to relate the research question to possible research designs and not simply to gather information about a lot of cases, which are often only included for pragmatic reasons.

2.3 The use of Comparative Analysis in Political Science: Relating Politics, Polity and Policy to Society

Usually the comparative approach to politics and society is defined both by its substance (the study of a plurality of societies or systems) and by its method (e.g. cross- and international, comparable cases, longitudinal, etc.; see Schmitter, 1993: 177; see also Figure 2.1). Such a description, however, undermines the necessary link between theory and method as well as the distinctiveness of the comparative approach in terms of what, when and how to compare. Theory here equals the propositions concerning the explanation of a relationship between politics in social reality and the societal developments that are (seen to be) affected by it. Method is then the most appropriate way to investigate the proposed relationships empirically. As we have stated before, comparing as such is one of the common tenets underlying much, if not all, research in the social sciences. Yet, one needs to realize all the time that this refers to the 'logic' of systematically finding answers to questions about the complexities of reality. This logic has a long history and was described by John Stuart Mill (1872) as the *methods of agreement and difference* (see also Janoski and Hicks, 1994: Chapter 1; Landman, 2003: Chapter 2). Comparison is then an instrument to verify or falsify relationships between two phenomena. Yet, here in this book we consider the logic as an integral part of the comparative approach by stressing the crucial importance of the link between the research question, on the one hand, and the research design, on the other. For this we need to reduce the complexity of reality and thus to control for variation – this is what the comparative method allows for.

As Sartori (1991: 244–5) stresses, we need to compare in order to control the observed units of variation or the variables that make up the theoretical relationship. In fact, what the researcher is attempting is to identify the necessary and sufficient conditions under which the relationship occurs in reality. This would entail the researcher assuming that all other things (or conditions) are equal except for the relationship under empirical review. This is what we call the *ceteris paribus* clause. The more 'true' the comparison, i.e. the more explicit the relationship between the research question and research design is of a comparative nature, the more positive the analytical results will be. If we look, for instance, at the relationship between 'class society' and the emergence of 'welfare states' the relationship is positive if we examine the developments in the UK, Sweden and Australia (Castles, 1978, 1985). However, the relationship could be negative if we focus instead on the Netherlands, Germany and Italy (Van Kersbergen, 1995) where the role of religion used to be the central focus of political behaviour. Hence, only when we take into account as many relevant and concurrent cases as possible can we reach a viable and plausible conclusion concerning socio-economic divisions in society and related consequences in terms of welfare regulation. Similarly, the question whether or not economic developments are also dependent on types of democratic governance and interest intermediation cannot be fully answered by studying one country, or – as Olson (1982) did – by comparing only the states within the USA. The basic message is thus that the degree of control of the environment or contextual features necessary to reach sound conclusions requires an appropriate number of cases, be it cross-sectionally or across time (depending, of course, on the research question; see Figure 2.1). From this point of view, it appears reasonable to conclude – as Dalton (1991) does – that it is almost impossible to conceive of serious explanatory work in political and social science that is not at least implicitly comparative.

Janoski and Hicks (1994: Chapter 1), for instance, point correctly to the distinction between *internal* and *external* analysis in the social sciences. Both types are considered important for comparative research. Internal analysis refers to the knowledge necessary to understand the cases under review *per se*, whereas external analysis is the analysis of the agreement or differences *between* cases. As we shall see later on, both types of analysis are useful for: (1) selecting the appropriate research design; and (2) evaluating the reliability and validity of the data gathered. Hence, from the perspective that the comparative approach is a crucial one in political and social science, depending on the definition of the core subject and research question asked, one must also take into account that knowledge of the cases as such, which make up the universe of discourse, is a vital prerequisite for accomplishing good comparative types of analysis. Hence, internal types of comparisons can be useful to execute external analysis of the same phenomenon (see also Mair, 1996).

The comparative approach to political science is thus not by itself exclusive, but if we follow the idea that concepts derived from theories about the real world need to be investigated by controlling variation as observed in the real world, we cannot abstain from this approach (Lijphart, 1971; Smelser, 1976; Mayer, 1989; Sartori, 1991). Actually, we could go even further by saying that the comparative approach is the fundamental point of departure for most theories that figure in political and social science. In addition, the comparative method then is not only preferred but required in those situations in which there is no possible recourse to experimental techniques or when the number of observations does not allow for the use of statistical techniques that are based on sampling. However, as we already saw in Figure 2.1, these limitations are the exception rather than the rule (see also Mayer, 1989; Keman, 1993d; Collier, 1993).

An important and crucial step in the use and application of the comparative approach is the issue of *concept formation*, which can travel across time, situations, or societies (Bartolini, 1993; Sartori, 1994). In other words, we seek to define crucial concepts and subsequently develop a systematic classification of variables that represent the theoretical relationship proposed and which are derived from the core subject of the discipline, i.e. the 'political' in a society.

The 'political' in a society can be described on the basis of three dimensions: *politics, polity and policy* (Schmidt, 1996; Keman, 1997). Politics is then what we would like to call the political process. On this level, actors (mostly aggregates of individuals organized in parties, social movements and interest groups) interact with each other if and when they have conflicting interests or views regarding societal issues that cannot be solved by them (i.e. deficiency of self-regulation). The process of solving those problems which make actors clash is more often than not visible through the political and social *institutions* that have emerged in order to facilitate conflict resolution (Scharpf, 1998).

Institutions – or the 'rules of political governance' – help to develop coalescence and to achieve a consensus among conflicting actors through compromising alternative preferences. These institutions manifest themselves in the *rules of the game* in a society. This is what is meant by the 'polity'. To put it more formally, rules are human-devised constraints that shape political interaction. Institutions are then considered to be both formal – as, for instance, in a constitution, which can be enforced – and informal, i.e. they evolve over time and are respected as a code of conduct by most actors involved. Hence, the rules – be they formal or informal – define the relationship between the 'political and society' (Braun, 1995; Czada et al., 1998). In short, a theory of the political process must assume that there exists a mutual and interdependent relation between politics and society, but that its organization is to a large extent independent of society. The issue at hand is then to investigate to what extent and in what way this process can be observed and affects social and economic developments of societies by means of comparison (Almond et al., 1993; Hix, 1999; Hague and Harrop, 2004). It should be kept in mind that the triad of 'politics–polity–policy' in itself is *not* a theory of the political process. It is instead a heuristic device to delineate the 'political' from the 'non-political' (and thus to distinguish politics from society). This description of the 'political', however, makes it possible to elaborate on the core subject of the comparative approach. That is to say that all those processes that can be defined by means of these three dimensions are in need of a comparative analysis in order to explain the process.

Box 2.1 Conceptualizing the 'political' in society

Political systems can be described by means of the politics–polity–policy triad.

Politics concerns the interactions between (collective) actors within a society on issues where actors (e.g. parties and organized interests) are strongly contested.

Polity is the available framework of the formal and informal 'rules of the game' – also called institutions – directing the behaviour of the political actors.

Policy denotes the political decisions made for a society (often called 'outputs'), which are subsequently implemented in society (also 'outcomes').

Theories and hypotheses in comparative political science usually refer to units of variation, i.e. political variables, policy variables and polity variables at the macroscopic level. The theories and hypotheses often apply to many units of observation (e.g. nations or parties, governments, etc.) and many time periods (e.g. decades or years).

The term 'unit of variation' can have two meanings, therefore: on the one hand, it signifies an elaboration of the theoretical argument and the related research question into meaningful concepts; on the other hand, it concerns the translation of the theory into a research design where variables are developed that can be observed empirically and are the units of analysis.

A number of comparative researchers have drawn attention to this confusing way of using the terms 'unit of variation' and 'unit of observation', which easily leads to equating description with explanation. Yet, it is quite important to know exactly what is under discussion if we wish to validate theoretical statements by means of empirical knowledge. Przeworski and Teune (1970: 50) propose a distinction between 'levels of observation' and 'levels of analysis', whereas Ragin (1987: 8–9) introduces the terms 'observational unit' and 'explanatory unit'. Both these distinctions between respectively empirical knowledge and theoretical statements appear useful, but may still be confusing to the practitioner. We prefer to follow the formulations as used in Chapter 1.

In summary: a comparative analysis of the 'political' in society begins with the formulation of the unit of variation by referring to relations at a macroscopic level (i.e. systemic level). By elaborating these units, one must always keep in mind that the units of observation (i.e. the (sub)systems or cases under review) that are employed are not identical, but are considered to be similar. Finally, the unit of measurement is not by definition equal to the analytical properties as defined in social theory and related research questions.

Box 2.2   Comparing as a means to control for contextual variation

Doing research in the social sciences, i.e. about people, societies, states, etc., *always* implies a reduction of the complexity of real life. The comparative method is useful in achieving this goal because it allows for controlling contextual variation. The issue is therefore how to select the *appropriate combination* of relevant cases and variables to validate theory without disregarding relevant contextual features.

To give an example: the study of the development of the welfare state is not, by definition, a topic of comparative political research. In our view, it becomes a comparative topic only if an attempt is made to explain this development by means of macro-political properties such as conflicting interests between socio-economic classes. These conflicts are, depending on the existing institutions of the liberal democratic state, fought out in parliament and other decision-making bodies and subsequently may result in a patterned variation of public policy formation at the system level of the state. Hence the core subject is not the welfare state, but instead the extent to which politics, polity and policy can be identified as properties of the political process that shapes the welfare state in a country. This being the case, the extent to which elements of this process are relevant explains the political development of the welfare state (Castles and Pierson, 2000; Scharpf and Schmidt, 2000). Table 2.1 lists some examples of how units of variation, observation and measurement are linked together in actual research in comparative politics.

To conclude our discussion of the study of the relationship between politics and society: the *theory-guided* question within any type of comparative analysis is to what extent the 'political', in terms of explanatory units of variation (= variables), can indeed account for and is shaped by the political actions in one social system compared to another. Conversely, the theory-guided question, or research question, needs to be refined so as to define the units of measurement (= indicators) and thus the units of observation (= cases) in social reality. This process and the attempts to explain it by systematic comparison distinguish the comparative approach from other approaches in political and social science. This conclusion brings us to the next issue: the steps that must be taken to properly relate the research question to an adequate research design, i.e. a design that is conducive to plausible conclusions. This is the subject of the next chapter.

Table 2.1 *Examples of units of variation, observation and measurement as used in the literature within comparative political science*

Unit of Variation	Unit of Observation	Unit of Measurement
Democratization	States	Available civil and political rights
Welfare states	National governments	Levels of public expenditure
Corporatism	Organized interests	Degree of tripartite consultation
Electoral volatility	Elections	Aggregate change of voters
Federalism	Subnational states	Constitutional design
Ideology	Parties	Contents of electoral programmes
Party government	Governments	Party composition of government
Social movements	Organized groups	Collective behaviour

2.4 Endmatter

Topics highlighted

- Theory comes before method, research questions before research designs.
- Selecting relevant cases across time and space.
- The study of the 'political' in relation to 'society' enables the comparativist to relate units of variation to units of measurement and units of observation in a meaningful way.
- The main advantage of the comparative approach in political and social science is to verify and to 'test' theories by controlling contextual variation.

Questions

- Can you explain why different research questions about welfare statism could well imply different research designs? See *European Journal of Political Research,* 31 (1–2): 99–114 and 159–68.
- If you look up the book by Landman (2003) and read Chapter 2, in particular the section on single-country studies, can you explain whether it is *developing* theory or *verifying* theory?
- In this chapter we discuss: space, micro and macro levels and inter- and intra-system comparisons (see Figure 2.1). Can you think of a topic of investigation that is solely comparatively researched on:

1 time without space?
2 micro-observations without macro-properties?
3 intra-system features without inter-system references?

Exercises

- Read Lijphart's article on 'Dimensions of democracy' and Duverger's article 'A new political system', and reformulate their research question in terms of the politics–polity–policy triad. (You can find Abstracts of these articles in the *European Journal of Political Research*, 31 (1/2): 125–46 and 193–204).
- An important feature of the 'art of comparing' is controlling for the contextual variation (or: exogenous variables). More often than not this is endeavoured by selecting the number of (proper) cases, which are supposed to be similar, but for the variation to be explained. If you take the article of Lijphart again (see above) can you tell from his list of cases *why* he thinks that these countries are indeed more similar than others and thus do enhance the matter of internal and external validity?

Further reading

Key texts: Ragin (1987), Lane and Ersson (1994).
Advanced texts: Mayer (1989), Marsh and Stoker (2002), Keman (1993c).

Meaning and use of the comparative method: research design

3.1 Introduction

There has been continuing debate about what, if and when, why and how to compare (e.g. Lijphart, 1975; Roberts, 1978; Dogan and Pelassy, 1990; Rueschemeyer et al., 1992; Keman, 1993d). Before we go into the comparative method as such in more detail, we shall first focus on the extant methodological controversies provoked by this debate (see also Collier, 1993; Landman, 2003).

What to compare? Rather than exclusively focusing on 'macro-social', 'societal' or 'contextual' entities, it should be clear from Chapter 2 that we propose to study the 'political' *vis-à-vis* the 'societal'. This further implies that the conceptualization of 'politics, polity and policy' as a heuristic tool is our major methodological concern with respect to using the comparative approach. The social and economic configuration of a situation or society is not the primary goal or meaning of comparison, instead capturing the *specifica differentia* of the 'political' across situations and across time will be our concern (albeit within the context of societal developments; Lane and Ersson, 1994).

Taking this point seriously, there are a number of implications for the controversies on the comparative method. It concerns questions such as (see also Table 2.1):

- whether research question and research design, i.e. the relationship between theory and reality, is embedded in the correct approach in terms of a variable-oriented (often equated with statistical) or a case-oriented research design (e.g. Lijphart, 1971, 1975; Przeworski, 1987; Ragin, 1987; Keman, 1993);
- whether or not causal or conditional explanations can be achieved by means of empirical and statistical corroboration (Ragin, 1987; Lijphart, 1975; King et al., 1994);
- whether or not comparisons are only meaningful by applying the longitudinal dimension and confining the number of relevant cases to be analysed (e.g. O'Donnell, 1979; Castles, 1989; Bartolini, 1993; Rueschemeyer et al., 1992).

The first issue is more or less reminiscent of the transition from the 'behavioural' dominance in political science and its attempt to achieve 'scientific' status (Mayer, 1972; Farr et al., 1995). The comparative method was considered to be the ideal platform, if executed on the basis of statistical techniques using data collections, variable construction and causal modelling, to achieve this status (e.g. Holt and Turner, 1970). This position strongly coincided with the search for a 'grand theory' of politics. Apart from the fact that for various reasons 'scientism' in the social sciences has lost its appeal, it simply induced a situation in which we lost track of what the substance or the focus of analysis, i.e. the 'political', is (Mayer, 1989: 56–7). Castles (1987), for instance, has succinctly pointed out that 'the major incongruity is not a matter of theory not fitting the facts, but of the facts fitting too many theories' (p. 198). In other words, 'grand' schemes appear to become meaningless if and when faced with 'facts' which are always derived from macroscopic phenomena. As Mayer (1972: 279) put it:

political science is at what might be called a pre-theoretic stage of development. Most of the existing theoretical work has been concerned with establishing logical relationships between non-empirically defined concepts or imprecisely defined classes of phenomena ... they have produced a plethora of generalizations that are incapable of being tested in terms of observable data.

Box 3.1 A definition of 'Theory'

In this book 'theory' is considered as a set of plausible research answers to a research question. These are stated as causal relations that are to be confirmed by means of empirical evidence, which refute or confirm the tenability of the proposed relations. From this perspective a theory can be either 'deductive' or 'inductive'. This definition implies that sheer description of events or an abstract argument without empirical footing is not sufficient. Defining theory in this way, the relevant findings can be enhanced or confirmed and theories can be developed. This process is, what we call *positive theory development*.

And precisely this tendency led to the idea that 'middle-range' theory was a more adequate and plausible way to go. Middle-range theories are those theories which claim to be explanatory for a certain class of cases (e.g. industrial societies, welfare states or parliamentary democracies) for which specific hypotheses are developed and specified in terms of variables (e.g. industrialism tends to produce welfare systems, or capitalism is conditional for democracy; see Lipset, 1963; Rueschemeyer et al., 1992; Dahl, 1998). In contrast to grand theories, middle-range theories are bounded by situation, time and location (see also Bartolini, 1995). However, even if one thinks one knows what to compare, the question remains of how to translate it into proper terms for empirical research. Hence, developing a research design is a crucial step in applying the comparative method to political and social science. How to do this is elaborated in this chapter.

3.2 The Problem of Variables, Cases and Interpretations

As we pointed out in the preceding chapter, the use of the term 'unit of variation' cannot and should not be solved by means of a methodological point of view alone, but instead ought to be primarily formulated by means of the core subject of comparative politics in terms of substantial relationships. However, this task remains unresolved by the definition of the core subject of the 'political' alone. It essentially means that one has to choose, on the basis of a topical research question that is formulated in terms of the 'political', the correct research design. The question of what to compare leads to the matter of how to compare, i.e. how to apply the comparative method.

Generally speaking, the 'logic' of comparative research goes back to the famous predicament of John Stuart Mill (1806–73) which has led to the equally well-known distinction between the 'most similar' and the 'most different systems research design for comparing (Przeworski and Teune, 1970: 32). Most comparativists agree on this distinction, but differ on the question of whether or not the research design should be based on as many similar cases as possible, or upon a (smaller) number of dissimilar cases. First, we should elaborate what distinguishes the 'most similar' from the 'most different' systems design. Let us therefore formulate what a theory-guided research design is:

$$C^* [X \to Y].$$

The relation $X \to Y$ denotes a substantial research question in terms of the units of variation. C denotes contextual factors, which are considered to be more or less constant. That is, we assume that most other factors in reality are more or less similar with respect to the cases under review (the *ceteris paribus* clause). Depending on the research question formulated, the researcher has to decide to what extent contextual factors can be kept constant by means of a 'most similar systems design' or a 'most different systems design' (see below). Hence, depending on the type of research question, a research strategy is chosen, which in turn directs the possible exclusion of contextual factors.

In other words, we have translated a theoretical question into a substantial research question, which in turn is characterized by an implicit or explicit causal relationship between X and Y. For instance: does a difference in electoral system (ES) produce different types of party systems (PS)? Or alternatively, do socio-cultural cleavages (SC) within a nation produce different types of party systems? These research questions are derived from theoretical ideas put forward by two political scientists, namely Duverger (1968) and Rokkan (1970). Hence, the first step in deciding what to compare and how, is to know the units of variation. In this example it concerns the variables of electoral systems, socio-cultural cleavages and party system characteristics. So the research design to apply could be represented by Figure 3.1. This design, if elaborated properly, should lead to answers for all cases concerned, i.e. the relevant set of units of variation. In this example it concerns those democratic systems where there is an electoral system and socio-cultural cleavages occur (in one way or another, to a greater or lesser extent; see Mair, 1996a). This is what we referred to in Chapter 1 as 'internal validity': the relationship under review is valid for all relevant cases (i.e. a middle-range theory). Yet, as we all know, in reality the world is much too complex, multifarious and varied to assume that one can study this kind of causal relationship in complete isolation. Hence, we need to make assumptions about how similar or different the cases or political systems under review are with respect to their context (= C). For instance, can we presume that socio-cultural differences have the same impact on a party system in the industrialized democracies of Europe as in the agricultural systems of the Third World? Or conversely, can we expect that electoral systems do indeed function the same in Asia today as in Europe fifty years ago? In other words, to what extent can we assume that the same variables (ES, SC and PS) will behave identically under varying conditions in different contexts? This question clearly has to do with the 'external validity' of the outcomes of the research, and thus the answer is vital for the direction of the research design to be used (i.e. whether the results are valid for other political systems that are not or could not be included). We need to control the context of the units of variation in order to be able to draw conclusions about the $X \to Y$ relationship, if and when analysed on

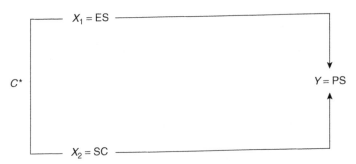

Figure 3.1   *Schematic representation of a research design: C, contextual factors; ES, electoral system; PS, party system; SC, socio-cultural cleavages*

the basis of comparable empirical evidence. The basic assumption underlying this type of comparative research design is then that most if not all other things are assumed to be equal (*ceteris paribus*).

At this point comparative researchers tend to agree that there is a plausible disagreement about what choice to make: on the one hand, one can argue that a few cases will suffice to answer the research question ($X \rightarrow Y$), since this research design allows the researcher to include only those cases that have as much context in common as possible. Hence, so it is argued, the control of the context is maximized (Lijphart, 1971: 692). Yet, on the other hand, others will argue that the internal validity may be high, but the external validity is not: too few cases are included and too many variables will have come into play in the comparison. Following this line of argument, one will opt to include as many cases as plausible. However, this implies that the number of variables that can be studied simultaneously is limited. In addition, such a choice implies that the context to be controlled is much more varied, and thus the assumed similarity of the cases involved will be in jeopardy (see also Landman, 2003: Chapter 2).

In short: in order to keep the context under control one has to choose between, on the one hand, a larger number of cases/systems that are contextually similar with only a few variables that differ amongst each other, and, on the other hand, maximizing control by using a smaller number of cases and a higher number of variables in which almost all contextual features are included in the research design. Whatever the choice the researcher makes with respect to the number of contextual comparable cases, it always implies a *most similar systems design* (MSSD; see also Przeworski and Teune, 1970; and, on its hazards, Przeworski, 1987). In our example concerning the explanation of the variation of party systems a MSSD approach implies that we can either include all political systems where there are free elections and parties competing for office, or we start by looking for those political systems which have all contextual features in common except the $X \rightarrow Y$ relationships under investigation.

The alternative choice concerns the *most different systems design* (MDSD). The crux of the logic of this approach is obviously opposite to an MSSD approach. Here the researcher is actually hoping not only that the contextual differences are omnipresent, but also that the units of variation – and thus the crucial relationships – do *not* vary regardless the contextual differences. The disadvantage is, then, that one is confronted with Popper's dilemma of the swans (we will never know whether or not they are *always* white) and this has a negative impact on the 'external validity' of the research (see Janoski and Hicks, 1994: 15).

It will be clear that the development of a proper research design is quite complex: the selection of cases drives the possible logic of comparison, which in turn is to a large extent driven by the type of variables (in particular, how they are measured). Hence the theory under investigation and the type of data available are important constraints to the research design possible.

A related issue in this respect concerns 'Galton's problem' (Lijphart, 1975: 171): few cases and many variables, which makes it difficult to arrive at conclusions of a causal nature. This is ultimately the result of 'diffusion' (i.e. processes of learning by adopting), which may lead to spurious relationships or to 'overdetermination' (i.e. even if cases are, to a large degree, similar, the remaining differences will be large because of the use of concepts that are broadly operationalized), and in turn this situation will affect the relation between apparently independent variables and the dependent phenomenon (Przeworski, 1987: 38–9). As far as we can see, there is, as yet, no proper solution to this problem. It is by and large due to the dynamic nature of social reality, which cannot be completely captured by means of controlled contexts. The comparative approach can only contribute to reducing the degree of erroneous statements here. Apart from consciously choosing either an MSSD or an MDSD approach, the reduction of errors is, of course, to be found in developing appropriate measured variables, applying the correct statistical techniques and – last but not at all least – interpreting the results in view of their internal and external validity (see Ragin, 1987: 9–10). This is one of the reasons for writing this book, and even perhaps its mission!

All in all, three issues with regard to method are to be observed when a research design is developed: firstly, the context of what is compared; secondly, the level of inquiry, i.e. the micro–macro link; and thirdly, the role of 'time and space' with respect to the problem under scrutiny and the number of cases involved. These issues are equally important and decisions made upon them will have a great impact on the plausibility, validity and quality of the outcomes of a comparative research project.

3.2.1 Context matters

Contextual variables are those variables that make up the environment of the core subject, i.e. of the 'political'. A 'most similar' design – as we stated earlier – is intended to reduce variation in the context to the barest possible minimum by means of selecting cases, or units of observation, that are by and large identical, except for the relations between variables under review that represent the research question, i.e. what is to be explained. For example, the analysis of the development of welfare states, mentioned earlier, is an example of how important the selection of cases is in relation to the analytical conclusions based on them. On the one hand, one can research 'welfare statism' across the world if and only if one seeks, for example, to answer the question under what conditions welfare states exist (or not: Schmidt, 1989). On the other hand, one can choose to limit the comparison to welfare states only, if one is interested in what type of politics they have in common (and why; see, for example, Esping-Anderson, 1990). Again, it is the theory-guided research question that directs our choices. In general, however, one can say that the number of contextual variables must be low in the eventuality of a research question that is akin to the most similar approach, and even in a most different design the number of 'contextual' variables should not be excessive, otherwise one would end up with conclusions that everything is indeed different and all situations are peculiar by definition. It is the enduring paradox of Scylla and Charybdis, and there is no easy solution (see Skocpol and Somers, 1980; Janoski and Hicks, 1994). In addition, one must realize that both the 'most similar' and the 'most different' approach not only are developed to control for the context, but also have implications for the 'logic' of interpreting the outcomes of the empirical results. To this we now turn.

3.2.2 Logics of comparison

As may be clear, the logic of comparative inquiry is closely linked to the issues of the level of inquiry (whether actors or institutions are involved within or across systems) and the units of observation (the type and number of cases).

The level of inquiry is not to be confused with levels of measurement (as used in statistics, nominal–ordinal–ratio–interval; this will be discussed in Chapter 4 of this book). Levels of inquiry signify the extent to which theoretical concepts are measured in more or less abstract categories (like the electorate is an abstract term for a collection of individuals, or party is a label that can cover various meanings with variable interpretations). In Section 3.5 we shall elaborate on this by discussing the difficult issue of 'stretching' concepts in order to make them travel across comparative units of observation.

The level of inquiry, however, indicates to what extent cases – countries, nations, years or other categories – are part of the 'universe of discourse' (i.e. the number of cases). And, as we have already seen, the type of inquiry and universe of discourse have implications for the logics of comparison. In the literature on the comparative approach one distinguishes four logics:

- method of difference;
- indirect method of difference;
- method of agreement;
- indirect method of agreement.

All these 'methods' refer to an implied logic as relating $X \rightarrow Y$ by means of comparison (see also Janoski and Hicks, 1994; Ragin, 2000; Landman, 2003). The

Table 3.1   *An example of a most similar systems comparison*

	Case 1	Case 2	Case 3	. . .	Case *n*
Independent variables					
X_1 = PR	yes	yes	yes		no
X_2 = SC	yes	no	yes		yes
Dependent variable					
Y = PS	yes	no	yes		yes

methods of difference and agreement were developed by John Stuart Mill in his *System of Logic* (1872). The basic idea is that comparing cases can be used to detect commonalities between cases. The *method of difference* focuses in particular on the variation of certain features amongst others that do not differ (dramatically) across comparable cases. Hence, co-variation is here considered crucial under the assumption of holding the context constant. This is what we call the 'most similar systems design': locating variables that differ systematically across similar systems, which account for observed political outcomes.

Conversely, the *method of agreement* compares cases (or systems) in order to detect those relationships between $X \rightarrow Y$ that are similar, notwithstanding the remaining differences on other features of the cases compared. Hence, all other things are different but for certain relationships are seen to be causal (or effect-producing). This is the so-called 'most different systems design'.

The indirect methods are basically the same, but more sophisticated versions of the original method. The *indirect method of agreement* eliminates those variables that all cases have in common, instead of focusing on an overall similarity *per se*. This elaboration is useful since it helps to avoid biased results by including more cases that are seemingly different (Janoski and Hicks, 1994: 14). Alternatively, the *indirect method of difference* can be seen as an extension of the cases under review: some crucial variables are positive (sharing some values) and others are negative. This extension helps to refine the analytical results. Both methods thus lead to either MSSD (indirect method of difference) or MSDS (indirect method of – agreement).

This 'logic of inquiry', or in our parlance the relationship between research question and research design, runs as follows: in an MSSD, where we assume that the cases have more circumstances in common than not, we interpret the research outcomes by concentrating on the variation *across* the cases, focusing explicitly on both the X and Y variables. Often this basis for explanation is called the 'cross-system variation'. This type of explanation on the basis of the 'method of difference' can be demonstrated in Table 3.1.

Let X_1 be 'PR electoral system' and let X_2 be 'socio-cultural cleavages'. The independent variable (Y) is 'type of party system' (i.e. polarized or not). Finally, the cases are considered similar because they represent constitutional democracies, warranting universal suffrage and freedom of organization as well as the right to contest elections: the type of democracy which Robert Dahl (1971) called 'polyarchy' (hence only polyarchies are compared). The research question is: what causes the differences across polyarchies in the development of party systems? The issue at hand is now: what do the research results tell us? The results tell us that the variation in type of party system is – assuming the context, i.e. polyarchy, to be constant – caused by the existence of socio-cultural cleavages (as Rokkan, 1970, contended) since X_2 systematically co-varies with the Y variable (yes/yes and no/no), whereas the other variable, X_1 – electoral system – does not co-vary with the dependent variable. Apparently, in reality the type of electoral system does not systematically produce a concurrent type of party system (as was put forward by Duverger). Hence, in an MSSD the focus is on the correspondence between the dependent and independent variables on the basis of their variation *across* the cases under review.

Conversely, the most different systems approach is based on the (indirect) method of agreement. An example of this 'logic of inquiry' can be found in the study of the relationship between capitalism and democracy (Rueschemeyer et al., 1992) and in Moore's (1966) treatise on democracies and dictatorship. In both studies the research design started from the idea that the comparison is meant to confront positive (yes, there is a relationship between capitalism and democracy) and negative outcomes (no, there is not). This method of agreement is also called the 'parallel demonstration of theory' (see Skocpol and Somers, 1980) and is demonstrated in Table 3.2.

Let X_1 be 'capitalism' present or not (yes/no) and X_2 be 'middle classes' present or not (yes/no) and X_3 be 'economic development' high or not (yes/no). The dependent variable Y is here 'polyarchy' more or less present in a functional way, i.e. strong and weak (see Keman, 2002). From the research results it could be inferred that, if two of the three variables are present for a case then that particular system appears to be more polyarchic. Hence, case 1 in Table 3.2 is characterized by all three conditions, whereas case 3 has only one. In contrast to the MSSD approach, we observe a parallel demonstration of theory. In fact, one could put forward that if only capitalism is present polyarchy does not appear to develop. In addition, if a middle class exists the chances seem to increase. This example indicates that polyarchy appears to have emerged due to the rise of favourable conditions. This would not only support the hypotheses of Rueschemeyer et al. and of Barrington Moore, but also Dahl's theory. The conclusion is not that one of the variables causes polyarchy, but rather that the independent variables represent favourable conditions for the emergency of polyarchy. In addition, X_1 (capitalism), so it appears, is not a direct factor in explaining the occurrence of polyarchy. Finally, the method of agreement is often conducive to internally valid conclusions since the cases hardly ever cover the complete 'universe of discourse' (which in this example would be all the countries of the world, since the typology of polyarchy can be applied to all political systems; see Vanhanen, 1997; Keman, 2002a). However, since only a limited number of cases can be studied one should be aware that the case selection represents comparable but *different* cases. A way to avoid this problem is, of course, to extend the number of cases without losing too much information.

Table 3.2   *An example of most different systems comparison*

	Case 1	Case 2	Case 3	Case 4
Independent variables				
X_1 = Capitalism	yes	no	yes	yes
X_2 = Middle class	yes	yes	no	yes
X_3 = Economic development	yes	yes	no	no
Dependent variable				
Y = Polyarchy	strong	medium	weak	medium

This problem can be dealt with by using Boolean analysis (Ragin, 1987; Berg-Schlosser and de Meur, 1996). This type of analysis allows for the handling of qualitative information, or many variables for a relative high number of cases. In fact, it transforms qualitative information into simple scalable values (i.e. in terms of more, less, none or strong, medium, weak, etc.). In addition to Boolean logic, this approach has been developed into 'fuzzy set' logic (Ragin, 2000; Pennings, 2003a). These approaches are known in the literature as 'qualitative case analysis' (QCA). Boolean analysis and 'fuzzy set' logic will be explained and highlighted in Parts II and III.

To recapitulate the discussion on relating cases to variables and vice versa:

- We are always confronted with the dilemma of choosing for a research design in which we trade off internal and external validity, i.e. MSSD versus MDSD.
- If we opt for an MSSD approach we assume the context to be (more or less) identical across all the cases under review, whereas using a MDSD approach, not constrained by the contextual bias, different contexts of cases can be compared.
- An MSSD approach follows a logic of inquiry that is based on the co-variation between X and Y variables, i.e. focusing on cross-system differences, whereas the MDSD approach uses the parallel demonstration of cases aiming to eliminate contesting explanations.

3.3 The Role of Space and Time

Often cases are confounded with countries in the comparative approach to political and social sciences. This need not to surprise us, since most comparative political research focuses on macroscopic phenomena, which are more often than not defined at the national level. Cross-sectional analysis is therefore often considered to mean the same as cross-national. Likewise one will find in textbooks on the comparative approach that case studies are, by implication, using the historical method. Again, this may well be often the case but not by definition. In this book we therefore argue that comparisons are made across *systems* – which refers to any type of political and social (sub)system that has an organizational reference to territorial space. For instance, an analysis of the role of politics with respect to policy-making in the USA concerns a cross-sectional analysis of the American states, i.e. the cases are subsystems of the US federal system. Conversely, the cross-sectional study of welfare statism by Wilensky (1975) comprises the comparison of 66 national welfare states. In this case the cases are indeed nation-states.

Time as a part of a research design is not always clearly defined in the literature. On the one hand, the term 'time series' analysis is used, i.e. the cases are time units (e.g. years, days or even decades) and the comparative variation across time is of interest. On the other hand, we aggregate the information for a number of time units and replicate the cross-sectional analysis on the basis of this division over time (see, for example, Bartolini and Mair, 1990; Keman, 1998). This combination of sections of time (i.e. periods) and a cross-inspection of systems is commonly called 'diachronic analysis' (see also Figure 2.1). Hence, if the cases are defined as time units we see it as 'comparable cases' analysed on the bases of time series. If we compare cross-sections at certain intervals then we have multiple 'snapshots' (Castles, 1987). A combination of the two – using intertemporal and cross-sectional comparable data – is nowadays referred to as 'pooled analysis'.

In sum: both time and space are important dimensions in any research design. Depending on the units of variation (i.e. the $X \rightarrow Y$ relationship) under review, intertemporal and/or cross-sectional variation will define the type of cases that are needed to organize the comparative data. In addition, if time is the preponderant dimension then, more often than not, the underlying logic of inquiry is based on the method of agreement, whereas if space is the dominant dimension of comparison the (indirect) method of difference will be the guiding principle of interpretation (see also Bartolini, 1993).

Having outlined the basic problems with regard to space and time in relation to the development of a proper comparative research design, we shall now delve into these dimensions a little deeper. This is necessary since both dimensions are crucial with respect to any empirical-analytical studies in the social sciences, in particular when the 'political' as a core subject of the comparative approach is to be researched. First, we shall discuss the historical method and then the problems related to spatial analysis.

3.3.1 Time and history

Much comparative research is characterized by a research design using the historical method. This poses a number of problems which are related to the consequentiality of time itself, the number of cases that can be studied and, finally, the measurement of time in terms of variation (Flora, 1974; Bartolini, 1995). Bartolini notes that, surprisingly enough, the historical method is rarely disputed by social scientists. A major problem is that one is implicitly assuming that the structuration of time is a result of a few universal factors (e.g. the impact of processes of 'modernization'). Hence, time remains sequentially defined and is therefore potentially an overdetermining factor in relation to the logic of inquiry applied.

A possible solution, which is often advocated, is to incorporate time in the research design by means of a comparable case study design in order to enhance the internal validity (Abrams, 1982; Tilly, 1984; Skocpol, 1985; Ragin, 1991). As Bartolini correctly points out, there is no fundamental (or logical) difference between using a synchronic and a diachronic research design. In both cases the comparativist has to grapple with the fact of whether or not the observed variation is part and parcel of both the independent and dependent variables. A possible way is developed within the already mentioned QCA approach (De Meur and Berg-Schlosser, 1994). In effect this approach tries to break out of the dilemma of too many variables and too few cases. By reducing complexity within cases one can compare more cases than before. In addition, it allows for intertemporal analysis. This type of analysis, aiming at internal and external validity, is an underused research design within the comparative approach. Yet, it is a useful way to amplify the advantages of both types of analysis instead of seeing them as opposite and exclusive instruments of the 'art of comparing'. On the one hand, it can be quite helpful to corroborate findings across the board as a means of validation. On the other hand, it can be quite helpful to generate new hypotheses or to account for deviant cases.

3.3.2 Space and cross-sections

In contrast to the time dimension, as has been pointed out here, the problems with spatial analysis have been discussed at great length. Spatial analysis has to do with the level of measurement in relation to the selection of cases under review. Lijphart (1971) distinguishes three types of spatial analysis: statistically based; case-oriented; and the comparable case approach (see also Ragin, 1987; Rueschemeyer et al., 1992). Ragin, in particular, overstates the differences between the various methodological approaches. He develops a dichotomy that separates the 'case-oriented' from the 'variable-related' research design. The first approach would enable the comparativist to analyse the 'political' more comprehensively than would be possible by means of a 'few variables, many cases' approach. The latter method is, in Ragin's view, inferior to the 'comparable case' approach because the relationships observed are bound to be biased or 'overdetermined' as a result of empirical indicators which are either too generally constructed or measured at a highly aggregated level (see also Przeworski, 1987).

However valuable these insights may be and no matter how important it is to reflect on these issues, they concern an argument which is false. The differences between research designs are often exaggerated and often not based on logical arguments. They concern quality (i.e. historical knowledge) versus quantity (i.e. analytical empiricism), holistic explanations versus parsimonious modelling, interpreting patterned agreement (e.g. on the basis of a 'most different' design) versus judging patterned co-variation (by means of a 'most similar' design), detailed knowledge of the cases versus theoretical knowledge from relations, and so on. Yet, is there really such a difference between the two approaches that warrants such strong views on the rights and wrongs of either approach? It is obvious that we do not think this to be the case nor that it is necessary (see also Rueschemeyer et al., 1992: 27ff. on this point). Budge and Keman (1990: 194) have attempted to clarify this point about applying the logic of comparison to a research question as a means to develop a theory within the field of comparative politics, as follows:

> to construct a theory at all one has to simplify and generalize, rather than describe. There is no point in constructing a general explanation clogged up with minutiae of time and place. The purpose of a theory is to catch and specify general tendencies, even at the cost of not fitting all cases (hence one can check it only statistically, and it is no disproof to cite one or two counter-examples). The theory should, however, fit the majority of cases at least in a general way, and provide a sensible and above all an applicable starting-point for discussion of any particular situation, even one which in the end it turns out not to explain – here it can at any rate serve as the basis of a special analysis which shows which (presumably unique or idiosyncratic) factors prevent it from fitting.
>
> A general theory of this kind serves the historian by providing him with an entry point and starting-ideas. These, we would argue, he always brings to the case anyway; with a validated theory he knows they are reasonably founded and has a context within which he can make comparisons with greater confidence. As we suggested at the outset, there is no inherent conflict between historical analysis and general theory. Each can, indeed must, be informed by the other and supplement the other's efforts. Theory is therefore a necessary simplification and generalization of particular motives and influences, not simply a restatement of them, though complete loss of contact with historical reality will render it too abstract and ultimately irrelevant.

This argument is also aired by others and only demonstrates, once again, the need for a proper research design, in which both the time dimension and the spatial dimension are explicitly discussed in view of the research question that is under review. We have summarized the discussion of time and space with regard to the requirements of developing a research design in Table 3.3.

3.4 Developing a Research Design

The main argument presented in this chapter has been that the purpose of applying the comparative method in political science is to identify regularities regarding

Table 3.3 *Spatial and temporal aspects of a comparative research design*

Dimension	Cases	Type of analysis	Interpretation	Related problems
Space	Territorial units or (sub)systems	Cross-sectional	Method of difference	– Unit of variation (system-specific or not)
	Case studies (one or a few)	Comparable cases	Method of agreement	– Type of data available (qualitative/quantitative)
				– Internal validity
Time	Regular intervals (e.g. years)	Time series	Method of (indirect) difference	– Unit of variation (diachronic/event-related or not)
	Periodization (e.g. before/after an event)	Repeated cross-sectional	Method of (indirect) agreement	– Type of data available (level of measurement)
				– Sequential or synchronic
				– External validity
Time and space	(sub)systems and periods or intervals	Pooled time series	Method of difference	– Unit of variation (structural and sequential)
	Multiple case studies	Time series or QCA	Method of agreement	– Type of data available (qualitative or quantitative)
				– Internal and external validity

QCA = Qualitative case analysis.

the relationship between societal and political actors, the accompanying processes of institutionalization of political life, and the societal change that emerged simultaneously. In addition, the logic of comparison is seen as the 'royal way' to establish theoretical and empirically refutable propositions that explain these regularities in terms of causality.

Assuming that one knows what to compare and (foremost) why, a proper research design must be developed to allow for an analysis that accounts in a plausible way for the research question. In Chapter 2 we proposed that comparative approach to political science may be defined by the use of the *politics–polity–policy* triad, which involves an understanding of the following:

1 How are concepts derived from the 'political' in relation to the research question posed? Hence, which actors, institutions and types of performance are implied in the research question? This points to the relation Theory → Evidence → Interpretation.
2 How can these concepts be made to 'travel' from one system (in relation to the unit of analysis) to another? Hence, how can one operationalize properly the type of actor, the rules in, and for use of a system as well as its overall performance? This refers to matters of internal and external validity regarding the data analysis.
3 How can a set of units of observation or cases be developed within which systems may be properly compared and classified? Hence, rather than maximizing the number of cases beyond the *ceteris paribus* clause, which are the comparable cases? To put it another way, what is the adequate 'universe of discourse' in relation to the research question asked?
4 How and when does one compare similar and dissimilar systems, synchronically and/or diachronically? Hence, how does one take into account time and space as well as promoting the plausibility of making causal statements on the basis of comparison? This concerns the range of the theory *per se*.

The understanding of these 'steps' is vitally important for every student of comparative politics and distinguishes it from other approaches within political and social science. In order to develop a proper research design we need, first of all, to relate the contents or substance of the research question to the core subject of the 'political'. Thus are we investigating a problem that is referring to the politics–polity–policy triad as a whole or to parts of it? For instance, are we employing a research question in which both the political determinants and consequences of the welfare state for society form the core subject? This would then imply that the variables are measured on the level of both the political and the social system. In addition, the comparativist must decide whether or not the process is questioned or the distinctive features of various welfare states as comparable systems are under scrutiny.

This logically leads to the decision on how time and space are part of the research design as well as the number of cases that can and should be involved (from 'many' to 'few'). The final decision to be made – in relation to the earlier ones – is then to what extent the context of the variables under investigation is homogeneous or heterogeneous. This means the choice of a 'most similar' or a 'most different' research design. If, for instance, the research question is directed to the internal dynamics of the politics of the welfare state it would imply a homogeneous context. If it concerns a research question with regard to the political-economic conditions of the emergence of welfare statism, it may well lead to the investigation of regimes throughout the world, which implies a heterogeneous context (see Keman, 1993a, as an example of a most similar design, and Schmidt, 1989 for a most different design). In summary: the researcher must – on the basis of the research question – go through a number of steps in order to develop the proper research design. These steps are summarized in Table 3.4.

As was elaborated in Section 2.3, the 'political' as a core subject of investigation refers to three dimensions: *politics* = actors and behaviour; *polity* = rules defining the room to manœuvre for these actors; *policy* = outcomes of the decision-making process. As can easily be understood, politics can be measured on the individual level, for instance voters' attitudes at an election, or the behaviour of a party during and after an election. Polity concerns the institutions of the systems under review: for example, the type of electoral system or the type of democratic system in which citizens parties operate (e.g. Lijphart's distinctions of 'consensus democracy' and 'majoritarian democracy'; Lijphart, 1999). Finally, policy always refers to what has been decided by the political authorities and upon which they will act (i.e. public policy-making; Castles, 1998; Keman, 2002b). Yet, most important for our purposes here, the student must understand what is central in his/her research. That is, what are the units of variation and their supposed relationship? Is it purely politics, polity or policy-oriented, or is it a mix? The answer to that question determines the level at which the core subject is to be observed. For example, if we wish to know more about the relations between voters, parties and policy actions, then we strive for observations of individuals (voters), political actors (parties), and public policy (e.g. social expenditures) within the rules (i.e. institutions) of the political system. Hence, we use individual observations (micro level), actor-related ones (meso or group level) and the system level (public governance). The main interactions we wish to investigate are then those between politics and society at various levels of measurement. It goes almost without saying that this is quite a complex and delicate matter in terms of operationalization and data analysis. In general, the levels of measurement are more straightforward to determine if the research question at stake is directed to the political process itself. These situations refer to the rows 2 and 3 in Table 3.4.

The second row explicitly refers to research questions in which the units of variation are systemic, or intra-system, features related to the behaviour of political actors. The study of government formation, for example, is directed by the 'local' rules within a given polity. Hence, we can compare the actual working of these rules over time in one or a few cases from a diachronic point of view. The units of variation concern then the process of government formation, and by definition this occurs within a homogeneous context (Keman, 1995). This implies that circumstances will be more or less constant, and thus deviations can easily be detected and discussed in terms of 'exceptions to the rules' (if not, then we need to reconsider both theory and probably the research design!).

Table 3.4 *Choices to be made in developing a research design*

Unit of variation of the political	Unit of observation and level	Time dimension	Number of cases	Contextual variables	Type of comparison
1. Politics, polity and policy	Political system	(a) Synchronic (b) Diachronic	Many Few	Heterogeneous Homogeneous	Cross-sectional Pooled
2. Politics and polity	Intra-system	(a) Synchronic (b) Diachronic	Many Few	Homogeneous Homogeneous	Cross-sectional Time series
3. Polity and policy	Inter-system	(a) Synchronic (b) Periodic	Many Fewer	Heterogeneous Homogeneous	Cross-national Cross-time

The third row points to a research design in which the units of analysis are focused at the variation system level: policy-making is then studied at the level of the system *per se* and thus should be compared with other systems. This is why it is called an inter-system comparison which – more often than not – is synchronic in nature (i.e. cross-sectional, if not cross-national). Yet, of course, one may also opt for fewer cases for which it is easier to assume that the context remains constant. This is particularly useful if the researcher aims at the explanation of a complex policy area and uses predominantly qualitative data (e.g. Héritier, 1993).

All in all, Table 3.4 demonstrates that the student – applying the comparative approach to political and social science – is bound to make choices on the basis of the research question under review. Therefore the main point of this scheme is that a student of comparative politics learns how to develop his or her research design by systematically assessing which options are available on the basis of the research question under review. Such a research design must thus be conceptualized in terms of the 'political' that is competent not only answering the specific question under review, but also enhances our (meta)theoretical understanding of the political process, the 'core subject', such as whether or not conflicting political actors are capable of achieving an optimal decision given the rules of the political game (Keman, 1997).

Examples of comparative research which can be categorized within this framework are the cross-national analysis of political performance (unit of variation no. 1 in Table 3.4) throughout the world by Powell (1982), the comparative analysis of the politics of government formation (2), and the development of the welfare state (3). In all these instances important choices are to be made relating the research question to a research design.

Budge and Keman, for instance, consciously choose to explain the process of government formation in terms of actors (i.e. political parties) in relation to their room for manœuvre due to existing modes of institutionalized behaviour (the 'rules of the game'). The level of observation is 'intra-system' oriented, and they increase the number of meaningful cases within a 'most similar' strategy of comparison (i.e. reducing the contextual variables which are assumed to be homogenous). The diachronic perspective is preferred here to a case-based strategy or a mere country-based comparative approach. Two arguments justify this decision: firstly, countries are not the units of analysis but parties and governments, and the time dimension is considered to be constant; secondly, given the point of departure used as a mode of the explanation and the wish to validate the research question empirically, as many cases as possible had to be collected as units of observation (Budge and Keman, 1990; see, for a comparable research design, Bartolini and Mair, 1990).

Hitherto we have discussed the basic structural features of developing a research design. These features – like units of observation or number of cases, and type of analysis – must be seen as (necessary) steps of reflection in view of the research question under review. Recall that a research question in our view always implies a relationship ($X \rightarrow Y$) representing a (middle-range) theory. In Chapter 1 we defined the unit(s) of variation as the variables (here X and Y) that enable us to develop a data matrix. Before collecting and analysing the relevant data one must also take a decision about the kind of data that are called for. Again, as for instance with the issue of many versus few cases, we are confronted with a contested topic amongst comparativists: the constructing of values or indicators (i.e. units of measurement) that are and remain comparable across the 'universe of discourse' (i.e. the units of observation). This debate is now known as the issue of 'concept travelling and stretching' (Sartori, 1970; Dogan and Pelassy, 1990; Collier and Mahon, 1993) and refers to the matter of operationalization.

3.5 Transforming Concepts into Units of Measurement

The process of operationalizing means the translation of theoretical concepts into what Sartori (1970) called 'travelling' concepts by means 'of stretching': the units of measurements are considered too broad to allow for inspecting the *specifica differentia* across systems or even across time. Hence, the development of 'truly' comparative units of variation is an awkward and often tricky business. Sartori pointed to this problematic as the 'ladder of generality', i.e. enhancing a wider use of a theoretical concept by extension (of its initial meaning) or by means of intension (limiting observations to specified categories). This procedure obviously will reduce the applicability of a concept in comparative research, but, equally obviously, will increase its internal validity. Conversely, extension will have the opposite effect, and here the question is whether or not the wider use (i.e. in number of cases to be compared) impairs the external validity of the analysis. The 'ladder of generality' is depicted in Figure 3.2 (adapted from Collier and Mahon, 1993).

The choice to be made and the matter of dispute is then how broadly or extensively we can define and measure the units of analysis without a serious loss of meaning. A good example of how *not* to do it is the comparative analysis of 'pillarization'. Originally this concept referred to Dutch society in which, on the basis of the religious cleavage (Catholics versus Protestants), social and political life was organized separately for each group in a vertical fashion (see Daalder, 1974). By means of this concept Lijphart (1968) was able to explain stable government under heterogeneous socio-cultural conditions in the Netherlands. Other studies used this concept to explain the degree of (in)stability in other segmented societies (such as Austria, Germany, Norway, Italy). The initial operationalization by Lijphart was too strict to apply across western Europe and thus the researchers resorted to the method of categorizing by means of 'family resemblance' (Collier and Mahon, 1993: 846–8). In its simplest fashion this method extends the initial concept, i.e. pillarization, by adding cases which share some attributes designated to indicate pillarization. How far this type of extension can go depends, first of all, on the research question asked, and secondly on whether or not the remaining contextual features can be kept reasonably constant (in an MSSD, of course).

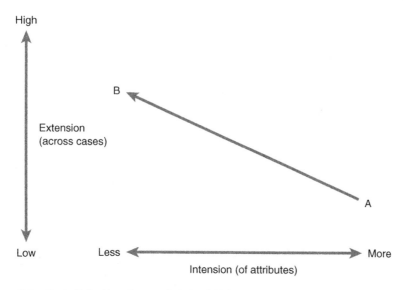

Figure 3.2   *Sartori's 'ladder of generality'. A = initial unit of variation as defined (theoretical concept); B = eventual unit of variation as operationalized (which can 'travel')*

Another method of going up the 'ladder of generality' is by the use of radial categories. Here the basic idea is that each step of extension, and thus including new comparable cases, is defined by a hierarchy of attributes belonging to the initial concept. Take, for example, the concept of 'polyarchy' as introduced by Dahl (1971). Central to his concept are the degrees to which the population at large is free to participate in political decision-making. Initially Dahl focuses on electoral rights to participate in decision-making and freedom to exercise opposition. In addition he lists a number of attributes that make up the optimal mode of democratization in order to compare the existing democracies in terms of his concept polyarchy (see: Dahl, 1971: Chapter 10). Now, by requiring that the core attributes must be available (opposition and participation) one can develop a categorization of democratic systems in which more or fewer of the other features are available. The more generally the requirements are defined, the more cases can be included. Hence radial categorization implies extension by relaxing the initial definition. Again – as with the method of family resemblances – it depends on the Research Question ($X \rightarrow Y$) to what extent this is still valid and will induce viable conclusions (for an application, see Keman, 2002a, see also Part III).

Figure 3.3 demonstrates the two possible strategies for extension. Family resemblance requires commonalities and, in this example, produces three cases in comparison with one under the initial categorization, by sharing two out of the three defining features. The radial method requires that the primary attribute (A) be always included. In Figure 3.3, this means two cases instead of the initial one.

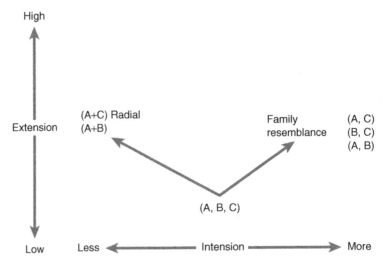

Figure 3.3 *Radial categorization and family resemblance. (A, B, C) = requirements/attributes of the original definition*

In summary: the process of operationalization for comparative purposes implies conscious decisions not only on how to develop the proper indicators, but also on the issue of the extent to which the process of operationalization as applied in observable characteristics can be relaxed to increase the units of observations (or cases) without losing its original meaning or definitions given the research question.

3.6 Conclusion

It is vitally important that an understanding of the 'rules' for systematically doing comparative research forms an essential part of learning and training – not only in comparative politics in particular, but also in political science in general. Ultimately this is one of the reasons why a grounding in comparative politics is so essential to a wider political science education. In general, political science, which has been accurately defined as 'an academic discipline which seeks to systematically describe, analyse and explain the operations of government institutions and overtly political organizations' (Finer, 1970), must necessarily include the comparative approach, if only by virtue of its explanatory intent.

And if we are to know other countries or systems, and, through this, to begin to understand how politics works, then it is essential that we promote an understanding of how to do comparative political analysis, and of how to become 'conscious' comparativists. And this, more than anything else, requires us to systematically develop a research design that enables the student to come to valid, reliable and plausible answers. Vitally important is it then – in our view – to relate theory to empirical evidence. This is a task that requires an adequate knowledge of data collection and related modes of analysis. How to do this is the core of Part II, to which we now turn.

3.7 Endmatter

Topics highlighted

- The structure and meaning of a research design: $(C^* [X \rightarrow Y])$ representing the research question.
- Interpreting empirical evidence from a most similar or most different systems design, methods of agreement and difference, regarding the interpretation of results.
- Space and time as dimensions of a research design: cross-sections, case studies and diachronic approaches.
- Choosing the proper research design on the basis of the unit of variation (derived from the core subject).
- Conceptualization and operationalization in view of striving for 'truly' comparative knowledge: concept travelling and stretching.

Question

Read the article by Lijphart and Crepaz (1991) and the rejoinder by Keman and Pennings (1995), both published in the British Journal of Political Science. What are the methodological issues in dispute? (Think of: reliability and validity; concept stretching and travelling, see Figure 3.2; radial and resemblance, see Figure 3.3.) Whose side are you on regarding the methodological issues raised in this chapter?

Exercises

We would like you to develop a research design of your own using one of the Research questions listed below. You should do the following:

1 Elaborate the relation between theory and the research question.
2 Cast your research question into the form $C^* [X \rightarrow Y]$ and infer from that whether or not you choose to use an MSSD or MDSD approach or a case-based comparison.
3 Develop the requirements of the research design in terms of time and space.
4 Try to operationalize the core of your research question (X and Y), and discuss your indicators in terms of concept travelling and stretching (i.e. internal and external validity!).

The research questions from which you can choose are:

1 Do parties matter with respect to the development of the welfare state?
2 Do variations in party systems matter with respect to the composition of governments and policy performance?
3 How do democracies differ in terms of their design and performance?

To answer, you can make use of the following literature: Castles and McKinlay (1979),
Budge and Keman (1990) and Lijphart (1994).

Further reading

Key texts: Dogan and Pelassy (1990), Hague and Harrop (2004).
Advanced texts: Mair (1996b), Ragin (2000).

Part 2

Statistics in Political Science

4

Concepts, cases, data and measurement

This chapter focuses on the measurement of political concepts. A concept has been measured whenever data have been found that indicate whether, or to what degree, the concept applies to an observed case. A measurement is simply defined as an assignment of a value (or datum) to an observed case (or an observed unit) on a variable (a concept). One measurement of the concept bilateralism, for example, is obtained by assigning the value 'yes' to Germany, another by assigning the value 'no' to New Zealand.

Whether it makes sense to ask not only whether a concept applies, but also which degree of the concept applies, depends not only on its definition but also on its level of measurement. The previous chapter showed also that the units (cases) to which a concept applies are by no means trivial in comparative political science.

Measurements always presume the availability of data. Various types of available data – e.g. data from statistical agencies, or survey data – will be discussed in Section 4.1. Separate measurements might be represented as the entries (or cells) in a rectangular data matrix with the units (cases) as rows and the variables (concepts) as columns (see Figure 1.1). This rectangular data matrix which brings together the various measurements for a set of concepts with respect to a set of units, is treated in Section 4.3. The problem of generalizability of research findings, which arises when the available data constitute only a subset of all conceivable data, is introduced in Section 4.2. Often a variety of data is useful to judge whether a single concept applies to a given unit. Scalability analysis (Sections 4.4 and 4.5) can be used to test the reliability of multiple indicators.

4.1 Data and Data Collection in Political Science

Political science is in our view an empirical science. Its inspiration may well hinge on philosophies of the good world, but more or less irrefutable facts constitute its basis. The relevant facts can be gathered from different sources.

4.1.1 Data obtained from official statistical agencies

An obvious source for comparative information on political processes is the data published on a yearly or quarterly basis by national and international statistical agencies, such as the IMF, the World Bank and the OECD, although the focus of these data is on economics. The statistical yearbooks from the *Encyclopaedia Britannica*, the yearbooks from SIPRI on military expenditures and warfare, and the Yale University *World Handbook of Political and Social Indicators* are additionally useful. All types of data sets with respect to political and social indicators compiled by political scientists and sociologists have been made publicly available. Some journals in the field of political science, for example the *European Journal of Political Research* publish data sets collected by political scientists also. Table 4.1 gives an overview of available data sets for comparative political science. Most university libraries provide online access to these databases.

Table 4.1 *Commonly used data sets from statistical agencies in political science*

IMF (www.imf.org)	International financial statistics Direction of trade statistics
OECD (www.oecd.org)	Historical statistics Employment outlook OECD economic surveys (country reports)
ILO (www.ilo.org)	Labour force statistics
Encyclopaedia Britannica (DVD, also www.eb.com)	Yearbooks, Statistical Addendum (comparative data on government, elections, economics and demography)
Worldwide Elections (http://sshl.ucsd.edu/election/world.html)	Comparative data on parties contesting elections and election outcomes
SIPRI (Stockholm International Peace Research Institute) (http://databases.sipri.se)	Yearbook of world armaments and disarmament
ICPSR (www.icpsr.umich.edu)	Archive of (partly comparative) data sets gathered by political scientists
LexisNexis (www.lexis.com)	Archive of textual accounts of the political process (e.g. newspapers, magazines)
IPU (www.ipu.org)	Comparative database on the features of parliaments and electoral systems around the world
Parties and elections (www.parties-and-elections.de)	Database of all elections in Europe since 1945 and on political parties
Comparative political data sets (http://www.ipw.unibe.ch/mitarbeiter/ ru_armingeon/CPD_Set_en.asp)	Data on politics and expenditures in all OECD countries and other central and eastern European countries

*Most university libraries have licenses to access these databases.

The compilers of data sets that enable comparisons between nations have usually obtained their data from national statistical agencies. Third World countries, in particular, do not have the statistical agencies to deliver the required data. When data from national agencies are available, they might not match the definitions of the international agencies precisely. Often the data obtained from statistical agencies do not allow for the distinctions desired by political scientists. The data set NIAS.SAV, which is used throughout this book, was compiled by a group of researchers visiting the Netherlands Institute for Advanced Study in the Humanities and Social Sciences in 1995/1996 and updated afterwards by the first author of this book.

4.1.2 Verbal and visual accounts, content analysis

Verbal accounts from politicians, eyewitnesses, journalists and contemporary historians constitute an important source of information for political scientists. These verbal accounts are accompanied in a growing number of cases by visuals on photographs, films and video. Verbal and visual accounts of the political process are provided by the participants in the process as well as by observers and interpreters.

Many contributions of the participants in the political process towards decision-making are recorded officially (e.g. party programmes, parliamentary proceedings). Politicians will use the media to pursue their ends, and will use press conferences, press reports, and 'sound bites' in television programmes to provide additional evidence, or at least additional images, of their daily pursuits.

Altogether the amount of available verbal and visual accounts from the political sphere is overwhelming. Citations, paraphrases and sound bites are the traditional means of mastering, or at least reducing, this overwhelming excess of information. It often remains an open question, however, whether the same citations, or even citations with the same purport, would also have been selected by other citation experts when complex policy documents, party programmes or parliamentary debates are at stake. The *reliability* of citations is low.

The term 'content analysis' refers to 'any technique for making inferences by objectively and systematically identifying specified characteristics of messages' (Holsti, 1969: 14). Content analysis thus aims at data with respect to verbal and visual messages that are more reliable than citations and paraphrases. Content analysis data typically enable systematic comparisons of verbal and visual accounts delivered by one actor at various points in time, or between various sources. Two basic types of content analysis can be distinguished: thematic content analysis and relational content analysis (Roberts, 1997; Popping, 2000).

Thematic content analysis aims at an assessment of the (frequency of the) presence of specified themes, issues, actors, states of affairs, words or ideas in the texts or visuals to be analysed. Which themes, issues or actors are sought depends completely on the theoretical concepts to be operationalized. The themes, issues or actors sought should be mutually exclusive (no overlaps). The complete set should be exhaustive (no unclassified texts). A mutually exclusive set of themes, issues or actors constitutes a nominal variable, since it does not exhibit a rank order. The frequency distribution of such a nominal variable indicates which themes, issues, facts or actors were mentioned more or less frequently in the texts or visuals being analysed. In the Manifesto research project (Budge et al., 2001), for example, a thematic content analysis has been performed of more than a thousand party programmes from industrialized countries (1945–98). Sentences from party programmes were classified into 54 predetermined issue areas, such as 'social justice', 'military positive', 'military negative' or 'economic orthodoxy'. Data from this content analysis will be used in many places in this book.

Relational content analysis aims at an assessment of the relations between actors, issues, ideas, etc., according to the texts or visuals being analysed.

For example, relations between nations are being sought in a content analysis project (COPDAB) by analysing newspaper articles. Its aim is to reconstruct the 'real events' underlying them. Roughly 350,000 events from the period 1948–1978 were construed on the basis of news reports in 77 international newspapers and news magazines, predominantly from the USA and the Middle East. The database consists of subject-nation/predicate/object-nation relationships. Hence, by classifying this type of information it is possible to compare the degree of cooperation or conflict between actors (here: national states) in a reliable and valid fashion.

4.1.3 Questionnaires and surveys

When the personal experiences, perceptions, opinions, attitudes and reported behaviours of persons are crucial to answering a research question, questionnaires and surveys come into play. In questionnaires and surveys the unit of measurement is usually an individual. Influential individuals might be asked, however, to act as the mouthpiece of their company, their party, or even their nation. In the latter case these organizations will usually become the units of analysis.

Here we will use the term *questionnaire* to denote a set of personalized questions that will be posed to a single actor on the basis of a preliminary investigation with respect to the actor's experiences, policy and world view. Usually the interview design allows subsequent questions to be asked that were not foreseen in the interview script. Subsequent questions will depend on the answers of the subject that are the starting point for an interview with a person. Questionnaires and interviews are at the heart of journalism. Political scientists will use them to reveal inside views of the political process. The reliability of answers obtained during an interview relies on an exchange between the interviewer and the respondent. Elite subjects willing to give an interview often want to stress their policy views once more, whereas the interviewer wants to have answers to preconceived questions. Friction in elite interviews is often enhanced by abstract, overarching questions that do not account for the multitude and diversity of daily experiences of elite persons on the basis of which answers to these questions have to be assembled. The question 'how much power has A in your opinion?', for example, is a confusing question. Policy experts might be as confused with respect to the various faces of 'power' as political scientists. Abstract, ambiguous and vague questions evoke abstract, ambiguous and vague answers.

The term *survey* is used to denote a standard list of questions that will be posed to a great number of individuals. Usually not the population of all individuals, but a sample from it will be interviewed. Interviews might be conducted by telephone or in a personal setting with an interviewer, usually at the homes of the interviewed persons. Examples of surveys in many countries are the National Election Studies. Commercial marketing agencies conduct surveys on a regular (daily or weekly) basis so as to monitor trends in opinions and behaviours on the basis of which their clients – firms, ministries, and to a minor extent also political parties – base their marketing decisions. A *panel survey* is a special type of survey where the same respondents are interviewed repeatedly over time. Comparative surveys in several countries are relatively rare. A sociological example, which *is* also useful in the context of comparative research of political values, is provided by the world value survey designed by Inglehart and colleagues (Inglehart, 1997). Eurobarometer provides comparative data on political attitudes and political behaviour in the European Union. Since many textbooks are available on survey research, we will not delve into it here.

4.2 Sampling and the Basics of Statistical Testing

Usually it is unnecessary to gather measurements on all the empirical cases to which a theory applies. Efficient research bears on a few crucial cases only or on a sample of cases from the population of all cases to which a theory applies. We will start the discussion of sampling here, before the statistics comes in. Sampling inevitably gives rise to the generalizability question. Is it reasonably safe to infer that the research results with respect to the sample will hold for the population of all cases to which the theory applies? An answer to this question depends, of course, on known characteristics of the relationship between the sample and the population.

In a *random sample* every individual from a given population has the same probability of being sampled. Most statistics presume random samples, although random sampling is an ideal type only. Research results that hold for a random sample may not hold for the population as a whole. Interesting research results on the basis of a sample are matched against a dull *null hypothesis* maintaining that in the population as a whole the result does not hold. A first type of error (*type I error*) is to keep maintaining that the interesting result holds for the population as a whole, whereas actually the null hypothesis holds. The aim of statistical testing is to reduce the probability of a type I error to less than a specified level, commonly set at 5 per cent. A *type II error* is made when interesting research results on the basis of a sample are discarded in favour of the null hypothesis, but the null hypothesis is false after all. The so-called 'power' of statistical tests is their ability to reduce type II errors. The power of various statistical tests is too complicated a subject to be discussed in this book.

4.2.1 Statistical inference from a random sample

If in the population the numbers '0' and '1' (e.g. representing 'girls' and 'boys') occur with the same frequency, then selecting a sample of 4 elements from this sample will definitely result in one of 16 sequences with equal probability: 1111, 1110, 1101, ..., 0000. Each of these 16 sequences has a probability of 1/16. By counting aspects of these 16 sequences it is easily verified that the probability of getting a sample distribution of either boys only or girls only is 1/8 (1/16 for the sequence 1111 + 1/16 for 0000). Although girls occur precisely as often in the population as boys, the chance of encountering an equal number of boys and girls in a sample of 4 amounts to 3/8 only (6 of 16 sequences only, namely 1100, 1010, 1001, 0110, 0101, 0011). One is more likely to obtain three times as many exemplars of the one sex than of the other (Probability 1/2, corresponding to 8 from 16 sequences, namely 0001, 0010, 0100, 1000, 0111, 1011, 1101, 1110). If one has found either no girls at all or no boys at all in a sample of 4, and one is willing to accept erroneous assertions one out of five times (type I error of 20 per cent), then statistically speaking the conclusion is warranted that boys and girls do not appear equally frequently in the population, since the chance of finding no boys at all or no girls at all amounted to 1/8 (= 12.5 per cent) only. Statisticians are usually more conservative in the sense of accepting erroneous assertions with respect to the population distribution for less than 5 per cent of the possible number of samples only (type I error < 0.05).

Let us emphasize three aspects of the statistician's line of thought in this simple example. First it should be noted that the statistician's tests are based on counts in an imaginary universe of all conceivable samples that might have been drawn. The second aspect to be noticed is that an important ingredient in the calculus of the statistician is the *sample size*. As long as the number of children in the sample is limited, giving birth to children of the same sex only is no reason to falsify the hypothesis that the odds of getting boys and getting girls are equal.

The third aspect to be aware of is that counts in an imaginary population to which the null hypothesis applies mount up to a *probability distribution* of all counts. Selecting at random sets of children from a school class of boys and girls gives a Newtonian or binomial distribution of the numbers of each gender in the sets. Once the probability distribution is known, statistical testing is straightforward from a mathematical point of view. The question of which probability distribution is appropriate under which circumstances will recur in Section 5.6. Distributions such as the Gaussian or normal distribution, the t-distribution, the chi-square distribution and the F-distribution play a central role in these sections. Why each distribution applies is a matter for mathematical statistics. Here we will use specific probability distributions on the authority of mathematical statisticians.

4.2.2 Random samples and non-random samples

Most samples are not random. Two types of non-random samples will be discussed here: the stratified sample and the cluster sample. The *stratified sample* intends to be more representative of the population as a whole than a random sample would be. Statistical tests based on random-sample assumptions will be too conservative for a stratified sample. The key to stratified sampling is the use of known population distributions in the sampling plan. If it is known that 50 per cent of mankind are women, and that 20 per cent of men and 22 per cent of women are older than 65, then it is quite natural to draw a stratified sample with 10 per cent of elderly men, 11 per cent of elderly women, 40 per cent of men under 65, and 39 per cent of women under 65. One should keep in mind, though, that the variables of interest are often not the variables on which the sample is stratified. Samples are usually stratified with respect to demographic characteristics, but the advantage of a demographically stratified sample over a random sample vanishes when the variables of interest are related only remotely to demography.

The *cluster sample*, or multi-level sample, is less representative of the population than a random sample. At the first level, clusters are selected, e.g. municipalities within a nation. At the second level, individuals within the first-level clusters, e.g. inhabitants of a selected municipality, are selected. A special type of a cluster sample is the snowball sample, where a set of individuals is sampled randomly and next the population of relatives of the interviewed person is asked to participate in the interview. The statistical inference problem is double-edged now. In principle one has to infer whether results holding for a sample of inhabitants would hold for the municipality as a whole and next whether results that hold for the sample of municipalities hold for the population as a whole. Cluster sampling is often preferred for pragmatic reasons over random sampling. Progress has been made during the last decade with respect to statistics for multi-level samples (Bryk and Raudenbush, 1995; Snijders and Bosker, 1999; Snijders, 2003; Skrondal and Rabe-Hesketh, 2004), but in this book we will only deal with statistics that assume random samples.

Many economists and political scientists will even perform statistical tests that assume a random sample, when the units of analysis at their disposal amount to the complete population. Economists studying quarterly data will perform statistical tests that assume a random sample, although the population from which these quarters are randomly drawn is metaphysical. Political scientists using data on all democracies for which data are available (western democracies) will perform statistical tests also. The attraction of statistical tests is their property of taking research results more seriously as the number of units of analysis increases. Since increasing the number of units of analysis will also be a means to cancel out random measurement errors and casual interpretation errors, statistical tests that assume a random sample are often used even when this assumption is obviously false.

4.3 Operationalization and Measurement: Linking Data with Concepts and Units

The *operational definition* of a concept prescribes which measurements are appropriate to measure a theoretical concept. The operational definition of a concept bridges the gap between the general definition of a concept and the available data (see Section 3.5). Concept definition is the first filter in the funnel from concepts to data, as Figure 4.1 depicts. *Operationalization* is defined as the set of efforts to obtain an acceptable operational definition, which renders a *valid* transformation that can be *reliably* measured.

The operational definition embedded in the measurement procedure is the next filter. Separate measurements have to be in accordance with the operational

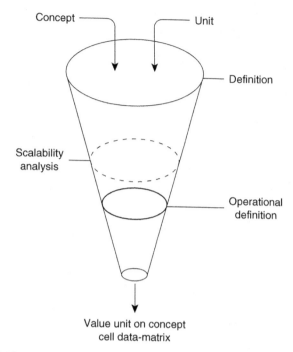

Figure 4.1   *The funnel of operationalization: from a concept and a unit towards a value*

definition, whereas the operational definition has to match the definition of the theoretical concept. The 'salience of an issue for a party', for example, might be defined on a theoretical level as the importance of an issue relative to the importance of other issues according to the policy statements of a party (Budge et al., 2001). If party manifestoes are used as the single source of available data to measure 'issue saliency', then an operational definition might be 'the percentage of sentences in a party manifesto devoted to a given issue'. Usually, various data and, as a consequence, various operational definitions can be imagined to measure a theoretical concept. Alternative operational definitions of issue salience, for example, could refer to speeches in parliament. As compared with the concept definition the operational definition is restricted to the specific method for data collection to be used. An operational definition of policy viewpoints designated to be used in a content analysis of party platforms will differ significantly from an operational definition designated to perform an elite survey among party officials.

Sometimes operational definitions are provided implicitly in the form of an elaborated measurement procedure, coding scheme, or classification scheme. Operational definitions may well include additional guidelines to apply general definitions to a specific empirical context.

Box 4.1 Levels of measurement

Levels of measurement are important for judging what type of statistics can be used or not. Without a proper understanding of these levels a correct choice of technique is impossible. These techniques will be discussed in Chapters 5 and 6 and applied in Part III in examples of existing research.

Measurement level	Meaning of numbers assigned to categories	Examples to be treated in this book
Dichotomous, binary	Different number = different category	Either use data analysis techniques for nominal scales or use (possibly adjusted) techniques for interval scales
Nominal	As dichotomous, binary	Frequency table or contingency tables
Ordinal	Higher number = higher rank	Either use data analysis techniques for nominal scales (e.g. if number of categories less than 5) or use techniques for interval scales
Interval	Equal interval between numbers = equal difference between categories	Frequency distribution, (rank order) correlation and regression analysis
Ratio	x times as far from zero = x times more	Logit and probability statistics
Absolute	Number = number	

Measurement is defined as the assignment of a value on a variable to a unit of measurement in accordance with an operational definition. The measurements within comparative political science map its theoretical concepts into databases that are accessible for data analysis. The assigned values may be visual (e.g. colour graphs on a monitor representing real-time approval of political speeches by members of a focus group), nominal (e.g. yes/no, communist/socialist.../conservative) or numerical. Length, for example, is measured in numbers of metres and centimetres, the gravity of a war is measured by the number of deaths, and political participation by the number of distinct types of activities aimed at political influence. Distinct visual and nominal codes can be represented as distinct numbers also. The visual, verbal and numerical values for separate units of measurement form a measurement scale with nominal, ordinal, interval or ratio level of measurement (see Section 4.1.2)

Table 4.2 *Data matrix of countries (units of analysis) by population characteristics (columns)*

Country	Year	Population (000s)	Turnout (%)
Italy	1960	50,198	93.7
Italy	2002	57,474	81.2
Sweden	1960	7,480	85.9
Sweden	2002	8,925	80.1
UK	1960	52,373	78.7
UK	2002	60,242	59.4

Each measurement fills in a slot in a data matrix with units (of measurements) in the rows, and variables (indicators of concepts) in the columns. As an example, part of a data matrix with 'population' and 'turnout' as variables and stacked country–year combinations is presented in Table 4.2. The value for 'turnout' in Italy in 2002 was measured as 81.2 per cent, for example.

Putting units of measurement in the rows and not in the columns is a matter of convenience reinforced by statistical packages. Successful measurements result in a completely filled rectangular array, since, for each combination of a unit of measurement and an indicator, a value will be obtained.

The reader should keep in mind that the data matrix in the final analysis often results from data at a lower level. The value of turnout for the Italian population as a whole (unit of analysis), for example, is actually an aggregation of the voting behaviour of individual Italians (unit of measurement in the first stage). The ultimate data matrix with units of analysis in the rows and concepts in the columns often results from a (rowwise) aggregation of data on units of measurement and/or a (columnwise) combination of indicators of the ultimate concepts (see Table 4.2).

4.3.1 Handling missing data

Measurements should ideally result in a completely filled rectangular data matrix. However, often many values in the data matrix remain missing.

Many data are simply not available. In the comparative research of nations it may be impossible to retrieve (recent) data on specific economic or political indicators for the complete set of countries. Next, not all indicators may apply to all units of measurement. Survey interviews often have filter questions, e.g. 'did you vote at the last elections?'. The follow-up question – which party was voted for – will be posed only to respondents who answered that they did indeed cast their vote. A third type of missing value results from rest categories in the measurement process. Substantial hypotheses on parties belonging to one of the ten ideological 'party families' distinguished by Gallagher et al. (2001) do not apply to parties which were coded as 'other parties'. A content analysis classification of issues raised in party programmes may have 'uncoded' as a category. Many questions in survey research allow for 'don't know' as an answer. Four strategies to deal with missing values will be discussed here.

Inclusion in tables as missing values is appropriate when the number and distribution of missing values is interesting. To answer the simple question 'have the poor a greater propensity to vote leftist?', it would be a good idea to include in the cross-table to answer this question the percentages of the poor and of the wealthy who abstained from voting, since, for the poor, abstention might be an alternative for a vote for the left.

Listwise deletion means that units of measurement with a missing value on one or more of the variables relevant for an analysis are excluded from the analysis. Listwise deletion is appropriate when the excluded units are not extremely important in the research design. When the number of units of measurement is large compared with the number of missing values, this solution is often preferred.

Pairwise deletion is an alternative to listwise deletion in multivariate data analysis when more than two variables with missing values enter the data analysis. As a first step, the bivariate relationships between separate variables might be based on all the cases with non-missing values for the two variables. Next the multivariate analysis will be performed on the bivariate relationships. The advantage is that fewer units of measurement will be discarded. The disadvantage is its obscurity. It is not always easy to reconstruct which units of measurement bear a special weight for the outcomes of data analysis.

Substitution of the missing values by approximations is a third possibility when it is known that a value for the variable must exist. The missing values might be filled in by predicting the true scores on the basis of causal relationships, by intrapolation or extrapolation, or by cross-sectional mean substitution. If, for example, the exact amount of military expenditure of a specific country is unknown, but the gross national product and the number of military personnel are known, and causal relationships between gross national product, military personnel and military expenditures are also known, then an estimate of military expenditure might be given. The estimated expenditures might be predicted from gross national product and military personnel. Intrapolation and extrapolation are obvious means to fill in the gaps in time series. A warning is, however, in order. Intrapolation and extrapolation may result in erroneous estimates of the statistical properties of time series models: data based on intrapolation and extrapolation give rise to a serious underestimation of the jerkiness of changes (see Section 6.7.5).

In sum: missing values create problems. Each treatment has pros and cons. It depends on the research question and the research design which treatment is to be preferred.

4.4 Criteria to Evaluate the Quality of Operationalization and Measurements

Many criteria may be applied to judge the quality of the measurements of a concept. The *efficiency* of measurements relates the quality of measurements to the time and money invested in getting the data. The *compatibility* of the measurements refers to their usefulness not only in the main research project but also in related research projects that use slightly different data (other nations, other time periods, slightly different data collection methods). The major criteria to judge the quality of measurements are *validity* and *reliability,* however. Measurements that are not valid or not reliable cannot be efficient or compatible with other data either.

The *validity* of measurements, often referred to as *construct validity*, is defined as the degree to which one actually measures whatever concept (or 'construct') the measurement procedure purports to measure. It refers to the closeness of the correspondence between the measurements and the concept being measured. But how to establish this correspondence?

Measurements possess *face validity* when they are perceived as indisputable facts with respect to the measured concept in the scientific community. Assessments of face validity are often based on the agreement of measurement results with common-sense expectations, regardless of the precise definitions of the concept.

Correlational validity (or 'internal validity') is obtained by using a traditional, but imprecise, measurement device as a yardstick to verify the correspondence between the measurements and the concept being measured. Newer measurement devices, e.g. an electron microscope, should be able to reproduce the measurements of the older ones, e.g. a lens microscope, albeit with greater precision. The refined results should, however, correlate highly with the old results.

The *predictive validity* (or 'external validity') of measurements refers to their usefulness in making correct predictions about real-world phenomena. A judgement with respect to external validity presupposes a causal theory with the concept being measured as an independent variable. Let us give an example. One might doubt whether counting the attention given to various issues in party programmes (e.g. Budge et al., 2001) renders valid measurements of the party agenda. An empirical demonstration that government expenditures on issues correspond to the attention given to these issues in the programmes of the governing party (but not with the attention given in the programmes of the opposition parties) renders an external validation for the measurements. Predictive validity is probably the most important hallmark of validity, since it relates the usefulness of the obtained measurements to the context of prevailing theories.

Students will notice that the word 'validity' is not only used in the context of the validity of measurements, but also in the context of the *validity of theories.* As was stated in Section 1.2, a theory is said to be 'internally valid' when it holds for the cases being investigated. A theory is said to be 'externally valid' when the theory also holds for the cases to which the theory applies which were not included in the data analysis. External validity of research findings is a synonym of generalizability of research findings.

Measurements are reliable to the extent that measurements with respect to the same units deliver consistent results. Reliability, however, cannot compensate for low validity. The *reliability* of measurements is related to the validity of measurement in the same way as a standard deviation from the mean is related to the mean. Measurements are not reliable when separate measurements have a large variance, i.e. when the precise measurement results for a given unit of measurement at a given time are shaky. It should be noted that a negligible variance of separate measurements does not imply that the measurements are valid: they may all be far from the truth collectively. Two varieties of reliability should be distinguished.

- *Intra-observer reliability* refers to the consistency between repeated measurements by the same observers using the same measurement devices with respect to the same units of measurement. Low intra-observer reliability is either a sign of a less than perfect task performance by the observer or a result of faulty, ambiguous or contradictory instructions with respect to the observation task.
- *Inter-observer reliability* refers to the agreement between measurements of different observers with respect to the same units of measurement. A lack of inter-observer reliability may indicate that the measurement procedure is too superficial (leaving room for additional interpretations of observers) or too complicated (encouraging personal heuristics) to overcome the subjective insights of observers. A mismatch between the phenomena to be observed and the concepts to be measured may also be at the heart of low inter-observer reliability. This type of mismatch will occur when classifications which were appropriate to the study of one specific country are transferred thoughtlessly to other countries.

Measures for the assessment of intra-observer reliability and inter-observer reliability are available for each level of measurement. Reliability measures start from ordinary measures of agreement between observers, but these measures have to be adjusted for agreement on the basis of mere chance. As an example, Scott's π (pi), a reliability measure for nominal variables, will be considered. In our example, Scott's π is equivalent to Cohen's (κ kappa), which is included in SPSS. As a starting point one can use the percentage of cases agreed upon as a first measure. If 100 cases are observed by two coders and identical observations show up for 98 cases then the agreement according to this intuitive measure would amount to 98 per cent. This intuitive measure does not take into account, however, that agreement may result from chance. If coders have two choices of code, then the probability of their agreeing by chance amounts to 50 per cent ($0.5 \times 0.5 + 0.5 \times 0.5$), at least when they make choices equally often. Things are even worse when they do not. Let us give a policy example. Suppose a new law is promulgated with rather vague criteria on special tax reliefs for firms stimulating environmental investments. Suppose that 100 firms demand special tax reliefs, but the civil servants enacting this law judge that only two firms deserve tax relief, because they know that enough money is available to grant two tax subsidies only. Agreement by chance as to whether the 100 firms should be granted tax relief now amounts to $0.98 \times 0.98 + 0.02 \times 0.02 = 0.96$. According to Scott's π the percentage of decisions agreed upon should be adjusted for agreement on the basis of mere chance:

$$\pi = \frac{\%\text{agreements} - \%\text{agreements expected}}{100\% - \%\text{agreements expected}}$$

Scott's π has a maximum value of 100 per cent. If the two civil servants pick out precisely the same two firms for tax relief, then this maximum will be reached. If they agree on 96 cases, but disagree precisely on the question of which two firms deserve tax relief, then Scott's π amounts to 0.49 only. This figure reflects common sense, since the civil servants disagree where the crucial question of which firms deserve tax relief is concerned, notwithstanding their amazing agreement that 98 out of 100 firms do not deserve tax relief.

When multiple indicators are available for one concept, the reliability of the measurements can be assessed by computing one way or another the agreement between these indicators. In the context of multiple-indicator research or 'scalability analysis' or 'item reliability research', which will be discussed in the next sections, the term scalability is used as a synonym for reliability.

4.4.1 Multiple indicators: the scalability (reliability) problem

Often a variety of related indicators of a concept can be imagined. One may choose one of these indicators as the best indicator on theoretical reasons. Often one will use *multiple indicators* to reconstruct a concept. In party manifesto research, for example, references to 'crime', negative references to 'social security' and references to 'economic orthodoxy' may be considered as signs of a rightist party ideology. In survey research, answers to a number of indicative questions will be combined to arrive at measurements of an abstract concept such as 'political efficacy'. To measure this single concept the survey respondent is asked whether he or she agrees or disagrees with a number of related statements such as 'Members of Parliament do not care about the opinions of people like me', 'Political parties are only interested in my vote and not in my opinions', 'People like me have absolutely no influence on governmental policy' and 'So many people vote in elections that my vote does not matter'. The operational definition of a concept should clarify whether a specific pattern is expected in the data with respect to the multiple indicators of the concept.

Multiple indicators may simply be intended as a *repeated measurements scale* of precisely the same concept. In survey research, several questions can be posed with respect to slightly different aspects of the concept (e.g. questions with respect to newspaper reading, watching television news and participating in political discussions to measure 'political interest'). In the case of repeated measurements one expects that each indicator gives rise to almost the same results.

Indicators may also build up to a *cumulative measurements scale*, however. The concept of 'political participation', for example, can be measured both with 'easy' indicators such as voting at elections (many citizens participate to this degree) and with 'difficult' indicators such as running for a political function (only a few citizens participate to this degree). Cumulative measurement scales resemble long jumping. An 'easy' indicator of one's jumping capacities is whether one can leap over a ditch 1 metre wide (many will pass this easy test), whereas a more 'difficult' indicator would be whether one can leap over a ditch of 3 or even 8 metres (fewer will pass these more difficult tests). Voting is an 'easy' indicator of political participation since most citizens tend to vote, whereas running for a political function is a 'difficult' indicator since fewer citizens *do so*. In the case of a cumulative scale one expects that passing the difficult threshold is a sufficient proof of being able to pass the easy thresholds. It is not to be expected that the world long jump record holder will fail to leap over a ditch of only 1 metre. It is not to be expected either that those who strive for a political career will not vote themselves.

In the case of an *unfolding measurements scale* or *proximity scale* the multiple indicators tap specific positions of an underlying continuum. If it is assumed that the three indicators 'nationalization of industries', 'no nationalization, no privatization' and 'privatization of government branches' are respectively a leftist, a centrist and a rightist indicator of the underlying left–right scale, then it is to be expected that parties will agree especially with indicators that come close to their own position on the underlying scale. The larger the distance between an indicator and the party position, the larger the disagreement with the indicators. Parties who endorse the centrist position will discard both 'nationalization' and 'privatization', for example. A party in favour of 'privatization' will surely resist the idea of 'no privatization' but will utterly detest the idea of 'nationalization', since the latter indicator of the left–right scale reflects the opposite end of the political spectrum as compared with its own position. In the case of an unfolding scale it is expected that the pattern of responses to indicators reflects the similarities between specific indicators and specific units of analysis. Here we will not discuss the large variety of advanced methods that are available to test whether indicators are consistent with a latent underlying cumulative or unfolding scale (Mokken, 1971; Van Schuur, 1994; Skrondal and Rabe-Hesketh, 2004).

Scalability analysis is a designation of research techniques to test whether the expectations can be corroborated which follow from the assumptions that multiple indicators build up to a repeated measurements scale, to a cumulative scale, or to an unfolding measurement scale. An overview of available techniques is presented in Table 4.3. Here these techniques will be mentioned only because scalability analysis is a highly technical area. To test whether indicators can be considered as repeated measurements, a variety of techniques are available, among them Likert reliability analysis (with Cronbach's alpha), principal components analysis and an array of variants of factor analysis. To test whether multiple indicators are consistent with an underlying cumulative scale, Guttman scale analysis and Mokken scale analysis are available. To test whether indicators are consistent with an underlying unfolding scale, relatively unknown procedures such as MUDFOLD analysis are available.

4.5 Scalability and Cluster Analysis

An introduction to all the techniques of scale analysis is beyond the scope of this book. The discussion will be confined to the most commonly used techniques:

Table 4.3   *An overview of techniques for scalability analysis*

Expected relationship between multiple indicators	Scale type	Variety of scalability analysis to test whether expected relationship is corroborated
Indicators of the same position on an underlying concept	'Repeated measurements scale' with equal weight indicators	Likert scale; Cronbach's alpha (SPSS)
	'Repeated measurements scale' with unequal weights	Principal components analysis; (one of the varieties of) factor analysis (e.g. principal axis factoring, maximum likelihood) (SPSS)
Indicators of the 'difficulty' of the position on an underlying concept	'Cumulative scale'	Guttman scale; Loevinger's *H* (special purpose program MSP5 (by Ivo Molenaar) available from http://www.scienceplus.nl, Stata module (by Jean-Benoit Hardouin, http://fmwww.bc.edu/repec/bocode/m/msp.ado)).
Indicators of various positions on an underlying concept	'Unfolding scale'	MUDFOLD (van Schuur, 1984) (Special purpose program available from http://www.scienceplus.nl)
Unknown resemblance between indicators		(One of the varieties of) cluster analysis

Likert-scale analysis with Cronbach's alpha as a measure of scalability, factor analysis and cluster analysis.

The first two methods have in common the assumption that the indicators are essentially repeated measurements of an underlying theoretical concept or dimension. They are assumed to measure the same thing. But what is meant by 'the same thing'? Cronbach's alpha assumes that all indicators are measured in the same direction. Thus, favouring the incumbent party in government and favouring the challenger do not measure the same political attitude according to Cronbach's alpha, because the indicators exclude each other. Moreover, all indicators are assumed to have the same variance. Principal components analysis and factor analysis automatically correct the indicators for such trivial types of not being the same. The latter techniques will also reveal that favouring the incumbent excludes favouring the challenger, but, more importantly, they will also reveal in the first place that favouring the challenger and favouring the incumbent are two measurements of the same political attitude, because these two responses exclude each other systematically. If Cronbach's alpha is used, then all indicators should be recoded in the same direction beforehand. Favouring the incumbent and opposing the challenger will amount to a high

Cronbach's alpha, whereas favouring the incumbent and favouring the challenger will not.

Likert scale analysis with Cronbach's alpha, principal components analysis and factor analysis share more, rather tricky, assumptions. One tricky assumption is that the direction of responses to an indicator (e.g. for or against the incumbent) is indicative of the position on the underlying concept of a political attitude. This may seem trivial. One may indeed conclude that a respondent in a survey does not share the political attitudes of the challenger if he or she favours the incumbent. But it is not certain whether a respondent endorses the political attitude of the challenger when he or she disagrees with the incumbent. The problem is that one may oppose an incumbent for different reasons: for being too 'leftist', but also for being too 'rightist', or for whatever reason. If the latter ambiguity is a serious one – which may be the case with political attitudes in multi-party systems – then unfolding analysis should be applied rather than the techniques being discussed here (van Schuur, 1993, 1995). Another tricky assumption is that the mean of all indicators should be the same. But often indicators differ with regard to their 'difficulty'. If the political attitude towards the incumbent is measured with an intention to vote, and an intention to sponsor the incumbent's campaign, then the measures being discussed here will indicate a fairly poor scalability, since *only a few* of those who intend to vote for the incumbent party are able and willing to sponsor the incumbent's campaign. In the presence of such indicators a cumulative scale should be applied to test whether the few who are willing to sponsor the incumbent's campaign belong only to the voters who intended to vote for the incumbent party.

When a bunch of possible indicators for a concept is available, one should first select those indicators that resemble each other fairly well, before a conclusive scalability analysis is performed. Both explorararaty factor analysis and cluster analysis are useful for this end. Both techniques will be discussed in this section, in addition to Likert scale analysis with Cronbach's alpha and 'confirmatory' factor analysis.

Even an introductory explanation of these techniques requires knowledge of elementary statistics such as means, variances, covariances and correlations at the undergraduate level. Students who feel that this knowledge has faded should brush up this knowledge. In addition to previously used textbooks, the first paragraphs of the next chapter may be used to obtain a quick overview of these statistics.

Why scalability analysis anyway?

If a scale analysis demonstrates that variables do not belong to one dimension, then adding together the values on these variables will give unintelligible results. The resulting sum will be some random number, almost independent of the values on the variables being added.

As an example, the national subsidies for municipalities in the Netherlands might be mentioned. The national law on municipal finances of 1955 opened the possibility for national ministries to enact Orders in Council which would allow municipalities to receive subsidies whenever they had some specific financial needs. Twenty-five years later, in 1980, more than five hundred Orders in Council dealt with special subsidies for specific financial needs of municipalities. A serious problem had evolved. The total effect of all these Orders was undesired, although each of the specific Orders had by and large desired effects. Let us rephrase the example in terms of scalability analysis. All subsidies should have been repeated measurements of one (or a few) underlying dimension(s) of legitimate financial municipal needs. But the civil servants of each of the separate ministries adhered to a faulty philosophy. They reasoned that one should enact a new Order in Council when a municipal financial need was detected that was independent of the remaining financial needs. Thus, a first Order in Council was enacted to subsidize municipalities with inner-city problems, a further one to subsidize municipalities in need of money to maintain their forests, a further one to subsidize municipalities which had to maintain their port, and so on. The problem was that inner cities, forests, ports, and roads are almost completely independent needs. Not a single municipality suffered from none of the subsidized problems, and not a single one suffered from all subsidized problems. The total amount of money a municipality received as a result of these five hundred subsidies was almost completely independent of any specific municipal need. Accruing a lump sum to municipalities would have had almost the same financial results, with far lower bureaucratic costs (e.g. enacting Orders, implementing subsidies, negotiations on subsidies). The abstract lesson to learn from this policy fiasco is that summing (non-scalable) indicators which are not repeated measurements of the same (position on the) underlying scale will result in a random number which is almost independent of the separate measurements. The aim of scalability analysis is to test whether indicators really 'add up'.

Which data to use in empirical illustrations?

The empirical examples to illustrate the use of scalability analysis and cluster analysis will be derived from a subset of the Manifesto research project (Budge et al., 2001) which was discussed in Section 4.1.2.

It should be noted that these data do not perfectly match the assumptions of classical test theory. Parties might choose not to address a specific issue area because they have addressed a related issue area in depth. The data from a questionnaire with respect to opinions on such related (but sometimes neglected) issue areas would show that the various issue areas amount to a strong scale. Since a party may pick up only one issue from a set of related issues in a given campaign, the content analysis data will often show no scales or rather weak scales, although related issues may have been one scale in the minds of the authors of the programmes. Therefore the 'strong' criteria for appropriate scales derived from experimental research and survey research should be relaxed.

As an example we will use the indicators for Laver and Budge's concept of 'state intervention' here (Laver and Budge, 1992: 23–5). Five of the 54 categories used in the content analysis project are assumed to measure state intervention, i.e. the percentages of programmes devoted to 'regulation of capitalism', 'economic planning', 'protectionism: positive', 'controlled economy' and 'nationalization'. The percentages devoted to these categories are simply added to measure 'state intervention'. Such an addition will amount to a random number if these indicators do not 'measure the same thing'. Laver and Budge assume on the basis of face validity that these indicators 'measure the same thing'. Laver and Budge use their measure 'state intervention' as one of their 20 measures to predict government coalitions. If the five indicators of 'state intervention' do not belong to the same scale after all, then 'state intervention' as measured by Laver and Budge is really a constant plus or minus a large random component. An even better prediction of future coalitions is to be expected by removing non-scalable items.

4.5.1 Likert scales and Cronbach's alpha

A Likert scale is a summative scale constituted by several unweighted indicators. These indicators are assumed to be identical, parallel, or 'repeated' measurements of one concept. The basic idea of a Likert scale is that a summative scale cancels out the errors in the separate indicators. Therefore the summative scale will discern the units of analysis more precisely than the separate indicators, since measurement errors in the latter hamper their discerning power. Cronbach's alpha is used to test whether summing separate indicators adds to the discriminating power of the theoretical concept. The simple idea that for a given case the various indicators should result in the same measurement outcomes implies that more or less the same measurement value should co-occur for all indicators. Equivalently, the covariances between the indicators should be high, as compared to the variances of these indicators. This idea is expressed in the formula for Cronbach's alpha by diminishing 1, the desired upper limit for Cronbach's alpha, in such a way that alpha decreases when the covariances between the indicators decrease as compared to the variances.

Let v_i denote the variance of the ith indicator, v_{ij} the covariance of the ith and the jth indicator. Then the sum of the variances v_i of the k indicators within the variance–covariance matrix is $\Sigma_i v_i$. This sum is divided by the sum of all the covariances v_{ij} and variances v_i in the variance–covariance matrix ($\Sigma_i \Sigma_j v_{ij}$), thus counting variances once and covariances twice. The result of this division is subtracted from one:

$$\alpha = \left(1 - \frac{\sum_{i=1}^{k} v_i}{\sum_{i=1}^{k} \sum_{j=1}^{k} v_{ij}}\right) \times \frac{k}{k-1}.$$

If the indicators co-vary to their maximal extent, then all entries in the variance–covariance matrix will become equal, and the outcome of this subtraction would become $1 - (k/k^2)$, or $(k-1)/k$. The postmultiplication by $k/(k-1)$ merely serves to guarantee that the upper limit of alpha is not $(k-1)/k$ but simply 1. The lower limit for alpha is not 0, nor −1, but minus infinity, which is reached when two indicators have exactly opposite values for each unit of measurement.

To test the reliability of separate indicators, for each item Cronbach's α is computed without the indicator itself. Cronbach's α should not increase by dropping an indicator.

It should be noticed that a proper computation of the variance of the summative scale, v_s, presumes correspondence of the *directions* of the indicators that are summated. If, for example, one dimension is supposed to underlie the answers to the question 'what do you think of the pro-choice movement?', as well as the answers to the question 'what do you think of the pro-life movement?' then the answers to one of these questions should be flipped over before summation, i.e. '(strongly) agree' with pro-life should be counted as '(strongly) disagree' with pro-choice.

The value of Cronbach's α tends to increase when the number of indicators increases, since errors are cancelled more easily when the number of indicators increases. As a rule-of-thumb test psychologists and survey sociologists use a minimum value for α of roughly +0.67. Within the context of the Manifesto content analysis of party programmes less stringent criteria should be applied, since authors of party programmes, as opposed to respondents in survey research, feel free to address only one theme from a set of more or less related themes according to researchers afterwards.

Since Laver and Budge added their five indicators of 'state interventionism' without giving them weights, a test of their scale using Cronbach's alpha would be a good idea. Table 4.4 presents the results. Cronbach's α is positive (+0.59), although too low by the standards for Likert attitude scales. The moderate value of alpha suggests that parties tend to address issues from the same issue group of 'state intervention' but that they will also often pick only one or a few of them. If one takes into account that parties were not forced in any way to address the themes that were put forward by the Manifesto researchers, the α-score of +0.59 is high enough to warrant unweighted addition of the issues.

To test whether all the indicators indeed belong to the same scale, values for Cronbach's alpha are also computed when specific items are removed from the scale. If Cronbach's alpha increases when a specific indicator is removed from the scale, then that indicator apparently did not belong to the scale. An inspection of the α-values for the scales with separate items deleted shows that the removal of 'protectionism' from the scale would improve Cronbach's alpha. Protectionism does not tap the same concept dimension as the other indicators. Apparently, not only leftist parties, but also many rightist parties favoured protectionism, for example to ensure the national balance of trade.

4.5.2 Factor analysis

Factor analysis has many variants. *Principal components analysis* is the simplest type, and is based on the same principle as Cronbach's α. The weighted scale should

Table 4.4   *Cronbach's alpha for five items of 'state intervention'*

Item	Percentage indicators $\alpha = +0.29$ (column below: α with indicator excluded)	Dichotomized indicators $\alpha = +0.59$ (column below: α with indicator excluded)
Protectionism: positive (406)	30	59
Nationalization (413)	18	52
Controlled economy (412)	17	52
Economic planning (404)	31	50
Regulation (403)	25	54

discern the units of analysis more pregnantly than the separate indicators, since measurement errors in the latter hamper their discerning power. The numerator of Cronbach's α indicated whether the discerning power (the variance) of the summative scale (v_s) exceeded the sum of the variances of the separate indicators $(\Sigma \Sigma v_i)$. The basic idea of principal components analysis is to find a linear combination S of the indicators with weights for the separate indicators such that the variance of the summative scale (v_s) is maximized. The aim is to find weights – labelled as *factor scores* – $u_1, u_2, \ldots, u_k$ for the k indicators of the component S, conceived as a linear combination of the indicators:

$$S = u_1 x_1 + u_2 x_2 + \cdots + u_k x_k,$$

such that the variance (discerning power) of this component S, v_s, is maximized. Thus, the factor scores – weights for the separate indicators – are ascertained in such a way that the discriminatory power (variance) of the underlying concept is maximized.

To understand principal components analysis (and factor analysis) one has to know the correct interpretation of the mathematical concepts of *eigenvalues* and *eigenvectors* in this context. The more general interpretation of these concepts, which are used throughout all areas of science where maximization in systems of linear equations is involved, does not concern us here. In effect the first eigenvalue is a measure of the maximum discriminatory power of the underlying concept being sought. As a first step the variables $x_1, x_2, \ldots, x_k$ are standardized so that each of them has a variance of 1. The first eigenvalue, usually denoted as λ_1, reduces to v_s/k, where v_s is the maximum variance (discerning power) of the cases under investigation over the concept to be measured and k represents the number of indicators. If $v_s/k<1$ then the underlying concept has a smaller discriminatory power than the indicators. The first eigenvalue expresses the discriminatory power of the concept as a multiple of the discriminatory power of separate (standardized) indicators. The larger the first eigenvalue, the higher the discriminatory power. The weights or *factor scores* $u_1, u_2, \ldots, u_k$ associated with this value are the elements of the *first eigenvector.*[1]

The question of which indicators qualify as reliable is usually answered by the rule of thumb that each indicator should 'load' on (correspond with) the first component found. As a rule of thumb the correlation coefficient between the indicator and the first component should be +0.35 at least. This requirement implies that roughly one-eighth ($0.35 \times 0.35 = 0.1225$) of the variance in the indicator should correspond with variance in the retrieved first component. These correlation coefficients between indicators and the retrieved component are often referred to as *factor loadings* or as the elements of the *factor matrix* (SPSS). From the requirement that each indicator should correlate linearly with the first component follows an overall measure for the reliability of the indicators. The variance in the indicators explained by the first component should be at least 1/8. The proportion of variance in the indicators that is bound by the first component is a simple function of the first eigenvalue, which denotes the variance of the concept starting from indicators with a variance of 1. The proportion of variance in the indicators bound by the first component amounts to the first eigenvalue λ_1, divided by the number of indicators k.

Some variance in the indicators will not be bound by the first component. The process might be repeated. Starting from the second eigenvalue and its associated second eigenvector, one might extract a second component which maximally explains the remaining variance. Indicators that did not load on the first factor might perhaps load on the second one. In the case of k indicators, a maximum of k components are retrievable, but most computer programs will not extract components with an eigenvalue of less than 1, since such components would have a smaller variance than the indicators on the basis of which the components are constructed. In the context of testing whether indicators represent one underlying concept with an interval level of measurement, the second and higher components do not have any substantive meaning. Output from statistical packages may be confusing because not just one eigenvalue, one eigenvector and one set of factor loadings are printed, but $k-1$ of them. Only the first series should be used.

The SPSS output from the principal components analysis for our now familiar example of five indicators for 'state intervention' suggested by Laver and Budge is printed in Figure 4.2. SPSS prints only one principal component, since the eigenvalues associated with the remaining ones are less than one. Components with an eigenvalue of less than one are not useful since their variance is lower than the variance of a single (standardized) indicator. The largest eigenvalue is $\lambda_1 = 1.91$. This eigenvalue indicates that the power of the resulting scale of 'state interventionism' to distinguish between the various party programmes under investigation is 1.9 times as high as the power of separate indicators to do so. Since five items were included in the component, this amounts to an explained variance in the values of the indicators by the ultimate values on the concept of 'state interventionism' of $1.91/5 = 0.382$, or 38.2 per cent. Since $100 - 38.2$ per cent of unique variation in the indicators remains, it is safe to conclude that the concept 'state interventionism' is not able to capture the larger part of the variation in the attention of parties for each of the separate five indicators of 'state interventionism'.

All factor loadings (the elements of the factor matrix) exceed $r = +0.35$. The worst indicator is D406, the now familiar troublemaker of protectionism. However, still roughly one-fifth of its variance (0.4486×0.4486) is bounded by the

Variable	Communality	*	Factor	Eigenvalue	Pct of Var	Cum Pct
D403	.37093	*	1	1.90968	38.2	38.2
D404	.46271	*				
D406	.20124	*				
D412	.42838	*				
D413	.44642	*				

PC   extracted   1 factors.

Factor Matrix:

	Factor 1
D403	.60904
D404	.68023
D406	.44860
D412	.65451
D413	.66814

Factor Score Coefficient Matrix:

	Factor 1
D403	.31892
D404	.35620
D406	.23491
D412	.34273
D413	.34987

Figure 4.2 *SPSS output from principal components analysis*

theoretical concept 'state intervention'. The factor scores (interpreted by SPSS as the elements from the first eigenvector divided by $\sqrt{\lambda_1}$), that are given below indicate indeed that D406 should be given a relatively low weight (0.23 instead of roughly one-third).

The factor scores represent the optimal weights for the indicators that were sought from the beginning (although the term 'weight' is slightly misleading here since they do not add up to one). The findings on eigenvalues, factor loadings, explained variances, and so on serve only as diagnostic materials. For each case under investigation the ultimate factor scores should be multiplied by the values on the standardized indicators to obtain for each case the values on the standardized concept being sought.

4.5.3 Principal axis factoring and confirmative factor analysis

The use of principal components analysis has been criticized because of its failure to signal that some indicators have a very large error component. Principal components analysis tries to capture *all* the variance in the indicators, regardless of whether this variance arises from the unreliability of the indicator or from the 'true' score on the first component. But which scores on an indicator are due to error and which ones reflect the 'true' score? One single answer to this question underlies all variants of 'true factor analysis'. The error part of an indicator does not correlate with the factor, whereas the true part does. The proportion of the variance of an indicator that is not due to errors, but is common with the factors sought, is referred to as the *communality* of an indicator. The aim of factor analysis is to find weights for the indicators such that the factors to be found do not account for all the variance in the indicators but only for the communalities of the indicators. The use of early computers made a method called *principal axis factoring* (PAF) popular. PAF is still widely used. It is an iterative method not based on an explicit maximization criterion. Because of its fuzziness from a mathematical point of view it is impossible to render PAF intelligible in a few sentences.

Since computing power is no longer a problem anymore, factor analysis variants that are more elegant from a mathematical point of view and therefore easier to explain than PAF, but computationally more demanding, gained predominance during the late 1970s and 1980s. In particular, Confirmatory factor analysis based on the *maximum likelihood* (ML) method has gained ground. ML starts from the core idea of item reliability analysis that the values of multiple indicators have to correspond with each other since they are manifestations of the same underlying concept. One expects the indicators to be highly correlated, since all indicators tap the same (unmeasured) concept. The amount of correlation to be expected between two specific indicators depends only on their (as yet unknown) factor loadings, i.e. on the correlations between the two indicators and the underlying concept. The correlation to be expected between two indicators is equal to the product of the factor loadings of these two indicators (not proved here). In the case of three indicators, it is not too difficult to determine unique factor loadings with paper and pencil. Let us call the factor F and the three indicators x_1, x_2 and x_3. Let us suppose that the correlations between the indicators amount to $r_{12} = 0.24$, $r_{13} = 0.3$ and $r_{23} = 0.20$ (see Figure 4.3). Let us denote the factor loadings of the three indicators as f_1, f_2 and f_3. Since a correlation between two indicators is simply the product of the factor loadings of the two indicators, one can also write $f_1 f_2 = 0.24$, $f_1 f_3 = 0.3$ and $f_2 f_3 = 0.20$. Elementary high school mathematics can be used to solve this system of three equations with three unknowns, which gives the solution $f_1 = 0.6$, $f_2 = 0.4$ and $f_3 = 0.5$. In the case of more than three indicators no unique solution is guaranteed. The principle remains the same, however. Unweighted least squares factor analysis ascertains the factor loadings in such a way that the sum of the squared differences between the observed correlations between indicators and their expected correlations (i.e. the product of their factor loadings) is minimized. ML factor analysis adds one complication to unweighted least squares factor analysis, however. ML estimation is a mathematical method to maximize the likelihood that the estimates of *population* characteristics based on sample data reflect the true population characteristics and not only the sample data. ML estimation justifies the general principle that low correlations in a sample should be given less weight, since low observed correlations in a sample are, unlike high observed correlations, easily produced by chance. Thus, ML factor analysis is weighted least squares factor

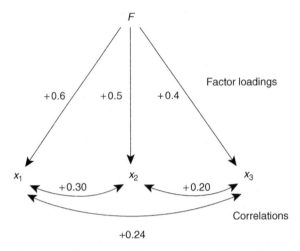

Figure 4.3   *A perfectly reproduced set of linear correlations between indicators. F, factor; x_1,*
x_2, x_3, indicators; single-headed arrows, factor loadings; double-headed arrows, correlations

analysis with weights dependent on the reliability (the height of the factor loadings)
of the indicators. The results of ML factor analysis are usually highly similar to
the results of PAF, *however*.

The proportion of variance extracted from the indicators by the PAF factor and
the ML factor is only 23.3 per cent, as compared with 38.2 per cent for the PC
component. According to PAF and ML, part of the 'explained' variance by
principal components analysis is simply measurement error. But for the
remaining part the conclusions remain the same. Just like Cronbach's alpha and
principal components analysis, both PAF and ML point out that 'protectionism'
(D406) is the poorer indicator.

4.5.4 Digression: an unknown number of dimensions

Thus far we have used principal components analysis and factor analysis as
confirmatory tools to *test* whether variables are reliable indicators of one concept
dimension to be measured. Factor analysis can also be used in a more exploratory,
inductive fashion to reveal how many dimensions and which dimensions would
underlie a series of indicators. All variants of principal components analysis and
factor analysis are suited to this end.

Procedures and criteria of exploratory factor analysis

The question of how many dimensions underlie indicators should be answered on
the basis of the eigenvalues of the extracted factors. As a first criterion, referred to as

the *Kaiser criterion* after the psychologist H.F. Kaiser, factors with an eigenvalue of less than one should be discarded, since these factors contain less variance than a single indicator. A more stringent, although mathematically not rigid, criterion is known as *Cattel's scree test* after its inventor, the psychologist R.B. Cattell. In order to apply the scree test the eigenvalues should be plotted in descending order. Factoring should be stopped at the point where the eigenvalues begin to level off, forming a straight line with an almost horizontal slope. As long as an eigenvalue is much smaller than its predecessor, the factor represented by it should be kept. But if an eigenvalue is only slightly smaller than its predecessor, then the factor represented by it, as well as all of its successors, should be discarded. Applying the scree test to the series of eigenvalues, for example, a series of eigenvalues (with rank orders in parentheses) such as 16.8 (1), 7.2 (2), 3.5 (3), 1.5 (4), 1.45 (5), 1.40 (6), ... would result in four factors, since 1.45 is only slightly less than 1.5, whereas 1.5 is much less than 3.5. The rationale of the scree test is that the discarded factors will usually have the variance of one indicator only (Kaiser criterion), plus some noise not explained by the 'true' factors. As a political psychologist Cattell was interested in the causes of war. In the early 1950s he wrote a then influential series of articles based on a factor analysis of data from official statistical agencies that revealed twelve cultural dimensions of 69 nations that would render these nations more or less prone to war.

The question of *which* dimensions underlie the indicators is far less easily answered. 'Rotating' the factors that were found by the sequential procedure described above – starting from the complete variance in all indicators, continuing on the basis of the residual variance not explained by the first factor, and so on – might facilitate interpretation from a theoretical point of view. Rotating does not affect the total variance explained by the complete set of rotated factors, but it may redistribute the explained variance over the various factors. The most widely used criterion for an optimal rotation is (*orthogonal*) *varimax rotation*. The theoretical idea of varimax rotation is that ideally each dimension will have its own subset of (non-overlapping) indicators. Therefore one would expect that some indicators will have high factor loadings on a factor, whereas the factor loadings of the other indicators will be zero. Varimax rotation strives for a maximum variance of the squared factor loadings on each factor. Even the results of varimax rotation – or any other rotation method – might be hard to interpret. The 'low' loadings will not be exactly zero, leaving open the question of whether a poor indicator is an indicator of a dimension or not. Moreover, there is no guarantee of course that variables which belong statistically to one factor are really indicators of one theoretical concept. The 'dimensions' found by Cattell in his pioneering work on the dimensions of nations, such as 'conservative patriarchal solidarity versus ferment of release', 'thoughtful industriousness versus emotionality' or 'bourgeois philistinism versus reckless bohemianism' were not very helpful for later generations of comparative political scientists, for example.

Example of exploratory factor analysis

As an example of (the problems with) inductive factor analysis the Manifesto data will be used once more. Laver and Budge (1992) wanted to use the data on party manifestoes to predict government coalitions between parties. They used 20 dimensions to characterize the policy space: 13 were simply the frequencies of the categories that were used in the content analysis; 7 were unweighted scales of these categories. The central dimension in our examples, 'state intervention', was one of the latter 7 dimensions. The question we wish to answer by inductive factor analysis is whether these 20 dimensions can be reduced to a smaller number of dimensions. Maximum likelihood factor analysis will be employed to this end, since the use of this method guarantees that indicators will only be accepted as belonging to one dimension when they correlate predictably.

An explorative factor analysis with all factors extracted, regardless of their eigenvalues, shows that the 20 dimensions might indeed be reduced in number. According to Kaiser's criterion (eigenvalues should exceed 1), 7 factors should be retained. According to Cattel's scree test, only 4 dimensions should be retained. Following the scree test, a factor analysis with a varimax rotation on the four dimensions is pursued. The factor loadings resulting from varimax rotation are given in Figure 4.4. Variable labels and underlining for 'significant' factor loadings (absolute value > 0.35) have been added manually. The results from varimax rotation are hard to interpret. Only one indicator contributes significantly to the first factor (capitalist economics). The same holds for the third factor (quality of life). The fourth factor can be interpreted as postmaterialism ('democracy' and 'human rights' against 'productivity and technology'), but it is hard to understand why 'the quality of life' is not included in this factor. The second factor makes sense: social conservatism (SOCCONS) against 'state intervention' and social justice (PER503).

Altogether, the first two dimensions seem to reflect the left–right dimension, but why should a factor analysis using varimax rotations result in *two* left–right dimensions? The answer to these questions is that the indicators might not be compatible with the assumption that these indicators tap *the same position* on the underlying (left–right?) scale. Themes in party manifestoes are simply not repeated measurements, but might be more in line with the unfolding model (van Schuur, 1995). Explorative factor analysis with varimax rotation will suggest *two factors* both representing the one underlying (albeit 'folded') dimension which would have been found if unfolding analysis had been applied (van Schuur, 1993, 1995).

4.5.5 Explorative cluster analysis

Whereas the aim of scalability analysis is to extract 'components', 'factors', 'dimensions' or 'latent variables' that account for the values of the indicators and for the correlations between indicators, the aim of *cluster analysis* is more modest: it is to cluster indicators on which units of measurement have almost identical values. The simplest type of cluster analysis is *hierarchical cluster analysis*. First indicators are clustered into one group whose members resemble each other extremely closely. The resulting group is considered as a new indicator. The new indicator (or cluster) receives scores by averaging the scores on the clustered

	Factor 1	Factor 2	Factor 3	Factor 4	
STATEINT	.23033	.48165	−.15706	−.02794	State intervention
QLIFE	.08187	.06833	.52864	.01964	Quality of Life
PEACE	.23543	.28417	.14916	.17843	Peace and cooperation
ANTIEST	.16698	.02284	−.19998	.14972	anti-establishment
CAPEC	−.95604	−.23512	−.16838	.03674	capitalist economics
SOCCONS	.10123	−.40294	−.22351	.16506	social conservatism
PRODTECH	−.00993	−.08199	.14894	−.39173	productivity, technology
PER104	−.04777	−.29170	−.07635	−.13787	Military +
PER108	.02065	−.25645	.24322	.10145	European Comm +
PER110	.08940	.24845	−.06688	.09937	European Comm −
PER201	−.04357	−.08673	.01096	.39428	Freedom-Hum Rights
PER202	.11063	.18577	.04089	.38796	Democracy
PER301	−.01439	−.02033	.28026	−.05369	Decentral +
PER303	−.00128	−.28899	.07358	.03803	Gov-Admin Efficiency
PER503	.15640	.40955	.04224	.19976	Social Justice
PER504	.05285	.24732	.21603	−.29257	Welfare +
PER506	.05971	.03154	.31936	−.24690	Education +
PER701	.22702	.13140	−.31572	−.02023	Labour +
PER703	−.06661	−.09280	−.17001	−.34183	Agriculture
PER705	.05788	−.00991	.29658	.11777	Minority Groups

Figure 4.4 *SPSS output (PAF, varimax rotation) of four factors underlying party manifestoes*

indicators. The cluster will resemble some of the remaining indicators. At each point the two 'closest' indicators are combined into a new cluster, a process that is iterated until all indicators belong to one cluster.

Many different measures of 'closeness' have been proposed. Actually, not measures of 'closeness', but opposite measures of 'distance' are used in cluster analysis. The three most widely used measures are probably city-block distances, Euclidean distances and correlation coefficients. The *city-block distance* between two indicators is equivalent to a simple sum of the *absolute* differences between the values of these indicators on the set of units. The *Euclidean distance* between two indicators is equivalent to the addition of the *squared* differences between the values of these indicators on the set of units. The *correlation coefficient* is one of the most widely used measures of association in the social sciences (see next chapter) and is also useful in cluster analysis. It is based on Euclidean distances rather than on 'natural' city-block distances. The correlation coefficient has −1 as its value when two indicators are each other's opposite and +1 when two indicators resemble each other perfectly. To use the correlation coefficient r as a distance measure, we have to use the value $d = 1 - r$.

Example: state interventionism

As an example we might apply hierarchical cluster analysis to our now familiar example of 'state interventionism'. The correlation coefficient will be used as the basis for the closeness measure, since the correlation coefficient was also (explicitly or rather implicitly) at the heart of the scaling methods discussed before. An intuitively appealing part of the cluster analysis output is the so-called *dendrogram*. The dendrogram is a horizontal tree. The horizontal axis denotes the (rescaled) distances between the indicators. The tree indicates which indicators branch together into one cluster given a specific (rescaled) distance. Figure 4.5 shows a dendrogram. The categories 'controlled economy' (D412) and 'nationalization' (D413) in party programmes resemble each other pretty closely. 'Economic planning' (D404) seems to belong to the same cluster. 'Economic regulation' (D403) and especially 'protectionism' (D406) are outliers in this cluster. Cluster analysis thus confirms the exceptional status of protectionism.

Digression: clustering units instead of clustering variables

Cluster analysis is also useful for clustering units that have almost identical values on indicators, rather than variables as in the previous example. From a technical point of view the only difference is that cluster analysis is now applied to the transposed data matrix (considering units as variables, and variables as units). Of course, variables of future analysis may also be applied to a transposed data matrix (McKeown and Thomas, 1980). As an example we will use the 20 indicators used by Laver and Budge to characterize party programmes to cluster parties in Germany in 1990. Such a cluster analysis reveals the closeness of the German parties in 1990 to each other. Laver and Budge use these cluster analyses to predict future coalitions. The dendrogram from the relevant SPSS output is presented in Figure 4.6. Since Laver and Budge use city-block distances, we will do the same here. The use of city-block measures to cluster units is recommended because the logic of more complex types of distances does not seem to apply to party programmes. The dendrogram indicates that the two green parties (Bündnis 90 and die Grünen) should cooperate immediately. Actually these two parties fused after the election. On the basis of their party programme the former communists of the PDS could easily cooperate with the greens. The FDP and the CDU could also cooperate. The SPD, however, seems to be somewhat isolated. The most likely partners would be parties to the left (the PDS and the greens). But the CDU/CSU and the FDP won the election, so a CDU/CSU/FDP coalition came into being.

Conclusion with respect to cluster analysis

The results of cluster analysis with respect to the similarity of indicators or, alternatively, the similarity of the units of analysis being studied, are intuitively appealing. When applied to the appropriateness of various indicators of state interventionism, cluster analysis reveals that protectionism is a dubious indicator of this concept, just like Cronbach's alpha, principal components analysis, principal axis factoring and confirmative factor analysis (ML factor analysis) did. Cluster analysis does not provide clear-cut criteria, however, to decide whether an indicator measures a concept or not.

Cluster analysis can be applied to assess the similarity of indicators (columns of the data matrix), but also to assess the similarity of units of measurements (rows of the data matrix). The latter has been done succesfully in the study of

Dendrogram using Average Linkage (Between Groups)

CASE		0	5	10	15	20	25
Label	Num	+ – – – – – + – – – – – + – – – – – + – – – – – + – – – – – +					
D412	4	– + – – – – – – – – +					
D413	5	– +		+ – – – – – +			
D404	2	– – – – – – – – – +		+ – – – – – – – – – – – +			
D403	1	– – – – – – – – – – – – – – – +				|	
D405	3	– +					

Figure 4.5 *SPSS output of a dendrogram resulting from hierarchical cluster analysis (Euclidean distances)*

CASE		0	5	10	15	20	25
Label	Num	+ – – – – – + – – – – – + – – – – – + – – – – – + – – – – – +					
green	1	– + – – – – – – – – +					
green	2	– +		+ – – – – – – – +			
pds	3	– – – – – – – – – +		+ – – – – – – – – – – +			
spd	4	– – – – – – – – – – – – – – – – – – – +				|	
fdp	5	– + – – – – – – – – – – – +					
cdu/c	6	– – – – – – – – – – – – – – – – +					

Figure 4.6 *SPSS output of a dendrogram resulting from hierarchical cluster analysis (city-block distances)*

coalition formation (Laver and Budge, 1992). Of course, one can also apply Cronbach's alpha and factor analysis to the rows rather than to the columns of a data matrix. We are not aware of any usage of Cronbach's alpha to cluster units of measurement rather than indicators of a concept, but the application of factor analysis to cluster units of measurement has a long history in psychology as a part of the literature on Q-methodology (McKeown and Thomas, 1988).

4.5.6 Summary

The various methods for scalability analysis are not easily compared, since they are based on a great variety of assumptions whose appropriateness is often hard to verify. As a start the decision tree from Table 4.3 should be used.

The empirical illustrations in this section indicated, however, that all the methods produced more or less the same outcomes, regardless of their precise assumptions. Of course this is only one illustration. But the suggestion is surely that researchers should not devote the bulk of their energy to the construction of optimal scales.

4.6 Conclusion

This chapter provided the linkage between theoretical concepts and units of analysis, on the one hand, and measurements, on the other hand. Concepts were operationalized. Data on units of analysis were eventually found by combining data on units of measurements. Data from content analysis, statistical agencies, and surveys and questionnaires were discussed. To evaluate the performance of measurements the criteria of validity, reliability, efficiency and comparativeness were introduced. Various types of scalability analysis to assess the reliability of multiple indicators were discussed. In the next two chapters the focus will shift from data gathering and measurement towards data analysis.

4.7 Endmatter

Glossary

- Aggregation: combining data on units of measurement to obtain data on the units of analysis, which are of theoretical interest.
- Data matrix: a rectangular matrix with cases (units of analysis) in the rows, concepts (variables, or units of variation) in the columns and values (scores) of cases on Concepts (Variables, units of variation) in its cells.
- Operationalization: combining data on indicators to obtain data on theoretical concepts (on the variables which are of theoretical interest).
- Scalability of indicators: Are the empirical relationships between indicators consistent with their presumed quality of tapping one and the same theoretical concept?
- Validity and reliability of indicators: Do indicators represent the theoretical concept which they purport to measure (validity)? Are measurement errors almost absent (reliability)?

Exercises

- Operationalize the concept 'mobility' (using indicators from the NIAS database such as pascarvn, comvehvn, rapakmvn, cakmflvn). Use an appropriate technique for scalability analysis to test whether one dimension of mobility is indeed present.
- Aggregate the concept of 'mobility' for the following units of analysis: (1) Nordic countries; (2) continental Europe; (3) Ireland, the United Kingdom and its former colonies; (4) Asian countries.

Further reading

General: White (1994), King et al. (1994).
Scale analysis methods: Mokken (1971), van Schuur (1984), Spector (1992), Skrondal and Rabe-Hesketh (2004).
Factor analysis: Kirn and Mueller (1978), Long (1983), Bollen (1994).
Cluster analysis: Everitt (1993).

Note

1 In SPSS output the term 'factor scores' is used slightly differently. On the basis of the SPSS 'factor scores' one will not obtain a first component with variance v_s/k but a standardized component with variance 1; mathematically this comes down to printing the elements of the eigenvector $u_1, u_2, \ldots, u_k$ divided by the square root of the associated eigenvalue, i.e. by $\sqrt{\lambda_1}$.

5

Explorative and descriptive statistics

The preceding chapter dealt with data gathering and with the art of obtaining valid and reliable indicators of theoretical concepts for a theoretically interesting set of cases (units of analysis). The next step is to become familiar with the data by exploring them with the help of elementary data analysis techniques. The chapter begins with the analysis of a single variable. Section 5.1 deals with the univariate analysis of nominal variables, Section 5.2 with variables having ordinal, interval or ratio levels of measurement. The distribution of cases along the categories or values of a single variable is the focal point here, e.g. the distribution of nations as cases over the categories 'yes' and 'no' of the dichotomous nominal variable 'bilateralism'. Considering data from a bivariate perspective means that for each category (or value) of the first variable the distribution of cases along the second variable is studied. Bivariate distributions of one nominal variable with another nominal variable will be discussed in Section 5.3. Bivariate distributions of two interval distributions (e.g. degree of postmodernism and level of economic growth) will be discussed in Section 5.4. In Section 5.5 the relation between a nominal variable and an interval variable will be discussed. The major methods for analysis discussed in Sections 5.3, 5.4 and 5.5 are respectively contingency-table analysis, regression analysis and analysis of variance. Multivariate extensions of these three data analysis methods will be discussed in Chapter 6.

Section 5.6 on inferential statistics widens the outlook from the data being explored to the universe of data which might have been studied. The focal question becomes whether the findings can be generalized. If data analysis is performed on data with respect to a sample from the population of cases, then the results may not hold for the population of cases. Statisticians have developed various tests to infer whether hypotheses which hold for a sample of cases are also plausible for the total population. Most inferential statistics assume that the sample is drawn randomly, but statistical tests which assume random samples may even be applied when the population of cases is analysed (see Section 4.2). Statistical significance tests indicate whether findings can be generalized. In this book on the methodology of political science, *only the ideas behind* statistical tests will be discussed. A multitude of voluminous statistical handbooks are available for the interested reader *to learn more on specific tests.*

5.1 The Univariate Distribution of a Nominal Variable

The obvious choice to represent a single (univariate) nominal feature of one's cases is the frequency distribution. The frequency distribution displays the actual values of a variable. The frequency of empirical occurrence is rendered for each of these values. A frequency distribution can be changed into a percentage distribution by dividing the frequency of occurrence of each particular value by the total number of occurrences. A pie diagram or a bar graph can be used to visualize the frequency distribution (see, for example, Figure 5.1).

Our example of a nominal frequency distribution bears on the type of macro economic policy of a country in a given year. The units of analysis are country–year combinations. Four different types of national macro-economic policy were prominent from the Second World War onwards: restrictive policy, monetarist policy, Keynesian policy and austerity policy (Keman, 1988: 101–26). Basically this fourfold typology derives from a cross-table of two dimensions: interventions to increase economic welfare and interventions to maintain or increase social welfare. Interventions in *economic welfare* are related to the ultimate pretensions of government policy. Will the central government intervene by means of an active macro-economic policy to neutralize market failures so as to stimulate economic growth? Or is the government just an accounting department looking merely at monetary indicators? Government intervention in *social welfare* is the second dimension of the typology. Does a government support and maintain extensive social security services and related expenditures?

A *restrictive policy* refers to macro-economic aloofness of the central government in combination with the absence of interventions in social welfare. A *monetarist policy*, also labelled as a *supermarket strategy* by Keman (1988), aims primarily at stable monetary indicators (no inflation, low interest rate, avoiding budget deficits), but does not exclude government interventions to maintain social welfare. Macro-economic interventions of the government to adjust the national economy are almost absent. A *Keynesian policy*, on the contrary, strives to provide a governmental stimulus for economic growth. One of the principal means of Keynesian policy is to create a buffer of effective demand due to social security expenditures that are expected to compensate for the lack of economic growth. An *austerity policy* is the combination of marginal interventions in social security so as to be able to keep the government expenditures balanced with economic growth.

Data for 18 OECD countries for the period 1965–1990 (26 years) with respect to macro-economic policy were taken from the NIAS.SAV data base. Hence the number of units of analysis amounts to $18 \times 26 = 468$. The type of macro-economic policy is referred to as the variable 'POP' (policy *output*) in the NIAS.SAV database.

Table 5.1 presents the frequency distribution of macro-economic policy. What we can learn from the frequency distribution is that the two most discussed macro-economic policies in the economic textbooks of the 1960s and 1970s, namely restrictive policy and Keynesian policy, were pursued less frequently than monetarist policy and austerity policy during the period 1965–90.

5.1.1 Measures of central tendency for nominal variables: the mode

The *central tendency* of a variable is the value on that variable that 'attracts' most of the cases. The value associated with the central tendency would be the best

Table 5.1 *Frequency distribution of macro-economic policy type (variable POP)*

Policy type	Frequency	Per cent
Restrictive	84	17.9
Monetarist	122	26.1
Austerity	157	33.5
Keynesian	105	22.4
	468	100

guess if you were asked to guess which value an unknown case would have on a variable.

Since the values (or 'categories') of a nominal variable have no rank order, the only thing to look for when the central tendency is at stake is the frequency of each category. The most frequently occurring category is called the *mode*. The mode indicates the central tendency of nominal variables. Austerity policy, for example, is the mode of macro-economic policy in OECD countries from 1965 until 1990 since its frequency of occurrence ($n = 157$, see Table 5.1) exceeds the frequency of all other policies.

5.1.2 Measures of dispersion for nominal variables: entropy and the Herfindahl index

The *dispersion* of a variable indicates to what degree the central tendency is indicative of the values of all cases. Measures of dispersion indicate how confident one can be that the value for a specific case is near to the central tendency of all cases.

Measures of dispersion for a nominal variable are also known as *concentration measures*, because they were used from the 1960s onwards to ascertain the effective number of equally matched firms in a branch of industry, i.e. the degree of business concentration. In comparative political science these measures have been adopted by Laakso and Taagepera to measure the 'effective number of parties', i.e. the degree of concentration of voters over parties. Measures of concentration have four aspects in common. A nominal measure of dispersion reaches its minimum when there is only one significant firm or party. Hence the minimum value of a concentration measure (in number equivalents) amounts to 1. When each party or firm is equally strong the maximum value of dispersion is reached. Thus, the maximum dispersion for a nominal variable with k values amounts to k.

Two measures of concentration which meet these four criteria have been proposed, namely the *entropy* and the *Laakso–Taagepera index*, also known as the *Herfindahl index* in the economic literature. To compute these concentration measures, first 'market shares' or 'frequency proportions' m_i for each of the k

values of a nominal variable should be computed. As an example we will once more discuss macro-economic policy (Table 5.1). The four 'market shares' ($k = 4$) of different types of macro-economic policy are $m_1 = 0.179$, $m_2 = 0.261$, $m_3 = 0.335$ and $m_4 = 0.224$. The dispersion will be a number *between* 1 and 4, since the market shares are unequal.

The Herfindahl index (in number equivalents) is defined as the inverse of the sum of squared market shares, thus as

$$Herfindahl_{N.E.} = \frac{1}{\sum_{i=1}^{k} m_i^2}.$$

In the 1960s the Herfindahl index came to be used to measure oligopoly and business concentration.

Since the 'market shares' of different types of macro-economic policy were as given above, the Herfindahl-index for the type of economic policy amounts to $1/(0.0322 + 0.0680 + 0.1125 + 0.0503) = 3.80$. What we learn from this number is that effectively almost four equally matched macro-economic policy types were available throughout the period 1965–90. In Chapter 8 we will use the Laakso–Taagepera index to measure the effective number of parties in a democracy.

The Herfindahl index is more often used in comparative political science than the entropy, but future research may well prefer the *entropy* measure because of its nice statistical features. The *entropy (in number equivalents)* is defined as the product of the inverses of market share raised to the power of that market share, thus as:

$$Entropy_{N.E.} = \prod_{i=1}^{k} \left(\frac{1}{m_i}\right)^{m_i}.$$

The entropy in number equivalents for the type of macro-economic policy is $1.361 \times 1.420 \times 1.443 \times 1.398 = 3.90$.

5.2 The Univariate Distribution of Ordinal, Interval and Ratio Variables

The frequency distribution is also useful to display the univariate distribution of variables with ordinal, interval or ratio levels of measurement when the number of different categories is small relative to the number of cases. The values should be ordered from the lowest to the highest. If the number of values of a variable is high relative to the number of cases, then the probability that a specific value will occur is zero. To obtain frequency distributions for such variables with an overwhelming number of values relative to the number of cases, the number of values should first be reduced by recoding subsequent values into value intervals.

5.2.1 Measures of central tendency

The central tendency is the 'typical' value of a variable. Whereas the mode, i.e. the most frequent value, is typical of a nominal variable, the average value is typical of an interval variable. The *arithmetic mean x* is adequate to assess the central tendency of an *interval* or *ratio* variable with values $x_1, x_2, ..., x_n$. If four persons have heights of 1.70, 1.85, 1.85 and 2.00 metres then their mean height amounts to the sum of their heights divided by 4, which reduces to 1.85 m. Actually, the symbol $\bar{x}$ denotes the *sample mean of the variable x*. A statistical proof maintains that the sample mean $\bar{x}$ is an unbiased estimate of the population mean, denoted as μ_x. For convenience the symbol $\bar{x}$ will be used in the formulae below. We write

$$\bar{x} = \frac{1}{n} \sum_{i=1}^{n} x_i$$

where n is the number of cases, and x_i is the value of the ith case on variable x. Alternatively, one might first count the frequency of occurrence of each specific value (or category) of the variable. In our example of the heights of four persons, three different heights are encountered with frequencies $f_1 = 1, f_2 = 2$ and $f_3 = 1$. Next one might compute the mean height as the mean of values weighted by their respective frequencies, thus as:

$$\bar{x} = \frac{\sum_{j=1}^{k} f_j x_j}{\sum_{f=1}^{k} f_j}$$

where k is the number of distinct values, x_j is the numeric value of the jth category, and f_j its corresponding frequency. The mean height is then calculated as $([1 \times 1.70] + [2 \times 1.85] + [1 \times 2.00])/(1 + 2 + 1) = 1.85$. Thus, the mean can also be computed as a weighted mean of means within subgroups, weighted by the frequency of subgroups. The formula for a weighted mean will be used regularly in the following sections. Its denominator is simply the sum of weights. The numerator is a sum of products of weights and corresponding values.

The arithmetic mean is influenced heavily by cases with extreme values. The average height of three persons with height 0.50, 1.85 and 2.00 (one baby and two adults), for example, is 1.45, although the height of the majority of persons is well above this average. A fairly intuitive measure of central tendency would be the *median* height, which is defined as the height of the person in the middle of the queue of persons sorted on the basis of their height. The median height of the three persons is 1.85. For strictly ordinal variables the median should always be preferred over the arithmetic mean, since the precise numeric values which are used to label the ranks of an ordinal variable lack substantial meaning by definition.

As an example we will consider the mean and median of public expenditure as a percentage of gross domestic product. The cases are once more country–year combinations. New Zealand and Japan are excluded since there were no reliable data for many years from the period 1965–2000. Therefore 576 cases (16 countries × 36 years) would remain, but for six recent cases (Canada 1999–2000, Switzerland 2000 and USA 1990–2000) data are missing which means that actually 570 will be used in the analysis. A *histogram* of public expenditures is presented in Figure 5.1. This is a frequency distribution, with nearby values recoded into classes. The horizontal axis of the histogram or frequency distribution displays public expenditures. The vertical axis displays the relative frequency of specific levels of expenditures. The frequency distribution shows that public expenditures vary between 19.7 per cent and 71.5 per cent of gross domestic product. Values between 30 per cent and 50 per cent are far more often encountered than values below 30 per cent or values above 60 per cent. The *mean* amounts to 44.1 per cent (see Table 5.2). There are no *outliers*, that is to say, no cases with extraordinarily low or high expenditures as compared with the other cases. A best-fitting *normal curve* is imposed on the histogram to display the dissimilarities of the empirical distribution from a normal distribution. The figure shows that the distribution of public expenditures is slightly skewed towards lower values, since the frequency of percentages near 30 per cent is somewhat higher than expected on the basis of a normal distribution. Therefore we would expect that the median is somewhat lower than the mean. Table 5.2 shows that this is indeed the case. The *median* amounts to 43.05.

5.2.2 Measures of dispersion

Intuitively the dispersion of variables with an interval or ratio level of measurement, which are not extremely skewed and have no outliers, is best measured with the mean deviation from the mean. Because absolute signs are undesirable in many types of further statistical calculations, instead of *absolute* deviations from the mean, *squared* deviations from the mean are used. The resulting measure is called the *variance* and denoted as σ^2. It is given by

$$\sigma_x^2 = \frac{1}{n} \sum_{i=1}^{n} (x_i - \overline{x})^2.$$

The *standard deviation*, denoted as σ, is defined as the square root of the variance. The standard deviation is easier to interpret than the variance. If the values of a variable are multiplied by a factor of 2, then the standard deviation will also become twice as large, but the variance will increase by a factor of 4.

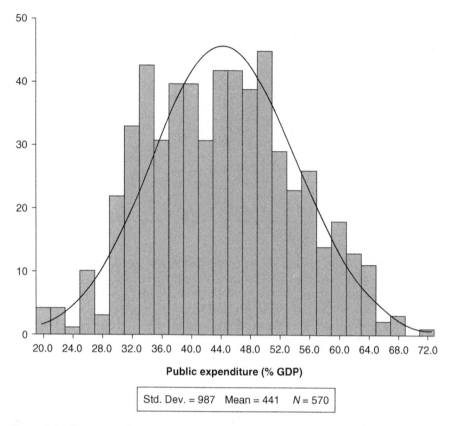

Figure 5.1   *Frequency distribution of public expenditure, with normal curve superimposed*

The formulae for the variance and the standard deviation presented here are used to measure the dispersion when the total population is investigated. If a *sample* of cases is analysed then one should not divide by n but by $n - 1$ to get an unbiased estimation of the population variance. Statistical packages such as SPSS assume that a sample is being analysed. The sample variance and the sample standard deviation are usually denoted as s^2 and s, respectively.

In a spreadsheet format the computation of the variance and the standard deviation is straightforward. We will perform these calculations in spreadsheet format here, since a good understanding of them is required for the understanding of correlation and regression analysis. Each row represents one case.

Table 5.2   *Central tendency of public expenditure*

	N	Mean	Median
Public economy (% GDP)	570	44.1	44.0

Table 5.3 *Computation of variance in spreadsheet format*

x_i	$x_i - \bar{x}$	$(x_i - \bar{x})^2$	x_i^2
-3	-2.8	7.84	9
-1	-0.8	0.64	1
0	0.2	0.04	0
1	1.2	1.44	1
2	2.2	4.84	4
Σ -1	0	14.8	15

$$\bar{x} = -0.2 \qquad \sigma^2 = 14.8/n = 2.96 \qquad (\Sigma x_i^2)/n$$
$$\sigma = 1.72 \qquad \sigma^2 = 3 - 0.2^2 = 2.96$$
$$s^2 = 14.8/(n-1) = 3.7$$
$$s = 1.92$$

In Table 5.3 a simple example of five countries is presented. In the first column, fictitious x_i-values are given. The sum of the column divided by n, the number of cases, represents the mean. Next two columns with $(x_i - \bar{x})$ and $(x_i - \bar{x})^2$ are given. The sum of the latter column, divided by n, represents the variance. To obtain the *sample* variance one should divide by $n - 1$. The (sample) standard deviation is simply the square root of the (sample) variance. In the example given here the sum of the squared deviations from the mean amounts to 14.8. Therefore, $\sigma^2 = 14.8/n = 2.96$ and $s^2 = 14.8/(n - 1) = 3.7$. Spreadsheet computations of the type presented above elucidate the logic behind the formula for the variance. This logic underlies correlation and regression analysis. High-school algebra suffices to simplify the formula of σ^2 further to $(1/n)\Sigma x_i^2 - \bar{x}^2$. Table 5.3 illustrates that this simplified formula also gives $\sigma^2 = 3 - 0.2^2 = 2.96$.

Standardized variables

The mean and the sample variance of variables are often used to *standardize* variables. Standardized values $z(x_i)$ of a variable are obtained by subtracting the mean value $\bar{x}$ from the original values x_i and dividing the result by the sample standard deviation s. These standardized values are also known as *z-scores*:

$$z(x_i) = \frac{x_i - \bar{x}}{s}.$$

Standardized variables have a mean of 0 and a sample variance of 1. If the data at hand cover the complete population then σ instead of s should be used to standardize. However, most computer programs, amongst them SPSS, will use s without offering the user a choice.

The use of standardized variables will often reduce the complexity of statistical computations, and sometimes even the interpretation of data and the interpretation

Table 5.4   *Dispersion of public expenditures*

			Percentiles	
	N valid	Std deviation	25%	75%
Public expenditure (% GDP)	570	9.1	36.6	50.9

of substantial outcomes of data analysis. For an American statistician the information that Anita from Amsterdam earns a standardized wage of –1.5 although her standardized level of education is +1.5 is easy to interpret. The original data that her net monthly wage amounts to €750 although she finished the HEAO is rather esoteric, however.

Standardized values should be used to compare the values of variables which would otherwise be hard to compare. But it is often too easily assumed that standardized values are easy to interpret. If the mean and the standard deviation are unknown or unstable because of small sample sizes or fast changes, then standardized values will be even more difficult to interpret than the original values. Comparative indices may be developed which are easier to interpret (e.g. all national expenditures measured as a percentage of gross national product; each policy emphasis measured as a percentage of total attention paid to all policy areas).

Dispersion of ordinal variables and variables that are not normally distributed

For strictly ordinal variables, for variables with outliers, and for heavily skewed or otherwise non-normal variables, the variance and the standard variation are often meaningless numbers. The distance between the closures of the first and the third quartile of the frequency distribution is often used as a measure of dispersion for these variables. Computation of this distance presupposes once more that the cases are ordered according to their values on the variable of interest. As an example, measures of dispersion of public expenditures as a percentage of gross domestic product have been included in Table 5.4. The standard deviation amounts to 9.1. If public expenditures had been a perfectly 'normal' variable, then 68 per cent of the observations would have fallen in the range 44.1 plus or minus 9.1, i.e. in the range 35.0–53.2. The actual distance between the first and third quartile is 36.6–50.9, which indicates that exceptional public expenditures occur less frequently than expected on the basis of a normal distribution.

5.2.3 The shape of the entire distribution of a variable with interval measurement

Numerical indicators of central tendency and dispersion are useful for characterizing a variable with ordinal, interval or ratio level of measurement,

Table 5.5 *Shapes of ideal-type distributions*

Name	Shapes of probability distribution (left) and corresponding cumulative distribution (right)	Functional form probability distribution
Symmetric		Normal distribution $y = c\,e^{-a(x-b)^2}$ $a>0;\ c>0;\ -\infty<x<+\infty$
Skew		Lognormal distribution* $y = c\,e^{-a[\log(x)-b]^2}$ $a>0;\ c>0;\ 0<x<+\infty$
J-distribution		Negative exponential distribution $y = c\,e^{-cx}$ $c>0;\ 0<x<+\infty$
Rectangular		Beta(1,1) distribution $y = 1$ $0<x<1$
U-distribution		Beta(a, b) function with $0<a<1$ and $0<b<1$ $y = cx^{a-1}(1-x)^{b-1}$ $c>0;\ 0<x<1$

*Requirements to ensure that probabilities add up to 1 not specified.

but a qualitative assessment of the *shape* of the distribution is also relevant. Table 5.5 lists a number of frequently occurring distributions in political science. These distributions are the normal distribution, the skew distribution, the rectangular distribution, the J-distribution and the U-distribution. For each distribution the shape of the *frequency distribution* is sketched. The *cumulative frequency distribution* is derived from the ordinary frequency distribution. The cumulative frequency distribution represents, for each value of a variable, the proportion of cases with values *lower than or equal to* this value. In the case of a variable *x* with four values 1, 2, 3 and 4 with respective relative frequencies of 10 per cent, 60 per cent, 25 per cent and 5 per cent, for example, the cumulative distribution amounts to 10 per cent, 70 per cent, 95 per cent and 100 per cent.

The *normal* distribution is the workhorse of statistical reasoning. The majority of data analysis techniques in this part of the book assume that the distributions of all variables have a 'normal' shape. Most of these techniques are fairly *robust*: when the normal assumptions are 'slightly' violated, these techniques and estimators may still produce reliable results. But techniques assuming normal distributions should usually not be applied to J-shaped or U-shaped distributions. This is another reason for a careful visual inspection of the shape of frequency distributions.

5.3 Relationships Between Variables with Nominal Measurement Levels

Frequency distributions do not tell us anything about *relationships* among variables. A simultaneous frequency distribution of two variables is required to examine relationships. We need to know how the empirical cases are distributed over the possible combinations of values on two variables. The *cross-table* of two variables displays empirical frequencies for a rectangle of all possible combinations of values on two variables which constitute the upper and left-hand side of the rectangle.

As an example, the relationship between macro-economic policy type (POP) and the economic situation will be examined. During the postwar period the world economy flourished until the late 1960s. The first oil crisis of 1973 marked clearly the end of the period in which growth was self-evident. During the late 1970s most economies suffered from inflation, low growth rates and rising interest rates. The second oil crisis of 1979 marked the end of this period. A world recession came along in the early 1980s, from which most economies recovered only slowly. It might be expected that the economic situation influenced the macro-economic policy, since governments will pursue specific macro-economic policies to restore economic equilibrium when the parameters of the world economy change. A cross-table is useful for exploring the precise relationship between the economic situation and macro-economic policy.

For three time periods and four types of macro-economic policy we will obtain a cross-table of 12 cells. The cross-table registers how the 442 nested units of years within countries are distributed over these 12 cells. It is common usage to display the separate values of the variable that is considered to be the *most interesting one*, or the dependent one, in the *rows* of the table. The columns of the table exhibit the values of the variable that is expected to 'explain' or 'predict' the variable of interest. Therefore the types of macro-economic policy are plotted in the rows, whereas the economic situation is plotted in the columns. The cells of the table contain the absolute frequencies of given policies in specific years. Absolute frequencies are hard to interpret, however. Since the cross-table should inform readers what the distribution of the variable of interest (in the rows) is for each of the values of the explaining variable (in the columns), it is most natural to compute a percentage distribution of the cases for each of the latter (column percentages). Table 5.6 exhibits this cross-table.

Since *column percentages* were used, the percentages *should be compared rowwise* to arrive at conclusions with respect to the question of whether the variable of interest does indeed depend on the explanatory variable. As compared with the earlier and later period, restrictive policy happened to be the most common policy type in the 1970s (23.5 per cent of cases in the 1970s as compared with 5.9 and 17.6 per cent, respectively). Monetarist policies and austerity policies were dominant in the 1960s (35.3, 41.2 per cent) as compared with the 1970s and 1980s (23.5 per cent, 29.4 per cent). Keynesian policies became gradually more prevalent (1960s 17.6 per cent, 1970s 23.5 per cent, 1980s 29.4 per cent). The data

Table 5.6 *Cross-table of macro-economic policy type by economic situation (column percentages)*

	Economic tide			
	1965–73 prosperity	1974–80 recovery from first oil crisis	1981–90 recession; slow recovery	Total
Restrictive	6	24	18	15
Monetarist	35	24	24	28
Austerity	41	29	29	33
Keynesian	18	24	29	24
	100 ($n = 153$)	100 ($n = 119$)	100 ($n = 170$)	100 ($n = 442$)

show that governments responded to the economic problems in either of two ways: either increasing the effective demand or reducing the budget deficit. No unidirectional, linear trend shows up. Although Keynesianism as a macro-economic theory was challenged by schools of thought such as monetarism, neo-classicism and rational expectations from the 1970s onwards, the data on economic policy as indicated by public expenditures do not support the belief that Keynesian macro-economic policy vanished. Presumably even governments with a monetarist or neo-classical ideology were forced, by corporatist institutions and Keynesian-inspired arrangements carried over from previous decades, to raise public expenditures (e.g. legal claims to higher social security expenditures when employment rises).

As a rough measure of the influence of the economic situation the maximum percentage difference in any *row* might be computed (column percentages assumed). In this table the maximum percentage difference amounts to $\varepsilon = 23.5$ per cent – 5.9 per cent = 17.6 per cent in the Keynesianism row. This value of ε indicates that the changing economic situation corresponded with a change of 17.6 per cent in the pursuit of Keynesianism. No relationship between the variables would have existed were the maximum percentage difference to have been zero.

For exploratory purposes bar graphs might be used instead of cross-tables to visualize relationships. As a first example the cross-table discussed here is presented as a bar graph in Figure 5.2. The bar graph shows at a glance that conflicting policies arose from the economic crises. Some countries pursued a more Keynesian policy whereas other countries did diametrically the opposite: they pursued a restrictive policy. Obviously, such conflicting policies will tend to cancel each other out in the world economy.

5.3.1 The chi-square measure of association in a cross-table

A percentage difference as computed above is an intuitively clear measure of association. However, it takes only two columns in one row of the table into

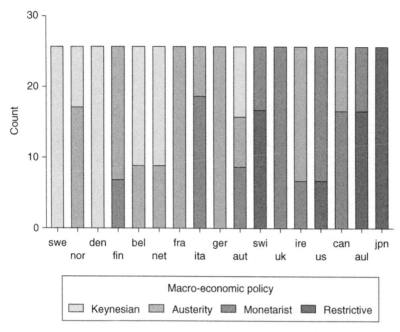

Figure 5.2 *Bar graph of macro-economic policy in various OECD nations*

account. Percentage differences are of little use in expressing parsimoniously the strength of association in larger cross-tables because of their sheer multitude. The number of different percentage differences for a cross-table amounts to $(r - 1)$ $(c - 1)$, where r is the number of rows and c the number of columns, since one row and one column of the table serve as reference categories to compute the remaining percentage differences 'freely'. This number of independent percentage differences $(r - 1)(c - 1)$, which is known as the *degrees of freedom* of a cross-table, will recur in Section 5.6.5 when a statistical test of the association in a cross-table is at stake.

A measure of association which takes all differences between rows and tables of the table into account could start from the definition that no relationship between variables exists when the percentage distribution of the first variable is precisely the same for each value of the second variable. The frequencies that would show up when no relationship existed are referred to as the *expected frequencies*. Expected frequencies can be computed from the univariate frequency distributions of the separate variables. As a matter of convenience the univariate frequency distributions of the row and the column variable are often displayed in the margins of the cross-table, thus on the right-hand side of the cross-table (row variable) and below the cross-table (column variable). For this reason the univariate distributions are often referred to as the *marginal distributions*. The expected frequency e_{ij} of the combination of value i on one variable and value j on the other is a function of the marginal frequencies $f_{i.}$ and $f_{.j}$ and number of cases $f_{..}$. Since the percentage distribution of the first variable is precisely the same for each value of the second variable when no relationship exists between the two variables, the ratio $e_{ij}/f_{i.}$ should be equal to $f_{.j}/f_{..}$. Therefore the expected frequency of a cell in a cross-table is simply the product of its marginal frequencies divided by the number of cases:

$$e_{ij} = \frac{f_{i.}f_{.j}}{f_{..}} = \frac{f_{i.}f_{.j}}{n}$$

The symbol $f_{i.}$ is used to denote the marginal frequency of value i on the first variable, regardless of the value on the second variable (thus $f_{i.} = \Sigma_j f_{ij}$). The symbol $f_{.j}$ is used to denote the marginal frequency of value j on the second variable regardless of the value of the first variable (thus $f_{.j} = \Sigma_i f_{ij}$). The symbol $f_{..}$ denotes the sum of frequencies, regardless of the values of the first and the second variable (thus $f_{..} = \Sigma_{if.j} = \Sigma_i f_{i.} = n$).

Table 5.7 *Frequencies and expected frequencies*

			Y		
			Y_A-value	Y_B-value	Total
X	X_A-value	Count	3	1	4
		Expected count	2	2	
	X_B-value	Count	2	4	6
		Expected count	3	3	
Total		Count	5	5	10

Whether a relationship exists between two variables is revealed by the (absolute or squared) differences between the observed frequencies f_{ij} and the expected frequencies e_{ij}. Chi-square, denoted as χ^2, is defined as the sum of ratios of squared differences between observed and expected frequencies to the expected frequencies. Thus,

$$\chi^2 = \sum_i \sum_j \frac{(f_{ij} - e_{ij})^2}{e_{ij}}.$$

Table 5.7 may serve as a simple example. The table consists of 10 cases. For each cell of the table the expected frequency is computed. χ^2 is easily computed as $(3 - 2)^2/2 + (1 - 2)^2/2 + (2 - 3)^2/3 + (4 - 3)^2/3 = \frac{1}{2} + \frac{1}{2} + \frac{1}{3} + \frac{1}{3} = 1.667$.

Regrettably the value of χ^2 is not easily interpreted, since its value is not restricted to a maximum. But for a 2 × 2 cross-table the square root of χ^2 divided by n, referred to as ϕ (phi), has a maximum of one:

$$\phi = \sqrt{\frac{\chi^2}{n}}.$$

For Table 5.7, ϕ amounts to the square root of 1.667/10, which equals 0.408. For larger tables Cramér's υ should be used, to ensure that the maximum value will not exceed 1:

The denominator within Cramér's υ is not simply n, but depends also either on the number of rows or on the number of columns, depending on the question of whether there are fewer rows or fewer columns. In a cross-table with dichotomous variables, υ reduces to ϕ.

$$\upsilon = \sqrt{\frac{\chi^2}{n\,(\text{smallest number rows/colums}) - n}}.$$

5.4 The Bivariate Distribution of Two Ordinal, Interval or Ratio Variables

Cross-tables are not very useful for describing the relationship between variables with an interval level of measurement, since the ordering of the values on the variables is not taken into account. Many relationships between such variables are of the type 'the higher x, the higher (or the lower) y'. When relationships between variables with an interval level of measurement are examined, the typical question is whether the values of y increase or decrease *monotonically* when x increases. As a matter of convenience it is often assumed that linear relationships can be expected. A perfect linear relationship between a dependent variable y and an independent variable x is represented by the equation $y = bx + a$. The complication that relationships in the empirical sciences are usually probabilistic does not need to worry us for the moment. In the language of the empirical social sciences the slope coefficient b in this linear equation is known as the (unstandardized) *regression coefficient*. The regression coefficient indicates by how many units y will change on the average when x increases by one unit. Linear relationships are even frequently assumed when ordinal variables with many values are at stake, although for ordinal variables the concept of a slope coefficient is overly precise since the variables can be stretched or shrunken arbitrarily. The regression coefficient is closely related to the correlation coefficient. The latter coefficient of association indicates by how many standard deviations a given variable changes when another variable changes by one standard deviation.

Cross-tables may be used to examine the relationships between variables with an ordinal level of measurement. A measure for the association of two ordinal variables is obtained by applying the correlation coefficient to the rank order of the measured values rather than to the measured values themselves. High-school algebra suffices to prove that this so-called rank order correlation coefficient, due to Kendall, reduces to a fairly simple formula. We will not discuss other measures of rank order association such as gamma, Kendall's tau B or Kendall's tau C.

As an example we will examine the relation between the level of imports and exports, on the one hand, and the level of public expenditures, on the other.

Katzenstein (1985) developed the theory that countries with an open economy, characterized by high imports and exports, such as Belgium and Ireland, are relatively vulnerable to swings in the world economy. Thus the export/import ratio, operationally defined here as IMEX2 = 50 × (imports + exports)/(gross domestic product), may well serve as an indicator of the economic openness of a nation in a given year. The multiplication by 50 rather than by 100 serves only to ensure that the import/export ratio has 100 per cent as its maximum (the variable IMEX in the NIAS.SAV database is multiplied by 100, however). Countries with a relatively open economy tend to use public expenditures more extensively than other countries, as a buffer to tone down shocks from outside. The higher the export/import ratio is, the higher public expenditures will be. The dependent variable, public expenditures (PE), is operationalized as central government expenditures as a percentage of GDP. Data are taken from the NIAS.SAV database. The units of analysis in the example are 17 OECD countries in 1988 (New Zealand is left out of consideration because of missing data).

5.4.1 Exploring the bivariate distribution: the scattergram

A feeling for the data must precede any serious data analysis. The 1988 data for 17 countries on openness of the economy and public expenditures are presented in Table 5.8.

The question to be answered with regression analysis is roughly to what degree countries whose openness exceeds the average (IMEX2 > 31.45) also have

Table 5.8   *The openness of the economy (IMEX2) and public expenditures (PE) (n = 17)*

Country	IMEX2	PE
swe	31.55	58.10
nor	37.05	52.50
den	30.75	60.20
fin	24.75	44.00
bel	70.75	57.30
net	52.65	56.30
fra	21.45	50.00
ita	19.30	50.30
ger	26.80	46.30
aut	37.50	50.60
swi	36.30	30.40
uk	25.05	37.90
ire	58.40	47.10
us	10.05	32.50
can	26.15	42.50
aul	17.05	33.60
jpn	9.15	31.60

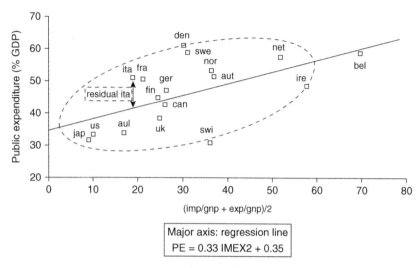

Figure 5.3 *Scattergram of openness of economy (IMEX2) and public expenditures (PE)*

public expenditures above the average (PE > 45.95). To answer this question tentatively, one may, for example, first have a closer look at the three countries with either extremely high or extremely low values on each of the variables. Inspection of the data informs us that Belgium, the Netherlands and Ireland have extremely open economies, whereas Japan, the USA and Australia have more closed economies. Sweden, Denmark and, again, Belgium rank highest on public expenditures, whereas Switzerland and, again, Japan and the USA rank lowest. Thus, Belgium, Japan and the USA behave according to Katzenstein's theory. Australia also behaves according to the theory, since it ranks third in the list of countries with low expenditures and fourth in the list of countries with low public expenditures. The Netherlands and Ireland should have high public expenditures. The Dutch economy ranks fourth on public expenditures, but the Irish economic model clearly constitutes an exception. Ireland's public expenditures are roughly average (PE = 47.1), in spite of its openness. Another exception is Switzerland, which ranks lowest on public expenditures although it is a relatively open country. Denmark is the country with the highest public expenditures, although its openness is modest. Such casual observations suffice to warrant the conclusion that Katzenstein's hypothesis is a probabilistic one, reflecting a tendency with many exceptions.

The relationship between two interval variables is easily visualized in a scattergram (see Figure 5.3). In a scattergram the variable, of primary interest, usually the 'dependent' variable, is plotted on the vertical axis (public expenditures, PE), whereas the independent variable (economic openness, IMEX2) is plotted on the horizontal axis. The scattergram reveals at a glance the probabilistic relationship between economic openness and public expenditures. The countries are arranged in an imaginary *ellipse*. Generally speaking, the major axis of the ellipse, which is known as the *regression line*, represents the rule whereas the vertical distances from this line represent the exceptions. The major axis of the ellipse suggests a positive relationship between economic openness and public expenditures, running from Japan and the USA (closed, low public expenditures) to Belgium (open, high public expenditures). Countries such as Denmark and Sweden (fairly closed, but high expenditures) and Switzerland (fairly open, but low public expenditures) are located at a large vertical distance from the regression line. The larger the ratio of the length of the major axis of the imaginary ellipse to that of its minor axis, the higher the *correlation* between the two variables is said to be. First we will concentrate on the major axis of the ellipse, the regression line.

5.4.2 Bivariate regression analysis

Regression analysis is a means to assess the slope of the major axis of the imaginary ellipse in the scattergram. It is assumed that for each case i the value Y_i on the dependent variable Y (here public expenditures, PE) is linearly dependent on the value X_i of the same case i (here country) on the independent variable X (here economic openness, IMEX2):

$$Y_i = \beta_0 + \beta_1 X_i + \varepsilon_i.$$

The expected values $\hat{Y}_i$ for each case i are precisely located on the regression line:

$$\hat{Y}_i = \beta_0 + \beta_1 X_i.$$

The *regression slope coefficient*, or simply *regression coefficient* β_1 indicates how much the dependent variable Y increases (if β_1 is positive) or decreases (if β_1 is negative) on average when the independent variable X increases by one unit. The regression coefficient will be zero if Y does not depend on X. If the imaginary data ellipse in a scatterplot is perpendicular to the X-axis, then the regression coefficient will be zero. The *regression constant* or *intercept* β_0 indicates the average value of Y when X equals zero. If the imaginary data ellipse is centred on the intersection of the axes of the coordinate system – thus, when $X = 0$ and $Y = 0$ – then the intercept will surely be zero. The *regression line* $\hat{Y}$ represents the expected (average) value of Y for each value of X. But some cases will not be precisely located on the regression line. ε_i represents the *residual* or the *error term*. The residual is the *vertical* distance of a case from the major axis of the data ellipse:

$$\varepsilon_i = Y_i - \hat{Y}_i.$$

Residuals are perpendicular to the X-axis, not to the axis of the ellipse. Figure 5.3 highlights the residual for Italy as an example. Since the estimation of the parameters β_0 and β_1 aims at the minimization of the residuals, the parameters

β_0 and β_{x1} are derived by minimizing the (sum of squared) differences between the actual values Y_i and the expected values $\hat{Y}_i$:

$$\text{Minimize} \sum (Y_i - \hat{Y}_i)^2$$

Elementary calculus – setting the first partial derivatives of $\sum(Y_i - \hat{Y}_i)^2$ with respect to β_0 and β_1 equal to zero (not to be pursued here) – suffices to derive the least squares estimators of β_0 and β_1:

$$\beta_0 = \bar{y} - \beta_{x1}\bar{x}, \quad \beta_1 = \frac{\sum_i (x_i - \bar{x})(y_i - \bar{y})}{\sum_i (x_i - \bar{x})^2}.$$

These estimators are often referred to as the ordinary least squares (OLS) esti- mators. To get a feeling for a regression analysis it is helpful to understand the formulae of these estimators.

The parameter β_1 represents the slope coefficient of the regression line. The coefficient indicates the number of units that the dependent variable is expected to increase when the independent variable increases by one unit.

Dividing both the numerator and the denominator by the number of cases n clarifies the regression coefficient further. A formula results with the variance σ_x^2 in the denominator:

$$\beta_{x1} = \frac{\sum_i (x_i - \bar{x})(y_i - \bar{y})}{\sum_i (x_i - \bar{x})^2} = \frac{n^{-1} \sum_i (x_i - \bar{x})(y_i - \bar{y})}{n^{-1} \sum_i (x_i - \bar{x})^2} = \frac{\sigma_{xy}}{\sigma_x^2}.$$

The fact that the variance appears in the denominator implies that the slope coefficient is measured in units of variance of the independent variable. Increasing the variance of the independent variable artificially (e.g. by expressing imports and exports not as percentages but as permillages of gross domestic product) will increase the denominator and therefore decrease the slope coefficient, since the change in the dependent variable associated with one unit of change in the independent variable diminishes.

The resulting numerator σ_{xy} is referred to as the *covariance* of the variables. The covariance is the sum of products, over all cases, of deviations from the mean values on the dependent and the independent variable. The product of deviations from the mean will be positive when the two variables co-vary in the same direction: that is to say, either when both variables are positive, or when both variables are negative (since plus times plus, as well as minus times minus, is plus). The product will be negative when positive deviations from the mean on the one variable coincide with negative deviations from the mean on the other variable. This supports the intuition that the regression coefficient will be positive when x and y move in the same direction, but negative when x and y move in opposite directions.

Related measures I: residual variance, explained variance R^2, F-ratio and adjusted R^2

Since empirical cases will not usually lie precisely on the regression line, the residuals ε_i, defined as $Y_i - \hat{Y}_i$, will not usually be precisely zero. As a measure of fit between the actual values of the dependent variable Y_i and the values $\hat{Y}_i$, predicted on the basis of the regression equation, the variance of the residuals σ_e^2 might be compared with the original variance σ_y^2 of the dependent variable. The explained variance R^2 is based on this idea:

$$R^2 = 1 - \sigma_e^2/\sigma_y^2.$$

When the ratio of the residual variance to the original variance is small, the explained variance is high. The explained variance has 0 as its minimum and 1 as its maximum. When the ratio of the residual variance to the original variance is high, the explained variance is low.

R^2 is probably the most widely used yardstick to assess the predictive power of a regression model in comparative political science. An R^2 of about zero indicates that it is impossible to predict with any precision *for a specific case* the value on the dependent variable on the basis of the regression model. An R^2 near 1 indicates that predictions of the values of separate cases on the basis of the regression model are near perfect.

R^2 should not be used as the only yardstick of predictive power, however. What predictive power is needed depends entirely on the *research question*. A model with an R^2 near zero may still be an extremely powerful predictive model when the research question asks for the prediction of an average trend, rather than for a prediction of the values of separate cases. In campaigning research for a political party with a new left ideology, for example, a regression model with a low R^2 maintaining that stressing classical leftist issues rather than environmentalist issues increases the probability of voting for the party is still a powerful predictive model. A party is faced with a political macro-question, i.e. how to maximize the sheer number of votes, rather than with a psychological micro-question, i.e. how to ensure that citizen A rather than citizen B will vote for the party. A model with an R^2 of almost 1, on the other hand, may hide a failure to predict when some of the variables in the model are uninteresting. In regression models based on time series data the research question is often to what degree an exogeneous variable is predictive of the future value of a dependent variable. An R^2 of almost 1 is usually easily obtained by assuming that the value of the dependent variable will resemble by default the value of the dependent variable from last year, last month, or even yesterday. An R^2 of almost 1 in such an *autoregressive model* (see Section 6.7.5) is no proof that the research question has been answered successfully.

One of the pitfalls of regression is that decreasing the number of cases will usually increase the explained variance, since it becomes easier to fit a straight line. Increasing the number of explanatory variables (thus moving from bivariate regression analysis towards multiple regression analysis) will increase the explained variance by definition. R^2_{adj} is a measure which adjusts R^2 in such a way that – all other things being equal – decreasing the number of cases and/or increasing the number of explanatory variables will not result in an artificially higher R^2. To ensure that an increase in R^2 is not due to a smaller number of cases and/or a higher number of explanatory variables, comparative political scientists routinely report R^2_{adj} rather than R^2. Here we will not expound the seemingly odd formula of R^2_{adj}, which takes into account that fitting a regression equation becomes artificially easy when *degrees of freedom* (see Section 5.6.5) are lost because of a decrease in the number of cases n or an increase in the number of explanatory variables k:

$$R^2_{adj} = 1 - (1 - R^2)\frac{n-1}{n-k}.$$

R^2_{adj} has 1 as its maximum, just as R^2, but whereas R^2 has zero as its minimum, R^2_{adj} will drop below zero when degrees of freedom decrease unduly, thus when n is small and/or k is high.

The *F-ratio* is closely related to R^2_{adj}. Whereas the variance explained by regression is divided by the *total variance* to obtain R^2, it is divided by the *unexplained variance* to obtain the *F*-ratio. The *F*-ratio takes the degrees of freedom of the explained and unexplained variance into account. R^2_{adj} is easy to interpret, since its maximum is 1, but the *F*-ratio is useful in statistical tests.

Related measures II: the correlation coefficient

The correlation coefficient is a measure of the strength of a bivariate relationship. It is a measure of association. The 'strength' of a bivariate relationship is related to the ratio of the minor axis of the imaginary data ellipse in the scatterplot to the long axis. If this ellipse is really a circle, then the strength of the relationship amounts to zero. If the two-dimensional ellipse collapses to a one-dimensional regression line – i.e. when all residuals reduce to zero – then the strength of the relationship reaches its maximum.

The correlation coefficient is defined as the *standardized covariance* – the ratio of the covariance between two variables to the product of the standard deviations of these variables:

$$r = \frac{\sigma_{xy}}{\sigma_x \sigma_y}.$$

Linear transformations of the variables – e.g. using metres instead of inches, or using percentages instead of proportions – do not have any effect on the correlation coefficient, because they have an equal effect on its numerator and its denominator.

One should note that the regression coefficient and the correlation coefficient have their numerator in common. The correlation coefficient standardizes the covariance so as to render a measure of strength which is independent of the original measurement scales, whereas the regression coefficient expresses the covariance in the variance of the independent variable so as to render a measure of the effect, on the dependent variable, of a one-unit change on the measurement scale of the independent variable. The correlation coefficient is a measure of association or strength (a measure of the shape of the data ellipse), whereas the regression coefficient is a measure of effect (a measure of the direction of the major axis of the data ellipse). The correlation coefficient varies between −1 and +1, whereas the regression coefficient can take any value.

Only in bivariate regression analysis does the correlation coefficient equal the square root of the explained variance: $r = \pm\sqrt{R^2}$. This equality shows that a correlation coefficient of 0.4 corresponds to an explained variance of 16 per cent only. In multivariate regression analysis (see Section 6.7) the relationship between r and R^2 is less simple. Correlation coefficient of the independent variables with the dependent variable, add up to k^2 only when the correlation coefficient between the independent variables are zero.

In explorative data analysis it is common usage to inspect the matrix of correlation coefficients between the variables that are of interest in some way or another. Since correlation coefficients are measures of bivariate association only, one should avoid drawing any direct causal conclusions on the basis of such an inspection. Many techniques for multivariate data analysis – such as multivariate regression analysis, factor analysis, discriminant analysis and the analysis of structural relationships (see Chapters 6 and 7) – are available to test causal hypotheses accounting for the observed pattern within the correlation matrix.

Related measures III: standardized regression coefficients

A regression coefficient estimates by how many units of measurement the dependent variable will increase when the independent variable is increased by one in the units in which the latter is measured. Regression coefficients are thus expressed in the units of (often rather arbitrary) measurement scales of the dependent and independent variables. Regression coefficients are hard to interpret when the measurement scales which were used are unknown, unfamiliar or contingent upon time or space.

One solution to the problem of incomparable regression coefficients arising from incomparable measurement scales is the use of *standardized regression coefficients*. Standardized regression coefficients express the size of an effect as the number of standard deviations by which the dependent variable will change as a result of a change by one standard deviation in the independent variable. Although it is hard to compare the unstandardized effects of national corporatism and the effect of world trade on national unemployment directly, a comparison in terms of standardized regression coefficients may still be possible.

One may compute standardized regression coefficients by computing ordinary, unstandardized regression coefficients on the basis of variables that were standardized first (thus by computing regression coefficients from the z-scores). As an alternative one can compute the ordinary, unstandardized regression coefficients first and multiply them by the ratio σ_x/σ_y of the standard deviations of the independent and the dependent variable.

> Standardized regression coefficient
> = unstandardized regression coefficient computed from z-scores
> = unstandardized regression coefficient $\times \sigma_x/\sigma_y$.

In bivariate regression analysis the standardized regression coefficient $(\sigma_{xy}/\sigma_x^2 \times \sigma_x/\sigma_y = \sigma_{xy}/\sigma_x/\sigma_y)$, equals the correlation coefficient $(\sigma_{xy}/\sigma_x\sigma_y)$, but this equality does not hold in multivariate regression analysis.

Standardized regression coefficients have been used rather unthinkingly as indicators of effect size. Especially in comparative research and in time series research, effects expressed in units of standard deviations are often harder to interpret than effects expressed in units of the original measurement scales. Standardized regression coefficients have even more pitfalls when the research question asks for a comparison of effect sizes in different countries (or different groups). Suppose that it is found that the standardized regression coefficient of the tax level on inflation is 0.5 in Germany and 0.25 in Italy. An unthinking interpretation would be that higher taxes yield higher inflation in Germany than in Italy. Policy advice based on this interpretation would be that the Italian government should feel freer to increase taxes than the German government. This interpretation is utterly wrong, however: first, because taxes were used far more often as a policy instrument in Germany than in Italy (which comes down to a larger σ_x in Germany than in Italy); and secondly, because the inflation level varied for other reasons far less in Germany than in Italy (which comes down to a smaller σ_y in Germany than in Italy). When there is reason to expect that standard deviations of the variables of interest will vary through time or between cross-sections, one should avoid relying on standardized regression coefficients.

A computational example: the effect of economic openness on public expenditures again

To get a feeling for regression analysis it is instructive to present the required computations in spreadsheet format (Table 5.9). This format is identical to that used for the computations of variances and standard deviations (see Table 5.3).

Table 5.9 Spreadsheet computation in bivariate regression analysis

	$X = IMEX2$	$Y = PE$	$X - \bar{x}$	$Y - \bar{y}$	Covar XY	Var X	Var Y	$\hat{Y}$	ε	ε^2
swe	31.55	58.10	0.10	12.15	1.22	0.01	147.62	45.99	12.11	146.77
nor	37.05	52.50	5.60	6.55	36.68	31.36	42.90	47.82	4.68	21.94
den	30.75	60.20	-0.70	14.25	-9.97	0.49	203.06	45.72	14.48	209.70
fin	24.75	44.00	-6.70	-1.95	13.07	44.89	3.80	43.72	0.28	0.08
bel	70.75	57.30	39.30	11.35	446.05	1544.49	128.82	59.03	-1.73	3.01
net	52.65	56.30	21.20	10.35	219.42	449.44	107.12	53.01	3.29	10.83
fra	21.45	50.00	-10.00	4.05	-40.50	100.00	16.40	42.62	7.38	54.42
ita	19.30	50.30	-12.15	4.35	-52.85	147.62	18.92	41.91	8.39	70.43
ger	26.80	46.30	-4.65	0.35	-1.63	21.62	0.12	44.40	1.90	3.59
aut	37.50	50.60	6.05	4.65	28.13	36.60	21.62	47.97	2.63	6.94
swi	36.30	30.40	4.85	-15.55	-75.42	23.52	241.80	47.57	-17.17	294.69
uk	25.05	37.90	-6.40	-8.05	51.52	40.96	64.80	43.82	-5.92	35.07
ire	58.40	47.10	26.95	1.15	30.99	726.30	1.32	54.92	-7.82	61.20
us	10.05	32.50	-21.40	-13.45	287.83	457.96	180.90	38.83	-6.33	40.05
can	26.15	42.50	-5.30	-3.45	18.29	28.09	11.90	44.19	-1.69	2.85
aul	17.05	33.60	-14.40	-12.35	177.84	207.36	152.52	41.16	-7.56	57.13
jpn	9.15	31.60	-22.30	-14.35	320.01	497.29	205.92	38.53	-6.93	48.01
Sum/n	31.45	45.95	0	0	85.33	256.35	91.15	45.95	0	62.75

$\beta_{xy} = 85.33/256.35 = 0.333$.
$\beta_0 = 45.95 - 0.333 \times 31.45 = 35.48$.
$r = 85.33/(\sqrt{256.35} \sqrt{91.15}) = 0.558$.
$R^2 = 0.558^2 = 0.312$ or
$R^2 = 1 - 62.75/91.15 = 0.312$.

The three basic steps to compute the regression coefficients are:

1 Compute the means of the dependent variable and the independent variable (summation and division by n, represented in an extra row).
2 Compute deviations from the mean (columns $X - \bar{x}$ and $Y - \bar{y}$) and from these the product of deviations (column Covar XY) as well as squared deviations from the respective means (columns Var X and Var Y). Put the result of summation and division by n in the extra row.
3 Compute the regression coefficients from the results in the extra row.

The correlation coefficient is also computable from the results in the extra row. In the case of bivariate regression the explained variance R^2 is simply the square of the correlation coefficient. An alternative way to compute the explained variance would be to compute the unexplained, residual variance explicitly. The basics steps are:

4 Compute the predicted values of the dependent variable from the original variables and the regression coefficients (column $\hat{Y}$).
5 Compute the residuals by subtracting the predicted values from the original values of the dependent variable (column ε) and from these residuals the squared residuals (column ε^2). Put the result of summation and division by n in the extra row.
6 Compute the explained variance from the results in the extra row by applying a formula for R^2.

The reader is encouraged to perform these steps – either by hand or using a spreadsheet program – on a database of four or five cases to learn the steps. At the cost of loss of transparency, the computational efficiency can be increased, amongst other ways, by rewriting the formulae for variance and covariation as functions of original values, squared values and multiplied values.

From Table 5.9 it is evident that the values in the column Covar XY, which represent the products of deviations from the means of the dependent and the independent variable, are predominantly positive. Thus, the dependent and the independent variable move in the same direction for 12 out of 17 countries. The Covar XY column shows five exceptions (Denmark, France, Italy, Germany and Switzerland). From this observation the sign of the regression coefficient and the correlation coefficient is already apparent, since both regression analysis and correlational analysis are based on the simple arithmetical fact that the product of two deviations from the mean will be positive when both numbers are either both positive or both negative. The further computations serve only to state these observations based on the column of products of deviations from the mean in neat numbers. The regression line becomes PE = 0.333 × IMEX2 + 35.48. If a country increases its exports and imports by 1 per cent, then the best guess is that public expenditures will be increased by 0.333 per cent. Exports and imports are by no means the only source of variation in public expenditures, since only 31.2 per cent of the variance in public expenditures is due to imports and exports ($R^2 = 0.312$). In the case of bivariate regression the standardized regression coefficient and the correlation coefficient do not provide additional information, since these coefficients can simply be computed as the square root of the explained variance.

5.5 The Relation Between an Interval or Ratio Variable and a Nominal Variable

Many empirical investigations are concerned with the relationship between an interval variable and a nominal variable. Political scientists may, for example, wish to compare public expenditures (interval) before or after the oil crisis of 1973 (nominal), changes in gross national product (interval) after 'treatments' with various macro-economic policies (nominal variable POP, Table 5.1), or public expenditures (interval) in various countries (nominal variable). Most research questions ask for a *comparison of the mean value* of the interval variable between the various categories of the nominal variable. One may, for example, make a cross-country comparison of the *mean* level of public expenditures (interval) within specific countries (nominal) over some time period. More sophisticated comparisons can also be made. A research question regarding the rigidity of public expenditures may require a between-country comparison of the *variance* of public expenditures within these countries over the last thirty years, or even of the *precise time paths* of the levels of public expenditures within these countries. Here we will concentrate on a comparison of the *mean* level of the interval variable for the various categories or values of the nominal variable. Adopting the language of psychologists, biologists and medical scientists, who have developed the explorative research techniques which will be discussed in this section, these values or categories of this nominal variable are also labelled as the 'groups'. The 'groups' in comparative political science do not usually consist of individuals, however, but rather of countries (cross-sectional analysis) or of time points (longitudinal analysis).

5.5.1 An interval variable and a bivariate nominal variable: the comparison of two means

An obvious way to compare the means of *two groups* is to assess the magnitude of the difference between the two means. When this difference is fairly large, as compared with the standard deviation of the interval variable within the two groups, then the two means differ substantially from each other. As a trivial example of this line of reasoning, the level of public expenditures within European and non-European OECD countries will be compared. Table 5.10 (produced by SPSS from the NIAS.SAV database) presents the basic results. The mean level of public expenditures as a percentage of GDP for non-European countries is 10.2 per cent less than for European countries. A difference between the *means* of these two groups does not imply, however, that each country within the European group has higher expenditures than each country within the group of non-European OECD countries. To determine the degree to which differences between groups hold for all cases within the groups one should compare the

Table 5.10 *A comparison of group means*

Variable	Number of cases	Mean	SD	SE of mean
Public expenditure (% GDP)				
non-European	103	35.5	5.8	0.57
European	520	45.7	9.6	0.42

difference between the means of the groups with the standard deviation of public expenditures *within* the two groups. If many exceptions exist to the rule that European countries have higher expenditures than non-European OECD countries, then the standard deviation of public expenditures within the European countries, and the standard deviation of public expenditures within the non-European countries, would be large compared with the difference between the mean expenditures within the two groups. Since the difference between the two groups amounts to 10.2 per cent, which is larger than the standard deviations within the two groups (5.8 and 9.6 per cent, respectively), it appears to be safe to conclude that there are not many exceptions to the finding that European OECD countries have higher expenditures than non-European OECD countries.

Two fairly abstract lessons from this trivial example should be kept in mind. The first lesson is that exploring the relationship between a (dependent) variable with an interval level measurement and a nominal (independent) variable consisting of a few 'groups' (or nominal values, or 'categories') comes down to the comparison of group means. The second lesson is that the difference between the group means serves as a sufficient summary of the differences between the cases from the groups to the extent that the difference between group means is large compared with the variance within groups.

5.5.2 Analysis of variance: an interval variable by a nominal variable with j values

The label 'analysis of *variance*' is slightly confusing, since its aim is to assess whether group *means* differ substantially from each other. The label expresses that this aim is best achieved by comparing the differences between group means with the variance within groups. The variance between group means is used as an indicator of the mean magnitude of the pairwise differences between the group means, since the number of pairwise differences increases disproportionately when the number of groups increases. J groups would give rise to $\frac{1}{2}j^2 - \frac{1}{2}j$ pairwise comparisons between groups. One would have to compare 136 pairs of means, for example, to test whether public expenditures in a given period differ between 17 countries. The group means differ from each other when the variance of group means is substantial. Thus, analysis of variance presupposes that group means are different from each other when the variance between groups is substantial compared with the variance within groups. If the variance of group means σ_{bt}^2 is substantial compared with the variance within the various groups σ_{wh}^2 then there will be only a few exceptions to the rule that, on average, cases from one group have higher (or lower) scores than cases from another group. The *explained variance* R^2, often labelled as η^2 (eta squared) in the context of the analysis of variance, is defined as the ratio of the variance between group means σ^2_{bt} to the total variance of the interval variable σ^2_{tt}:

$$R^2 = \eta^2 = \frac{\sigma^2_{bt}}{\sigma^2_{bt} + \sigma^2_{wh}} = \frac{\sigma^2_{bt}}{\sigma^2_{tt}}.$$

The total variance is simply the variance of the interval variable. The variance between groups σ^2_{bt} is computed as the sum of squared deviations of group means from the grand mean $\overline{Y}$, where the jth group is weighted by its number of cases n_j. Thus,

$$\sigma^2_{bt} = \frac{\sum_j n_j (\overline{y}_j - \overline{Y})^2}{n} = \frac{SS_{bt}}{n}.$$

where $\overline{Y}$ is the grand mean, the mean value on the dependent variable y across all cases, and $\overline{y}_j$ its mean within the jth group. The variance within groups simply defined as the sum of squared deviations of each value from its own group mean, divided by n:

$$\sigma^2_{wh} = \frac{\sum_j \sum_i (y_{ij} - \overline{y}_j)^2}{n} = \frac{SS_{wh}}{n}.$$

This knowledge suffices for the understanding of the principles of the analysis of variance, but it is not sufficient to understand the output of most statistical packages. Instead of using the variance between group means divided by the total variance as a measure of difference between group means, one may also use just the variance within as the denominator. Since both the variance between means and the variance within groups have n in the denominator it is convenient to consider just the numerators; statistical packages will usually print just the sum of squares between (SS_{bt}) and the sum of squares within (SS_{wh}).

A further complication concerns the fact that in order to arrive at an unbiased estimator of the variance one should divide the sum of squared deviations by $n - 1$ rather than by n, the number of cases (see Section 5.2.2). Since the means of j groups are compared with the grand mean in the numerator, $j - 1$ is the proper divisor of SS_{bt} to arrive at an unbiased estimator of the variance between groups. To arrive at an unbiased estimator of the variance within a specific group j the proper divisor would be $n_j - 1$. Summation over all groups gives $n - j$ as the proper divisor of SS_{wh} to arrive at an unbiased estimator of the variance within. The divisors $j - 1$ and $n - j$ are known as the *degrees of freedom* between and the degrees of freedom within, respectively. The ratio of SS_{bt} divided by its degrees of freedom $j - 1$ to SS_{wh} divided by its degrees of freedom $n - j$ is known as the F-ratio:

$$F = \frac{SS_{bt}/(j-1)}{SS_{wh}/(n-j)}.$$

In the analysis of variance the F-ratio plays an important role in statistical tests.

Example: an analysis of variance of public expenditures in 17 countries

As an example of the analysis of variance we present a fairly common explorative question in comparative political science. If pooled time series data are available, an important question is always whether the variation in the dependent variables is due to time or due to cross-sectional variation. If the variation through time is negligible (the institutional sclerosis hypothesis) then one could just as well employ data on cross-sections at one point in time. If the variation between cross-sections is negligible (the global economy hypothesis), then one could just as well study time series data for one specific case.

Here we will explore whether variation in public expenditures (as a percentage of gross domestic product) is mainly longitudinal or mainly cross-sectional. The graphical tool to split variation in pooled time series data in longitudinal and cross-sectional variation is called the *sequence plot* (available within SPSS; see Figure 5.4). The sequence plot shows the time path from 1965 to 2000 for each cross-section. It shows at a glance that countries such as Sweden had high public expenditures all along, whereas countries such as the USA and Switzerland had low public expenditures throughout, as was expected on the basis of the *institutional sclerosis* hypothesis. A closer inspection of the time paths shows that in most of the countries public expenditures rose in the 1960s, fell in the 1980s, then rose again in the early 1990s.

The analysis of variance is the appropriate statistical technique to refine this visual impression. It decomposes the variation in pooled time series into variation through time, variation across cross-sections and remaining 'unexplained' variation due to independent – or idiosyncratic – national policies that result in an independent national time path. First an analysis of variance is pursued to assess the viability of the institutional sclerosis hypothesis, i.e. to establish the degree to which the variance is cross-sectional. What percentage of the variance in public expenditures is maximally due to cross-sectional variation between countries? The results (SPSS output) are presented in Figure 5.5. The SPSS output follows the standard format of analysis of variance output. The columns SS (sums of squares), DF (degrees of freedom) and F (the F-ratio) have been discussed before. Here we will concentrate on the SS column. The figure of 29 301.26 in the SS column represents the sum of squared deviations of the mean public expenditures within a country from the overall mean of public expenditures in all countries, where

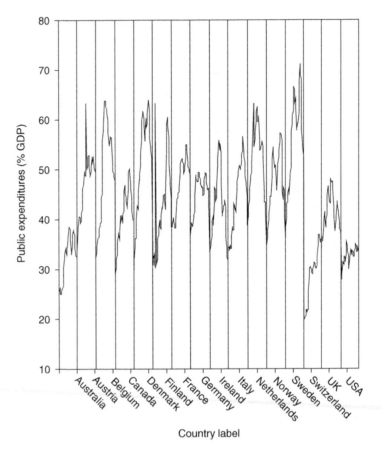

Figure 5.4 *Sequence plot of public expenditures by country and year*

each country is weighted by the number of observations from it (here 36 years). The number $55\,381.25$ represents the sum of squared deviations of the mean public expenditures in specific countries from the mean public expenditures in all countries in all years. The proportion of explained variance is obtained by dividing the sum of squares between countries by the total sum of squares. The explained variance amounts to $R^2 = 29\,301/55\,381 = 0.529$. Thus, the data clearly support the hypothesis of institutional sclerosis. Some 53 per cent of the variation in public expenditures over the period 1965–2000 in OECD countries is due to structural differences between countries.

An analysis of variance with the year as the independent nominal variable reveals that another 26 per cent ($R^2 = 0.256$) is variation through time, independent of the specific country. This implies that the global economy hypothesis is also confirmed, although the explained variance is twice as low. National economic policies which deviated both from the global trend and from the policies induced by national institutions at an earlier point in time explain

Source of Variation	SS	DF	MS	F	Sig of F
WITHIN CELLS	26080.00	554	47.08		
COUNTRY	29301.26	15	1953.42	41.50	.000
(Model)	29301.26	15	1953.42	41.50	.000
(Total)	55381.25	569	97.33		
R-Squared =	.529				
Adjusted R-Squared =	.516				

Figure 5.5 *SPSS output for the analysis of variance of public expenditures, 1965–2000*

merely some 10 per cent of the variation in public expenditures. The bulk of the variation in public expenditures was due to the global economic development (roughly 30 per cent) on the one hand and to national constraints on the other (roughly 60 per cent).

Summary

Exploratory analysis of the relationships between variables depends on the level of measurement of the variables. Cross-tables and measures such as chi-square, phi and Cramér's v are appropriate when the relationship between nominal variables is at issue. Regression analysis and the analysis of variance assume that the dependent variable has an interval level of measurement. Analysis of variance assumes a nominal independent variable only, whereas in regression analysis the independent variable has interval level of measurement. The concepts of explained and unexplained (residual) variance are central concepts both in the analysis of variance and in regression analysis. The unexplained variance is the proportion of the variance in the dependent variable which is independent of variations in the independent variable.

5.6 Populations, Samples and Inferential Statistics

Unfortunately the results of an exploratory data analysis are almost always based on available data that may not be the only data that can be imagined to mirror the research topic. Therefore, statistical tests to assess whether the results may hold for a larger population enter the picture. Whether one feels confident about the results found on the basis of available data depends on whether other results would have been found if other data had been employed. Although the latter question appears to be rather philosophical at first sight, it is precisely this question which is routinely answered by the use of statistical tests. Statistical tests narrow down the philosophical question by asking how likely it is that another sample of data from the same 'population' (or 'reality') would have given rise to completely different results (see Section 4.2). Statistical tests do not question the inherent quality of the available data. Questions of reliability and validity have to be addressed by other means (see Section 4.4).

In the last sections of this chapter we will first repeat the essentials of statistical testing (see Section 4.2). Next, additional concepts such as estimators, desirable aspects of estimators such as unbiasedness and efficiency, and degrees of freedom will be discussed. The chapter concludes with a discussion of the use and misuse of statistical tests.

5.6.1 The urn model

The urn model, which provides the basis of elementary statistical testing, was introduced in Section 4.2. The model starts from the assumption that there is an unknown population from which a sample of data has been drawn. Statistical tests are designed to *disprove a null hypothesis* H_0 that contradicts an interesting hypothesis H_1. The aim is to show that the null hypothesis is untenable as it leads to an unsatisfactorily small probability of being compatible with sample data. Unlike comparative political scientists, statisticians never set out to prove an interesting hypothesis. The best they can do is to demonstrate that the likelihood of a null hypothesis which is not in line with an interesting hypothesis is negligible in the light of the available sample data. This knack is extremely useful, however, to prove that the obtained results are not artefacts of (limited) available data.

A statistical test rests on the thought experiment of drawing *all possible samples* with a sample size precisely as large as the actual sample size from a population in which the null hypothesis holds true. The thought experiment continues with the computation of a *test statistic*. A test statistic is a summary of the sample data that is indicative of the tenability of the hypothesis.

As an example, the hypothesis may be considered that proportional representation systems have higher turnout rates in elections than majoritarian electoral systems, since minorities will not vote in majoritarian countries because the two major parties will seek to please the median voter rather than some minority. Logically the null hypothesis must be that there is no difference between the turnout rates in these systems. Suppose that data on turnout rates in 40 elections – 20 from proportional representation and 20 from majoritarian systems – are available. The relevant test statistic here is the difference between the mean turnout in proportional representation systems and the mean turnout in majoritarian electoral systems. The thought experiment of the statistician would be to compute this test statistic, i.e. the difference between the mean turnouts in the two systems, for each possible sample of 40 cases which could have been drawn from a population in which the null hypothesis holds. Most samples will show up negligible differences between the two groups of systems, since such a difference does not exist in the imaginary population from which the samples were drawn. Mere chance dictates, however, that some samples will show far higher turnout rates in proportional representation systems, whereas others will show far higher turnout rates in majoritarian systems. Therefore the thought experiment results in a *probability distribution of the test statistic*. Statisticians have proven that the probability distribution of the test statistic in our example, i.e. the difference between the mean turnouts in the two systems, is a symmetric distribution. Actually it is a 'normal' or 'Gaussian' distribution (see Figure 5.6).

Moreover, the mean value of the differences which will be found between the two types of electoral system in all possible samples will be precisely zero. To put it another way, the mean value of the test statistic, i.e. the difference found between the mean turnout in proportional systems and the mean turnout in majoritarian systems, hits the mark precisely, regardless of the sample size. *The test statistic is unbiased.*

However, the variance of the test statistic decreases as the sample size is enlarged. The smaller a sample, the more variant and shaky the results are. If the sample size amounts to 500 elections, then the set of all possible samples will contain only a few samples with large differences between the two types of systems if actually the null hypothesis is true which maintains that in the population the difference between the two systems is zero. If one is drawing all hypothetical samples of only 10 elections then one will find in many samples differences between the groups of electoral systems even when the null hypothesis holds.

Statisticians have proven that increasing the sample size has diminishing returns. Given the sample result that women live 5 years longer on the average, the probability that there is no difference between the mortality rates of men and women in the population decreases sharply when the sample sized is increased from 10 to 1000. A further increase of the sample size to 2000 will decrease the probability that there is no difference in the population only slightly further.

To sum up, statistical testing rests on a thought experiment of drawing all possible samples of a given size from a population in which the null hypothesis holds. The concepts of an estimator, a test statistic and a probability distribution of the test statistic are important in understanding the thought experiment. A few more things have to be said about features of estimators before the general procedure employed in hypothesis testing is discussed. This additional discussion involves the concepts of (un)biasedness, (in)efficiency and robustness of estimators.

5.6.2 Unbiasedness, efficiency and robustness of an estimator

An estimator or test statistic is a function of sample data that is used as an approximation of a population parameter. One may use the sample mean as an estimator to estimate the population mean, for example. In comparative political science, as in any other branch of science, estimators should give 'correct' results. The correctness of estimators is operationalized using the concepts of unbiasedness, efficiency and robustness.

An estimator is *unbiased* when its approximations are on the average precisely to the point. An estimator is *biased* when its approximation of the population parameter is consistently beside the point. The sample mean from a random sample is an unbiased estimate of the population mean. It is not always true, however, that a sample parameter is an unbiased estimator of the corresponding population parameter. To arrive at an unbiased estimate of the population variance, for example, one should divide the sum of squared deviations from the sample mean by $n - 1$ rather than by n. The reason why an unbiased estimator of the population variance requires division by $n - 1$ rather than by n is that one free observation – one degree of freedom – has to be offered to calculate the sample mean before the actual calculation of squared deviations from it may start. Degrees of freedom will be discussed further in Subsection 5.6.5. An estimator is *asymptotically unbiased* if it is unbiased provided the sample size is sufficiently large. Dividing the sum of squared deviations from the sample mean by n may result in a biased estimator of the variance, but it does result in an asymptotically unbiased estimator, since division by n rather than by $n - 1$ does not make a difference when n is sufficiently large.

Unbiased estimators may still produce faulty approximations of population parameters. Being to the point on average is compatible with being faulty at any time. The variance of the estimates should also be taken into account. Estimators with a small variance are called *efficient* estimators; estimators with a small variance when the sample is large are called *asymptotically efficient*. The ordinary least square estimator of the regression coefficient which was introduced in Section 5.4, for example, is an efficient estimator of population regression parameters in most circumstances. But in Section 6.7 notable exceptions will be discussed (e.g. heteroscedasticity, autoregression).

The third aspect of estimators to be discussed is their *robustness*. The robustness of an estimator refers to its quality of producing more or less the same estimate when small changes in the sample data are introduced.

A problem in statistics is that many estimators do not combine the three desirable properties of unbiasedness, efficiency and robustness. The research on the robustness of estimators suggests a simple conclusion. Estimators that use the complete set of data at once, such as ordinary least squares estimators in regression analysis, or the F-test in variance analysis, are fairly robust. Hierarchical estimators, which first use subsamples of the data to draw inferences from them, are far less robust. To sum up, the choice of an estimator should depend on its (un)biasedness, (in)efficiency and (un)robustness. Intuitive plausibility and mathematical elegance are additional considerations.

The ordinary least squares estimator of the regression coefficient was introduced in Section 5.4 simply because of its plausibility. As an alternative one may derive mathematically which estimator has the maximum likelihood of estimating population parameters correctly on the basis of sample data, given a number of assumptions with respect to the population distribution. Maximum likelihood estimation is the holy grail of mathematical statistics. One problem with maximum likelihood estimators is that they may not be robust when the precise assumptions on the data have not been met. The assumption of a Multivariate normal distribution is a strong one, which is seldom warranted by the data. *Parameter-free tests* are designed to keep the number of assumptions with respect to the population to a minimum. But tests that do not rest on any assumption at all do not exist. Many parameter-free tests assume that the rank order of values in the sample reflects precisely the rank order in the population, whereas the values themselves do not. The latter assumption is no less dubious, especially when measurement errors are extant as is usually the case in comparative political science. For this reason we will not discuss parameter-free tests in this book.

5.6.3 The general procedure used in hypothesis testing

Hypothesis testing involves a number of steps (see Kanji, 1999). As a preliminary step the theory at stake should be broken down into testable hypotheses. As a further preliminary step one should decide on the magnitude of the type I error one is willing to risk making. Type I error is defined as the probability of rejecting the null hypothesis, even though the null hypothesis is true. As a matter of convenience we will abide by the convention that in the social sciences type I errors that exceed 5 per cent are not acceptable.

For each hypothesis the following steps should be taken.

1a State the *object of a hypothesis* in statistical terms. Usually the statistical object of a substantial hypothesis is a *population parameter* (e.g. the population mean, the regression coefficient in the population).

1b Determine whether the hypothesis is one-sided or two-sided.

1c Formulate a *null hypothesis* which excludes the stated hypothesis. Typical null hypotheses are that there is no difference at all or no relationship at all. Compute a *test statistic* (T), that is a function of the sample data, with a known probability distribution (when the null hypothesis holds). Statisticians have derived what the distribution of the values of the test statistic will be over the infinite number of samples of a given size that might be drawn from the population.

As a next step the *standard error* of the estimate is usually computed. The standard error refers to the variance of the estimates of the population parameter that would be obtained if the null hypothesis holds and an infinite number of samples of the given sample size were drawn from the population.

As a further step to compute the test statistic the estimate of the population parameter on the basis of sample data is 'compared' with the standard error on the basis of the null hypothesis. The test statistic is a value on the x-axis of the probability distribution of the estimator.

2 Derive from the table of the probability distribution of the test statistic (or from computer output) the *significance level*, i.e. the percentage of the possible samples from the population for which the test statistic is compatible with the null hypothesis. One should take into account whether the hypothesis was one-sided or two-sided when looking up this percentage, although most computer programs will assume that the test is two-sided.

3 Decide whether the null hypothesis should be rejected by determining whether the probability found at step 2 is lower than the accepted magnitude of type I errors (usually set at a maximum of 5 per cent).

5.6.4 Four common probability distributions of test statistics

Consider the probability distribution of the mean age according to samples. Ages in the western world vary between 0 and 120 years. But the mean age according to a sample of 10 humans will not vary that much. It is unlikely, although not impossible, that a random sample of size 10 from the world population will include only newborn babies. In the majority of cases the sample mean will be near to the population mean. Although the age distribution is highly skewed, with many babies and only a few old people whose age exceeds 100 years, the distribution of the means of a host of imaginary samples from this skewed population will *nevertheless* be symmetric. When the sample size is sufficiently large ($n > 120$) the probability of the sample mean is a *normal* distribution with a standard deviation that is much smaller than the standard deviation of the population distribution, regardless of the precise shape of the population distribution. On the authority of mathematical statistics we accept that the standard deviation of the sample mean, also known as the *standard error*, equals the standard deviation of the population distribution, divided by the square root of the sample size. Thus, if the standard deviation of the population distribution equals 1, and the sample size is 100, then the standard error will be $1/\sqrt{100} = 0.1$. A standard error of the sample mean of 0.1 indicates that on the average the mean of a sample will deviate 0.1 standard deviations from the population mean. To obtain a standard error of 0.01 a sample size of 10 000 is required. Thus, increasing the sample size has diminishing returns. Figure 5.6 depicts a standardized normal distribution. The normal distribution is also known as the Gaussian distribution and as the z-distribution.

The area beneath the standardized normal curve indicates the proportion of cases with specific values. Roughly 68 per cent of the cases are located within one standard deviation of the mean. Five per cent of the cases exceed the mean by more than 1.645 standard deviations. Five per cent of the area beneath the curve is located either to the left of −1.96 or to the right of 1.96. Therefore 1.645 standard deviations is a crucial value in one-sided statistical tests with the normal curve, whereas 1.96 standard deviations is a crucial value in two-sided statistical tests. In our example with a standard deviation of 1 in the population, which resulted in a standard error of 0.1, a sample mean which deviates more than $1.96 \times 0.1. = 0.196$ standard deviations from the hypothesized mean in the population would be enough to conclude that the null hypothesis is unwarranted.

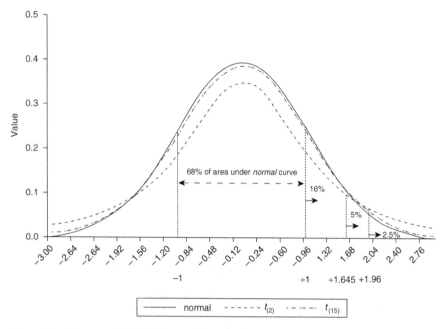

Figure 5.6   *The normal distribution and the t-distribution*

In the case of a sample size of 10 000, a deviation of the sample mean from the hypothesized mean of $1.96 \times 0.01 = 0.0196$ would be sufficient to draw the same conclusion.

A slightly different distribution for the sample mean results when the sample size is small (less than about 100): the tails of the resulting probability distribution are somewhat thicker than the tails of a normal distribution. This normal-like distribution is called the *t*-distribution. As the sample sizes decrease, or in the language of statistics, as the *degrees of freedom* (df) decrease, the *t*-distribution becomes flatter (degrees of freedom are related (but not identical) to the sample size). Actually there is not a single *t*-distribution, but a class of *t*-distributions depending on the degrees of freedom. When the sample size increases ($df > 100$) the resulting *t*-distributions become almost completely identical to the normal population. Figure 5.6 depicts $t_{(2)}$ and $t_{(15)}$, the distributions with 2 and 15 *df* respectively; $t_{(15)}$ is already practically indistinguishable from the normal distribution by the naked eye. Many other test statistics also have a *t*-distribution, e.g. that for the test of whether a regression slope coefficient differs significantly from zero.

The sample variance has quite a different distribution. Suppose that a sample of size 1 is drawn from a population. The variance calculated on the basis of this sample would be zero by definition. To put it more generally, if the sample size is small, then the variance calculated on the basis of sample data will generally be smaller than the population variance. This is the reason why statistical laymen and researchers consistently underestimate the variance of processes on the basis

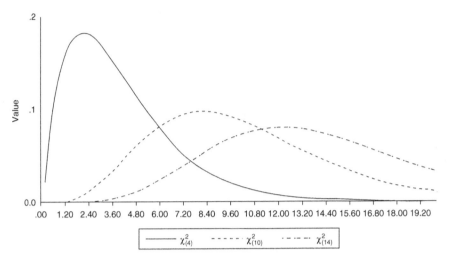

Figure 5.7 *Chi-square distribution with 4, 10 and 14 degrees of freedom*

of their limited personal experience. It is also the reason why case studies should be dealt with cautiously when the research question asks for the assessment of the variability of events, policies, processes or institutions. The distribution of the sample variance statistic, known as the *chi-square distribution* or χ^2-distribution, is not symmetric, but *skewed*. Again there is a family of chi-square distributions, each characterized by its degrees of freedom. Figure 5.7 shows $\chi^2_{(4)}$, $\chi^2_{(10)}$ and $\chi^2_{(14)}$, the chi-square distributions with 4,10 and 14 *df* respectively. When the number of 'free' observations increases, the skewness gradually disappears. $\chi^2_{(14)}$ already resembles a normal distribution, although it is still visibly skewed. When the number of free observations exceeds 100 the chi-square distribution becomes almost equivalent to the *z*-distribution. The point at which the χ^2-distribution reaches its maximum increases with the sample size. The $\chi^2_{(df)}$ distribution with *df* degrees of freedom reaches its maximum for *df* – 2. As can be seen from Figure 5.7, the $\chi^2_{(4)}$, the $\chi^2_{(10)}$ and the $\chi^2_{(14)}$ reach their maximum at the values 2, 8 and 12, respectively. The chi-square probability distribution applies to many other test statistics, e.g. to test whether a cross-table exhibits a relationship.

Many tests involve the comparison of two variances. The analysis of variance (Sections 5.5.2 and 6.6), for example, is based on the comparison of the variance between groups with the variance within groups: the *F*-ratio is defined as the *ratio* between the variance between group means and the variance within groups. The probability distribution of a division between two sample variances, is known as the *F*-distribution. Since variances follow a χ^2-distribution the *F*-distribution is actually the distribution of the division of two χ^2-distributions. Since the *F*-distribution has a sample variance with its associated degrees of freedom in the numerator, but also a sample variance with its associated degrees of freedom in the denominator, the *F*-distribution has two different degrees of freedom (df_1 for the numerator and df_2 for the denominator). In the case of the analysis of variance the degrees of freedom in the numerator are related to the number of groups to be compared, whereas the degrees of freedom in the denominator are related to the number of units within these groups.

5.6.5 Degrees of freedom

The t-distribution, the χ^2-distribution and the F-distribution are actually classes of distribution. Figure 5.6 presents the $t_{(2)}$ and the $t_{(15)}$ specimens of the t-distribution, while Figure 5.7 presents $\chi^2_{(4)}$, $\chi^2_{(10)}$ and $\chi^2_{(14)}$. The parameters to specify precisely which distribution is at hand are labelled as *degrees of freedom*. To specify the F-distribution, two degrees of freedom are required: one for the numerator and one for the denominator. Degrees of freedom are derived from sample sizes, and refer to the sample size diminished by the number of units that have to be offered to calculate the test statistic. Degrees of freedom designate the number of units that are still freely available once the required test statistic has been computed from the sample data.

Let us *consider* the difference between two sample means. To compute a mean, you need at least one unit from the sample. To compare two sample means, two units have to be offered beforehand. The degrees of freedom for the t-distribution of the difference of sample means when variances are known amounts therefore to $n - 2$. As another example, the t-distribution of a regression coefficient might be used. At least two units of analysis are required to pin down a regression line since a straight line is denned by two points. Therefore the degrees of freedom for the t-distribution of the regression coefficient statistic also amount to $n - 2$.

To compute a variance at least one observation is required. The χ^2-distribution of the sample variance therefore has $n - 1$ degrees of freedom. Chi-square also applies to the comparison of r samples from a nominal distribution with c values. The degrees of freedom for the χ^2-distribution of differences between samples from a nominal variable amount to $(r - 1)(c - 1)$. This number corresponds precisely with the number of different percentage differences which can be calculated from one cross-table. One conception of a cross-table of r rows and c columns is that r samples were drawn from a nominal variable with c values. To test whether these r samples might have been drawn from the same nominal distribution, one may choose one sample as the base rate and compare the other $r - 1$ samples with it. To be able to tell something about a sample distribution of a nominal variable, one value of the nominal variable is required as the base rate category, thus leaving $c - 1$ columns freely available. Altogether this results in $(r - 1)(c - 1)$ comparisons.

To test whether two variances are different from each other, the question can be answered whether the ratio of these variances, which follows an F-distribution (see the previous subsection), differs from 1. The F-test has a number of degrees of freedom for the numerator, as well as for the denominator. The F-distribution of the ratio of two sample variances therefore has $n_1 - 1$ degrees of freedom in the numerator and $n_2 - 1$ degrees of freedom in the denominator. For the outcome of the test the question of which sample is labelled as the first one is irrelevant. The same logic holds for the computation of the degrees of freedom for the F-test in the analysis of variance. This F-test compares the variance between k group means to the variance within these groups. To compute the variance around the mean of the k group means at least one observation is needed to compute the mean of the group means. Therefore the degrees of freedom for the numerator of the test amount to $k - 1$. To compute the variance within these groups, first the means of k different groups have to be computed, which requires k observations. The degrees of freedom for the denominator amount therefore to the number of observations n minus the number of groups k, thus to $n - k$.

5.6.6 Sense and nonsense of statistical tests

Statistical tests are often employed although the assumptions that underlie them are violated. Statistical tests are used, for example, when data are only available for successive years, or when the sample consists of data on the complete population of nations. Statistical tests that assume normal distributions of variables are used even though tests indicate that the variables are not normally distributed.

One should be aware that the unwarranted use of statistical tests renders significance levels meaningless. The decision to discard a hypothesis when the probability that the null hypothesis is true amounts to $p = 0.073$, as well as the decision to maintain a hypothesis when this probability amounts to $p = 0.029$, are completely arbitrary from a mathematical statistician's point of view when the assumptions of the tests are violated.

At least two arguments can be used to make a case for the use of statistical tests even when the precise assumptions of the test are violated. The first justification is that even statistical tests whose assumptions have not been met precisely are based on the common-sense principle that the credibility of research results increases as the number of investigated cases increases. Statistical tests prevent comparative political scientists from jumping to conclusions on the basis of a few cases only. The second justification is the *robustness* of many statistical tests. The outcome of a robust test will still hold when the assumptions are not completely met.

Statistical tests should always be interpreted cautiously. It is an exception rather than a rule that conclusions with respect to the tenability of theories in comparative political science can be based straightforwardly on statistical tests. Nevertheless, statistical tests are important because they are usually more critical than common sense when it comes to an evaluation of theories in the light of available data.

5.7 Summary

This chapter has concentrated on elementary methods for exploratory data analysis. The choice of techniques for data analysis depends crucially on the level of measurement of the variables. The sequence in exploratory data analysis is usually to start with univariate data analysis and to continue with bivariate data analysis.

The reason is that one needs to develop a feeling for the separate variables first, before the bivariate relationships which are of theoretical interest can be sorted out.

Univariate analysis centres on measures of central tendency and measures of dispersion. The mode, the median and the mean were discussed as measures of central tendency for nominal, ordinal and interval variables, respectively. The Herfindahl index, also known as the Laakso–Taagepera index, and the entropy were discussed as measures of the dispersion of nominal variables. The variance and standard deviation were discussed as measures of the dispersion of interval variables.

The analysis of cross-tables is appropriate for the study of the bivariate relationship between nominal variables. Chi-square, phi and Cramér's υ can be used to express the strength of association in a single number. Correlation and regression analysing were dealt with as techniques for analysing the relationship between two variables with an interval level of measurement. Measures such as the regression coefficient, the standardized regression coefficient, the correlation coefficient, the explained variance, and the unexplained variance were introduced. The analysis of variance was introduced to analyse the relationship between an interval variable and a nominal variable. In an analysis of variance the question of association is reduced to the question of whether the mean value of the interval variable varies for the various categories of the nominal variable (which are labelled as 'groups' in the analysis of variance). Concepts such as the variance between groups, the variance within groups, sums of squares between, sums of squares within, the explained variance and the F-ratio were introduced.

Almost inevitably the data analysis will end up in the question of whether the 'findings' really are findings. Statistical tests to answer the question of whether theoretical beliefs can stand up in the light of the available data have been discussed in Section 5.6. Relevant concepts were (unbiasedness, efficiency and robustness of) estimators, test statistics, the normal distribution, the t-distribution, the chi-square distribution and the F-distribution. Statistical tests prevent one from declaring summer when a swallow has been seen. The ground for statistical tests is often soggy, however, since the precise assumptions of these tests are seldom met in comparative political science.

The next chapter will elaborate on the elementary methods discussed in this chapter. The methods will be generalized to the analysis of multivariate relationships between variables. The focus will shift from exploratory purposes towards the causal analysis of political processes.

5.8 Endmatter

Topics highlighted

- Measures of central tendency (mode, median, mean): assessment of the most likely, typical value.
- Measures of dispersion (entropy, Laakso–Taagepera index, variance, standard deviation): assessment of the typical departure from the central tendency.

- Measures of association (percentage difference, χ^2, ϕ, Cramér's v, correlation coefficient): assessment of the degree to which knowledge of one variable is helpful to predict the value of another variable.
- Explorative univariate data analysis: computation of the central tendency and the dispersion of separate variables.
- Explorative bivariate data analysis (by means of cross-tables, analysis of variance, regression analysis). Assessment of the degree to which two variables go together.

Exercises

- Compute measures of central tendency and dispersion for the parties which gained office in agriculture (variable AGRICULT in the NIAS.SAV database) and social affairs (variable SOCIAL) in Belgium. *Hint*: determine which measures of central tendency and dispersion are appropriate given the level of measurement of the party in office. Use SPSS or another statistical program to display a frequency distribution. Compute the appropriate measures by hand from the frequency distribution.

    Which issues (agricultural or social ones) are more disputed in Belgium? *Hint*: is a low or a high dispersion of the parties holding office a measure of political dispute?

    Which party behaves most vehemently as the 'issue owner' of agriculture in Belgium? *Hint*: What is the central tendency of the parties in office on agriculture?
- Compute measures of central tendency and dispersion of the percentage unemployed in OECD countries in 1965 and 1990 (using the same steps as above).
- Compute the central tendency and the dispersion of public expenditures as a percentage of GDP (variable PE in the NIAS.SAV database) in OECD countries in 1965, 1978 and 1990.

    - Determine whether public expenditures were cut down on average (1) as a reaction to the first oil crisis, (2) as a reaction to the recession of the 1980s.

        Did convergence between the economic policies of OECD countries increase (1) as a reaction to the first oil crisis? (2) as a reaction to the recession of the 1980s? *Hint*: convergence is opposite of divergence; divergence = high dispersion.

- Test whether the party group holding office on social affairs (SOCIAL2) has an effect on the type of economic policy (POP).

    - Construe a cross-table, and compute Cramér's v.
    - Interpret the results in the light of substantive theory.

- Apply an analysis of variance to test whether public expenditures (PE) depend on the party group holding the ministry of social affairs (SOCIAL2).
- Use regression analysis to test whether in 1992 the percentage of elderly in a country (variable AGE65 in the NIAS.SAV database) has an upward effect on the percentage of public expenditures (e.g. health care, pensions, lower productivity).

- Apply the language of statistics – probability distributions, degrees of freedom – to explain why statistical laymen with little knowledge or experience in a given field consistently tend to underestimate the diversity, the variety of emprical phenomena in that field; and to overestimate the strength of the connections, the relationships between these phenomena.

Further reading

Elementary text: Babbie (2004).
General texts: King et al. (1994); Tacq (1997); Shively (2001); Kaplan (2002).
Statistical tests: Kanji (1999).

Multivariate analysis and causal inference

The research methods discussed in this chapter are useful for a causal analysis of political processes. The univariate and bivariate methods of Chapter 5 will usually be applied as a first step in data analysis, and the multivariate analysis techniques of this chapter will be applied afterwards. Many research questions can be answered simply by using the techniques discussed in the previous chapters, but multivariate analysis is indispensable to answer research questions concerning the disentanglement of the effects of several variables on a political phenomenon of interest. Examples will be presented in Part III.

Starting from the discussion of most different and most similar cases (see Part I), the concept of causality will be discussed and applied in the context of multivariate relations in Section 6.1. The introduction of more variables makes data analysis more complex. Variables can be interwoven in many ways, even when only three variables are considered. A third variable may simply add to the explanation of the phenomenon of interest, but it may also determine the nature of the relationship between the other two variables (an interacting variable). Section 6.2 presents an overview of methods for multivariate analysis, which will be elaborated in the remaining sections. First a distinction is made between methods for many variables but a limited number of cases (units) and methods for the analysis of many cases but a limited number of variables. If the number of cases is limited – e.g. less than 15 units of analysis – then a researcher will strive for a completely deterministic, albeit complex, explanation for most if not all cases. The approach is *case-oriented*. But no meaningful deterministic explanation might be found to be consistent with the data on a large set of cases. Simple (although probabilistic) reasoning, dealing with a limited number of variables, dominates the discussion over the explanation of patterns found in large data sets. The typical research question for a limited number of cases – how to account completely for the data on these cases – often shifts towards the question of whether the role of a few crucial variables in a huge variety of cases can be understood *parsimoniously*. The approach shifts towards a *variable-oriented* one. The case-oriented approach will be dealt with in Section 6.3. The four subsequent sections focus on the variable-oriented approach. The choice of the research method depends not only crucially on the number of cases and the number of variables, but also on the level of measurement of the variables (nominal or higher). The research techniques used most often in political science, i.e. cross-table elaboration (nominal variables only) and multivariate regression analysis (interval variables only), will be elaborated more thoroughly than the less frequently used techniques. Special attention will be given to variants and extensions that are especially useful for comparative political science, e.g. pooled time series analysis for the analysis of nations whose political characteristics change through time.

6.1 Causality and Multivariate Relations

The relation of cause and effect to which the concept of *causality* refers is a complex one. Yet it appears to be a simple type of relation because we make use of it in almost every instance of our daily and political lives. Our daily activities are aimed at the causal production of results. Causes are manipulated in order to achieve desired effects after a while. Concepts such as action, production, consumption, political power, political influence and political authority all presume the ability to harvest desired future effects above mere chance. They all presume a sequential timely order between a means and an end, between a cause and an effect. These and other observations led John Stuart Mill to state that causation 'is but the familiar truth that invariability of succession is found by observation to obtain between every fact in nature and some other fact which has preceded it'. Unfortunately, invariability of succession is rarely observed in political science. But some timely successions are far more likely than others in a probabilistic sense. The fundamental assumption of the comparative method is that the only baseline to assess whether a cause produces an effect beyond chance in a given case is provided by comparable cases to which the same cause does not apply. Causal statements in comparative political science rest on a comparison in time, in space or in both.

If particular combinations of values on two separate variables occur more frequently than expected on the basis of the frequency distributions of the separate variables, then these variables are related to each other in a statistical sense. A causal relationship assumes not merely a statistical relationship, but also a time dimension and a direction. A causal effect of a variable x on a variable y implies that changing the value of x will produce another value of y after a (short or long) while. The concept of causality implies the concept of an *independent* variable and a *dependent* variable. A causal relationship is a unidirectional relationship ($x \rightarrow y$). Reciprocal causal relationships ($x \rightleftarrows y$) can be understood as two separate causal unidirectional relationships. A variable x is said to have an effect on a nominal variable y when changing x's value will, after a while, increase the chance that variable y will show a particular value. In the case of an ordinal, interval or ratio dependent variable y, causality means that changing x's value increases the chance that y will increase (or decrease) after a while. A linear causal relationship exists when the ratio of the resulting change in the dependent variable to the preceding change in the independent variable is a given constant, regardless of the starting values of the dependent and the independent variable, or the precise history of the causal process. Linear causal relationships are assumed as the default in comparative political science.

Pure additivity, intervention, spurious correlation and interaction

This chapter deals with multivariate causal relationships. The relationships between a multitude of variables will be studied. As a first step towards the analysis of multivariate causal relationships we will consider the various ways in which a third variable z that is 'causally relevant' for the causal explanation of a dependent variable y might have an effect. A third variable might be causally relevant in four ways, summarized in Figure 6.1.

Pure additivity. First, variable z may simply *add* to the explanation of y, without changing the effect of x on y. The effect of z on y does not affect the effect of x on y.

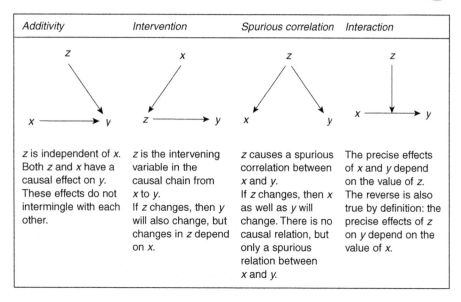

Additivity	Intervention	Spurious correlation	Interaction
z is independent of x. Both z and x have a causal effect on y. These effects do not intermingle with each other.	z is the intervening variable in the causal chain from x to y. If z changes, then y will also change, but changes in z depend on x.	z causes a spurious correlation between x and y. If z changes, then x as well as y will change. There is no causal relation, but only a spurious relation between x and y.	The precise effects of x and y depend on the value of z. The reverse is also true by definition: the precise effects of z on y depend on the value of x.

Figure 6.1   *Four types of multivariate relationships*

The total effect on *y* is precisely the sum of the separate effects of variables *x* and *z* on *y*. Variables *x* and *z* are causally *independent* of each other.

Intervention (or 'mediation'). A variable *z* intervenes in the causal relationship between an independent variable *x* and a dependent variable *y* when *z* is influenced by *x*, and influences *y* in turn. The third variable *z* depends on *x* in the intervention model, whereas *x* and *z* were independent of each other in the additive model. If *z* is held constant – or 'controlled for' in the language of social science methodology – the association between *x* and *y* will cease to exist.

Spurious correlation. A variable *z* introduces a spurious correlation (spurious association) between *x* and *y* when it is the cause of *y*, as in the additive model, but also the cause of *x*. *x* and *y* will move in the same direction in response to their common cause. But their association is spurious: the association would vanish if *z* were held constant. One should note the similarity between the spurious correlation model and the intervention model at this point. Both models predict that the association between *x* and *y* will vanish when *z* is held constant.

Interaction (or 'modification'). A variable *z* interacts with variable *x* when the effect of *x* on *y* depends on the level of the other variable. The magnitude or even the direction of the effect of *x* on *y* depends on *z*. An increase in social expenditures (*y*) may depend on the number of leftist seats in parliament (*x*). A simple theory of leftist influence in multi-party systems is that leftist parties will especially succeed in increasing social expenditures when the coalition government includes leftist parties. In this example the inclusion of a leftist party in the coalition government is the interacting variable *z*.

The four models discussed here are only ideal type models. Usually political reality is something in between. Independent variables are often *collinear* instead

Table 6.1 *An overview of methods for causal data analysis*

Orientation	Measurement level of dependent variable	Measurement level of independent variable	Preferred method of data analysis
Case-oriented			Single case study (see Yin, 1996) Comparative qualitative analysis (*Section 6.3*)
Variable-oriented	Nominal	Nominal	Cross-table elaboration (*Section 6.4*)
	Nominal	Interval/ratio	Discriminant analysis (*Section 6.5*)
	Interval/ratio	Nominal	Analysis of variance (*Section 6.6*)
	Interval/ratio	Interval/ratio	Regression analysis (*Section 6.7*)

of purely additive, for example. Collinear variables overlap each other. Therefore their joint influence is less than the sum of their separate influences, and disentangling their separate influence becomes tricky. Researchers do not test every conceivable model. They confine themselves to specific causal hypotheses which derive from a research question.

6.2 Overview of Multivariate Data Analysis Techniques

Table 6.1 gives an overview of frequently used methods for causal data analysis. Only two of the possible criteria for selecting a method of analysis are highlighted in Table 6.1: the number of cases and the level of measurement of the variables.

The first criterion is whether the number of cases considered is small or large compared with the number of variables being considered. If the number of cases is small, then researchers usually want to describe and to explain them as fully as possible. If the number of cases increases, a full, extensive description and explanation of each separate case tends to become rather cumbersome or even impossible. The researcher will attempt to explain most variation in all cases (or groups of cases) parsimoniously, albeit incompletely, by a few variables of theoretical interest only. We call this distinction the distinction between case-oriented and variable-oriented research, following Ragin (1987). Related, albeit not completely identical, distinctions are exploratory versus hypothesis-testing research and inductive research versus deductive research. *Case-oriented* research aims at a full understanding of a few cases using as many variables as necessary. *Variable-oriented* research aims at a full understanding of the role of a few variables in a multitude of cases.

Within the class of case-oriented methods, methods for pure case studies where one case is studied in depth and methods for a limited number of cases (typically less than 15) can be distinguished. Methods for the study of one case will not be treated here (but see Yin, 1996) because they serve as a first step for comparative research only. Methods for the study of a limited number of cases usually rely on John Stuart Mill's causal insights (see Chapter 3). Recently Charles Ragin (2000) has proposed a new approach, known as qualitative case analysis (QCA), by means of the fuzzy set methodology (see Sections 6.3 and 9.3).

In variable-oriented research the choice of the appropriate method depends on the levels of measurement of the dependent and independent variables. Elaborations of cross-table analysis are appropriate when both the dependent and the independent variables are nominal variables (see Section 6.4). Discriminant analysis is appropriate when the dependent variable is nominal but the independent variables have a higher level of measurement (see Section 6.5). If the independent variables are nominal variables but the dependent variable has a higher level of measurement then analysis of variance can be recommended (see Section 6.6). If all variables are measured with interval or ratio precision then one of the many variants of regression analysis is possible (see Section 6.7).

6.3 The Case-Oriented Approach

If the occurrence of a phenomenon or an event is studied for a small number of cases then the aim of the investigation is to achieve a complete explanation. The aim is to identify precisely the conditions that led to the phenomenon or event, or at least to identify sets of conditions that might have led to it. A slightly more modest aim is to identify various sets of circumstances that preceded it or accompanied it. Ragin's *qualitative comparative analysis* (Ragin, 1987; Berg-Schlosser and Quenter, 1996) has been developed as a method to formalize this approach.

The *variables* used to explain the occurrence of an effect are assumed to be dichotomous. Essentially the variables refer to the presence (1) or absence (0) of a condition or of an event. Whether the event of interest occurs or not is also a dichotomous variable. Each dichotomous variable can be represented as a letter of the alphabet. Capitals correspond with the value 1, lower-case letters with the value 0. We may ask ourselves, for example, why some democracies in inter-war Europe broke down (B) while others did not (b). Variables of interest might be the political role of the military (M is substantial, m is almost absent), the level of social unrest (U or u), the level of economic development (E or e), the level of integration into the world market (W or w), social homogeneity (H or h) and the domestic representation of commercial interests (C or c). In this example a possible combination of variables might be listed as $MuewHc \rightarrow B$: once upon a time a democracy broke down (B) when the political influence for the military was substantial (M), social unrest was low (u), economic development was slow (e), the integration into the world economy was poor (w), social homogeneity was high (H) and commercial interests were poorly represented (c). Suppose that democracy broke down in one other case only, namely when the combination

MUEWhC → *B* occurred. Intuitively one would conclude that a breakdown of democracy (*B*) is associated with a political role for the military (*M*), but that the other factors are not important at all, since democracy collapsed both when they occurred and when they were absent. A political role for the military seems to be a necessary, albeit not necessarily sufficient, condition of the breakdown of democracy (*M* → *B*). If democracy never survives in cases where *M* is high, then *M* → *B* would be a completely satisfactory explanation. *M* would be QCA's explanation of *B*.

An explanation in QCA is technically just a parsimonious listing of the constellations which give rise to the presence (or absence) of the phenomenon of interest. Three types of explanation can be conceived: disjunctive explanations, conjunctive explanations and explanations with both disjunctive and conjunctive elements. A *disjunctive* explanation entails that circumstance A or circumstance B must have been present. A *conjunctive* explanation entails that both A *and* B must have been present. Disjunctive explanations are represented by the plus sign (+), whereas conjunctive explanations are represented by a multiplication sign (or no sign at all). One possible explanation of the collapse of democracy could for example be listed as:

$$c = M + hUw.$$

This explanation entails that democracy will collapse (*c*) when the role of the military in politics is substantial (*M*), or when three factors emerge simultaneously: poor social homogeneity (*h*), considerable social unrest (*U*), and a low integration into the world market (*w*).

To get a feeling for QCA a formal approach is helpful. With six explanatory variables, as in the previous example (*M, U, E, W, H, C*) the number of possible constellations amounts to $2^6 = 64$ (*MUEWHC, MUEWHc, ... , muewhc*). In the case of *k* independent variables of interest, 2^k possible constellations can be listed. Depending on the empirical characteristics of the cases being studied, each of these 2^k constellations can be classified into one of four classes:

1 Only cases with high values on the dependent variable belong to the constellation (in our example, constellations characterized by *B*, the breakdown of democracy).
2 Only cases with low values on the dependent variable belong to the constellation (constellations characterized by *b*, the absence of a breakdown).
3 Contradictions: both cases with low and cases with high values on the dependent variable belong to the constellation.
4 Logical remainders, missing constellations: not a single case belongs to the constellation. All constellations that are not encountered in the empirical data are labelled as *logical remainder cases*.

Thus, the 2^k constellations can be divided into four groups that are defined by the presence or non-presence of high and/or low values on the dependent variable. The constellations belonging to each group can be listed exhaustively. The idea

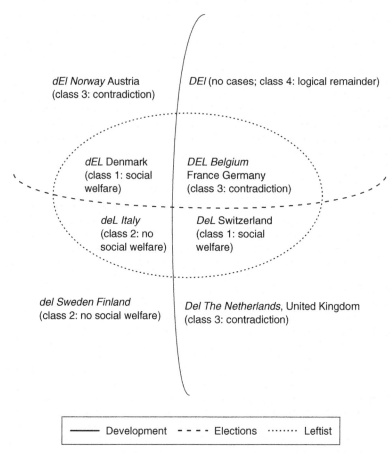

dEI *Norway* Austria
(class 3: contradiction)

DEI (no cases; class 4: logical remainder)

dEL Denmark
(class 1: social
welfare)

DEL *Belgium*
France Germany
(class 3: contradiction)

deL *Italy*
(class 2: no
social welfare)

DeL Switzerland
(class 1: social
welfare)

del *Sweden Finland*
(class 2: no social welfare)

Del *The Netherlands*, United Kingdom
(class 3: contradiction)

Development - - - - Elections ········ Leftist

Figure 6.2 *Example of qualitative case analysis*

of *Boolean minimization* is simply that variables whose presence or absence apparently has no effect on the dependent variable can be neglected. Two complications render this task slightly less trivial than one might think at first. The first complication is that a parsimonious listing of the presence of the variable of interest (class 1) should not include constellations belonging to class 2. The second complication has to do with the logical remainders (class 4), thus with the class of conceivable constellations which are empty from an empirical point of view. Parsimonious explanations of the phenomenon of interest may include some but not all logical remainders. Suppose, for example, that the research question is to explain Z using the variables A, B and C. Suppose that empirically the constellations $ABC \rightarrow Z$ and $Abc \rightarrow Z$ are found, whereas constellations ABc and AbC are logical remainders, since they do not exist empirically, A parsimonious explanation of Z would be $A \rightarrow Z$, since it seems irrelevant whether B and C are present. This explanation entails that the logical remainders are included in the set of constellations which would produce phenomenon Z.

Example: social welfare provisions in 12 nations in 1900

We will use a simple example from Berg-Schlosser and Quenter (1996), with three independent variables only. The dependent variable in the example is the development of social welfare provisions. The cases, or units of analysis, are 12 nations in 1900. Some of them have a low level of welfare provisions (italic font) whereas others have extended welfare provisions. The research question asks for an explanation of the development of social welfare provisions. Figure 6.2 gives an overview of the data on the available cases. Three independent variables are considered in the example. The curved y-axis represents the level of economic development. Values to the right of this axis represent a high level of economic development (D), whereas values to the left represent poor development (d). Values above the curved x-axis represent the fact that almost everybody is entitled to vote in national elections (E), whereas values beneath represent the absence of parliamentary democracy (e). The ellipse represents the strength of leftist parties. Outside (l) represents weak leftist parties, whereas inside (L) represents a strong leftist block. Three independent variables result in $2^3 = 8$ possible constellations.

As a first step each of the 12 countries is classified as belonging to one of the eight constellations. Consequently these constellations are classified into four classes of constellations:

Classes of constellations	Constellations included	Simplified formula for constellations included
1. Only high values (roman font) on the dependent variable	*DeL, dEL* ($n = 2$) including Denmark, Switzerland	No simplification, but $D+E$ with class 4 included (outcome *may* occur when $D + E$, when D or E occurs)
2. Only low values (*italic* font) on the dependent variable	*deL, del* ($n = 2$) including Italy, Sweden, Finland	*de* (outcome will surely *not* appear when *de*, when *d* and *e* occur simultaneously)
3. Neither high nor low values on the dependent variable (the empty class, 'logical remainders')	*DEl* ($n = 1$) empty	No simplifcation
4. Both high and low values on the dependent variable (contradictions, both roman and *italic* font)	*dEl, DEL, Del* ($n = 3$) including Norway, Austria, Belgium, France, Germany, The Netherlands, UK	No simplification

Each class of constellations consists of a list of (either zero, one or more) constellations. The class of nations where social welfare provisions will surely come into being (class 1: *DeL* + *dEL*) cannot be simplified to *L*(*D* + *E*), since the latter formula includes *DEL*, whereas the constellation *DEL* contains Belgium as an exception. Class 2 consists of *del* and *deL*, which can be simplified to *de*. Apparently leftist parties cannot produce social welfare provisions when neither economic development nor parliamentary democracy helps. One could also ask, of course, in which nations social welfare provisions *can* emerge. Effectively this comes down to merging classes 1 and 3, thus to minimizing *DeL* + *dEL* + *dEl* + *Del* + *DEL*. If the logical remainder class is added (*DEl*), then the list *DEL* + *DEl* + *DeL* + *Del* + *dEL* + *dEl* arises, from which it is clear that *L*(eftist party strength) is an irrelevant variable. These constellations can be simplified to *D* + *E*. Thus, either economic development or universal suffrage is enough to create the possibility of social welfare provisions.

The example shows clearly that QCA can offer intriguing, asymmetric insights. Strong leftist parties were irrelevant to the explanation in which nations social welfare provisions *do* come about. But weak leftist parties were essential to explain why in some nations social welfare provisions *do not* come about.

The QCA approach is useful when the number of cases is small compared with the number of variables. If the number of variables is small compared with the number of cases (e.g. less than a tenth) and the relationships between the variables are probabilistic to a certain degree, then almost all constellations tend to belong to the class of contradictions. There is little left to explain for binary deterministic data analysis models such as QCA. In Section 9.3 we will discuss the newest development in configurational analysis to cope with this problem, namely the fuzzy set methodology (Ragin, 2000).

6.4 Nominal Dependent and Independent Variables

An introduction to cross-tables was given in Section 5.3 using the relationship between the economy (before the oil crisis of 1973, before 1981, after 1981) and macro-economic policy (restrictive, monetarist, austerity, or Keynesian) as an example. Here we will incorporate the electoral system of a nation as a third variable into this example to extend the use of cross-tables from bivariate analysis to multivariate analysis.

The causal model to be tested

Electoral systems can be divided into proportional systems (e.g. the Scandinavian countries, Switzerland, Austria, Italy, the Netherlands, Belgium), on the one hand, and majoritarian systems (e.g. Great Britain, USA, Canada, France) and semi-proportional systems (e.g. Australia, Ireland, Japan, Germany), on the other hand. Minorities in proportional systems have a good chance of being represented in parliament. Proportional electoral systems tend to lead to multiparty systems, whereas majoritarian systems and semi-proportional systems are often dominated by two or three parties. Voters are more dispersed over parties in proportional systems than in majoritarian and semi-proportional systems, as is indicated by the Herfindahl index in number equivalents. For the period 1965–90 this index amounts for the proportional electoral systems to 4.3 parties and for the other systems to 2.6 parties only ($n = 442$ nested country–year units). A proportional system favours consensus democracy, in which 'all significant political parties and representatives of the major groups in society share executive power' (Lijphart, 1984: 46).

The *hypothesis* to be tested here is that proportional electoral systems are conducive to Keynesian macro-economic policy, whereas majoritarian systems enhance a restrictive macro-economic policy. In proportional electoral systems, parties that promote the interests of a homogeneous segment of the population only in order to get some seats (rather than the majority of seats) can survive. Parties in proportional electoral systems can and will relatively often plead for public expenditures to favour their own group. The dominant parties in majoritarian systems will have to make broad appeals to a heterogeneous electorate with conflicting interests. They are therefore expected to favour broad tax cuts instead of public expenditures to help specific, homogeneous groups. In Figure 6.3. this hypothesis is depicted as a direct arrow from electoral system to macro-economic policy.

Let us add a second hypothesis. In Section 5.3 the conclusion was that the economic crisis had opposing influences on macro-economic policy. Some countries shifted towards a more restrictive policy, others towards a Keynesian policy. This effect is visualized as a direct effect from economic tide to macro-economic policy in Figure 6.3. One expects that the type of reaction to a worsening economy is dependent on the electoral system. Or, to put it another way, the economy also determines the *strength* of the effect of the electoral system on the type of macro-economic policy. In times of economic prosperity even politicians in majoritarian systems will often favour help for specific societal groups, since the electorate as a whole will not have to suffer because of it. This effect is visualized as the *interaction effect* from the economy on the direct effect from the electoral system on the type of macro-economic policy.

6.4.1 Cross-table elaboration

The method of analysing multivariate relationships with cross-tables is called cross-table elaboration. Here we will illustrate the method for three variables. The general idea is that the relationship between the two variables of primary interest, x and y – in our example, the relationship between the electoral system and the type of macro-economic policy – should be split up for each category of the remaining nominal variable z – in our example, for each state of the economy. Thus, the dependence of macro-economic policy on the electoral system is depicted in partial tables for each value of the economy. In the jargon of cross-table elaboration, the economy is held constant. Each partial table reflects only one particular state of the economy.

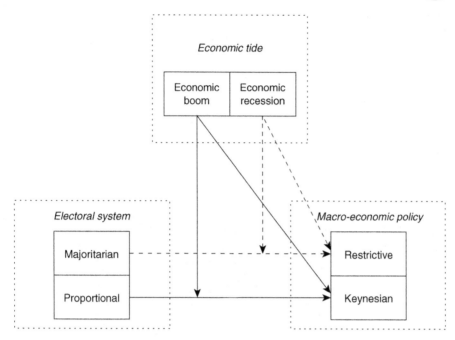

Figure 6.3   *Causal model of electoral system, economy and macro-economic policy*

All partial tables will show an association of the same magnitude when the variable being controlled for is an additive variable that explains variance in the dependent variable, but is independent of the primary independent variable. The association in the uncontrolled cross-table will have the same magnitude as the association in the partial tables.

When the variable being controlled for is either an intervening variable or an exogeneous variable responsible for spurious correlation, the associations in the partial tables will be small compared with the bivariate association. The column percentages in corresponding cells of the partial tables will be equal to each other.

When the variable being controlled for is an interacting variable the association should be strong in some partial tables but low in others.

First the overarching cross-table between economic tide and macro-economic policy will be inspected, regardless of the state of the economy (Table 6.2). Next, for each of the three values of the economy, the partial tables between these two variables could have been presented, but for simplicity's sake only the partial tables for the period before the oil crisis of 1973 and the crisis period of the 1980s will be presented (Table 6.3). The actual relationship between the type of electoral system and the type of macro-economic policy is in line with the hypothesis. Keynesian policy is pursued in proportional election systems only ($\varepsilon = 44.9$ per cent). A restrictive macro-economic policy is pursued more often in majoritarian systems ($\varepsilon = 24.0$ per cent $- 7.3$ per cent $= 16.7$ per cent).

Table 6.2 *Cross-tabulation of electoral system by macro-economic policy*

| Macro-economic policy type | Economic tide | | | |
	1965–73	1974–80	1981–90	Total
Restrictive	5.9%	23.5%	17.6%	15.2%
Monetarist	35.3%	23.5%	23.5%	27.6%
Austerity	41.2%	29.4%	29.4%	23.8%
Keynesian	17.6%	23.5%	29.4%	23.8%
Total	100%	100%	100%	100%
	(n = 153)	(n = 119)	(n = 170)	(n = 442)

Table 6.3 *Electoral system by macro-economic policy elaborated for economy (period 1974–9 not considered)*

| Economy | Macro-economic policy type | Electoral system[a] | | |
		Majoritarian or semi-proportional	Proportional	Total
1965–73	Restrictive	12.5%	0%	5.9%
(economy still	Monetarist	37.5%	33.3%	35.3%
flourishing)	Austerity	50%	33.3%	35.3%
	Keynesian	0%	33.3%	17.6%
Total		100%	100%	100%
		(n = 72)	(n = 81)	(n = 153)
1981–90	Restrictive	25.0%	11.1%	17.6%
(recession;	Monetarist	37.5%	11.1%	23.5%
economy	Austerity	37.5%	22.2%	29.4%
recovering slowly)	Keynesian	0%	55.6%	29.4%
Total		100%	100%	100%
		(n = 80)	(n = 90)	(n = 170)

[a]*Source:* Lijphart (1984).

The partial cross-tables show clearly that the economy is neither an intervening variable nor an exogeneous variable causing spurious correlation, since the percentage differences in the partial tables do not fall to near zero. The economy is an interacting variable, however. In the good old prosperous years before the oil crisis of 1973 the relationship between the electoral system and the macro-economic policy pursued is clearly extant, but relatively weak as compared to the years of crisis in the 1980s. Before the oil crisis Keynesian policy was pursued in proportional electoral systems only, whereas a restrictive policy was pursued in majoritarian electoral systems only. The percentage difference for Keynesian policy was 33.3 per cent, the percentage difference for restrictive policy 12.5 per cent. The years of crisis tightened up the differences between the electoral systems. In the 1980s the percentage differences had grown. They show an increase for Keynesian policy of 55.6 per cent and for restrictive policy of 25.0 − 11.1 per cent = 13.9 per cent. Before the oil crisis the association measure ϕ between the electoral system and the type of economic policy amounted to 0.49; in the 1980s it had increased to 0.62.

The partial cross-tables are also consistent with an autonomous, additive effect of the economy on macro-economic policy. Restrictive policy became more popular in the early 1980s, as is indicated by an increase from 0 per cent to 11.1 per cent in proportional systems and from 12.5 per cent to 25.0 per cent in majoritarian systems. The worse the economy, the more popular a restrictive macro-economic policy tends to become, regardless of the electoral system.

6.5 Nominal Dependent Variable, Interval *Ind*ependent Variables

If the variables have an interval level of measurement then they will have many values. Consequently, the number of cases in each separate cell of the cross-table analysis will be small, which will render percentage differences and association measures such as χ^2 shaky and therefore meaningless from a statistical point of view.

When the independent variables have a higher level of measurement, but the dependent variable is still nominal, the question becomes whether the value which the nominal dependent variable takes is predictable from the values on the independent variables. Discriminant analysis is one of the oldest data analysis techniques to provide an answer to this problem (many newer techniques have been developed, with fancy names such as neural network classification, maximum entrophy network and so on). Since each party can be considered as one value of the nominal variable party choice, discriminant analysis can be used to answer the question to what degree party choice in multi-party systems is dependent on various ideological and socio-economic variables with an interval level of measurement (education, income, sympathy ratings of electoral leaders, and so on).

Discriminant analysis will be discussed only cursorily here, because the combination of a dependent nominal variable and independent interval variables does not apply often. The mathematical and statistical properties will be left aside.

Discriminant analysis assumes a linear, unidirectional model. The probability that a case has a given value on the nominal dependent variable is modelled as a linear function of the independent variables. Discriminant analysis assesses the direct effect of each separate variable controlled for the effects of the other variables. When the independent variables correlate with each other the direct effects of each separate variable may deviate strongly from what would have been expected on the basis of bivariate inspections of the data.

When the dependent variable is a dichotomous one, discriminant analysis is equivalent to multiple linear regression analysis with a dichotomous dependent variable (see van de Geer, 1986), but this equivalence is hidden by most statistical packages. The printed output for discriminant analysis will typically contain various overviews and details that are not printed in the case of regression analysis and vice versa. Even to sort out the exact correspondence of discriminant function coefficients with ordinary regression coefficients is non-trivial since regression coefficients and discriminant function coefficients tend to be standardized differently (even within the same statistical package). When the number of values of the dependent nominal variable is three or higher, the precise correspondence with multiple regression analysis is lost.

6.5.1 Discriminant analysis example: explaining the type of government

One of the nominal variables in the NIAS.SAV database is the type of government (TOGORI). This variable has four categories: single-party governments, minimal winning coalitions, surplus majority coalitions that rest on the official parliamentary support of more parties than strictly necessary for survival, and (various subtypes of) minority governments. Caretaker governments will be excluded from consideration here. A variety of explanations of the type of government have been offered (see de Swaan, 1973; Budge and Keman, 1990; Laver and Shepsle, 1996). Many theories emphasize aspects of coalition governments that are not captured by the single variable TOGORI (e.g. whether coalition partners occupy a smallest region in issue space, the distribution of cabinet portfolios among the coalition parties). The aim of the analysis presented here is simply to investigate whether a non-exhaustive number of selected variables with an interval level of measurement add to the explanation of the rough type of government. Due to missing values in the NIAS.SAV database, data are only available for 392 government–year combinations (16 OECD countries, period 1965–1990).

Once more the theory of the effects of the type of electoral system is useful. Majoritarian electoral systems will tend to produce two parties only. Single-party governments are likely. As compared with politicians in multi-party systems with the same ideology, party politicians in majoritarian systems will attempt to appease heterogeneous groups with low taxes and low social contributions. Thus, the existence of many parties (as measured by the Laakso–Taagepera index) as well as high taxes and high social security contributions will decrease the likelihood of a single-party government. A majority coalition will presumably result when party ideologies are deemed less important than national unity. One indicator of such a state of emergency is the number of strikes. Strikes increase the likelihood of a majority government. Polarization between parties, as measured by the distance between left-wing and right-wing parties (as measured in turn by party manifestoes), on the other hand, hampers government coalitions with centrist parties and will increase the likelihood of a minority coalition.

As a first step the plausibility of these hypotheses can be verified by means of a bivariate analysis of variance. Table 6.4 depicts for each type of government the

Table 6.4 *Mean values of independent variables per type of government*

	Type of government (TOGORI)			
	Single-party government	Minimal winning coalition	Majority coalition	Minority government
	Mean	Mean	Mean	Mean
Electoral system (1 = majoritarian, 2 = proportional)	1.2	1.8	1.8	1.8
Effective number of parties (Laakso–Taagepera index)	2.2	3.9	4.4	3.7
Taxes	33.5	37.5	34.3	42.2
Social security contributions	3.9	10.1	10	7.4
Left–right polarization	2.03	1.79	1.84	2.91
Number of strikes (ILO)	3571	1428	3387	2325

mean scores on the independent interval variables. The mean values per type of government are roughly in line with expectations. The mean value of single-party governments on 'electoral system' of 1.2, as compared with 1.8 for other types of government, indicates that majoritarian electoral systems do indeed produce single-party governments. Remember that the variable 'electoral system' takes the value 1 in the case of a majoritarian system and 2 in the case of a proportional system. Single-party governments emerge when the effective number of parties is low (2.2 on average), whereas majority governments emerge when the number of parties is extremely high (4.4 on average). Thus, fragmented societies with a proportional electoral system seem to produce political elites which tend to cooperate in large majority coalitions. On average, low tax rates and low social security contributions do indeed correspond with single-party governments (33.5 and 3.9, respectively). Polarization does indeed favour minority governments (mean polarization of 2.91). Majority coalitions are indeed associated with a relatively high number of strikes, but the number of strikes is even higher when 'stubborn' single-party governments take office.

Discriminant analysis is the appropriate technique for assessing to what degree the combination of these variables suffices to explain and to predict the type of government. A central concept in discriminant analysis is the (*canonical*) *discriminant function*. A discriminant function is a *division function* which is interpreted as dividing the cases which belong to two particular sets of categories of the dependent nominal variable on the basis of their values on the independent variables. The number of discriminant functions is one less than the number of categories of the dependent variable. In our example of four categories, there are three discriminant functions. Each of them makes a statistically significant contribution to the explanation of the type of government. Figure 6.4 shows the essentials of the SPSS output for the application of discriminant analysis to our example. The meaning of the discriminant functions should be discerned by interpreting the 'rotated standardized discriminant function coefficients' of the

Rotated standardized discriminant function coefficients
Based on rotation of structure matrix

	Func 1	Func 2	Func 3	
ELSYS	.36258	.13412	.75953	Electoral system. Lijphart (1984)
EFFNOP	.74963	−.03528	−.51300	Effective number of parties
TAX	−.49170	.65792	.50833	Taxes
SSC	.54635	−.91833	.03132	Social security contributions
POLAR	.24842	.58169	.31833	Polarization left–right
NRSTRIKE	.10818	.57047	−.32482	Number of strikes (ILO)

Canonical discriminant functions evaluated at group means (group centroids)

Group	Func 1	Func 2	Func 3	
1	−1.53184	.33075	−.51097	Single-party government
2	.25861	−.48301	.21869	Minimal winning coalition
3	1.32335	−.59363	−.35458	Surplus majority coalition
4	.07335	1.13661	1.00438	Minority government

Classification results

Actual Group	No. of Cases	Predicted Group Membership			
		1	2	3	4
Group 1	105	91	12	0	2
Single-party government		86.7%	11.4%	.0%	1.9%
Group 2	114	21	41	32	20
Minimal winning coalition		18.4%	36.0%	28.1%	17.5%
Group 3	103	0	25	71	7
Surplus majority coalition		.0%	24.3%	68.9%	6.8%
Group 4	70	11	5	4	50
Minority government		15.7%	7.1%	5.7%	71.4%
Ungrouped cases	24	2	2	7	13
		8.3%	8.3%	29.2%	54.2%

Per cent of 'grouped' cases correctly classified: 64.54%

Figure 6.4 *SPSS output of discriminant analysis to predict the type of government*

dependent variables with regard to the three discriminant functions. The discriminant function coefficients of the independent variables on the discriminant functions in discriminant analysis are comparable to the factor loadings of variables on the factors in factor analysis. As a further means to clarify the meaning of the discriminant functions, a glance at the location of each of the group means (group centroids) with respect to these division lines is useful. Classification results can be trusted once the meaning of the discriminant functions is interpreted in the light of the available theory.

First the *division lines* or, in the jargon of discriminant analysis, the *canonical discriminant functions* that are constructed by discriminant analysis to explain the type of government should be interpreted on the basis of the available theory. To get a feeling for these *discriminant functions*, a glance at the group centroids is useful.

The first discriminant function separates single-party governments (average position −1.53 with respect to first discriminant function) from the other types of governments, especially from majority coalitions (position +1.32 with respect to first discriminant function). A look at the (rotated standardized) *discriminant function coefficients* shows that positive positions relative to the first discriminant function are associated with a proportional electoral system (+0.36), a high number of effective parties (+0.75) and high social security contributions (+0.55). Negative positions relative to the first division line are associated with low taxes (−0.49). These results are pretty much in line with the basic theory. The first discriminant functions distinguishes between majoritarian electoral systems with a few parties only and low taxes and, on the other hand, proportional electoral systems with a great many parties and high social security contributions.

The second discriminant function separates the minority governments (average position +1.14) from the minimal winning coalitions and especially from the majority coalitions (position −0.59). Positive positions with respect to the second discriminant function are associated with high taxes (+0.66), a high degree of polarization (+0.58) and strikes (+0.57). Negative positions are associated with low social security contributions (−0.92). The second division line has at its positive side the minority governments that arise when political agreements between coalition partners become impossible due to a high degree of possible polarization, societal tensions as indicated by strikes, and taxes that are already too high. Thus, the second discriminant function can also be interpreted fairly easily.

The third discriminant function is less easily interpreted on the basis of theory. Apparently it captures the idea that majority coalitions (average position −0.35) provide a political answer to labour unrest and strikes (−0.32) when the effective number of parties is high (−0.51). Note that the three minus signs merely indicate here that strikes, many parties and majority coalitions are on the same side of the third discriminant function. In discriminant analysis, these signs are arbitrary (one may multiply them by −1). When the higher-order discriminant functions are completely random from the point of view of substantial theory, the number of discriminant functions should be reduced a priori, even when these higher-order functions are statistically significant.

To assess the quality of the overall explanation of the nominal dependent variable the *classification results table* is useful. Overall the type of government was predicted correctly for 91 + 41 + 71 + 50 = 253 cases, which amounts to 64.5 per cent of the 392 cases without missing values. This percentage is fairly impressive, since it is much higher than could be expected on the basis of the frequency of the modal type of government (the relative frequency of minimal winning coalitions amounts to 114/392 = 29.1 per cent).

The rows of the classification table should be inspected to get a feeling for the strengths and weaknesses of the explanation. Single-party governments are predicted quite well on the basis of the model (86.7 per cent correct). Majority coalitions and minority governments are predicted correctly for roughly two out of three cases. Surplus coalitions are often predicted when actually a minimal winning coalition came into being (24 per cent). The model provides poor predictions of the realization of minimal winning coalitions (36 per cent correct guesses). This poor prediction reflects the fact that some minimal winning coalitions are politically attractive whereas others are absurd, depending on the policy distances between the parties within the minimal winning coalition (de Swaan, 1973).

It is worthwhile to examine the quality of predictions not only from a quantitative point of view but also to examine precisely for which cases the model performs well or badly. To save space we will not print casewise predictions here. It will come as no surprise that the casewise predictions show that the model presented here has no difficulty in explaining the trivial facts that Great Britain has single-party governments while Switzerland has surplus majority coalitions. For some countries the model performs extremely poorly, however. Austria, for example, is predicted to always have minimal winning coalitions, but in reality Austria has all types of governments. Nevertheless the simple discriminant analysis model presented here predicts some shifts in the type of government remarkably accurately. For Belgium the model predicts correctly, for example, the succession in 1966 of a majority coalition by a minimal winning coalition. For the Netherlands the succession in 1977 of a majority coalition by a minimal winning coalition is predicted, whereas this shift came about in 1978 (at least according to the annual data). For Italy the succession in 1987 of a majority government by a minority government is correctly predicted.

6.6 Interval Dependent Variable, Nominal Independent Variables: Analysis of Variance

Models for the analysis of variance (ANOVA) have a dependent variable with an interval level of measurement. In Section 5.2.2 an ANOVA model with one independent nominal variable was presented. More complex ANOVA models have been developed of course. First, *multiple* independent nominal variables can be entered. Next, models with *interactions* between the various nominal independent variables have been introduced. Third, *covariates* – variables with a higher level of measurement – can be introduced as additional independent variables to explain the value of the independent interval variable. Many other complications, such as repeated measurements or varying contrast groups, can also be handled within the context of ANOVA models. Here we will not delve into the analysis of variance, since regression analysis can be used in many circumstances as an alternative.

The analysis of variance with one independent nominal variable with j categories is equivalent to regression analysis with $j - 1$ dummy variables as independent variables. An obvious way to set up these dummy variables is to select one of the j groups as the reference category and to construct for each of the remaining groups a variable that has the value +1 when a case belongs to that group and the value 0 otherwise. Let us take a simple example. Suppose one wishes to examine the effect of one's 'religion', conceived as a nominal variable with three values, namely 'Christian', 'none', and 'other (e.g. Islam)', on the interval variable 'trust in government'. The regression approach to this problem would be to construct a variable 'Christianity' with value 1 when the nominal variable takes the value 'Christian' and 0 otherwise. Furthermore, a variable 'other religion' could be construed (1 = other religion, 0 = Christian or no religion). The regression equation to be estimated would be:

$$\text{Trust} = b_1 \text{ Christianity} + b_2 \text{ Other Religion} + a.$$

Instead of the binary 0–1 'contrast' to code a dummy variable, other numerical 'contrasts' can be used. If not belonging to a specific group is considered not only as absence of group membership, but more strongly as group avoidance, then the value −1 is preferable to the value 0, for example. Many other contrasts have been used in the literature. One should keep in mind that the precise contrasts do have effects on the unstandardized regression coefficients, since the measurement scale of the independent variables is altered, but not on the explained variance, since the latter is independent of linear transformations in the independent variables.

An interaction effect of two nominal variables implies that each specific combination of the values of these two variables is associated with a particular level of the dependent variable. In regression analysis the (first-order) interaction terms can be constructed by multiplying each dummy used to represent the first variable with each of the dummies used to represent the second variable. If two variables have j and k values, respectively, then $j - 1$ and $k - 1$ dummies, respectively, should be created to deal with them in multiple regression analysis as independent variables, and $(j - 1)(k - 1)$ dummies should be constructed to represent the interactions between the two nominal variables. To study the combined effect of religion and class – conceived of as a dichotomous nominal variable – on trust in government, for example, one should first construct a binary variable 'class' with value 1 for the upper class and value 0 for the lower class. The regression model without interactions is:

$$\text{Trust} = b_1 \text{ Christianity} + b_2 \text{ Other Religion} + b_3 \text{ Class} + a.$$

A model with interactions allows for the fact that especially citizens from the higher class exhibit trust in government. In our example $(3 - 1)(2 - 1) = 2$ interaction variables should be created to enable a full regression analysis with interaction effects:

$$\text{Trust} = b_1 \text{ Christianity} + b_2 \text{ Other Religion} + b_3 \text{ Upper Class} \\ + b_4 \text{ Christian Upper Class} + b_5 \text{ Other Religion Upper Class} + a,$$

where Christian Upper Class = 1 if Christianity = 1 and Upper Class = 1, otherwise 0; and Other Religion Upper Class = 1 if Other Religion = 1 and Upper Class = 1, otherwise 0. The regression representation of analysis of variance readily allows for the possibility of including covariates, defined as other variables with a higher level of measurement, as independent variables in the regression equation. Interaction in regression models will be discussed in Section 6.7.4.

Thus, from a mathematical point of view, analysis of variance is equivalent to regression analysis. Nevertheless the required input and the printed output from both subroutines will be quite different in most statistical packages. The printed output of regression analysis concentrates upon regression parameters of separate (dummy) variables (that might or might not represent (interactions between) categories of nominal independent variables), whereas the printed output of the analysis of variance deals primarily with the statistical significance of complete nominal variables and their interactions. Thus, if one is interested in general questions such as whether nominal variables or their interactions have an effect on the dependent variable at all, ANOVA output should be requested. If one is interested in the precise effects of specific conditions, as most comparative political scientists are, then the regression approach is to be preferred. In this book we will concentrate on the regression approach.

6.7 Interval Dependent and Independent Variables: Regression Analysis

Regression analysis is probably the most frequently used technique for data analysis in political science. Various extensions of bivariate regression analysis (Section 5.4) will be discussed in this section. Regression analysis is the appropriate technique whenever dependent and independent variables have an interval level of measurement.

In Section 6.7.1 the linear multiple regression model will be discussed. The precise assumptions of the linear multiple regression model are dealt with in Section 6.7.2. Sections 6.7.3 and 6.7.4 serve to translate the general principles of testing causal theories, which were presented in Section 6.1, to variables with interval and ratio levels of measurement. The use of multiple regression analysis to deal with additive relationships, intervention and spurious correlation (see Section 6.1) is discussed in Section 6.7.3. Interactions in the framework of a multiple regression model will be discussed in Section 6.7.4.

A thorough discussion of the assumptions of regression analysis (Section 6.7.2) is required to prevent its unwarranted use. Moreover, knowledge of the assumptions of the technique is useful to understand the background of extensions of regression analysis. Almost without exception these extensions were developed to tackle violations of the assumptions of the pure linear regression model. In this book the focus will be on extensions of regression analysis to deal with time series (Section 6.7.5), pooled time series (Section 6.7.6), and reciprocal relations between variables (Section 6.7.7).

Time series data and pooled time series data are essential to test causal theories, since they give a clue to the temporal sequence of events. Nevertheless, time series data pose a serious problem to regression analysis, called *autocorrelation*. Autocorrelation means that the dependent variable displays a rigidness that is not accounted for by the independent variables. If autocorrelation exists, then a poor explanation at one point in time is predictably followed by a poor explanation at the next point in time. Prediction on the basis of a regression equation is tricky when autocorrelation exists. Various remedies to cure autocorrelation will be discussed in Sections 6.7.5 and 6.7.6. These remedies amount either to more advanced estimation techniques or to an alternative specification of the regression model which allows for hypothesis testing.

Reciprocal relationships constitute chicken and egg puzzles. Which party gets its way in a government coalition, for example? Who influences whom? A chicken and egg puzzle can only be solved when data on exogeneous variables are available. If one takes for granted that a party in government tries to implement its own party manifesto, then it is a good idea to find out which coalition partner wrote the party manifesto that resembles current government policy most closely. To put it in a more abstract form, if A and B reciprocally influence each other, then a third factor C that directly influences A but does not directly influence B is required to estimate the strength of the reciprocal relationships between A and B. Models and estimation techniques for reciprocal relationships will be discussed in Section 6.7.7.

6.7.1 The multiple regression model

The linear multiple regression model is a straightforward generalization of the bivariate model. Instead of one independent variable, more than one independent variable is assumed to have an influence on the dependent variable. The value for case i on the dependent variable, Y_i, is assumed to be a linear combination of the values of case i on the independent variables $X_{1i}, X_{2i}, \ldots, X_{ki}$, except for a *residual*, ε_i, that is not accounted for by the independent variables. The residual for case i is the difference between the value of the dependent variable, Y_i, and the predicted value, $\hat{Y}_i$:

$$Y_i = b_0 + b_1 X_{1i} + b_2 X_{2i} + \cdots + b_k X_{ki} + \varepsilon_i.$$

In the case of k independent variables $X_1, X_2, \ldots, X_k$ the *predicted value* for case i, $\hat{Y}_i$, is a linear function of $X_{1i}, X_{2i}, \ldots, X_{ki}$ multiplied by their respective regression slope coefficients $b_1, b_2, \ldots, b_k$, and the regression constant b_0

$$\hat{Y}_i = b_0 + b_1 X_{1i} + b_2 X_{2i} + \cdots + b_k X_{ki}$$

The *ordinary least squares* procedure to estimate the *regression coefficients* $b_0, b_1, b_2, \ldots, b_k$ prescribes that the sum of all squared residuals, ε_i^2, also denoted as *SSR*, should be minimized:

$$\text{minimize } SSR, \text{ where } SSR = \sum_i (Y_i - \hat{Y}_i)^2.$$

The formulae for the regression coefficients $b_0, b_1, b_2, \ldots, b_k$ which follow from this minimization procedure are rather cumbersome when k becomes large. Numerical procedures to minimize *SSR* are fairly efficient, however.

Dividing SSR by SS, the sum of squares of the values with respect to their mean $\bar{Y}$, gives the proportion of unexplained variance. The proportion of explained variance, R^2, is computed as one minus the proportion of unexplained variance:

$$R^2 = 1 - SSR/SS, \text{ where } SS = \sum_i (Y_i - \bar{Y})^2.$$

The nature of a regression coefficient in multivariate regression analysis

A regression coefficient in multivariate regression analysis reflects the influence of a variable X_k on Y when the other independent variables are *held constant* or are being *controlled for.* To compute a single regression coefficient in multiple regression analysis, only those variations in X_k and Y are considered that do not depend on variations in the remaining independent variables. The disturbing influences of the remaining variables are filtered out by, first, computing the residuals in X_k that cannot be accounted for by the remaining independent variables from the original regression equation $(X_1, \ldots, X_k)$, by computing the residuals in Y. These residual variables will be denoted here as RX_k and RY. The regression coefficient b_k in the regression equation with Y as the dependent variable and the complete set of independent variables, $X_1, \ldots, X_{k-1}, X_k$, is identical to the *bivariate* regression coefficient of RY with RX_k.

Regression of Y dependent on $X_1, \ldots, X_k$:

$$Y_i = b_0 + b_1 X_{1i} + b_2 X_{2i} + \cdots + b_k X_{ki} + \varepsilon_i.$$

Regression of Y on remaining $X_1, \ldots, X_{k-1}$:

$$Y_i = c_0 + c_1 X_{1i} + c_2 X_{2i} + \cdots + c_{k-1} X_{k-1,i} + RY_i.$$

Regression of X_k on remaining $X_1, \ldots, X_{k-1}$:

$$X_{ki} = d_0 + d_1 X_{1i} + d_2 X_{2i} + \cdots + d_{k-1} X_{k-1,i} + RX_{ki}.$$

Bivariate regression of obtained residuals: $RY_i = e_0 + e RX_{ki} + \varepsilon_i.$

then $b_k = e.$

A bivariate regression line is easily visualized in the plane. Predictions in multivariate regression do not amount to a straight line as in bivariate regression. In a regression analysis with two independent variables the predictions amount to a flat surface in three-dimensional space. In a regression analysis with three independent variables the regression equation amounts to a three-dimensional object in an unintelligible four-dimensional space. It is impossible to visualize the regression coefficients in multiple regression analysis directly. But for each independent variable the *partial regression* with the dependent variable can be visualized. A partial regression plot of X_k with Y is a plot of RX_k as the independent

Table 6.5 *Regression coefficients: an example*

	b (unstandardized coefficients)	Std error	Beta (standardized coefficients)	t	Sig.
(Constant)	12.15	13.69	–	0.89	0.39
IMEX2[a]	0.28	0.13	0.48	2.26	0.04
AGE65[b]	1.83	0.94	0.41	1.95	0.07

[a] (imp/gnp + exp/gnp)/2.
[b] % population > 65.

and RY as the dependent variable. Instead of the original variables X_k and Y, the residual variables RX_k and RY along the X-axis and the Y-axis, respectively, should be plotted.

Example: effects of an old population on public expenditures in addition to imports/exports

The responsiveness of the political system to the growing share of elderly citizens poses a serious policy question in western democracies. Nations with an old population will tend to have high public expenditures since the elderly no longer work and so do not contribute to the gross domestic product. They are in need of health care and pensions instead. As an example, throughout this section the relationship between the percentage of the population older than 65 (AGE65 in NIAS.SAV) and public expenditures as a percentage of gross domestic product (PE) will be considered.

Since the influence of high imports and exports on public expenditures has already been discussed in the introductory section on regression analysis (Section 5.4) the regression question to be answered here is whether an old population (AGE65) helps to explain high public expenditures (PE) in addition to imports and exports (IMEX2).

$$PE_i = b_0 + b_1 IMEX2_i + b_2 AGE65_i + \varepsilon_i.$$

As in Section 5.4 we will confine ourselves to data on the year 1988 for 17 countries. But the precise percentage of people older than 65 for Japan in 1988 is missing in the database. Therefore the regression model will be tested for 16 countries only. Table 6.5 presents the regression coefficients as computed by SPSS. The table reveals that $b_0 = 12.15$, $b_1 = 0.28$ and $b_2 = 1.83$, which gives rise to the regression equation

$$PE = 12.15 + 0.283 IMEX2 + 1.834 AGE65.$$

Thus, public expenditures (as a percentage of gross domestic product) tend to increase, on average, by 1.83 per cent when the percentage of elderly rises by one percentage point. This is what was to be expected: it is the elderly who boost public expenditures. When imports and exports increase by 1 per cent, then public expenditures tend to increase also, on average by 0.28 per cent. One should note

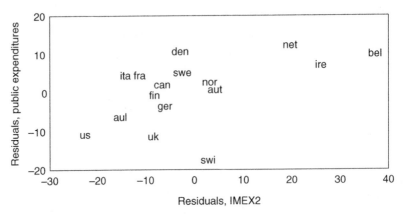

Figure 6.5 *Partial regression plot of openness of economy (IMEX2) and public expenditures (PE) controlled for the percentage of elderly (AGE65)*

that 0.28 is slightly less than 0.33, which was the regression coefficient found in the bivariate regression analysis of Section 5.4. Regression coefficients in multivariate regression analysis are lower than in bivariate regression analysis when the additional variables are collinear to a certain degree, which is almost always the case. Multivariate regression coefficients will be precisely identical to bivariate regression coefficients when the independent variables show zero correlations among each other.

The *t*-coefficients in Table 6.5 indicate that both regression coefficients are significant when a one-sided test is applied, although not when a two-sided test is applied (see Section 5.7.4; critical value at the 5 per cent significance level, $n = 16$, $df = 14$: $t = 1.746$). One-sided tests should be applied here since the hypotheses prescribe precisely the direction of effects (positive for both variables). The significance levels printed by SPSS refer to two-sided tests, which are applicable when no a priori assumptions with respect to the direction of a regression coefficient are made. The explained variance (not printed in Table 6.5) amounts to $R^2 = 0.41$.

To get a feeling for multivariate regression analysis it might be helpful to compare Figure 6.5, which represents the partial regression plot between IMEX2 and PE controlled for AGE65, with Figure 5.3, which represents the bivariate regression plot between IMEX2 and PE. Only small differences show up. Since the correlation between IMEX2 and AGE65 is almost absent ($r = +0.03$) only small differences are to be expected. The regression coefficient would have been hard to interpret had IMEX2 and AGE65 been highly correlated. The bivariate regression plot between IMEX2 and PE would have differed enormously from the partial regression plot between IMEX2 and PE controlled for AGE65 in the latter case. Multicollinearity is the technical name to label the problem of high correlations between independent variables (see Section 6.7.2).

6.7.2 Assumptions of the ordinary least squares estimation method

Regression coefficients computed by the ordinary least squares method may give a false impression of precision. Regression analysis assumes linear relationships. Regression coefficients are meaningless when relationships are *non-linear*. If relationships are severely non-linear, then linear regression coefficients will tell a misleading story. The OLS method which is used to estimate regression coefficients may be inappropriate to estimate population regression coefficients when the data exhibit nasty properties. These properties have been given appealing names such as outliers, heteroscedasticity, multicollinearity and autocorrelation. OLS estimates will be biased, inefficient or non-robust in their presence (see Section 5.6.2 for a discussion of unbiasedness, efficiency and robustness of estimators). The nature of these properties will be discussed in this subsection.

Non-linear relationships

Linear relationships are a basic assumption of multiple regression, but some theories give rise to non-linear relationships. Sometimes a non-linear relationship is still linear in the parameters to be estimated, for example, the parabolic relationship $Y = b_0 + b_1 X + b_2 X^2$. In the construct X^2 might be treated as an ordinary variable.

Sometimes a non-linear relationship between an independent variable and the dependent variable can be changed into a linear relationship by a numerical transformation of the variables. Exponential relationships, which are quite common in rational theories of economic, political and social conduct (e.g. Coleman, 1991), such as the so-called Cobb–Douglas production function

$$Y = b_0 X_1^{b_1} X_2^{b_2},$$

can be turned into the linear relationship $\ln(Y) = b_0 + b_1 \ln(X_1) + b_2 \ln(X_2)$ by taking logs of the separate variables. Taking logs is also a standard device in comparative political science when the original variables are expressed as quantities, whereas the theory deals with relationships between percentage changes.

Unfortunately, it is impossible to transform all non-linear relationships into linear ones. The logistic relationship (the S-curve)

$$Y = \frac{1}{1 + e^{-b_0 - b_1 X}}.$$

which is often used to model the probability of binary events, is an example of a pure non-linear relationship. Most statistical packages have a separate procedure for *logistic regression analysis*. Moreover, they have more or less flexible procedures to model other types of non-linear relationships. Non-linear regression will not be treated here any further.

Unbiasedness and efficiency of regression estimates

In the mathematical statistician's thought experiment of an infinite number of samples from the same population, an estimate is said to be unbiased when on average it hits the mark precisely. Ideally an estimate should also be efficient (recall Section 5.6). Fortunately, ordinary least squares estimates are indeed unbiased and efficient when the variables involved in regression analysis are distributed normally, and relationships between them are linear. The (fairly simple) mathematical statistician's proof of this conjunction, based on the maximum likelihood procedure, is beyond the scope of this book. Many other assumptions also lead to the conclusion that OLS estimates are unbiased and efficient. The general claim is that OLS estimates are robust against violations of normality assumptions.

There are some noteworthy exceptions, however. Nasty properties of the data which will render OLS estimates dubious or even simply mistaken will be discussed in this subsection. Four aspects of the data which give rise to biased or inefficient regression estimates will be discussed: outliers, multicollinearity, heteroscedasticity and autocorrelation:

- *Outliers* are single cases which have a disproportionate effect on the slope of the regression line. Generally these cases have extreme values on the dependent or on the independent variables in the regression model. In the presence of outliers a regression coefficient does not tell a story about the majority of cases, but a story about a few outliers.
- *Multicollinearity* means that two or more independent variables are almost inextricable. Disentangling almost inextricable variables will result in regression estimates that depend on small residual variations in the variables which may well be measurement errors.
- *Heteroscedasticity* means that the residual variance is much larger for some values of the independent variable (e.g. for cases with high values on the independent variable) than for others (e.g. for cases with low values).
- *Autocorrelation* often arises in the context of regression analysis with time periods as units. Autocorrelation entails that a failure to explain the state of the dependent variable at one point in time carries over into subsequent time periods. The residual from the regression equation at one point in time depends upon the residual at the previous point in time. The number of independent observations is in fact smaller than the number of time periods.

In the following paragraphs the nature of the problem, the diagnosis, and the solution to outliers, multicollinearity, heteroscedasticity and autocorrelation will be sketched.

The outlier problem

An *outlier* is a case which affects the slope of the complete regression line disproportionately. An example is given in Figure 6.6. Six data-points (P1–P6) are plotted in the x–y plane. Without case P6 the slope of the regression coefficient

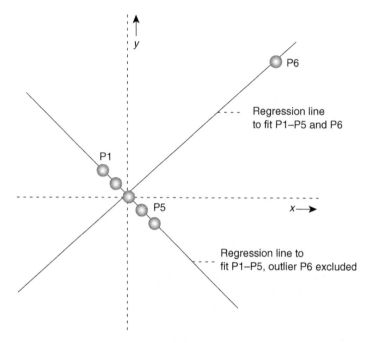

Figure 6.6   *Example of an outlier which changes the regression slope coefficient*

would be negative ($y = -x$), but with case P6 included the slope coefficient will turn positive ($y = +x$).

The concept of an outlier should be clearly distinguished from the concept of a large residual. From Figure 5.3 it is apparent that public expenditures of the Swiss national government cannot be accounted for by imports and exports only. Switzerland has a large negative residual. But Switzerland is not an outlier, since the slope of the regression coefficient is not affected heavily by the precise size of Switzerland's residual. In Figure 5.3 the slope of the regression coefficient is not determined completely by a single outlier.

Two problems concerning outliers should be distinguished. The first problem is an interpretation problem *given* the sample data. The story of Figure 6.6 cannot be told with one regression slope coefficient. Figure 6.6 suggests one story about the cases P1–P5 and another about the outlier P6. The second problem has to do with the statistical properties of regression estimates on the basis of a sample when the population contains outliers. The regression slope coefficient on the basis of a sample for a given population depends critically on the accidental inclusion or exclusion of outliers in the sample. To put it another way, regression estimates on the basis of a sample will *not* be *robust* when extreme values on the dependent or the independent variables are extant in the population.

Since outliers may influence regression coefficients enormously, the interpretation of regression parameters should be based on a careful analysis of outlier diagnostics. Especially in research based on small databases, outliers are a potential source of serious misinterpretations. In larger databases incidental outliers tend to cancel each other out.

Diagnosis   With Figure 6.6 in mind as a typical example of an outlier, a visual inspection of bivariate and partial regression plots will give a first impression of whether outliers are present. Inspection of *partial* regression plots is necessary since, in multiple regression analysis, outliers can result from high correlations between the independent variables (*multicollinearity*; see below).

Various measures have been suggested to quantify the influence of outliers on the regression slope coefficients. The simplest measure, DFBETA, is calculated for each case for each variable and for the constant in the regression equation as the difference between the regression prediction with and without the case included. Other measures such as Cook's distance are based on the DFBETA measure. The DFBETAs for the data from Figure 5.3 indicate that Belgium, Switzerland and Ireland have a disproportionate effect on the slope of the regression coefficient. Not a single case is strong enough to change the sign of the regression line, however.

Solutions   The therapy is less straightforward. One alternative is to develop an extended regression equation to model the outlier. Are the 'ordinary cases' and the 'outliers' both specimens of a more general theory?

Dropping the outliers from the regression estimation is the appropriate solution when the aim of the regression analyst is to tell a story about the majority of cases and there is no plausible theory available to account for the outlier. The claim that the ultimate story can be based on the remaining cases only may not be credible. The exclusion of outliers has to be accounted for in the research report, since research regression results depend critically on the inclusion or exclusion of outliers.

A technical alternative for dropping outliers completely is to create a dummy variable for each outlier, with a 0 for all cases but a 1 for the outlier. The slope coefficient for such a dummy variable indicates the difference between the value of the outlier on the dependent variable and the prediction for the outlier produced by the regression equation based on the remaining cases. It indicates precisely how much the outlier is different from the remaining cases, but it does not provide an explanation of why this is the case. To fit the data from Figure 6.6, for example, one might create a dummy variable, DP6. On this variable the value 0 is assigned to cases P1, P2, P3, P4 and P5, while the value 1 is assigned to case P6. The regression equation to produce a perfect fit would be $y = b_0 + b_1 x + b_2 \, DP6$. In comparative nation studies without a time dimension, a perfect fit can always be obtained by adding a separate dummy variable for all but one of the selected countries.

Technical solutions may, however, hide, the fact that the relevant story to tell may be the story about the outliers as compared with the remaining cases, whose internal differences are uninteresting on further consideration. The argument for maintaining the outliers is that their story is theoretically interesting as compared to a story on the minor differences between the 'normal' cases.

Heteroscedasticity

Homoscedasticity and heteroscedasticity are antonyms that refer to the correspondence of the *spread* of residuals with the independent variables. If the residuals have a constant variance, regardless of the value of the independent variables, we call them *homoscedastic*; but if their variance is variable, we call them *heteroscedastic*. Dependence of the residual variance on the independent variables is termed *heteroscedasticity*. Heteroscedasticity occurs often when variables based on raw counts (e.g. receipts and expenditures; gross national product and military expenditures measured in dollars) are related to each other. Low corresponds always with low, while a high value on the independent variable is necessary (but not sufficient) to produce a high value on the dependent variable. Therefore the residual variance is low for low values of the independent variable, but high for high values. Heteroscedasticity impairs the efficiency of OLS estimators of the regression coefficients, but these coefficients are still unbiased.

Diagnosis   A first means to trace heteroscedasticity is a visual inspection of bivariate and partial regression scatterplots. Most statistical packages can plot them. Heteroscedasticity is observed when the spread of the residuals increases or decreases with the values of the independent variables being plotted on the X-axis.

A generally accepted formal test is not available. When the residual variance is assumed to correspond linearly with an independent variable in the regression model, as in the examples given here, a split-half test on the basis of low and high values on this independent variable is often carried out. This popular split-half test is called the *Goldfield–Quandt* test. Two regression equations are estimated, one for values of X with a low residual variance and one for values of X with a high residual variance. Usually the group of cases with values beneath the median value of X is compared with cases having higher values on X. Heteroscedasticity is assumed when the two regression equations result in different explained variances according to the *F-test* to compare complete regression equations.

Solutions   What to do when heteroscedasticity is present? Often an insufficient, albeit necessary, *cause* is at the heart of heteroscedasticity. The obvious solution would be to incorporate interaction terms in the regression equation to discriminate between cases in which the cause being considered thus far brings about the expected result and cases in which it is insufficient.

Transformations of the variables in the regression equation may also reduce heteroscedasticity. Heteroscedasticity frequently occurs when the variables in the regression equation are based on counts (number of people, amount of money). Especially for high values of independent variables based on counts, the residual variance of other variables based on counts tends to be high. Taking logs of the dependent and independent variables is an obvious device. Taking logs comes down theoretically to a substitution of a theory regarding relationships between pure counts by a theory regarding relationships between percentage changes. It is apparent from Figure 6.7 that taking logs will reduce heteroscedasticity. Another obvious means to avoid heteroscedasticity is to use *relative figures*

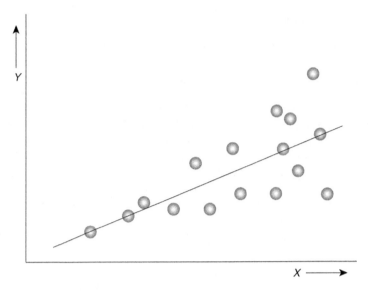

Figure 6.7 *Example of heteroscedasticity*

instead of raw counts as variables. In the NIAS database, for example, government expenditures are not expressed in US dollars, but as percentages of gross domestic product of a given nation in a given year. A disadvantage of the latter choice is that autonomous changes in the percentage base will affect the percentages. A sudden 'increase' in the percentage of public expenditures as a percentage of gross national product can be the result of a sudden economic recession which affects the economy negatively.

When theory-guided reduction of heteroscedasticity fails, one of several advanced estimation techniques developed by econometricians to improve the efficiency of estimates might be applied. The most widely used technique is *weighted least squares*. It is applicable when the residual variance is assumed to increase proportionally with the values of the independent variables in the regression equation. More advanced weighting procedures are also available (White, 1994: 209–17), but should be handled with care since these techniques are based on strong assumptions. They tend to produce quite chaotic results when regression analysis is applied to a few cases only.

Multicollinearity

The aim of multiple regression analysis is precisely to unravel the effects of collinear variables. Multicollinearity is the phenomenon of *highly* correlated independent variables. To understand why multicollinearity poses a problem, one should remember that a regression coefficient in multiple regression analysis is simply equal to the bivariate regression coefficient between the *residuals* from the dependent and the independent variable obtained by regressing the remaining independent variables on the dependent and the independent variable. If the

Table 6.6   *Diagnostics for multicollinearity*

Acceptable tolerance[a] (unexplained variance $1 - R_j^2$)	Corresponding variance due to remaining independent variables R_j^2	Acceptable correlation coefficient[b] among two independent variables r_{jk}
>0.50	<0.50	<0.71
>0.25	<0.75	<0.87
>0.10	<0.90	<0.95
>0.05	<0.95	<0.975
>0.01	<0.99	<0.995

[a] Rule of thumb: the accepted tolerance should be slightly larger than the proportion of the variance which is probably due to measurement errors.
[b] Upper bound of correlation coefficient corresponds only with bounds of other measures when only one pair of variables is highly correlated and the remaining independent variables are largely uncorrelated.

independent variables in a regression equation correlate highly, then the variance of these residuals will become small compared with the variance of the original variables. Often the remaining residuals are simply a swarm of measurement errors. Modelling residuals which are really measurement errors will result in a chaotic pattern of regression coefficients. To put it another way, the standard errors of the estimates increase. They are *inefficient*, although still unbiased.

Diagnosis   As a measure of dependence of one independent variable *j* on the remaining independent variables, R_j^2, the explained variance in the former due to the latter can be computed. A widespread measure of multicollinearity is the tolerance. The *tolerance* is defined as one minus the explained variance in one independent variable *j* due to the other independent variables in the regression equation $(1 - R_j^2)$. If the tolerance of a variable amounts to 0.01, then the corresponding regression coefficient is based on only 1 per cent of the variance in the measured variable. Since most variables in political sciences have not been measured with such precision, regression coefficients based on such a low tolerance will usually be unacceptable. If measurement errors of 10 per cent or even 25 per cent are deemed possible, then variables in a regression equation with tolerances lower than 0.1 or 0.25, respectively, should be mistrusted. Table 6.6 can be used to interpret tolerance levels.

For data which do not contain measurement errors, multicollinearity poses no problem. In research based on data from official statistical agencies, tolerances between 0.01 and 0.25 may still be acceptable, since these data are not prone to measurement errors (although they may exhibit systematic biases). In survey research one would generally not accept tolerances below 0.25 or even 0.5, since respondents often interpret survey questions differently.

Solutions   Many remedies for unacceptably low tolerances can be considered. When two or more independent variables measure almost the same concept, then the least interesting variable from a theoretical point of view can be omitted. If the independent variables are actually indicators of one latent dimension, then one should construct one scale and enter this scale as the independent variable instead of the separate indicators.

But often the conclusion should be that the data at hand are simply insufficient to unravel the effects of the various independent variables. *Additional data* should be gathered (either cross-sectional, longitudinal or both) to ensure that the independent variables do not always coincide with each other. One may also gather more *refined data* with smaller measurement errors that will warrant the acceptance of lower tolerance levels.

6.7.3 Direct causes, intervening variables and antecedent variables

A political analyst using regression analysis for causal analysis may either assume that the interrelationships between the independent variables do not represent a causal ordering, or assume one specific causal order between the independent variables. One should realize that the regression does not assume by definition a causal order between the independent variables.

In a conventional causal diagram a curved, double-headed arrow is used to represent a non-causal relationship, whereas a straight single-headed arrow is used to represent a causal effect (see Figure 6.8). A variable usually has not only a direct effect on the dependent variable, but also *indirect* effects through *intervening* variables. The size of an indirect effect is computed as the product of the regression coefficients belonging to the direct relationships which build up a causal path. The total effect is computed as the sum of all indirect effects and the direct effect. In Figure 6.8 this formula amounts to a total effect of X_3 on X_1 of $+0.2 + 0.4 \times 0.7 = 0.48$.

6.7.4 Interactions in the multivariate regression model

An interaction refers to a conditional effect. The size of the effect of an independent variable X_1 on Y depends on the value of a third variable X_2. To start the discussion we will first consider the case of a dichotomous interacting variable X_2 with values 0 and 1 (a binary or dummy variable).

As an example, the relationship between the percentage of the population older than 65 (AGE65 in NIAS.SAV) and public expenditures as a percentage of gross domestic product (PE) is considered here. An ageing population will lead to high public expenditures since the elderly no longer work and so do not contribute to the gross domestic product. Moreover, in welfare states the elderly are granted rights to receive pensions and health care, which require public expenditures. The precise relation may well depend on the electoral system. Party systems which are characterized by many different parties increase the chance that public

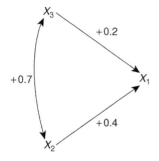 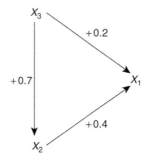

Curved arrow between X_3 and X_2; impossible to compute indirect effect of X_3 on X_1.

Straight arrow between X_3 and X_2; X_3 is the antecedent variable, X_2 is the intervening variable. Indirect effect of X_3 on X_1 amounts to $+0.28$; total effect amounts to $+0.20 + 0.28 = +0.48$.

Figure 6.8 *Regression analysis and causal analysis*

expenditures are raised. Even the sheer existence of left-wing parties in these party systems will increase the chance that other parties will agree with higher public expenditures to accommodate low-income groups. In proportional electoral systems at least one party will try to get the votes of the elderly. The sheer danger that such a party will become powerful will encourage other parties also to accommodate the elderly. In majoritarian electoral systems the chance that public expenditures are raised to meet the demands of the elderly is lower, since the two major parties will both have a strong incentive to promise lower taxes in order to accommodate a variety of electoral groups.

An interacting variable may influence the *slope* and/or the *intercept* of the regression line. If public expenditures in proportional systems are higher than those in majoritarian systems, regardless of the precise percentage of elderly, then only the intercept will be affected. If politicians are more sensitive to the percentage of elderly in proportional electoral systems, then the slope is affected.

The general regression interaction model for two interacting independent variables is

$$Y = b_0 + b_1 X_1 + b_2 X_2 + b_3 X_1 X_2 + \varepsilon,$$

and the example discussed here is

$$PE = b_0 + b_1 AGE65 + b_2 PROP + b_3 AGE65\ PROP + \varepsilon.$$

In the case of a binary variable X_2 this regression equation is equivalent to two regression equations; one for cases with $X_2 = 0$ and one for cases with $X_2 = 1$. To obtain these two equations, one should substitute $X_2 = 0$ and $X_2 = 1$, respectively, in the equation presented above. For $X_2 = 0$, we obtain

$$Y = b_0 + b_1 X_1 + \varepsilon,$$

or, for our example,

$$PE = b_0 + b_1 AGE65 + \varepsilon.$$

For $X_2 = 1$, the corresponding equations are

$$Y = (b_0 + b_2) + (b_1 + b_3)X_1 + \varepsilon.$$

and

$$PE = (b_0 + b_2) + (b_1 + b_3)AGE65 + \varepsilon.$$

If b_2 is significant and positive, then a proportional electoral system (X_2) has an effect on the intercept of the regression equation, indicating that politicians in proportional systems increase public expenditures more than do their colleagues in majoritarian systems. If b_3 is significant and positive, then a proportional electoral system has an effect on the slope. In proportional electoral systems politicians respond to an ageing population with higher additional public expenditures than do their colleagues in majoritarian systems. First, a binary variable PROP is computed. Semi-proportional electoral systems will be also considered as proportional ones in this subsection. The interaction term PAGE65 is computed as the product of PROP and AGE65. This simplifies our equation to

$$PE = b_0 + b_1 AGE65 + b_2 PROP + b_3 PAGE65.$$

Interaction and multicollinearity

The variables that are multiplied together to obtain an interaction term often correlate highly with the resulting interaction term. Multicollinearity easily comes in. In our example the correlation coefficient between $PAGE65$ and $PROP$ amounts to $r = +0.98$. Estimation of the regression equation above results in an unacceptably low tolerance of less than 0.05. As a technical solution to this problem various authors, amongst them the authors of the first edition of this book, suggested to subtracting the mean from each of the interacting variables before computing their product. Kromrey and Foster-Johnson (1998) have demonstrated, however, that this solution merely shunts the difficulties. In the end the conclusion is simply that available data which give rise to a high multicollinearity between the independent variable and the interaction term are insufficient to distinguish sharply between the autonomous effect of a variable and the part of its effect that results from the interplay with other variables.

6.7.5 Time series analysis: the autocorrelation problem

Time series analysis is ordinary regression analysis with points or periods in time as the units of analysis. The dependent variable y_t is measured at point t.

Since it takes some time before effects come into place, the independent variables in time series analysis are often measured at earlier points in time than the dependent variable. Time series regression analysis is a powerful tool for causal analysis, since the temporal order of a cause and its consequence can be expressed with a time lag between the independent variables and the dependent variable. A typical regression equation for time series analysis would be

$$y_t = b_0 + b_1 x_{t-1} + b_2 z_{t-1} + \varepsilon_t.$$

The availability of time series data allows one to construct an *autoregressive* model. The basic idea of an *autoregressive model* is that the current state of affairs y_t is dependent primarily on the state of affairs in the immediate past (y_{t-1}), although external influences (effects of x_t and z_t) and random shocks (ε_t), together with an autonomous trend (b_0), may amount to a change:

$$y_t = b_0 + b_1 y_{t-1} + b_2 x_t + b_3 z_t + \varepsilon_t.$$

The resulting R^2 from an autoregressive model should not be compared with the R^2 in an 'ordinary' model. Particularly when almost nothing changes compared with the previous point in time, the R^2 of an autoregressive model will be high, since a lack of changes (due to slowness of political changes and rigidities in political structures) will result by definition in a close correspondence between y_t and y_{t-1}. This contradicts the intuitive meaning of 'explained variance' for many political scientists.

Autocorrelation is defined as serial correlation between residuals. It occurs when the residuals in a given time period carry over into a later time period. First-order serial correlation is correlation between immediately successive points in time (between observations at time points t and $t - 1$), e.g. when an overestimate in one year is likely to lead to an overestimate in the next year. False predictions for one point in time will result in false predictions for the next point in time. If autocorrelation is present, then it is misleading to think of the consecutive time points as *independent* observations. Autocorrelation implies that the number of independent observations is smaller than the number of time points. Whereas the computation of standard errors of regression estimates in OLS is based on the available number of time points, this computation should be based – less optimistically – on the (unknown) number of independent observations. In the presence of autocorrelation OLS estimates of regression coefficients in non-autoregressive models are *inefficient*, although still *unbiased*. Autocorrelation in autoregressive models makes things even worse. Estimates will not only be inefficient but also biased.

Diagnosis

A straightforward diagnostic of first-order serial correlation would be the correlation coefficient $r_{t,t-1}$ between residuals in successive points in time. The *Durbin–Watson* statistic DW is based on this serial correlation coefficient between residuals. It is roughly equal to $2 - 2r_{t,\,t-1}$; it thus takes values between 0 and 4 rather than between −1 and +1. $DW = 2$ corresponds to $r = 0$, $DW = 0$ to $r = +1$, and $DW = 4$ to $r = −1$. DW-values in the neighbourhood of 2 indicate the absence of autocorrelation. Values near 0 indicate the presence of autocorrelation: it is likely that a deviation from the regression line at time t will be followed at time $t + 1$ by a deviation in the same direction. Values of DW between 2 and 4 indicate an oscillating pattern: if the actual value at time t is higher than one would expect on the basis of the regression equation, then it is likely that the actual value at time $t + 1$ is lower than one would expect on the basis of the regression equation.

DW-values are computed by most statistical packages, but it is usually still necessary to consult a table (such as Table A.6 in the Appendix) to find out whether a specific value indicates autocorrelation, no autocorrelation, or doubt, given a specific number of time points as units of analysis and a specific number of independent variables. DW has a critical region with a lower limit d_L and an upper limit d_U. The null hypothesis that no autocorrelation is present in the residuals from a regression analysis should be: rejected if the actual value of DW is lower that d_L; accepted if the actual value of DW is higher than d_U; and considered as undecided when the actual value of DW falls between d_L and d_U. Table A.6 shows that the DW-test becomes less undecided, that is to say, the region in between d_L and d_U becomes smaller, as the number of independent variables decreases and the number of observations increases.

The formula for $r_{t, t-1}$ requires separate standard deviations of ε_t, and ε_{t-1}, however. In the DW formula ε_t is used as a single estimate of the standard deviation. The formula then reduces to:

$$DW = \frac{\sum_t (\varepsilon_t - \varepsilon_{t-1})^2}{\sum_t \varepsilon_t^2}$$

The Durbin–Watson DW-test applies to non-autoregressive time series regression models, but should not be applied to autoregressive models. To indicate whether autocorrelation in the residuals from an autoregressive equation is absent, one should not use the ordinary Durbin–Watson test. One of the tests is Durbin's h-test:

$$h = \left(1 - \frac{DW}{2}\right)\sqrt{\frac{n_t}{1 - n_t[var(\hat{\beta}_{y_{t-1}})]}}$$

where n_t is the number of observations within the time series, DW is the ordinary Durbin–Watson coefficient, and $Var(\beta_{y_{t-1}})$ is the squared standard error of the OLS estimate of the regression coefficient of the lagged dependent variable. Some statistical packages, such as SPSS, will not report Durbin's h, but these packages can still compute the elements from which h can be computed according to its formula. To compute h one should first compute the ordinary Durbin–Watson DW and the (square of) the standard error of the OLS estimate of the regression coefficient of the lagged dependent variable. Durbin's h has a standard normal z-distribution; thus, one should not use the DW table to interpret Durbin's h! If the usual 5 per cent criterion is used, the assumption that serial autocorrelation is absent is tenable when $h < 1.645$.

If Durbin's h-test indicates that autocorrelation is present in an autoregressive regression equation estimated by ordinary least squares, then the conclusion should be that OLS ordinary least squares should not have been used. One must resort to *generalized least squares* estimation procedures, which are beyond the scope of this book, but which are implemented in most statistical packages. OLS estimates of regression coefficients can be used in autoregressive models, however, when Durbin's h-test indicates the absence of autocorrelation.

Solutions: do not explain positions (states) but explain motions (changes) instead

An often-used, rather intuitive solution to obtain independent observations would be to diminish the number of time points in the regression analysis, e.g. by aggregating quarterly data to yearly data, or by aggregating all time points before and after important historical events (e.g. the Second World War, the 1973 oil crisis, the 1989 velvet revolution). Two procedures may be used: simply pick out one time point per period or smooth the data within each time period (e.g. by computing average values for each time period). This intuitive solution is flawed, however. Meaningful variation within the aggregated time spans is easily ignored. Moreover, the periodization is often arbitrary, because each variable tends to have its own periodicity, its own rhythm of change. Here we will stick to solutions which retain all data points in the regression equation.

Let us first consider a non-autoregressive model which exhibits autocorrelation according to the DW test (DW far lower than 2). This indicates that the process being studied remains by and large in the same state as at the previous point in time. It may still be possible to explain changes, however. To explain changes relative to the status quo either a simple first-order difference regression model or a more advanced autoregressive model should be used.

In the *first-order difference model* the dependent variable is the change $Dy_t = y_t - y_{t-1}$ in y (the 'zero-order' dependent variable) compared with the preceding point in time. Regardless of the previous level y_{t-1}, Dy_t will become zero whenever $y_t = y_{t-1}$ (The difference model $Dy_t = b_0 + b_2 x_{t-1} + b_3 z_{t-1} + \varepsilon_t$ is equivalent to a model $y_t = b_0 + b_1 y_{t-1} + b_2 x_{t-1} + b_3 z_{t-1} + \varepsilon_t$ where b_1 is constrained to equal 1. In the latter formulation, y_t may be considered as the dependent variable, with y_{t-1} as an independent variable). An analogy from physics may be helpful. In a first-order difference model the motion of an object is the dependent variable, whereas in a zero-order model the position of an object is the dependent variable.

In an *autoregressive* model $y_t = b_0 + b_1 y_{t-1} + b_2 x_t + b_3 z_t + \varepsilon_t$ the regression coefficient for the lagged dependent variable y_{t-1} is not constrained to equal 1, but empirically estimated. The autoregression coefficient b_1 gives information about what exactly is being influenced by the remaining independent variables. An empirical estimate of $b_1 = 0$ is equivalent to an ordinary regression model with y_t as the dependent variable. An estimate of $b_1 = 1$ is equivalent to the first-order difference model. Empirical estimates of b_1 will often result in a value between 0 and 1. An estimate of $b_1 = \frac{1}{2}$ would indicate that the remaining independent variables in the model have an influence on $y_t - \frac{1}{2} y_{t-1}$.

To compare a non-autoregressive model ($b_1 = 0$), a first-difference model ($b_1 = 1$) and an autoregressive model (say, with $b_1 = \frac{1}{2}$) it is helpful to think of the 'shocks' or 'innovations' required from the remaining independent variables to keep y at an extreme high (or low) level. In a first-order difference model a continuation of the shocks which brought about today's level of y_t is superfluous to preserve the status quo. For this reason a first-order difference model is also known as a *random-walk* model. A random-walk process resembles a walker who time and again takes a step so as to keep a tail wind from the independent variables, regardless of where he came from or where he wants to go. He will stay where he is when it is dead calm. In a non-autoregressive model our walker will return home immediately once there is not a breath of wind. This property of a non-autoregressive model is known as *regression towards the mean*, which means that without continued external shocks the mean will be restored. An autoregressive model with an autoregressive parameter of 0.5 resembles a walker who returns half-way home when the wind drops.

The solution for autocorrelation in an autoregressive regression equation (as indicated by Durbin's h) or in a first-order difference model (as indicated by the ordinary DW-test) is subject to debate, both from a theoretical and from a statistical point of view. One solution would be to develop a second-order difference model, which has as dependent variable the rate of change of the change in the original dependent variable. A second-order model from physics would be a model with the *acceleration* of an object – rather than its position (zero order) or its motion (first order) – as the dependent variable. Second-order theories in political science are rarely available, however. A better alternative is possibly to use, instead of OLS, more advanced econometric estimation techniques which go beyond the scope of this book.

Example: public expenditures in France

A multiple regression analysis on the basis of cross-sectional data for 16 nations in 1988 revealed that public expenditures were dependent both on exports and imports and on the percentage of elderly. Here we will test whether time series data for France give rise to the same conclusion. Data on the relevant variables are available in the NIAS.SAV database for the period 1965–88 ($n = 24$ consecutive years). A preliminary question to be answered is how long it takes before changes in exports/imports and changes in the percentage of elderly amount to changes in public expenditures. What is the length of the time lags? Computation of the so-called *cross-correlation function* reveals for each lag of the independent variable what the correlation between the dependent and the independent variable is. Figure 6.9 exhibits a graphical representation of the cross-correlation function between openness of the economy, on the one hand, and public expenditures, on the other. The horizontal axis displays a number of lags and leads of the independent variable IMEX2. The size of the correlation

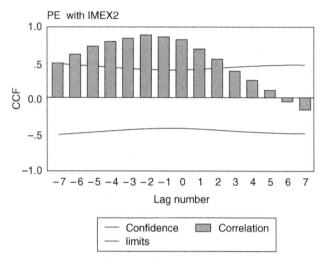

Figure 6.9 *Cross-correlation function for openness of economy (IMEX2) and public expenditure (PE)*

coefficient is plotted on the vertical axis. Figure 6.9 reveals that it takes the French government roughly 2 years to respond with public expenditures to the level of imports and exports. Correlation is highest when the independent variable IMEX2 is lagged with 2 years. The cross-correlation function between the percentage of elderly (65 years or older) and public expenditures (not displayed here) reveals that the French public expenditures also respond to changes in the percentage of over-65s. Only after five years the correlation between age 65 and public expenditures reaches its maximum. To put it bluntly, it is not so much those over 65 as those over 70 years who are boosting public expenditures. The cross-correlation functions suggest that the following regression equation be tested:

$$PE_t = b_0 + b_1 IMEX2_{t-2} + b_2 AGE65_{t-5} + \varepsilon_t.$$

The regression results are (*t*-values in brackets):

$$PE_t = -7.146 + 0.818\ IMEX2_{t-2} + 2.812\ AGE65_{t-5} + \varepsilon_t$$

$$(-0.32) \qquad (+1.96) \qquad\qquad (+1.24)$$

$R^2 = 0.851$, $DW = 0.438$, $t = 1967–1988$ (1965 and 1966 missing due to lags).

Table 6.7 shows the SPSS output with respect to the regression estimates. These results are confusing. On the one hand, they seem to indicate that the theory is confirmed. The F-test for the regression equation as a whole (not printed here) reveals that a significant portion of public expenditures has been explained. The explained variance R^2 amounts to 0.851. The regression estimates suggest an

Table 6.7 *Public expenditures as a function of IMEX2 and AGE65 in France (OLS)*

	b (unstandardized)	Std error	Beta (standardized)	*t*	Sig.	Tolerance
(Constant)	−7.15	22.02	–	−0.32	7.49	–
IMEX2$_{t-2}$	0.82	0.42	0.57	1.96	0.06	0.08
AGE65$_{t-5}$	2.81	2.28	0.36	1.24	0.23	0.08

even stronger relationship than the cross-sectional estimates (0.818 and 2.812 compared with 0.283 and 1.834, respectively).

The independent variables are fairly multicollinear in France, but since measurement errors in these macro-economic variables will be less than the tolerance (tolerance = 8.3 per cent), we will not concern ourselves with multicollinearity here. The regression coefficient for IMEX$_{t-2}$ is hardly significant (one-sided, $p_{H_0} \approx$ 0.064/2 = 0.032) whereas the regression coefficient for AGE65$_{t-5}$ is insignificant ($p_{H_0} \approx$ 0.115). Although the OLS regression estimates are still unbiased, the OLS standard errors, t-values and significance levels are completely meaningless, since the Durbin–Watson test indicates serious autocorrelation ($DW = 0.438$; critical value $d_L(n = 24, k = 2) > 1.19$). It is misleading to think of the consecutive years as *independent* observations. The autocorrelation of the residuals implies that the observations are serially dependent.

A first-order difference model An appealing procedure to get rid of most types of autocorrelation is to consider the first-order difference $dY_t = Y_t - Y_{t-1}$ as the dependent variable. A first-order difference model is equivalent to an ordinary regression model with Y_t as the dependent variable and Y_{t-1} as an additional independent variable with a regression coefficient fixed to 1. One should realize that Y_{t-1} behaves as a pigeonhole for all structural long-term effects on Y_t. All effects on Y_t which were already incorporated in Y_{t-1} will be attributed to Y_{t-1}. Only effects which were not incorporated in Y_{t-1} will be attributed to exogenous variables. A first-order difference model is blind to cumulative long-term influences. It is not surprising, therefore, that the cross-correlation functions (CCFs) with the first-order difference dPE_t as the dependent variable reveal relatively short time lags. The CCFs suggest that yearly *changes* in public expenditures are primarily dependent on imports and exports in the preceding year and on the percentage of elderly two years before:

$$dPE_t = b_0 + b_1 IMEX2_{t-1} + b_2 AGE65_{t-2} + \varepsilon_t.$$

The empirical results indicate that both regression coefficients are insignificant, whereas the Durbin–Watson test still indicates autocorrelation. One simple reason is that short-term effects on public expenditures as a percentage of gross national product depend as much on public expenditures as on the development of gross national product. Economic growth (EG) will have a negative impact on public expenditures as a percentage of gross national product when public expenditures remain constant. Therefore results will be discussed with respect to a regression equation with economic growth (EG) included. It is expected that the regression coefficient of economic growth is negative:

$$dPE_t = b_0 + b_1 IMEX2_{t-1} + b_2 AGE65_{t-2} + b_3 EG_t + \varepsilon_t.$$

The regression estimates are presented below, with t-values in brackets:

$$dPE_t = -5.91 - 0.394 IMEX2_{t-1} + 1.257 AGE65_{t-2} - 0.731 EG_t + \varepsilon_t$$
$$(-0.81)(-3.04) \qquad\qquad (+1.82) \qquad\qquad (-4.90)$$
$$R^2 = 0.599, DW = 1.73, t = 1966\text{--}1989 \ (n = 24).$$

The Durbin–Watson test now indicates that autocorrelation is absent (critical value $d_U (n = 24, k = 3) > 1.66$). The regression coefficients of economic growth (negative) and the percentage of elderly (positive) are in the expected direction. The regression estimate of imports and exports is in the wrong direction, however. Whereas the correlation coefficient between $IMEX2_{t-1}$ and dPE_t amounted to +0.29, the regression coefficient is –0.394. Multicollinearity between imports and exports, on the one hand, and economic growth, on the other ($r = -0.82$; tolerance = 0.12), is the technical reason for this negative regression coefficient. Doubt with respect to these results has the upper hand.

A first-order autoregressive model   A model, which is fairly equivalent to the first-order difference model tested above, is the first-order autoregressive model

$$PE_t = b_0 + b_1 IMEX2_{t-1} + b_2 AGE65_{t-2} + b_3 EG_t + b_4 PE_{t-1} + \varepsilon_t$$

with the first-order lag of the dependent variable included as an independent variable. The regression results indicate, however, that $IMEX2_{t-1}$ and $AGE65_{t-2}$ are non-significant. $IMEX2_{t-1}$ becomes significant only when EG_t is dropped, but even then $AGE65_{t-2}$ remains non-significant. After dropping the insignificant variables the following regression equation remains:

$$\text{standard error } PE_{t-1} = 0.0773; \text{ thus Durbin's } h = 2.37$$

The regression results indicate that two variables leave only 2 per cent of the variance in public expenditures unexplained. The regression coefficient of $IMEX2_{t-1}$ has the expected sign. Its magnitude exceeds the cross-sectional regression coefficient (0.283, see Table 6.5). Public expenditures will increase by 0.39 per cent if imports and exports increase by 1 per cent. Durbin's h indicates that there is still significant autocorrelation left (since 2.37 exceeds the critical z-value 1.645). The ordinary DW-test is not appropriate in autoregressive models.

Epilogue   Time series data are a perfect means to assess the causal order, because of their temporal order. Therefore they are superior to cross-sectional models. However, the example discussed here is fairly typical of the difficulties one encounters when regression analysis is applied to the fairly short time series which are the rule rather than an exception in political science. The regression models based on the original variables typically suffer from the autocorrelation defect. Difference models and/or autoregressive models will often cure the auto-correlation disease, but difference and autoregressive models are usually not robust. At least three origins of this lack of robustness can be mentioned.

Autoregressive models will usually leave only a small portion of the variance in the dependent variable unexplained. Estimates of exogeneous influences are shaky when the remaining unexplained variance is small, as compared to the magnitude of the typical measurement errors.

A second reason why autoregressive models and difference models often fail to retrieve the obvious is their fixation on short-term changes. Long-term shocks in exogeneous variables which have already influenced the lagged dependent variable will not be attributed to exogeneous variables but to the endogeneous lagged dependent variable.

The third, and most important, reason is simply the limited number of time points. Data on 25 consecutive years are insufficient when autocorrelation is present. Twenty-five years may shrink to 5 'independent' years when most years are almost perfect copies of their predecessors. Time series data for postwar France are insufficient, for example, to estimate with any precision which combination of variables is responsible for public expenditures. One way out of this difficulty in time series analysis is to test elaborated theories for many time series simultaneously, which brings us to the topic of the next section.

6.7.6 Pooled time series analysis: autocorrelation and heteroscedasticity

The advantage of time series analysis for political science is its ability to assess the time dependency of causal relationships. Often the data available amount to short time series only (e.g. 40 points in time or even less). More often than not, various plausible models will account for the data in such a short time series. One way out is to increase the quantity of data used for testing.

Pooled time series analysis combines time series for several cross-sections. The data are stacked by cross-section and time point. The NIAS database used throughout this book, for example, is a pooled time series database of 828 units stacked by 18 countries over 46 years. Instead of studying the effects through time of various variables on public expenditures in each country, these effects may be studied for a number of countries simultaneously. Instead of testing a time series model for one country using time series data, or testing a cross-sectional model for all countries at one point in time, a pooled time series model is tested for all countries through time. Much more refined tests of theories will become possible, since the available units of analysis increase from T (number of time points) to NT (number of cross-sections times number of time points). Pooled time series analysis captures not only variation that emerges through time, but variation across different cross-sections as well.

Regrettably, pooled time series analysis also has a serious drawback. Since pooled time series analysis is still time series analysis, the problem of *autocorrelation* must still be dealt with. But in addition to autocorrelation within cross-sections, heteroscedasticity between cross-sections comes in. Heteroscedasticity will usually arise because the appropriate models for the various cross-sections will not be precisely identical. Therefore a model to explain all cross-sections will usually do better for some than for others, which amounts to unequal variances of the residuals for the cross-sections (which is heteroscedasticity by definition). The tendencies which led to higher public expenditures in the 1970s manifested themselves in all capitalist countries. Nevertheless the precise effect of an increasing percentage of elderly on public expenditures may depend on polity variables such as the electoral system, and on policy and legislation with respect to health-care technology, health-care insurance and pensions for the elderly. If one model is tested for all cross-sections at all time points, then heteroscedasticity comes in, since the residuals for 'extreme' countries will be large compared with the residuals for mainstream countries.

The combination of autocorrelation and heteroscedasticity in sample data may result in inefficient, although unbiased, estimates of the true population parameters.

Diagnosis of heteroscedasticity and autocorrelation in pooled time series data

The diagnosis of autocorrelation and heteroscedasticity in pooled time series analysis is fairly straightforward, but not all statistical software packages are ideally suited for its implementation (STATA is, but SPSS is not).

The degree of heteroscedasticity due to pooling, e.g. unequal residual variances within cross-sections, is obtained by examining the residuals of the pooled model within cross-sections. A sequence plot of the residuals for the various cross-sections (comparable to Figure 5.4) will give a first visual impression. Ideally the average of the residuals within each cross-section should be equal to zero.

A simple diagnostic test on the robustness of the pooled model is to run the same model on its own residuals for each cross-section through time, and on its residuals for each time unit over cross-sections. If the same model holds for all cross-sections and all time points, then the pooled model will not be able to explain its own residuals split up by cross-section and time unit. Thus, for a regression model tested on 80 units stacked by 8 cross-sections over 10 years, $8 + 10 = 18$ regressions should be performed on the residuals from the pooled model. The model should not be able to explain significant proportions of the variance within its own residuals in more than 5 per cent of the cases. Thus, the pooled model from our example should not be able to produce significant regression estimates within its own residuals in more than four time units or cross-sections. If the model is able to explain additional variance in its own residuals for a large number of time units or cross-sections (more than four in our example) then the suspicion should be that the original model does not hold for all cross-sections and time-units equally well.

Solutions

The solutions to the problems raised by pooled time series analysis might be divided into two groups. The first group is directed at the improvement of the models to fit pooled time series data. The second group is directed at the development of statistical estimation procedures to improve on OLS deficiencies when a combination of autocorrelation and heteroscedasticity is present.

Let us start with model improvements to get rid of heteroscedasticity between cross-sections. When the mean of the residuals for one or more specific cross-sections is unequal to zero, then one should add variables to the model so as better to explain these cross-sectional differences.

A non-theoretical model to get rid of heteroscedasticity between cross-sections completely would be to add one dummy variable to the model for each cross-section except one. This model is called the least squares fixed dummy variable model in the jargon of pooled time series analysis. A more advanced variant would be to assume that each cross-section has a randomly distributed intercept associated with it (the random coefficients model). We would advise against these non-theoretical solutions, since atheoretical dummies and random intercepts that are added to a regression model will usually be collinear with some variables of theoretical interest. The explanatory power of the variables of theoretical interest will easily get obscured.

To get rid of serial autocorrelation the same model ramifications (first-order difference model, autoregressive model) should be considered as in ordinary time series analysis.

A rather different question is which estimation technique should be used when autocorrelation and heteroscedasticity have not been banished completely. How to deal with the fact that OLS estimates will be inefficient; that is to say, with the fact that they will usually underestimate the standard errors of the regression estimates? The econometric literature advises more advanced estimation techniques than OLS, such as (feasible) generalized least squares (Greene, 2003). These estimation techniques will in effect test a difference model, rather than a model in the original variables. Instead of using a generated least squares difference model rather than the original model to cope with technical issues such as heteroscedasticity and serial autocorrelation, one may also use OLS to test the parameters of an autorregressive model or a difference model that is warranted for theoretical reasons. When the time series are relatively short, as is the case with yearly or even quarterly data, then OLS estimates are more robust than more advanced estimates (Beck and Katz, 1995, 2004). Beck and Katz (1995) showed that OLS estimates of regression coefficients are more robust than more advanced estimates when sample sizes are small. Katz and Beck have developed a formula to compute *panel-corrected standard errors* which encompass autocorrelation and heteroscedasticity in the computation of the standard errors of the OLS regression estimates. Panel-connected standard errors for cross-section time series data are implemented in STATA. An SPSS macro using the matrix language of SPSS is available from the authors' website.

Example

In the epilogue from the section on time series analysis the conclusion was that time series data for France were insufficient to distinguish between rival theories. It was impossible to decide whether the level of public expenditures in France was due to the level of imports and exports, to the percentage of elderly in need of social support and health care, to economic decline, to the number of strikes, or to the emphasis on welfare provisions in the party programmes of governing parties. The same research question can be asked for all countries. The NIAS.SAV data file contains data with respect to the variables mentioned above for the period 1971–88 (18 years), for 12 countries – France, Sweden, Norway, Denmark, the Netherlands, Italy, Germany, Great Britain, Ireland, the USA, Canada and Australia. The number of units of analysis is $12 \times 18 = 216$ units of years stacked within nations.

A preliminary analysis of lag structures using the CCF (cross-correlation function) procedure from SPSS reveals that the relationship between strikes and public expenditures is a complex one. Cross-correlations with various time lags for various countries lead to the conclusion that the hypothesis that strikes are a cause of higher public expenditure and not a consequence of lower public expenditure is not clearly supported. Therefore we will postpone looking at the apparently reciprocal relationship between strikes and public expenditures until the next subsection. The influence of strikes on public expenditures will not be included in the pooled time series model. The cross-correlations also indicate that the time lags involved for the other independent variables differ for the 12 countries being investigated. For the pool of 12 nations the best assumption to make seems to be that there are no time lags at all. On average the variables investigated here seem to have an immediate effect on public expenditures in these 12 nations.

The first model to be tested considers the level of public expenditures as the dependent variable. As a first model all the variables IMEX (imports and exports), AGE65 (percentage of the population aged 65 and over), EG (economic growth) and GVT_WLF2 (percentage of party programmes of governing parties devoted to welfare state provisions) are entered into the regression equation. A 'backwards' procedure is used to drop all variables not significant at the 5 per cent level from the equation, starting with the most insignificant one. The results of statistical testing based on the appropriate panel-corrected standard errors (Beck and Katz, 1995) are compared with OLS standard errors in the output of the SPSS macro PCSE (available from the authors' website), as shown in Figure 6.10. The results show that OLS standard errors and panel-corrected standard errors give almost identical results. The dependence of public expenditures on each of the four variables examined is statistically significant at the 5 per cent level. Imports and exports, economic decline, the percentage of elderly and leftist party programmes explain almost three-quarters of the variance in the level of public expenditures in the 12 countries ($R^2_{adj} = 0.73$).

OLS								
	mse	R2	R2 adj	F	df1	df2	sig F	
PE	4.4625	.7368	.7318	147.6470	4	211	.0000	
		b	beta	se	T	sig T		
IEO		.1840	.5588	.0130	14.1229	.0000		
AGO		1.7485	.4641	.1450	12.0618	.0000		
EGO		-.6086	-.1571	.1394	-4.3666	.0000		
GVT_WLF2		.1472	.0978	.0633	2.3255	.0210		
const		12.8483	.0000	1.9582	6.5612	.0000		

_ _ _ _ _ _ _ _ _ _ Panel Corrected Standard Errors

n total: 216
n cross: 12
n time: 18
n vars: 5

   Dep: PE

PCSE								
	mse	R2	R2 adj	F	df1	df2	sig F	
PE	4.4625	.7368	.7318	147.6470	4	211	.0000	

PC_SE

	b	beta	pc_se	T	sig T
IEO	.1840	.5588	.0094	19.4796	.0000
AGO	1.7485	.4641	.1264	13.8315	.0000
EGO	-.6086	-.1571	.1555	-3.9136	.0001
GVT_WLF2	.1472	.0978	.0692	2.1284	.0345
const	12.8483	.0000	1.8576	6.9165	.0000

Figure 6.10   *SPSS macro output for panel-corrected standard errors, no autoregression*

As was to be expected from the notion that the level of public expenditures is fairly rigid, a model with the level of public expenditures as the dependent variable gives rise to severe autocorrelation in the residuals. The DW and Durbin h statistics – which are computed by the PCSE macro with the RESID = 1 option – show autocorrelation in the residuals from the specified model ($DW < 1$; Durbin's $h > 1.645$). This raises some doubt about whether the independent variables tap only cross-sectional variation but do not also explain the changes in public expenditures as compared with the previous year. Therefore an autoregression model is tested with, as independent variables, the same variables plus the lagged dependent variable. Entering the lagged dependent variable as an independent variable in the regression model has the advantage that independent variables really have to explain short-term shifts in order to become significant. They will tend to reduce the autocorrelation within residuals. But one should keep in mind that the lagged dependent variable catches all the long-term effects of slowly operating variables, such as party programmes as well as a growing percentage of the elderly. Since autoregressive models will attribute long-term

PCSE

	mse	R2	R2 adj	F	df1	df2	sig F
PE	1.5590	.9679	.9671	1265.3666	5	210	.0000

PC_SE

	b	beta	pc_se	T	sig T
LPE	.9072	.9099	.0221	41.1328	.0000
IEO	.0140	.0426	.0072	1.9590	.0514
EGO	−.4540	−.1172	.0547	−8.2966	.0000
GVT_WLF2	.0519	.0345	.0280	1.8509	.0656
const	4.5812	.0000	.8228	5.5681	.0000

Smalldw, for each time series: no_cross dw dh

11.00	1.56	.93	Sweden
12.00	1.31	1.47	Norway
13.00	1.03	2.06	Denmark
22.00	1.53	.99	the Netherlands
31.00	1.13	1.84	France
32.00	1.29	1.51	Italy
41.00	.56	3.07	Germany
51.00	.97	2.20	United Kingdom
53.00	1.32	1.45	Ireland
61.00	1.28	1.53	United States
62.00	1.41	1.25	Canada
63.00	1.32	1.45	Australia

Figure 6.11   *SPSS macro output for panel-corrected standard errors, autoregressive model*

effects of exogenous variables to the lagged dependent variable, they will underestimate long-term effects of exogenous variables.

The results given in Figure 6.11 show that even an autoregressive model exhibits the influence of an economic decline on rising public expenditures. The influence of higher exports and imports and leftist party programmes has borderline significance in each case: the likelihood that they do not have an influence on changes in public expenditures is less than 7 per cent (two-sided test; less than 3.5 per cent in a one-sided test). The explained variance amounts to 97 per cent. This figure may seem impressive, but one should remember that for an autoregressive model a high explained variance merely indicates that the current public expenditures can be predicted fairly well on the basis of last year's public expenditures.

An inspection of Durbin's *h* statistics indicates that, for most countries, no significant autocorrelation in the residuals remains. But for Germany, Denmark and the United Kingdom the correlation between changes in public expenditures in successive years is still not accounted for completely by the 12-country model. One may wish to create additional country-specific models to explain the remaining 3 per cent residual variance for Germany, Denmark and the United Kingdom. Here we will not pursue such an analysis.

6.7.7 Reciprocal causal relations: linear structural equation models

We have limited ourselves to unidirectional causal relations. Reciprocal relations might be expected, for example, when political actors interact with each other, and action–reaction spirals come into being. Two types of action–reaction spirals can be distinguished: the positive feedback loop and the negative feedback loop. An arms race is an example of a positive feedback loop. An increase in A's armaments will lead B to increase its armaments, which will make A do the same, and so on. A *positive feedback loop* between A and B will result in a high correlation between A and B, which is easily misconceived as a strong unidirectional causal relationship.

Negative feedbacks underlie cybernetics. A negative feedback loop exists when a behaviour of A causes B to produce signals that reverse A's behaviour which caused B's signals. The relationships between strikes by employees and government expenditures provide an example. Strikes by employees are often followed by higher public expenditures, which may appease employees and reduce strike activity. A *negative feedback loop* between A and B will result in a low correlation between A and B that is easily misconceived as the absence of a relationship between A and B.

As a matter of fact, lengthy data sets are required to test whether a seemingly strong unidirectinal relationship is really a (possibly weak) reciprocal positive feedback loop, or whether a seemingly absent relationship is really a (possibly strong) reciprocal negative feedback loop. Ordinary regression (OLS) is not suited to estimate the strength of reciprocal relationships. What is called for is structural equation modelling, which comes down to the simultaneous estimation of the parameters of more than one equation. Structural equation modelling (e.g. Bollen, 1994), which is beyond the scope of this book, may be carried out with add-ins to SPSS (AMOS, Lisrel) or with more versatile econometric statistical packages (STATA, Shazam). Although important in political theory, for example in the writings of Alexis de Tocqueville, feedback loops have not attracted much attention in the empirical political science literature.

6.8 Epilogue

This chapter fits somewhere between the elementary, bivariate methods of data analysis that were discussed in Chapter 5, on the one hand, and the advanced methods of data analysis that dominate political science journals, on the other. The discussion aimed at an assessment of the applicability of advanced methods in comparative political science. Almost no attention has been paid in this chapter to the statistical properties of the estimators used or to the mathematical background of the methods. No use was made of matrix algebra to set out the essentials of population parameters and their estimators concisely. More advanced estimation methods than OLS were only touched upon. Structural equation modelling was left aside. The reader who uses this book as a stepping stone to read monographs and specialized research articles with respect to the methods discussed here will still face a hard task. But the reader should have acquired an overview of the type of methods available to analyse available data with respect to political systems from a comparative point of view. The next chapters will set these methods to work in comparative political science research.

6.9 Endmatter

Topics highlighted

- Causality, a likelihood above mere chance that a dependent variable will change in a specific direction when the independent variable changes in a certain direction.
- Case-oriented analysis, aimed at a complete, non-statistical, description of relationships for a relatively limited number of cases.
- Variable-oriented analysis, aimed at a summative, statistical description of the relationships among a relatively limited number of variables for a huge number of cases.
- Basic techniques of quantitative hypothesis testing: cross-table analysis (dependent and independent variables have a nominal level of measurement), discriminant analysis (dependent variable nominal, independent variables interval or higher), analysis of variance (dependent variable has an interval level of measurement, independent variables interval or higher) and regression analysis (both dependent and independent variables have interval levels of measurement).
- Assumptions of regression analysis: linear relationships, no outliers, no multicollinearity, homoscedasticity, no autocorrelation of residuals.

Exercises

1 *Cross-table elaboration.* The relationship between macro-economic policy (POP) and electoral system (ELSYS, recode semi-proportional systems to proportional ones first) depends partly on the economic tide. Does it also depend on the position of the parties in government on a left–right scale? If so, what is the nature of the dependence (intervention, exogeneous variable, interaction effect?). Use the NIAS.SAV database to find an empirical answer. As a first step dichotomize the variable GVT_LR (or alternatively the variable GVT_WLF2) around its median.

2 *Discriminant analysis.* Perform an explorative discriminant analysis to find out which policy objectives of governments (as measured on the basis of the party manifestoes of the parties in government, variables GVT_LR, GVT_WLF2 and so on) are predictive of the type of macro-economic policy (variable POP). As a first step select the years 1970 (before the oil crisis of 1973), 1977 (after the oil crisis) and 1984 (during the economic recession).

3 *Analysis of variance.* Perform an analysis of variance to find out how the level of public expenditures (PE) depends on the nominal variables 'electoral system' (ELSYS, recode semi-proportional systems to proportional ones first) and the type of government coalition (TOGORI), and on the interaction between these variables.

4 *Interaction in regression analysis*. Test whether the political colour of the government (GVT_LR or GVT_WLF2) is an interacting variable in the apparent relationship between the percentage of imports and exports (variable IMEX) and public expenditures (PE). Do leftist governments respond more readily with higher expenditures to higher imports and exports? As a first step dichotomize the variable GVT_LR (or alternatively the variable GVT_WLF2) around its median.
5 *Time series analysis*. Test whether the conclusions for France in Section 6.7.5 hold also for Germany and the USA. If not, how can one explain public expenditures in these two countries?
6 *Pooled time series*. Test whether government expenditures on social security as a percentage of public expenditures depend on the same variables as public expenditures according to Section 6.7.6.

Further reading

Case study: Yin (1996). *Case-oriented approach*: Ragin (2000). Variable-oriented approach: Tacq (1997), Babbie (2004).
Regression analysis, general: Fox (1997), Berndt (1996), Greene (2003).
Special issues in regression analysis. Regression assumptions: Berry (1993), Fox (1991). Interaction in regression: Jaccard et al. (1990). Time series analysis: Greene (2003). Pooled time series analysis: Sayrs (1989), Beck and Katz (1995, 2004).
Elementary: Babbie (2004), Tabachnik and Fidell (2001).
Advanced: Kaplan (2002).

Part 3

Doing Political Research

Introduction to Part 3: Doing political research

This part focuses on the application of the methods and statistics that are discussed in the previous chapters: the nature of comparative politics (Chapter 1), the comparative methods (Chapter 2), the choices underlying research designs (Chapter 3) and, of course, the statistical techniques discussed in Chapters 4–6.

We do not claim blanket coverage but engage with a specific selection of central themes in political science. The themes are related to the politics of problem-solving in postwar democracies. We focus on socio-economic problems as they are central in the concerns of the public, the parties and governments in modern democracies (see Keman, 1997).

The way problems tend to be solved is cyclic: problems get on the agenda, parties and governments present (partial) solutions, and the effectiveness of these solutions is again potentially relevant for the political agenda. Hence we follow the well-known Easton model; however, we attempt to fully specify it (see Figure III.I). We have divided this process into three parts that correspond to the input–throughput–output–outcomes mechanisms of the political systems, as follows.

Chapter 7 concentrates on input-related variables. *Problems arise* when there is a growing awareness of certain problems: the media are covering them, politicians are concerned about them, the public is alerted, interest groups are demonstrating. In sum, the problem is being put on the political agenda. The problem is now in the hands of politicians. Political parties are mandated by the voters to develop solutions on the basis of their programmatic profiles (Budge et al., 2001).

Chapter 8 discusses research on the throughput side of the process. *Decisions are made* by political parties. The way parties handle problems is determined by their ideology but also by the institutional environment in which they are functioning. For example, the party system, federalism, presidentialism, and corporatism are patterned institutions that shape the room for manœuvre within which parties are operating and thus how politics is made.

Chapter 9 discusses the output side of the process. *The way problems are solved*, or the effectiveness of the solutions, is a complex mixture of actor-related and institutional factors. Problems are rarely completely solved, but there are variations in the degree to which problems are solved, or come back on the agenda. We will search for the factors that may explain these variations. In other words,

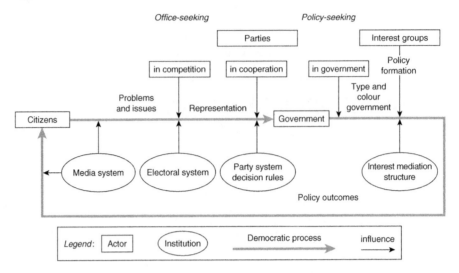

Figure III.1 *The chain of democratic control and command*

the focus is on the material and democratic performance of political systems (Heywood, 1997).

The cyclic process of the politics of problem-solving can be understood with the help of the so-called 'chain of democratic control and command' (Chapter 2 in this book). This chain represents an overall schematic and descriptive overview of the role that political actors such as parties play in the democratic process. Some basic assumptions on the role of parties in the democratic process are visualized in this scheme:

- Parties play *crucial* roles in the selection of problems that need to be solved and the transmission of preferences into decision-making. Hence, they are what is commonly called 'gatekeepers'.
- Parties play *institutionalized* roles: institutions provide the room to manoeuvre that parties can utilize in order to fulfil their democratic function. The type of electoral system and party system, for example, shapes the opportunities for policy formation.
- Parties play *differential* roles in the democratic process: these roles are competitive in relation to voters and cooperative in relation to government formation and functioning due to the institutional design within which parties operate – in particular, in the case of coalition government or of divided government (Weaver and Rockman, 1993).
- Parties play *reciprocal roles* in the democratic process, which is of a cyclic nature in the sense that the output/outcomes or material performance matter for the (renewed) inputs which in turn direct subsequent outputs/outcomes.

In sum, this part basically provides three things:

1 an overview of specific research methods and strategies that are relevant and basic for comparative political analysis;
2 relatively easy access to data and techniques in this field to perform comparative political analysis and enable the student to do it on his or her own by developing a research question of interest to him or her;
3 practical exercises and examples that stimulate the understanding of complex forms of analysis.

As our examples are a selection and presented in a summarized fashion, we provide additional references that may help students to get a deeper theoretical insight into the themes that are discussed. Generally speaking, we have tried to give a thorough overview of the theoretical background of the fields of research. The techniques that are used in this part are more fully explained in Part II:

* factor analysis (Section 4.5.2);
* scalability analysis (Section 4.5);
* cross-tabulation (Section 6.4);
* correlational analysis (Section 5.4.2);
* analysis of variance (Section 5.5.2);
* discriminant analysis (Section 6.5.1);
* multiple linear regression analysis (Section 6.7);
* time series analysis (Section 6.7);
* boolean analysis (Section 6.3);
* cluster analysis (Section 4.5.5).

These techniques are fairly representative of the techniques that are frequently used in quantitative political science.

Most of the data are made available so that students can replicate any (part of an) analysis and adjust elements of it (see the file methstat.zip that can be downloaded on http://research.fsw.vu.nl/DoingResearch). These data are related to a selection of modern classics in political science, among them Downs (1957), Sartori (1976), Olson (1982), Lijphart (1984), Budge et al. (1987), Bartolini and Mair (1990), Strøm (1990b) and Janoski and Hicks (1994).

In order to exemplify the working of the chain of democratic control and command we have decided to use socio-economic policy as the main field of policy. In addition, we use electoral data, democracy scales and public opinion data. Exercises will stimulate and direct students to practice the techniques. The emphasis is on *doing* political research in order to get a better understanding of the problem-solving capacities of political parties within the institutional context of modern democracies. We assume that the reader has read the preceding chapters before reading this part. Without doing so, this part is only accessible to advanced students in political science who have completed their basic courses on statistics.

Finally a few *practical hints* for using this part of the book. In most cases the following steps can help students to get a practical understanding of the techniques that are involved.

1   Replicate the SPSS mode of analysis on the data presented in the chapter.
2   Study the SPSS output. Study the SPSS Manual in order to get additional information about the statistics in the output. This extra information is indispensable for a correct understanding of the often elaborate output that is not fully discussed in the following chapters.
3   Try to grasp the decisions underlying the analysis that are presented in the book based on the nexus research design–research question–research answer as discussed in Part I.
4   Attempt to formulate at least one additional hypothesis which you wish to test.
5   Alter the presented analysis by adding, merging or recording variables on the basis of the new hypotheses.
6   Check whether the assumptions for the analysis are not violated.
7   Write a short paper in which the steps and results of the new analysis are presented correctly.
8   Let students present the results of their own analysis to the class, followed by a discussion.

Two helpful key texts for the general conceptual background to the chapters are Goodin and Klingemann (1996) and Katznelson and Miller (2002). The methodological concerns are largely covered by Dierkes et al. (1987) and Janoski and Hicks (1994).

How problems arise

7.1 Processes of Electoral Change

7.1.1 The problem of change

This chapter examines the trends in voting behaviour and preferences, shifts in party priorities and subsequent consequences for the political agenda. The shifting preferences of voters and parties are important for a correct understanding of why and how certain problems get on the political agenda and other problems do not, i.e. how societal problems become political ones. Both descriptive and explanatory research strategies will be utilized in this chapter by means of time series data on the preferences of voters (electoral data) and the preferences of parties (manifesto data based on the coding of the main party manifestoes of postwar democracies).

Electoral change affects the relationships between the three main actors in the democratic process: voters, parties and governments. In this chapter we will focus on voters and parties. Chapter 8 will also include governments. Countries in a given time period serve as the units of analysis since ultimately it is countries that are being compared. Parties are often the unit of measurement, as the data on seats and votes are linked to political parties.

Several forms of change are to be distinguished that stress different dimensions of changing relationships between parties and voters and among parties. We distinguish several types of indicators that can be used to measure, model and classify electoral change (see Chapter 4 – in most cases countries are the units of analysis and parties are the units of observation):

- party system indicators, e.g. the number of (effective) parties according to the Herfindahl index (see Section 5.1.2) – this indicator distinguishes between types of party systems, such as two- and multi-party systems;
- electoral system indicators, such as the fragmentation of seats and votes that can be used to distinguish among systems in terms of their degree of electoral proportionality;
- volatility indicators, such as *block volatility* (measuring electoral gains or losses of party blocks and families within a system) and *total volatility* (the net electoral change between consecutive elections) – these are commonly used indicators to distinguish between more and less stable systems;
- party organizational indicators (e.g. the number of party members, party finance) and party–voter indicators (such as party identification) – these are often used to distinguish between systems with a high and low potential for change.

These different types of electoral change are caused by sudden events (regime collapse, landslide elections) and also by more enduring factors such as dissolving cleavage structures, the waning of religion or the emergence of post-materialism (Inglehart, 1990). Electoral change can be limited to one party system component (so-called restricted party system change) or can have a more enduring impact on all party system components (so-called party system transformation). Figure 7.1 shows how party systems and electoral change are interrelated.

Figure 7.1 shows that electoral change not only affects the party–voter relationship, but also has potential consequences for the type and composition of government and the functioning of the party system. The indicators of electoral change that are mentioned above are devised to analyse the (inter)relationships which are shown in Figure 7.1.

In this chapter we will discuss examples of the measurement of electoral change, especially volatility (Section 7.1.2), the regression modelling of electoral change (Section 7.1.3), the comparison of the expert and Manifesto left–right scales plus scalability analysis (Section 7.2.2), factor analysis and regression analysis on party emphasis and the calculation of median voter positions (Sections, 7.2.3 and 7.2.4). These sections will introduce the main aspects of contemporary empirical research on processes of electoral and party change. A glossary will be found in Box 7.1. The exercises at the end of the chapter will deepen these insights and encourage reporting of this type of empirical research in a paper.

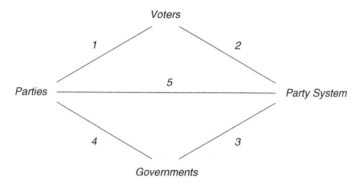

Figure 7.1 *Party systems and electoral change: 1, voter–party relationship (changing voter preferences evoke electoral change); 2, voter–party-system relationship (mediated by the electoral system); 3, party-system–government relationship (affects type and colour of government); 4, party–government relationship (parties are in or out of government); 5, party–party-system relationship (affects party competition)*

Box 7.1   Glossary of basic terms

- *Electoral system*: the set of rules that determines how votes are translated into seats.
- *Issue ownership*: the ownership (i.e. monopolization) of certain issues or policy areas by parties vis-à-vis others.
- *Left–right scales*: the positioning of parties between two poles that represent left and right issues on the basis of expert opinions or party manifestoes.
- *Median voter position*: the policy preferences of the voters, which are derived from the preferences of the parties they are voting for.
- *Median Voter Theorem for two-party systems* (Downs): Parties are assumed to move towards the median voter position and will thus converge to the middle of the distribution.
- *Party competition*: the moulding or profiling of parties in order to keep or achieve votes, policy goals and office.
- *Party system*: the cooperation and competition between political parties which it influences by the number of parties and their ideological distance.
- *Volatility*: how many parties win or lose per election (this includes all parties).

7.1.2 *Measuring electoral change*

In Chapter 4 we discussed the problems involved with measurement. This section focuses on one specific measurement problem, namely how to measure the degree and nature of electoral change. Bartolini and Mair (1990) analyse the levels of electoral stability in western Europe. Their ultimate concern is to account for variance in electoral stability/instability (the dependent variable) which is defined as the degree of electoral change between elections. Among the independent variables are electoral disproportionality (how votes are translated into seats), voter turnout, the number of parties contesting election, policy distance between parties and their ideological difference, societal segmentation, issue saliency, cleavages, party membership rates and trade union density.

Most prominent in the study of Bartolini and Mair is the total volatility (or system volatility): that is, volatility measured at the level of the individual party and added together for the party system as a whole (so-called 'total net electoral interchange'). The volatility measures are suited to comparative political analysis because they enable us to analyse electoral change for any selection of time points and countries and also to link the empirical analysis to the theory on party systems and cleavage structures. Although there are other indicators of electoral change, such as those based on election surveys, these alternative indicators are only available for a limited number of time points and countries.

The formula for total volatility is:

$$TV = \frac{|PV_1| + |PV_2| + |PV_3| + \cdots |PV_n|}{2}$$

where TV = total volatility; $|PV_i|$ = the absolute vote share change of party i. The formula divides the sum of the individual *party volatilities* by 2 in order to avoid a double-counting of the same electoral shifts: if one party loses 5 per cent of the votes and the other parties win 5 per cent in total, the net volatility is 5 per cent and not 10 per cent. The theoretical range of values runs from 0 (no change) to 100 (maximum change). The empirical (or actual) range is in reality much smaller and varies by political system (or 'polity') and period. This is clearly shown by Figure 7.2, which presents the mean volatility rates in 13 western European democracies (Siaroff, 2000). The graph indicates that there is a slightly rising trend in total volatility. The graph also shows that there are significant country differences: some countries are consistently unstable (i.e. a high level – France), others are consistently stable (i.e. a low level – Austria and Switzerland), whereas other countries vary in stability over time (Norway and Sweden).

The same index of total volatility can also be based on change at the level of blocks of parties – what Bartolini and Mair call *block volatility*. A 'block' of parties can be a party family, or it can refer to other distinctive groups of parties such as left and right, new and old, opposition and government, etc. Block volatility is more directly linked to the policy-making process than is total volatility: when the vote share of the liberal or conservative block goes up significantly we expect a more restrictive type of policy-making. Such a hypothesis could not be made solely on the basis of a rise (or decline) of total volatility. Block volatility is formally defined as follows:

where BV = block volatility, P_i = party i, V = votes.

$$BV = \frac{|PV_1 + \cdots + PV_k| + |PV_{k+1} + \cdots + PV_n|}{2}$$

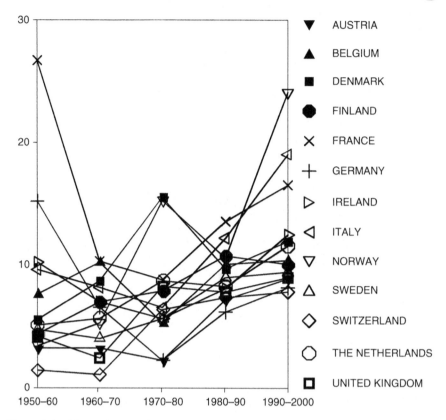

30

20

10

0

1950–60   1960–70   1970–80   1980–90   1990–2000

▼ AUSTRIA

▲ BELGIUM

■ DENMARK

⬤ FINLAND

✕ FRANCE

+ GERMANY

▷ IRELAND

◁ ITALY

▽ NORWAY

△ SWEDEN

◇ SWITZERLAND

◯ THE NETHERLANDS

◻ UNITED KINGDOM

Figure 7.2   *Total volatility in Europe (trends)*

Figure 7.3 shows the development of block volatility in $n = 13$ European countries (Armingeon et al., 2003). Block volatility is increasing, which is to the advantage of the protest parties, but to the disadvantage of the left and (even more so) for the religious party group. Gains by one party group always involve an electoral backlash against one or more other groups. In this particular case we see that the winning blocks of parties share a common property. If this property is ideology we speak of *party families*. Whereas block volatility measures the electoral interchange between blocks of parties, *within-block volatility* (WBV) measures the interchange within blocks. The WBV formula adds together the party net changes which have a sign contrary to that of the block as a whole. The total volatility is in fact the additive index of both scores. Concrete examples of how the measures are calculated are given in Figure 7.4. The figure shows the situation of two party blocks (e.g. left and right), each with three parties (A, B, C and D, E, F). On the basis of the party volatility scores it is possible to compute the block volatility, the total volatility and the within-block volatility.

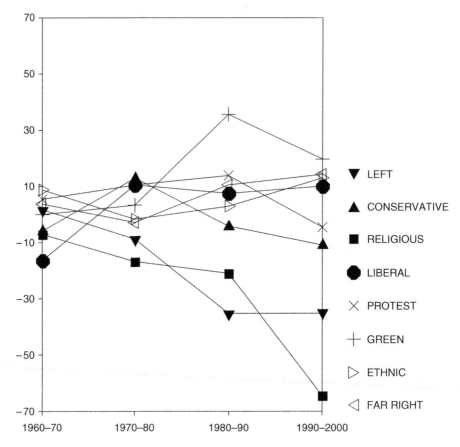

Figure 7.3 *Block volatility in Europe*
Note: *n* = 147 election years in 13 European countries.

In this subsection we have focused on total and block volatility. We have shown that it is important to decompose overall trends into periods and categories and not to trust averages that may well hide relevant variations. Total volatility and block volatility are crucial measures for the study of party behaviour. Total volatility is an indicator of the degree of electoral instability of party systems. Block volatility indicates the electoral strength of blocks, which has implications for the office-and policy-related room to manœuvre of political parties. There are, of course, more indicators of electoral change. Some of these other indicators, such as the effective number of parties, disproportionality and convergence, will be discussed in Chapter 8. In general, these indicators may help us to spot variations in electoral and party behaviour and also help to dispel certain generalizations or even myths on supposedly universal trends in party behaviour, such as overall convergence or catch-all-ism (i.e. the attempts to transgress the socio-economic and cultural

$$\text{Blocks} = \frac{1}{\begin{array}{ccc} A & B & C \end{array}} \quad \frac{2}{\begin{array}{ccc} D & E & F \end{array}}$$

$$PV = +6 -2 -1 \quad -5 -2 +4$$

$$BV = \frac{|+6 -2 -1| + |-5 -2 +4|}{2}$$

$$TV = \frac{|+6| + |-2| + |-1| + |-5| + |-2| + |+4|}{2} = 10$$

$$WBV = |-2| + |-1| + |+4| = 7 \,(= 10 -3)$$

Total volatility = Block volatility + Within-block volatility
Legend: PV = Party volatility, BV = Block volatility, TV = Total volatility,
WBV = Within-block volatility.

Figure 7.4   *Examples of the calculation of volatility scores (Bartolini and Mair, 1990: 24)*

cleavages among the electorate in order to attract a broader audience; see Krouwel, 1999).

7.1.3 Modelling change

In Chapter 4 the processes of measuring and modelling were presented as two complementary research activities. The modelling of electoral change is a necessary and logical step after we have measured electoral change by means of various volatility indicators. We again follow the arguments of Bartolini and Mair who apply the multiple regression technique that is explained in Section 6.7. In its simplest form the model looks like Figure 7.5.

The way Bartolini and Mair model electoral change is linked to the 'theory–method problem' as discussed in Chapter 1 and can be seen as theory-guided research questions. As we are basically interested in the system level, the conceptualizations and operationalizations are directed to this level. In some cases the operationalizations of systemic variables (meaning: part of a system) are based upon individual behaviour, which clearly confronts us with the problem of data aggregation as explained in Chapter 3.

The variables shown in Figure 7.5 are related to actors (such as electoral participation), institutions (such as change in electoral institutions) and the systemic features of democratic polities (such as cleavage closure) and they are all potential sources of aggregate volatility. Bartolini and Mair (1990: 37–40) describe these as follows:

- *Cleavage closure.* Cleavages are enduring dividing lines in a society based on socio-economic or socio-cultural divisions such as class, religion, language or ethnic differences. Societies with a distinct cleavage structure are called plural or fragmented. In systems where cleavages do not produce a full closure of relationships, there is a higher chance of electoral mobility. Bartolini and Mair restrict their analysis to one important cleavage in mass politics: that of class,

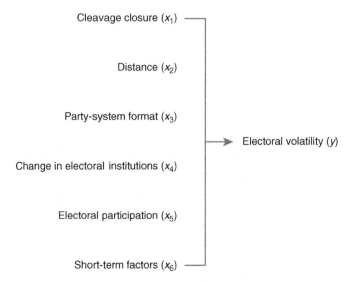

Cleavage closure (x_1)

Distance (x_2)

Party-system format (x_3)

Electoral volatility (y)

Change in electoral institutions (x_4)

Electoral participation (x_5)

Short-term factors (x_6)

Figure 7.5 *Determinants of electoral instability:* x_1 *to* x_6 *are the independent variables selected by Bartolini and Mair (1990)*

more specifically the class-left block volatility, being the aggregate block volatility of left parties. This measure is used to test the Lipset–Rokkan 'freezing hypothesis' which states that the cleavage structure has not fundamentally changed (has remained 'frozen') since it came into existence during the nineteenth and early twentieth century (Lipset and Rokkan, 1967).

- *Policy distance.* In the case of small distances between parties we expect more electoral volatility as party switches by voters are made easier. These distances are measured in several ways which will be shown in Section 7.2.2.
- *Party-system format.* This is operationalized as the number of effective parties, which takes both the number of parties and their relative weights into account. The more options are offered to the voter, the more voters will change their vote from election to election.
- *Change in electoral institutions.* This affects the structure of opportunities for the electorate at large and modifies the preference rankings of individual voters. These changes have a legal-institutional origin. Bartolini and Mair refer to the enfranchisement of new sectors of the population, a new electoral law, the introduction or abandonment of compulsory voting, and variations in the disproportionality potential (meaning the disproportionality between votes and seats) in different systems.
- *Electoral participation.* Changes in the level of electoral participation (rather than the levels as such) are assumed to increase electoral volatility, especially in cases where former non-voters add substantially to the pre-existing active electorate.
- *Short-term factors.* These refer to contingent factors such as specific salient issues, the appeal of individual candidates and exceptional and unforeseen

Table 7.1 *Aggregated categories in the Bartolini and Mair model*

Determinant	Variables
Institutional change	Occurrences of franchise elections plus occurrences of changes in the electoral system
Cultural segmentation	Ethno-linguistic plus religious heterogeneity
Organizational density	Party-membership rate plus trade union density
Party-system format	Number of political parties

Source: Bartolini and Mair (1990: 280).

events, e.g. scandals during the political campaign. These factors change from election to election, and their occurrence and impact are highly unpredictable.

The basic underlying assumption of the model (as in all models) is that the variance in total volatility will be significant to the extent that it is possible to disentangle the *relative* weight of the different components indicated in Figure 7.5. The assumption is justified only if the model is well specified, meaning that it is neither underspecified (i.e. missing significant relationships that are commonly assumed in the literature) nor overspecified (i.e. including too many relationships so that the model becomes too detailed and descriptive). The inclusion of actor-related, institutional and systemic variables in the model indicates that it presents an encompassing schematic overview of relevant independent variables.

Table 7.1 is an initial scheme based on theoretical considerations; it is not yet quite suited for regression analysis. In a step-by-step analysis the factors are analysed and sometimes abandoned if their effect can be largely attributed to the mediating effects of other variables (Bartolini and Mair, 1990: 279). The remaining independent variables are then combined into a set of more general indices. The regression analysis is based on a simplified (parsimonious) model of the determinants of electoral instability which incorporates the individual variables into the broader socio-political phenomena of which they are part.

Figure 7.6 shows the results of the regression analysis reported by Bartolini and Mair ($n = 231$ election years in 13 European democracies in the period 1918–85). The explained variance is 44.6 per cent. Apart from the short-term factors, they find moderate betas (lower than 0.35) for the direct effects of the institutional incentives (i.e. the party-system format and institutional change) and socio-organizational bonds (i.e. cultural segmentation plus organizational density). The amount of variation which is not explained by the model is assigned to the short-term factors. These factors turn out to be potentially crucial for the explanation of electoral instability.

The black-box character of the Bartolini and Mair model is invoked by the relatively strong effects of the unknown short-term factors. Although Bartolini and Mair are correct in stating that an exact measurement and modelling of short-term factors is difficult, it is nevertheless possible to select variables, that represent short-term developments which vary from election to election.

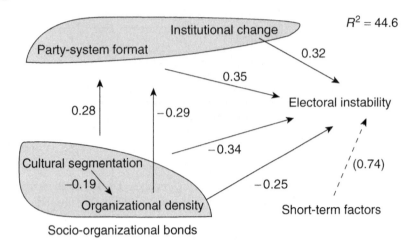

Figure 7.6 *Bartolini and Mair's final causal model. Source: Bartolini and Mair (1990: 282); n = 231 election years in 13 European democracies in the period 1918–85.*

Box 7.2 Hypotheses that underlie our model of the short-term factors in the Bartolini and Mair model

We assume that the total volatility is higher in situations where:

1 the bond between voters and parties is weak (a low party-membership rate represented by the variable 'gemmem');
2 the economic situation is weakening (variable 'misery');
3 the electoral support for left parties is weakening (variable 'leftv', the vote share of the left parties; if this share is high, then the impact of the overall decline of left parties on volatility is also higher);
4 the established parties are converging on the socio-economic left–right scale (variable 'partysys');
5 the economy is vulnerable because of its openness (variable 'imex');
6 the working population is dissatisfied with the working conditions (variable 'nrstrik').

We have constructed a new regression equation that includes (proxies for) short-term factors on the basis of the hypotheses shown in Box 7.2. These hypotheses have in common that they refer to socio-economic conditions and party–voter relationships that change from election to election. As such they differ from structural features such as institutional incentives and socio-organizational bonds that are not likely to change over short time periods.

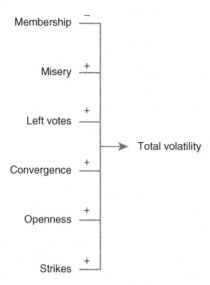

Figure 7.7 *Expected causal effects of the short-term factors*

Note that the variables are not based on an exact measurement of short-term trends as we *assume* that a relatively low average score of, for example, economic misery indicates that there is a gradual decrease in misery. Figure 7.7 presents the model graphically. Step-by-step those variables are omitted that appear to be insignificant: nrstrik and misery. The remaining variables give a model with an adjusted R^2 of 0.68 ($n = 13$ European countries). The results are presented in Table 7.2. All our hypotheses are confirmed, except one: the high level of convergence relates negatively to the degree of total volatility. Note that our model is not wholly comparable with Bartolini and Mair's model. Not only are our variables proxies (being 'stand-ins' for variables that are difficult to operationalize), but the units of analysis are also quite different (the regression is based on 13 cases as compared with $n = 231$ in the Bartolini and Mair analysis). The small number of cases renders our model vulnerable to small changes (see Section 5.6.2 on robustness). Adding or dropping one variable destroys the promising relationships we have found. It makes sense, therefore, to apply the model to time series data. This can only be done properly by correcting for errors that are related to autocorrelation. One modern technique to do this is the panel-corrected standard errors (PCSE) method, explained in Section 6.7. The results of the PCSE regression analysis show that our suspicion towards the 13-case model is justified. The betas and the adjusted R^2 in the PCSE model are much lower. The signs of the betas are identical in both types of regression analyses (two variables in the short-term factors model are not significant at the 5 per cent level).

Table 7.2   *Regression results of two models which seek to explain total volatility with solely short-term factors*

Proxies:	OLS regression results on the basis of aggregated data[a] ($R^2_{adj} = 0.68$)			PCSE regression results on the basis of pooled time series data[b] ($R^2_{adj} = 0.28$)		
	beta	t	Sig. t	beta	t	Sig. t
Membership	−0.67	−3.5	0.0078	−0.47	−8.65	0.00
Left votes	0.76	3.3	0.0106	0.40	4.4	0.00
Convergence	−0.62	−3.8	0.0054	−0.35	−8.3	0.00
Openness	0.44	2.1	0.0701	0.27	4.4	0.00
Constant	−	0.81	0.4402		3.7	0.00

[a] $n = 13$ European countries.
[b] $n = 299$ (13 European countries × 23 years).

Recent instances of electoral instability, such as landslide elections and heavy electoral losses by pivotal parties, cast some doubt on the overall validity of the Bartolini–Mair model. First of all, electoral volatility is only one way of looking at party-system change. There are more detailed ways of looking at recent forms of party-system change in a comparative manner, such as examining the effects of regime breaks or processes of redemocratization (Pennings and Lane, 1998). Secondly, Bartolini and Mair examine electoral change at the aggregate level. Looking at the individual level might reveal more change. This is shown by Ersson and Lane (1998) who examined volatility at the individual level. It is well known that the bonds between voters and parties are becoming weaker (Katz and Mair, 1992). Other forms of political participation and new potentials are arising (Kriesi and Koopmans, 1995) which have, for instance, led to the rise of protest parties.

The conclusion is as follows. In this section we have examined processes of electoral change along two lines: the type and degree of variation and the explanation of these variations with the help of causal modelling. The two subsequent steps of finding and explaining variations are crucial to comparative research. Without variations we cannot compare, and without explanation the art and craft of comparing loses most of its scientific significance. The problem is, however, that there is usually more than one way to find and explain variations. One way to cope with this problem is to relate the research question to earlier research on the topic. This is, in fact, also what Bartolini and Mair did, as their research builds on the work of Lipset and Rokkan. This type of theoretical basis has a structuring impact on the research question and research design to be developed by students in comparative political science.

7.2 Processes of Party Change

7.2.1 The role of parties

Parties have different functions and roles and related dilemmas (Strøm, 1990a): seeking votes, office and policy simultaneously.

- Parties that are solely vote-seeking are vote maximizers. It was Anthony Downs who proposed the vote-maximizing model of party behaviour (Downs, 1957).
- Office-seeking parties seek to maximize not their votes, but their control over political office. Office mainly refers to cabinet portfolios (Riker, 1962).
- Policy-seeking parties seek to maximize their effect on public policy. Policy-based coalition theory assumes that coalitions will be formed by parties that are 'connected' (Axelrod, 1970) or at least close to each other in policy space (we will come back to this in Section 8.4).

Strøm criticizes the three models on their static and non-institutional character. He proposes a unified model of party behaviour that focuses on the interrelations and trade-offs between the three party goals. Strøm argues that pure vote seekers, office seekers, or policy seekers are unlikely to exist. Party objectives are mostly mixed.

Figure 7.8 shows a three-dimensional space where each party goal is represented by one dimension. Strøm suggests that each case of party behaviour is a linear additive function of the three party goals,

$$B = w_1 V + w_2 O + w_3 P,$$

where B is position in behavioural space, V is vote-seeking behaviour, O is office-seeking behaviour, P is policy-seeking behaviour, and w_1 w_2, w_3 are coefficients representing the weights of each type of behaviour. The weights signify the relative importance of different types of party behaviour, analogously to the beta weights in regression analysis. The weights are constrained to sum to 1, so that all feasible forms of party behaviour fall in the triangle in Figure 7.8. A pure vote-seeking party would be located at point 1, a pure office seeker at point 2, and a pure policy seeker at 3. Parties that pursue all three objectives fall somewhere in the interior of the triangle. A party that places some value on votes and more on policy than on office, will fall inside the right-hand area of the triangle. Although there are no data available that can be used to test this specific model, the idea of party goals has proved to be useful. This book shows several examples of it, such as the 'chain of democratic control and command' and Robertson's 'two-stage factor analysis' (Section 7.2.3).

Strøm distinguishes between two sets of factors that systematically affect the trade-offs between votes, office and policy. One set of factors is to be found in the organizational properties of parties (such as the constraints on party leaders). The second set of variables is constituted by the electoral, legislative and governmental institutions. There is always a potential conflict between the different objectives, which often boils down to a trade-off between short-term and longer-term benefits. For example, a party may benefit from the decision to join a government, in terms of office, but suffer from it in terms of future votes. Given these conflicting aims, parties have to make choices and formulate priorities. How these choices are made depends on the functioning of the party as an organization (internal affairs) and on the impact of electoral, legislative and

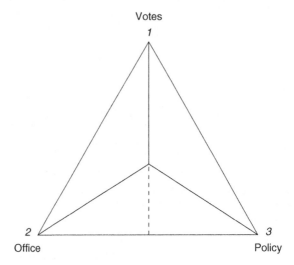

Figure 7.8 *Strøm's range of feasible party behaviours (Strøm, 1990a)*

governmental institutions (external environment). These institutions determine how votes are translated into seats, bargaining power into government status, and government status into office and policy benefits. In Chapter 8 we will examine several examples of the impact of institutions which can be seen as the 'rules of the game' determining the constrained opportunities for each party to achieve its goals (or not).

7.2.2 Parties and ideology scales

One main aspect of party change is ideological change. In this section we will demonstrate how this can be measured. According to Lipset and Rokkan, different ideologies stem from cleavage systems and result in different party families. Party families are groups of parties with similar ideological background or roots. One important cleavage in most parliamentary democracies is the class cleavage which is strongly linked to the left–right division in politics. Three kinds of scales are developed to measure left–right positions of parties: expert scales, voter scales and manifesto scales. The expert scales are based on the positions of parties on the basis of a selection of expert opinions. Three prominent expert scales are those of Castles and Mair (1984), Laver and Hunt (1992) and Huber and Inglehart (1995). An extensive summary of expert scales is presented in Laver and Schofield (1990: Appendix B). An example is presented in Figure 7.9.

The manifesto scales are based on the emphasis that parties put in their manifestoes on left and right issues. The party manifestoes (see Section 4.5) are

```
                                    DC,
  DP                PCI Rad PSI    PRI PSDI PLI                         MSI

  0.5               1.6  2.3  3.1   4.8  5.4  5.9                       9.1
  └─┴───────────────┴────┴────┴─────┴┴───┴───┴──────────────────────────┴─┘
  0                                  5                                   10
```

Figure 7.9   *The position of Italian parties on the Castles–Mair expert scale (1984): DC, Christian Democrats; DP, Proletarian Democrats; MSI, Nationalists; PCI, Communists; PRI, Republicans; PLI, Liberals; PSDI, Social Democrats; PSI, Socialists; Rad, Radicals*

coded for the relevant parties in most democracies for the postwar period – these are the parties gaining more than 5 per cent of the vote at any postwar election, together with all that were potentially pivotal in coalition bargaining (Laver and Budge, 1992: 17). Each sentence is assigned to one of the 54 coding categories. At the end of the coding process all the sentences are counted by category and the counts taken as a percentage of the total number of coded sentences. A recent example is a left–right scale that is constructed by summing up 13 left and 13 right items; and the latter are subtracted from the former. The result is an interval score for each party in each election (Klingemann et al., 1994: 40). Another example comes from Laver and Budge, who made the selection of left and right variables on the basis of factor analysis. This enabled them to combine the original 54 policy-coding categories into 20 in order to diminish the overlap between these categories (Laver and Budge, 1992: 24).

It is possible to compare both types of scales once they are put into the same format, notably the 10-point scale. Figure 7.10 gives the example of the Italian parties in 1992.

Manifesto scales tend to assign moderate scores to all parties, even if these parties are distinctive left or right parties. Expert scales, on the other hand, make sharper distinctions between the parties. A comparison of three scales in Figure 7.10 illustrates this point clearly. You can use the same set-up in Chapter7.sps to make a similar drop-line chart for any country or election year that is included in the party manifesto data set.

Another important difference is the dynamics of the scales. The expert scales are static. Apparently, they do not measure the positioning of parties at many points in time (mostly only at one). As a consequence there is not much variation between the expert scales in time. Most expert research in 1995 still produces more or less the same results as it did in 1984. The Castles–Mair and Huber–Inglehart scales differ in 23 cases (being parties), meaning that the positions of the parties differ by more than 1 point (Castles and Mair regard a difference of 0.5 as significant). It is striking that these differences in nearly half of cases apply to social democratic parties. The Huber–Inglehart scale places these parties more to the right than the Castles–Mair scale. This might imply that there is a bias in these scales, but it also means that there has been a movement to the right of social democratic parties. The Laver–Hunt and the Huber–Inglehart scales differ for 22 parties. This time

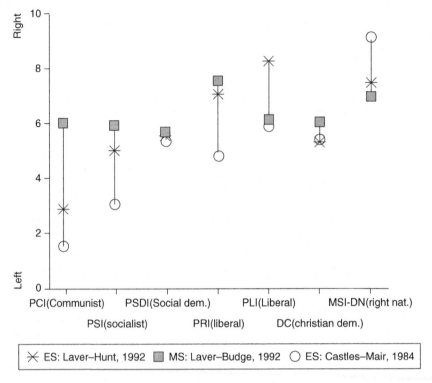

Figure 7.10 *Position of Italian parties on expert-scales (ES) and manifesto scale (MS). Source: Laver and Schofield (1990, p. 260)*

there is no 'bias' towards one particular party family, but there appears to be a more 'nationalistic' bias as the differences apply to many Belgian parties. Laver (1995) applies the Laver–Hunt expert scale also to the Dutch elections in 1994. Inglehart's analysis originates from the end of 1994, which is approximately the same point in time as Laver used. It is striking that Huber and Inglehart place all parties further to the left than Laver does.

We conclude that there are remarkable differences between the ranges of the expert scales and the manifesto scales. Between the expert scales are more differences in the scaling of parties than is generally assumed. The (dynamic) manifesto scales have a centripetal bias, whereas the (static) expert scales are more centrifugally oriented. The fact that both types of scales have pros and cons does not imply that either scale will do for any research. If in doubt, it is always better to compare several scales in order to grasp the degree of consistency between them. The analytical comparison of two or more scales should be based on their reliability (as demonstrated in Section 4.5), on the number of parties included and on the external validity of the scales (i.e. do the scales produce roughly the same results?).

Another topic that needs attention is the scalability of the manifesto scales. Most of the scales are constructed on theoretical and not empirical grounds.

This implies that these scales – as they are used and applied in the publications of the Manifesto Research Group – may contain items that do not fit into the scale very well. We will present an example here of the construction of a left–right scale (with the help of the SPSS procedure Reliability) that results in a Likert scale (see Section 4.5.1). We limit the analysis to the Labour and Conservative parties in the UK. We select the economic variables in the Manifesto data set.

The first step in the analysis is to recode the scores on the items. In the original data set all scores are positive. The construction of a left–right Likert scale is only possible if contrary signs are assigned to the left and the right issues (here we assigned negative signs to the left items). The main criterion is Cronbach's α: one by one we delete those items with the highest score on 'Alpha if item deleted' when this additional alpha exceeds alpha for all items (see Section 4.5.2). In our example we start with a selection of 13 items and end up with a selection of 10 items with an alpha score of 0.79 and a standardized item alpha of 0.80.

The final left–right scale is an additive index of these ten variables (this index is presented in the file Chapter7.sps). The SPSS procedure 'descriptives' reveals that the scale ranges from –23 (left) to +26 (right). By computing the additive index we have created a score on the left–right scale for both parties for all election years. These scores are plotted in Figure 7.11. The figure shows that the two parties consistently move on their own side of the party system and that there is a cyclical movement towards both convergence (1945–70) and divergence (1970–92). Both conclusions have far-reaching consequences for our thinking on parties. The results are not so obvious as they seem. This can be illustrated by comparing these empirical results (which are not unique to the UK! – see also the two-stage factor analysis on the US data in the next section) with the theoretical assumptions and predictions of Anthony Downs (Figure 7.12).

Electoral volatility is the change of vote between parties and thus must be explained within the context of choices offered by parties. Especially on the basis of the Bartolini–Mair discussion (see Section 7.1), emphasizing movement between left–right party blocks, it is useful to define choice in left–right terms. This also gives us the opportunity to present a spatial representation of such movements. One of the most widely discussed hypotheses on vote-seeking party behaviour was formulated by Downs (1957). His main assumption is that parties are moving, and that the electoral preferences are more or less fixed. On the basis of the party manifestoes it is possible to confront Downs' long-term expectation of party convergence, as represented in Figure 7.13, with actual party movement. This is done with the left–right scales discussed in the previous section. Most of the graphical presentations which have been made on the basis of the manifesto scales show that parties are, for instance, not 'leapfrogging', as they stay in their own ideological segment and are thus ideologically fixed (Laver and Budge, 1992; Budge et al., 2001).

How can we explain these characteristics of party behaviour? One explanation lies in the parties' information shortage. Parties do not know exactly where the

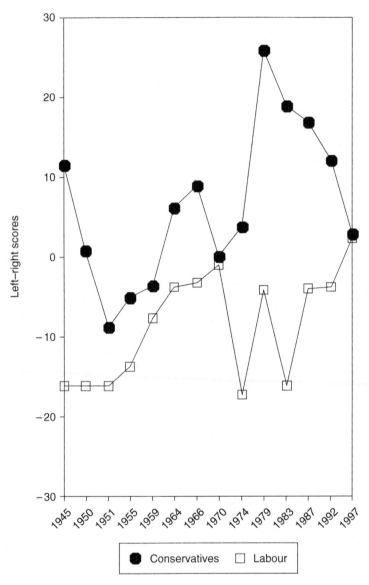

Figure 7.11   *Movement of British parties on the left–right scale, based on the SPSS procedure Reliability. Source: Comparative Manifestoes Project, Budge et al. (2001).*

voters stand. Consequently, parties rely on their own ideology. If parties do not move, volatility must be explained by voters moving or by the rise of new cohorts of voters. Note, however, that volatility is limited. The best predictor of the next election result is the previous result. Sometimes enough electors get concerned about a problem which is 'owned by' a different party than the one they have

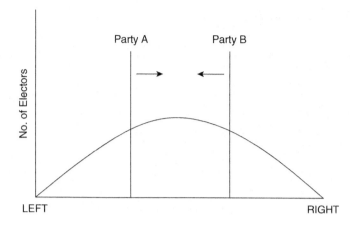

Figure 7.12 *Downs' model for two-party competition (Downs, 1957)*

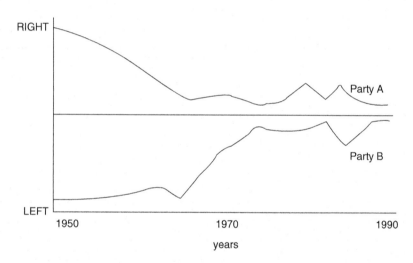

Figure 7.13 *Downs' single election model leads to the expectation of convergent party positions over time (Downs, 1957)*

been voting for. This may cause enough imbalanced movement at the aggregate level to change the election result. The saliency theory of party competition (nowadays often labelled as the 'issue ownership theory' – see Petrocik, 1996) is designed to allow understanding of the impact of issues 'owned by' parties. When the saliency of issues changes, this gives an electoral advantage to those parties which 'own' the salient issues (Budge and Farlie, 1983).

7.2.3 Parties and issues

Issues are societal problems that need to be solved, although not necessarily by means of government policy. They play an important role in the competition between parties. Parties seek to present themselves to the voters by means of specific issues that enable voters to identify themselves with these parties. The way parties select issues is clearly patterned. This pattern is linked to the party family concept. In this chapter we will use factor analysis to illustrate the paradoxical relationship between parties and issues: many parties 'own' specific issues in the sense that they are the natural bearers of this ideology, but at the same time, parties are also inclined to change and modernize their ideology and presentation of issues in order to stay attractive to the voters (van der Brug, 2004). It is clear, for example, that the Christian ideology is very much at the heart of what Christian democratic parties stand for, but if these parties did not adapt this ideology to modern circumstances, they could not survive. The same goes for the socialist and the liberal party ideologies, which need constant adaptation to modern conditions and preferences.

One seminal study in this field is Budge et al. (1987). Their approach is spatial, i.e. dimensional. On the basis of positive and negative associations between percentage scores they have identified sets of related policy areas. Each set can be represented spatially by a line, thus becoming a dimension of some space (Budge et al., 1987: 29). This only holds when there are no more than three clusters of dimensions.

Each manifesto is located on each dimension by the percentage of references made to the issue areas associated with it, multiplied by the 'loading' of these areas on the dimension (factor loadings higher than 0.30 are considered by these authors as an indication that a policy area is important). The factor analysis (see Chapter 4) brings to the fore the paradoxical relationship between parties and issues:

1 Parties compete on the basis of a fixed set of issues that belong to dimensions of conflict. The *first stage* of the factor analysis examines these cleavages.
2 Parties change their positions over time, meaning that the relative position of election programmes within the multi-dimensional space is not stable. The *second stage* of the factor analysis examines the movements of parties within the substantive domains.

Although factor analysis is primarily a data-summarizing technique, one still needs some theoretical assumptions that structure the data. An analysis of 54 issue categories would produce blurred results, difficult to interpret and statistically dubious as the number of variables would outnumber the number of cases (as the analysis is performed at the country level). For this reason Budge et al. use the two leading factors in each of the seven domains as new variables for the second-stage factor analysis in order to get a simple description of the overarching structure of party competition.

Table 7.3 is an example of the first-stage factor analysis. The table shows a summary of the results of factor analysis in the economic domain. In technical terms it is based on principal axis factoring (PAF) with communality estimates in the

Table 7.3 *Results of the factor analysis in the economic domain*

Factor	USA 1	USA 2	UK 1	UK 2	NZ 1	NZ 2	Australia 1	Australia 2
Eigenvalue	3.3	2.4	2.7	1.3	1.9	1.7	1.3	1
% of variance explained	30%	22%	27%	13%	21%	19%	14%	11%
Variable								
401 Free enterprise	−0.89	−0.07	0.69	0.53	−0.23	−0.63	−0.28	0.28
402 Incentives	0.19	−0.21	0.34	0.89	0.93	−0.21	0.39	0.09
403 Regulation of capitalism	0.69	−0.07	−0.39	−0.22	−0.01	0.63	0.38	−0.30
404 Economic planning	0.46	0.48	−0.52	0.02	−0.09	0.87	0.31	−0.04
406 Protectionism	−0.46	−0.10			−0.06	0.37	−0.02	0.10
408 Specific economic goals	0.59	−0.39	0.03	−0.41	0.15	−0.16	0.51	−0.11
410 Productivity	0.29	−0.45	0.04	0.27	−0.27	0.07	0.22	0.89
411 Technology and infrastructure	0.65	−0.07	0.42	−0.48	−0.66	−0.14	−0.04	0.02
412 Controlled economy	0.17	0.94	−0.44	−0.26				
413 Nationalization	0.07	0.92	−0.61	0.10				
414 Economic orthodoxy	−0.85	0.01	0.80	0.01	0.59	0.11	−0.69	−0.06

Source: Budge et al. (1987: 55). A blank means that a variable is omitted from the analysis.

main diagonal, followed by varimax rotation. The set-up for this analysis is included in the file Chapter7.sps. Table 7.3 shows the following results:

1   the two factors for four countries – these are the two dimensions that represent the variables in the economic domain;
2   the factor loadings of the variables on these factors;
3   the explained variance of the two factors;
4   the eigenvalues – these represent the degree of association between the factors and the variables that they represent.

The results indicate that the structure of party competition on economic issues differs from country to country but also that, despite these differences, the left–right dimension is clearly present in all four countries. The American parties compete along two dimensions, the first being *laissez-faire* versus regulation of capitalism, which accounts for 30 per cent of the variance; the second dimension contrasts controlled economy and nationalization on the one hand with productivity on the other hand. In the case of the UK the first factor is a classic left–right clash; within the second factor a stress on economic goal attainment is contrasted with economic ideology *per se* (incentives and nationalization). For New Zealand the first factor contrasts two classic 'right-wing' economic symbols (namely incentives and economic orthodoxy versus technology and infrastructure and productivity); the second factor shows the contrasts between conservative and socialist economic issues (free enterprise versus planning and

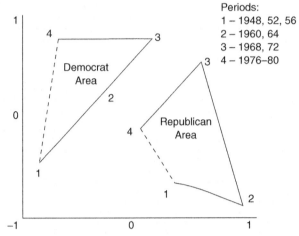

Second stage factor 2
Welfare and economic regulation

Periods:
1 – 1948, 52, 56
2 – 1960, 64
3 – 1968, 72
4 – 1976–80

Second stage factor 1: Republican versus democrat issues

Figure 7.14 *US party positions, 1948–80. Source: Budge et al. (1987)*

regulation). The first Australian dimension is a left–right clash, and the second is a unipolar and single-category stress on productivity.[1]

In the first stage of the analysis the seven domains are split into two factors that represent what parties are competing for (their policy-seeking goals). This reduces the 54 categories in the party manifestoes to 14 variables (an exception is domain 2, of which the original scores are used). In the second stage these 14 variables are fed into the factor analysis. The set-up that does this job for the USA is included in the file Chapter7.sps

In Figure 7.14 the means that result from the second-stage analysis are presented in two-dimensional space. The figure confirms the basic hypotheses on how party competition works: the movement of parties is restricted, but at the same time this rigidity does not mean that parties do not change. They are constantly adapting their party goals, and this is done in a more or less cyclical movement as shown in Figure 7.14. In terms of Strøm's categorization of party goals, we have been mainly looking at the changes in the policy-related goals of parties. These changes indirectly also affect the vote- and office-seeking goals of parties. The degree to which this is the case depends on the electoral and party systems. In the case of the USA, the parties' room to manœuvre is affected by the characteristics of the two-party system. If, for example, a third relevant party were to be introduced into the American party system it would certainly affect the policy positions and the movements of the established parties.

Although the results of the two-stage factor analysis appear convincing for the USA, it is not the technique as such that invokes these kinds of results, it is the ideas, theories and assumptions of the researchers. Even the smallest changes in the selection of years or variables would produce different results (you can test this statement by adapting the set-up slightly and rerunning the factor analysis for the period 1948–92). David Robertson (Budge et al., 1987) not only used factor analysis as a data-reducing technique, but also as a theoretically guided (and manipulated) tool in order to corroborate the hypothesis that the division into left and right matters in the USA. This particular use of factor analysis requires an experienced outlook on the subject in order to be useful and reliable. Simpler examples of factor analysis will be given in Sections 8.2 and 9.4.

7.2.4 Public opinion and party responsiveness

Hitherto we have mainly concentrated on party positions as such. A relatively new topic in party literature is the so-called party responsiveness: the degree to which parties are responsive to external factors such as voter opinion and shifting problem intensities.

The saliency theory of party competition, or issue ownership theory, claims that parties are mainly ideologically driven (ideology refers here to left–right positions) and not very responsive to sudden shifts in problems and public opinion. This challenging hypothesis is tested by confronting the salience theory with alternative explanations of party behaviour. In this way we can determine to what extent the saliency model is the best-fitting model of party emphasis.

Basically, there are three competing models:

- The Downsian model predicts that parties are neither ideologically driven nor problem-driven. Instead, parties are following public opinion and voter preferences in order to *maximize* their votes. Parties are very responsive to voter preferences ('competition-driven').
- The saliency issue model (Budge et al., 1987) predicts that parties are ideologically driven. The implication of this is that parties are characterized by ideological rigidity and are not responsive to voters or problems ('cartellization-driven').
- The combined model predicts that parties will be driven by both ideology and public opinion. This model is based on the hypothesis that most parties base their choices on both ideological and electoral considerations.

These three models are tested by means of regression equations on the basis of pooled time series data. As the research question focuses on trends and variations in party behaviour we obviously have to adopt a cross-national and cross-temporal perspective. The first step is to define the dependent variables. We haven chosen the emphasis of political parties in four policy domains which are fundamental to party competition. The operationalization of these variables is explained in Budge et al. (2001) and in Table 7.4.

One independent variable is the so-called median voter position on the planning and market variables that are defined in Table 7.4. The median voter position is a measure of the ideological position of a particular electorate that is comparable across countries and across time. It is the central ideological tendency among voters. If parties are following voter preferences, then we expect them to move towards the median voter positions, especially when they are (potential) cabinet parties. The calculation of the median voter position is based on a well-known formula that incorporates the policy positions and the votes shares for the relevant political parties (Bohrnstedt and Knoke, 1982: 52; Kim and Fording, 1998: 79). For each party the midpoint is calculated between the one immediately to the left of it and the one immediately to the right of it. It is assumed that voters on the left of this interval will vote for the party on the left and the ones on the right will vote for the party on the right of it:

$$M = L + \{(50 - C)/F\} \times W,$$

where M is median voter position (ideological score), L is the lower end (ideological score) of the interval containing the median, C is the cumulative frequency (vote share) up to but not including the interval containing the median, F is the frequency (vote share) in the interval containing the median, and W is the width of the interval containing the median (ideological score).

The three elements needed to perform the calculations are:

1   the mean scale positions of the parties;
2   the vote percentages of the parties;
3   the scale positions of each party.

We now give a short example of how this formula works for a country with a left party (A), a centre party (B) and a right party (C). The ideological score refers to either the left–right scale, the planning positions or the market positions. Suppose that the median voter in this country in a particular election year is in party B, because by the time we move through party B, we have covered more than 50 per cent of all voters. Having identified party B we can figure out that L, the lower ideological score of B, is the midpoint between party A and B. The value of W equals L minus the midpoint of the ideological scores of B and C. The value of C is the sum of all votes to the left of party B. The value of F is the vote percentage of party B.

We will also give a more empirical example of the calculation of the median voter position of the left–right scale for a multi-party system, Sweden. The data stems from the *International Almanac of Electoral History* (Mackie and Rose, 1991). The rows comprise the parties. The columns comprise the (interpolated) vote percentages of the election years and the in-between years.

Firstly, we line up the parties from low to high on the scale of interest. This is done by means of the command 'sort cases' which orders the parties from a high score to a low score. As the parties do not account for 100 per cent of the votes, we also calculate the adjusted vote shares by recomputing the vote percentage by dividing each by the sum and multiplying by 100. The next step, which is also taken in the case of a two-party system, is to determine which party has more than 50 per cent of the votes: the median party. After these steps have been taken

Table 7.4   *Regression analysis on (combined) models that predict the party emphasis on four policy areas (n = 1991)*

Y: Party emphasis on	X	Beta	t	Sig. t	Adj. R²
Market economy	Median voter	0.29	12.5	0.00	0.23
	Left–right	0.38	16.6	0.00	
Planned economy	Median voter	0.37	15.9	0.00	0.22
	Left–right	−0.26	−11.4	0.00	
Welfare	Median voter	0.52	24.8	0.00	0.37
	Left–right	−0.27	−13.0	0.00	
International peace	Median voter	0.44	19.7	0.00	0.27
	Left–right	−0.28	−12.4	0.00	

Left–right: (per104+per201+per203+per305+per401+per402+per407+per414 +per505+per601+per603+per605+per606)–(per103+per105+per106+per107 +per403+per404+per406+per412+per413+per504+per506+per701+per202).

Planned economy: per403+per404+per412.

Market economy: per401+per414.

Welfare: per503+per504.

International peace: per102+per105+per106.

The variable names per101 to per706 are explained in Budge et al. (2001) and in the file Chapter7.sps

n = 1991 election years in 25 countries (the full data set).

we are ready to calculate L, C, F and W. The main results for Sweden (1948–98) are reported below as an example (Budge et al., 2001):

1948 −20.20	1964 −31.67	1979 −15.22	1991 −2.59
1952 −13.74	1968 −34.09	1982 −17.12	1994 26.60
1956 −30.37	1970 −38.19	1985 −13.14	1998 −1.71
1958 −5.66	1973 −6.38	1988 −21.34	
1960 −34.59	1976 −11.03		

Note that these computations have to be adapted for each particular party system and each different policy scale (Y) in order to correct for different numbers and positions of parties on the policy scale. Assuming that the given example in the file Chapter7.sps gives an impression of how the median voter position is computed, we continue with the data analysis on the determinants of party responsiveness (Budge et al., 2001; McDonald et al., 2004).

The second independent variable is the left–right ideology scale in Budge et al. (2001). As indicated above, the models that represent the main theoretical positions in the debate on party responsiveness are (Y = the party emphasis policy area):

- the Downsian model: $Y = a + (b \times \text{median voter position}) + e$;
- the salience model: $Y = a + (b \times \text{ideology}) + e$;
- the combined model: $Y = a + (b \times \text{ideology}) + (b \times \text{median voter position}) + e$.

The Downsian and salience models are quite unequivocal. The combined model combines the other two models by predicting that the emphasis on a policy area is a function of both ideology and public opinion. Table 7.4 shows the results of a regression analysis on the combined models for four policy areas. The results on the basis of these computations do provide more support for the Downsian model than for the saliency model. Although parties are to a large extent ideologically driven, there is also a consistent and far-reaching party responsiveness to shifting problem intensities and voter preferences.

We conclude that voter preferences do affect party priorities (in general) to a certain extent. But at the same time the role of parties is more encompassing than just to reflect what the voters want. The saliency theory of issues argues that non-responsiveness is electorally more rewarding than responsiveness, as rigidity makes parties reliable and credible in the eyes of the voters (McDonald et al., 2004). Other theories, like the cartel theory, explain non-responsiveness out of the integration of the party elites within the state so that parties have lost their feeling for society. The welfare state regime explanation explains it by picturing parties as bounded actors operating within the historical boundaries of welfare state regimes. So, we conclude that what various theories on party behaviour have predicted has been only partly confirmed in the regression analysis, and it is not possible to conclude solely on the basis of the regression analysis whether or not these theories provide empirically sound and plausible alternative explanations (i.e. too many theories fitting too few data).

7.3 CONCLUSIONS

In this chapter we have discussed aspects of the 'input side' of the chain of democratic control and command, with an emphasis on electoral and party change. We have shown that in order to be able to analyse electoral change we need a range of indicators that capture the phenomena under study. As the comparative method aims at explaining cross-national variations, we need a comparative research question and research design in order to be able to come up with plausible explanations. Table 7.5 gives an overview of the main research questions, research designs and research answers that are discussed in this chapter.

Chapters 1–6 have focused on the theoretical, methodological and technical aspects of comparative research, of which several are summarized by the first two columns of Table 7.5. In this chapter we have applied comparative methods and statistics to research questions which relate to changes in the preferences and behaviour of voters and parties. In doing so, we have illustrated that the quality of the research answer strongly depends on the preceding steps in the research: the research question, the hypotheses, the operationalizations, the specification of the model, the interpretation of the results. The most important guide in this process is theory, i.e. a clear and consistent set of hypotheses that guides the researcher through all the necessary steps. These steps are part of an iterative process of choice (how to operationalize and analyse) and interpretation (how to make sense of the results by relating them to existing knowledge). Starting from

Table 7.5 *Overview and examples of the main stages in comparative research on the preferences and behaviour of parties and voters*

Research question	Research design	Research answer
§7.1.2. What variations in electoral volatility are there?	Operationalization of Y; indicators of change; examination of trends by means of descriptive techniques such as graphical presentations	The aggregated, country-specific and party family-specific results show cross-national and cross-temporal variations which can only be explained by means of theory
§7.1.3. How do we explain variations in electoral volatility?	Operationalization and modelling of X and Y; time series and regression analysis	Variations in electoral change are partly explained by institutional and socio-organizational factors. The plausibility of this answer depends on the specification of the model that is used to analyse the data
§7.2.3. What are the underlying dimensions of party competition?	Conceptualization and operationalization of issues that belong to dimensions of political conflict, and application of factor analysis to them	The left–right dimension is one of the most prominent conflict dimensions. This answer is based on the interpretation of factor scores
§7.2.4. What drives parties: voter preferences or ideology?	Operationalization of median voter positions and party emphasis on dimensions of party competition (left versus right, market versus planning) plus the modelling of X and Y	Both voters and ideology seem to be important drivers for parties. There is more than one theory to interpret this result

one and the same research question there is more than one road to a plausible answer. This gives the researcher the freedom to explore but it also necessitates a full and detailed elaboration of all the steps taken. A short checklist which examines whether these steps are correctly taken includes the following:

1 The research question. Does it refer to variations in a dependent variable and to possible explanations of these variations, e.g. by means of hypotheses or assumptions?

2 The research design. Are the cases properly selected, the variables clearly operationalized and integrated in a well-specified model? Is the choice of the technique related to the levels of measurement and the type of research question?

3 The research answer. Do the interpretations and conclusions give a correct and plausible answer to the research question, and are they related to the findings of similar research projects?

7.4 Endmatter

Topics highlighted

- The problem of electoral change: how to measure and model it with the help of regression analysis:

  What variations in electoral volatility are there?
  How do we explain variations in electoral volatility?

- The problem of party change: how to measure and model it with the help of factor and scalability analysis:

  What are the underlying dimensions of party competition?
  What drives parties: voter preferences or ideology?

Exercises

The exercises cover some of the main subjects in this chapter. The formulated research questions in the exercises are suited to the writing of a short research note. Exercise 7.1 focuses on the problem of the research answer. The other exercises focus on statistical and methodological aspects of the research design.

- 7.1. Measuring electoral change

Files: bartmair.sav, nias.sav, poL4.sav.

How correct is Bartolini's and Mair's finding that there is not much change in western European party systems? Answer this question by means of an extensive descriptive analysis (by examining the trends and variations of crucial party system variables).
    Suggested steps: 1. Select several indicators of electoral change. 2. Examine the trends of these indicators by means of 'plot' or 'graph'. 3. Examine the country-specific trends by comparing the period before and after 1970, with the help of the command 'aggregate'.
    Background reading: Bartolini and Mair (1990), Pennings (1998b).

- 7.2. Modelling electoral change

Files: poL4.sav, nias.sav.

Construct a multivariate regression equation that explains the variation of the block volatility of left parties. One assumption behind this equation is that the vote share of left parties is more stable when their rank-and-file are well organized (and when these organizations are incorporated in cooperative forms of decision-making). Test your model by means of multiple regression. Integrate the relevant scores of the regression analysis into a table that is understandable for outsiders. Extend your model by introducing an interaction term into the equation. Examine whether the assumptions for regression are violated. Concentrate on linearity and multicollinearity (see Chapter 6 for those tests).

Perform also a second analysis, this time for total volatility as the dependent variable. Integrate one interaction term into your model. Study the residuals of the total volatility model. Are there significant outliers?

Suggested steps: 1. Formulate several hypotheses that can be modelled and that explain either left volatility or total volatility. 2. Add an interaction effect to the hypotheses. 3. Test the models (check the violation of assumptions, especially tolerance).

Background reading: Bartolini and Mair (1990), Mair (2002).

- 7.3. The Budge et al. left–right scale

Perform a reliability test on the Klingemann et al. (1994) scale. This scale was originally computed as:

> compute left
> = per103 + per105 + per106 + per107 + per202 + per403 + per404
> + per406 + per412 + per413 + per504 + per506 + per701.
> compute right
> = per104 + per201 + per203 + per305 + per401 + per402 + per407
> + per414 + per505 + per601 + per603 + per605 + per606.
> compute scale = right–left
> variable label scale 'left–right scale Budge et al. 2001'

The data are included in Budge et al. (2001).

Suggested steps: 1. Recode the issues into the same direction (namely either left or right). 2. Perform the reliability analysis by dropping variables with the highest score on 'alpha if item deleted'.

Background reading: Budge et al. (2001).

- 7.4. The Median voter position

Compute the median voter position on the left–right scale position for at least one election year in both a multi-party system and a two-party system. You can compute the median voter positions manually or with the help of SPSS.

Suggested steps: 1. Determine which party is the median party. 2. Calculate L (the lower ideological score), C (the cumulative frequency), F (vote share of the interval containing median), W (width of this interval). 3. Insert the numbers into the formula.

Background reading: Budge et al. (2001), Kim and Fording (1998).

Further reading

- *General*: Bartolini and Mair (1990).
- *Specific*: Budge et al. (2001), Laver (2001), Laver and Budge (1992).

Note

1 This use of factor analysis is only sound when there are no issues involved that are typical of parties in the middle of the party system. If this is the case, then factor analysis will produce two related left–right dimensions whereas only one is present. Therefore, one has to delete the issues in the middle before one starts this type of analysis (van der Brug, 2001).

How decisions are made

8.1 Introduction

Chapter 7 indicated that the behaviour of voters and parties should be understood within their institutional context. In this chapter several of these contexts (and relations between them) will be explored. As institutions shape the behaviour of actors, these institutions are important for the decision-making process. This chapter, like all the chapters in this part of the book, aims to improve the understanding and the accessibility of data and the techniques. We will not discuss all the background to and details of the techniques (this has already been done in Chapters 4–6) but focus on how to use and apply them within cross-national research designs that aim at answering substantial research questions.

We focus on the institutional and constitutional foundations of modern democracies. These foundations are summarized by Lijphart (1999). This chapter starts with an overview of Lijphart's operationalization of the main characteristics and variations of political institutions in modern democracies (Section 8.2). Special attention will be given to the factor analysis that Lijphart uses and that leads to the division between consensus and majoritarian democracies. This division is crucial – in his ideas – for understanding variations in political behaviour and the functioning of democracy.

In the following sections we will explore the working, trends and effects of several institutions that are central to the functioning of democracies. A good overview of the main concepts from a comparative perspective can be found in Gallagher et al. (2001). See also our definitions of the basic terms in Box 8.1. First, we will discuss the party system typologies and ways to study party system change (Section 8.3). Party systems can be seen as the main institutional environment of party competition and cooperation. We will compare the party system typologies of Lijphart and Sartori which originate from the same period but are very different in their assumptions. Sartori (1976) assumes that sooner or later pluralism inevitably leads to instability. Lijphart (1977) emphasizes the possibility that elites may handle conflicts properly so that plural societies remain stable.

Box 8.1 Glossary of basic terms

- *Consensus democracy*: the set of intertwined institutional arrangements that enhance elite cooperation and coalition-building in the parliamentary arena.
- *Minimal winning coalitions* (MWC): cabinets that are based on more than 50% of the parliamentary seats ('winning') and that are devoid of unnecessary partners ('minimal').
- *Median legislator*: this median position is found by adding up the number of seats that each party controls from the left to the right.
- *Distributional coalitions*: the alignment of pressure groups at various levels of government in ways that are Pareto suboptimal (i.e. at the expense of collective welfare).
- *Corporatism*: institutionalized cooperation ('concentration') of trade union federations, employers' organizations and the state by means of non-parliamentary consultation in order to avoid or reduce suboptimal (zero-sum) outcomes of policy.
- *Federalism*: a state structure with a high degree of geographical autonomy *vis-à-vis* the political centre, which is expressed by means of constitutionally sharing power between the federal state and its parts.
- Centralism: the degree to which aspects of policy-making are directed from the central political institutions.
- *Institutional autonomy* (or devolution index): the degree to which decentralized governing units, like local communities, have powers to control policy-making independently of the centre (i.e. forms of self-regulation).

Why do party systems matter? They have an enduring impact on party behaviour, both during and after elections, which leads to different types of interaction between parties. In Section 8.4 we will therefore discuss the different forms of cabinet formation and functioning of government with reference to coalition theories that make predictions on the composition of governments given the vote shares of parties and/or their policy stance. We will apply regression analysis (both linear and logistic) to the possibility that minority governments are formed as well as to the duration of governments in general.

A related topic is the degree and nature of interest intermediation. In Section 8.5 the focus will be on the concept of corporatism (i.e. the structure of interest intermediation), its operationalization and its relationship with consensus democracy. It will be shown that both concepts should be distinguished because they are too different to be amalgamated into one score, like the one that was proposed by Lijphart and Crepaz (1991).

There are more institutions which affect the nature and degree of state intervention and policy formation. The degree and nature of regional and institutional autonomy are indicated by the federal or unitary state structure, in particular since the implementation is differently organized. In Section 8.6 the variations and policy effects of federalism, centralism and autonomy are discussed and analysed with the help of regression analysis. Executive–legislative relations are also crucial determinants of decision-making because the separation of powers is differently organized. Two major institutional variants of these relationships are presidentialism and parliamentarism. Section 8.7 analyses the variations of presidentialism and its effects on democratic performance. This is done by applying the most different design (comparing the democratic performance of all systems in the world) and the comparative case study (explaining the special character of American presidentialism).

This chapter ends with a set of exercises that relates to the subsequent paragraphs. These exercises may help students to assess the ins and outs of the application of statistical techniques to the working, effects and change of political and socio-economic institutions.

8.2 Types of Democracies

This section focuses on the main features of democratic political systems in the world, on the basis of quantitative and statistical aspects of identifying system properties. The basic institutional framework that structures the decision-making process is the type of democratic system. Lijphart (1999) describes two extremes, majoritarian democracies versus consensus democracies, which are presented as 'ideal types' (i.e. sketched in their archetypal or perfect form). These types are described on the basis of ten differences with regard to the majoritarian and consensus principles which are listed in Table 8.1. All ten variables are expected to be closely related because they belong to anti-poles.

The first dimension (executives–parties) groups five characteristics of the arrangement of executive power, the party and electoral systems, and interest

Table 8.1 *Overview of the ten characteristics of majoritarian versus consensus democracies*

Majoritarianism	Consensus democracy	Indicator
Executives–parties dimension		
1 Concentration of executive power in single-party majority cabinets	Executive power-sharing in broad multi-party coalitions	Proportion of time during which minimal winning cabinets and one-party cabinets were in power
2 Executive dominance	Executive–legislative balance of power	Executive dominance: average cabinet durability
3 Two-party system	Multi-party system	Effective number of parties: Laakso–Taagepera index
4 Majoritarian and disproportional electoral system	Proportional representation	Difference between vote and seat shares of parties, aggregated according to Gallagher's index of disproportionality
5 Pluralist interest group system	Corporatist interest group system	Extent of interest group pluralism (Siaroff index)
Federal–unitary dimension		
1 Unitary and centralized government	Federal and decentralized government	Index of degree of federalism and decentralization
2 Unicameral legislature	Bicameral legislature	Index of bicameralism
3 Flexible constitution	Rigid constitution	Index of constitutional rigidity
4 Judicial review by legislation	Judicial review by supreme or constitutional court	Index of the strength of judicial review
5 Central banks dependent on executive	Central bank independence	Mean of three indices of central bank independence

Source: Lijphart (1999).

groups. Most of the five differences on the second dimension seem to be associated with the contrast between federalism and unitary government, so that Lijphart calls it the federal–unitary dimension. He signals that it is the weakest one, probably because it is not fully clear how the five items fit into it and it is hard to explain why this dimension should be so clearly distinct from the other dimension. He finds a persuasive explanation of the two-dimensional pattern in the distinction between 'collective agency' and 'shared responsibility', on the one hand, and divided agencies and responsibilities, on the other. These are both

Table 8.2 *Varimax orthogonal rotated factor matrix of the ten variables distinguishing majoritarian from consensus democracy in 36 democracies, 1945–96*

Variable	Factor I	Factor II
Effective number of parliamentary parties	−0.90	0.02
Minimal winning one-party cabinets	0.93	−0.07
Executive dominance	0.74	−0.10
Electoral disproportionality	0.72	0.09
Interest group pluralism	0.78	−0.01
Federalism–decentralization	−0.28	0.86
Bicameralism	0.06	0.74
Constitutional rigidity	−0.05	0.71
Judicial review	0.20	0.73
Central bank independence	−0.07	0.71

Note: The factor analysis is a principal components analysis with eigen values over 1.0 extracted.

forms of diffusion of power, but the first dimension of consensus democracy with its multi-party face-to-face interactions within cabinets, etc., has a close fit with the collective responsibility form. In contrast, both the four federalist characteristics and the role of central banks fit the format of diffusion by means of institutional separation of power. Viewed from this perspective, the first dimension could also be labelled the joint-power dimension and the second the divided-power dimension.

Lijphart summarizes the relationships among the ten variables by means of factor analysis (see Part II). The same two clusters seem to emerge from this analysis (Table 8.2). The factor loadings are very high within each of the two clusters and much lower in most cases outside of the clusters. The percentage of minimal winning one-party cabinets again turns out to be the strongest variable in the first dimension. The effective number of parties is an almost equally strong element. The federalism variable emerges once more as the strongest element in the second dimension with a factor loading of 0.86. The remaining factor loadings within the two clusters are lower but still strong.

The two-dimensional pattern formed by the ten basic variables allows us to summarize where the 36 individual countries are situated between majoritarian and consensus democracy. Their characteristics on each of the two sets of five variables can be averaged so as to form just two summary characteristics, and these can be used to place each of the democracies on the two-dimensional conceptual map of democracy shown in Figure 8.1. The horizontal axis represents the executives–parties dimension and the vertical axis the federal–unitary dimension. Each unit on these axes represents one standard deviation; high values indicate majoritarianism and low values consensus.

In Lijphart's view, most of the prototypical cases of majoritarian and consensus democracy are in their expected positions on the map. The United Kingdom and New Zealand are in the top right-hand corner. The United Kingdom is slightly more majoritarian on the executives–parties dimension. Switzerland is, as expected, in the bottom left-hand corner but not quite as far

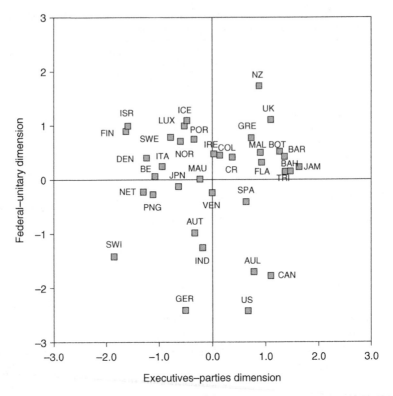

Figure 8.1 *Two-dimensional conceptual map of democracy*

down as several other countries, mainly due to its one non-consensual characteristic – the absence of judicial review. It is still the clearest consensual prototype, however, because it is further from the centre on both dimensions than Germany. Belgium is the one exemplar case not to be in an extreme position, mainly because it only became fully federal in 1993; it does, however, have a strong consensual position on the executives–parties dimension.

In Lijphart's view the two-dimensional map also reveals prototypes of the two combinations of consensus and majoritarian characteristics. In the top left-hand corner, Israel represents the combination of consensus democracy on the executives–parties dimension but, albeit somewhat less strongly, majoritarianism on the federal–unitary dimension (an unwritten constitution and a unicameral parliament, moderated, however, by intermediate characteristics with regard to federalism and central bank independence). In the bottom right-hand corner, Canada is the strongest candidate for the opposite prototype of majoritarianism on the executives–parties and consensus on the federal–unitary dimension: on the one hand, dominant one-party cabinets, a roughly two-and-a-third-party system, plurality elections (the winner takes all), and interest group pluralism, but, on the other hand, strong federalism and judicial review, a rigid constitution, an independent central bank, and a bicameral parliament (albeit of only medium strength). Germany's location on the clearly consensual side of both dimensions confirms that it is a 'grand coalition state' (Schmidt, 2002).

On the correspondence between the conceptual and geographical maps Lijphart concludes that such a relationship exists as far as the consensus side of the executives–parties dimension is concerned: most continental European countries are located on the left-hand side of the map. On the right-hand side, the three Latin American democracies are close together and only slightly to the right of the centre. Considerably further to the right, the four Caribbean countries are located near one another. But most of the countries on the right-hand side of the conceptual map are geographically distant from one another. Instead, the striking feature that many of these countries, including those in the Caribbean, have in common is that they are former British colonies. According to Lijphart, it is the presence or absence of a British political heritage that appears to explain the distribution on the left and right of the executives–parties dimension better than any geographical factor. According to others (e.g. Armingeon, 2002: 151) there is a clear geographical concentration since almost all consensus democracies appear to be located in Europe.

Although Lijphart argues that these empirical results confirm his theoretical assumptions, a quick examination of Table 8.3 reveals some problematic cases. This is especially true for the federal–unitary dimension which includes some non-federal countries like Spain, the Netherlands and Japan. Furthermore, a study of his conceptualization, operationalization and factor analysis shows that his interpretation is based on assumptions which are not necessarily adequate or the only ones that are plausible.

The main problem is that Lijphart's two-dimensional map is quite encompassing, and the federal–unitary dimension in particular is not (always) intrinsically related to the majoritarian–consensus divide (Armingeon, 2002: 149). This dimension includes variables such as unicameralism, fiscal centralization and constitutional flexibility which measure the degree to which segments are autonomous or minorities are protected. But also the executives–parties dimension includes variables that are not conditions for consensus democracy, such as executive dominance, since cabinet durability seems more likely to be an effect than a feature of democratic systems.

In addition, one might wonder if his polar approach to democracies is becoming (partly) outdated as most systems nowadays are (becoming) mixed systems (Dunleavy and Margetts, 1995). These mixed systems might not function according to most of Lijphart's descriptions. This confronts us with the changing conditions of consensus and majoritarian democracy. These changes can be examined by selecting the theoretically most convincing institutional variables and studying the developments over time. It can be argued that three factors are inextricably linked to the division between consensus and majoritarian democracy:

Table 8.3 *Factor scores of Lijphart's two basic dimensions of consensus democracy, 1945–96*

		Executives–parties dimension	Federal–unitary dimension
Consensual–federal			
SWI	Switzerland	1.88	1.44
NET	Netherlands	1.30	0.24
PNG	Papua New Guinea	1.12	0.29
JPN	Japan	0.63	0.15
GER	Germany	0.52	2.44
AUT	Austria	0.34	1.04
MAU	Mauritius	0.24	0.01
IND	India	0.20	1.28
VEN	Venezuela	0.01	0.26
Consensual–unitary			
FIN	Finland	1.62	−0.89
ISR	Israel	1.60	−0.99
DEN	Denmark	1.25	−0.39
BEL	Belgium	1.09	−0.03
ITA	Italy	0.94	−0.23
SWE	Sweden	0.77	−0.78
NOR	Norway	0.59	−0.70
LUX	Luxembourg	0.51	−0.98
ICE	Iceland	0.49	−1.05
POR	Portugal	0.34	−0.73
Majoritarian–federal			
SPA	Spain	−0.64	0.44
US	United States	−0.66	2.45
AUL	Australia	−0.78	1.73
CAN	Canada	−1.09	1.82
Majoritarian–unitary			
IRE	Ireland	−0.04	−0.46
COL	Colombia	−0.14	−0.42
CR	Costa Rica	−0.38	−0.39
GRE	Greece	−0.74	−0.72
MAL	Malta	−0.90	−0.47
NZ	New Zealand	−0.90	−1.69
FRA	France	−0.94	−0.29
UK	United Kingdom	−1.12	−1.08
BOT	Botswana	−1.28	−0.47
BAR	Barbados	−1.36	−0.39
TRI	Trinidad	−1.38	−0.12
BAH	Bahamas	−1.49	−0.12
JAM	Jamaica	−1.59	−0.21

Extraction method: principal component analysis. Explained variance is 35.6% (executives–parties dimension) and 27.6% (federal–unitary dimension).

1   the degree of disproportionality;
2   the effective number of parties;
3   the type of government.

These three indicators have in common that they are related to the functioning of electoral systems. In proportional systems, we expect a high degree of proportionality, which enhances a high number of effective parties and thus (indirectly) the formation of coalition governments. In majoritarian systems, on the other hand, we expect the opposite: a low degree of proportionality, a low number of parties and majority governments.

Factor analysis can be used to combine these conditions for consensus and majoritarian democracy into one single factor score. First, the nominal variable type of government has to be recoded into a dichotomous (interval) variable with score 1 for the consensual types of government and 0 for the majoritarian ones (Woldendorp et al., 2000). The next step is to perform the factor analysis on the OECD data (1965–98, $n = 578$) which throws up one factor with an explained variance of 50%. The factor loadings are 0.76 for the type of government, 0.79 for the effective number of parties, and –0.56 for electoral disproportionality. These scores are in line with our expectations. A high factor score indicates favourable conditions for consensus democracy. On the basis of the constructed factor it is possible to examine trends by country or by clusters of countries. We refer to Exercise 8.1 for further details on this longitudinal approach (see also Pennings, 1997). By restricting the factor analysis to the three crucial indicators of consensus democracy, the outcomes of this analysis are easier to interpret as one factor is extracted instead of two.

In this section, we have questioned aspects of the operationalization and analysis of the conditions for consensus democracy. Nonetheless, the analysis of these data is still an effective way to get acquainted with the main characteristics of modern democracies. We have illustrated how a more pronounced longitudinal approach is possible with these data by means of factor analysis. This section also underlines the relevance of the 'checklist' at the end of Chapter 7 for the evaluation of research.

8.3 Party Systems

Party systems comprise different kinds of relationships between parties in terms of competition, coalitions and ideology, which lead to patterned interactions. A party system has certain properties that distinguish it from other party systems, e.g. the number of parties, electoral disproportionality, fragmentation, centripetal (towards the centre) or centrifugal (towards the extremes) party competition (Gallagher et al., 2001). Party systems structure the type of competition and representation, on the one hand, and the consensus-building and mode of governance, on the other hand.

Three main questions have dominated the party-system literature: What party systems are there? What countries are characterized by what systems? How do

Table 8.4 *Lijphart's typology of democratic systems*

Elite behaviour	Structure of society	
	Homogeneous	Plural
Coalescent	*Depoliticized* Austria (1966–)	*Consociational* Belgium, Netherlands, Switzerland, Austria (1945–66)
Adversarial	*Centripetal* Finland, Denmark, UK, USA, Norway, Sweden, West Germany	*Centrifugal* France, Italy, Canada

Source: Lijphart (1977).

Table 8.5 *Sartori's typology of party systems*

Ideological distance	Party system fragmentation	
	Low	High
Low	*Two-party* Canada, USA, Austria, UK	FRG, Switzerland, Netherlands, Denmark, Belgium, France V*
High	*Predominant* Norway, Sweden	*Extreme and polarized* Finland, Italy, France IV*

Source: Sartori (1976: 314).
*France IV and France V are the French Fourth and Fifth Republics (1946–58 and 1958 – present respectively).

party systems change over time? Party system typologies seek to answer the first two questions. We will concentrate here on two well-known typologies of Lijphart (Table 8.4) and Sartori (Table 8.5). For the use and limitations of typologies, we refer to Chapter 3.

In Sartori's typology the two dimensions are ideological distance between political parties and party-system fragmentation (indicated by the number of 'relevant parties' – parties with either coalition potential or blackmail potential; see Sartori, 1976: 121–3). These dimensions are dependent as they co-vary directly: the higher the number of parties, the larger the ideological distance – and consequently the range of the party system – is assumed to be (Sartori, 1976: 291). The number of parties and the ideological distance are positively correlated: Sartori expects more polarization in countries with a high number of parties. This linear correspondence between these two dimensions enables us to reformat Sartori's typology into a one-dimensional scale that combines the two original dimensions. In this new dimension, the predominant type (low number of parties and ideological distance) is the opposite of the polarized type (high number of parties and ideological distance).[1] This particular type of one-dimensional scale is also applied by Sartori himself (Sartori, 1976: 283). The resulting one-dimensional scale is incorporated into Table 8.6.

Table 8.6 *Typologies of party systems*

Sartori	Lijphart
Predominant Norway, Sweden	*Centrifugal* France, Italy
Two-party Austria, UK	*Centripetal* Finland, Denmark, Norway, Sweden, UK, West Germany, Ireland
Moderate multipartism Germany, Switzerland, Netherlands, Denmark, Belgium, France V*, Ireland	*Consociational* Austria, Belgium, Netherlands, Switzerland
Polarized Finland, Italy, France IV*	

Adapted from: Von Beyme (1985), Lange and Meadwell (1991), Keman (1995).
*France IV and France V are the French Fourth and Fifth Republics (1946–58 and 1958 – present respectively).

Lijphart's typology of democratic systems represents perhaps the most important alternative to Sartori's typology of party systems. Although Lijphart's typology is strictly speaking a classification of *democratic* systems, it has far-reaching implications for the ways in which party systems are assumed to function. Recall that Lijphart's main hypothesis is that segmental cleavages at the mass level can be overcome by elite cooperation (Lijphart, 1977). Lijphart proposed a typology that is based on the structure of society (homogeneous versus plural) and the behaviour of elites (coalescent versus adversarial). The elites behave in a cooperative and stabilizing manner by means of four practices: grand coalition, segmental autonomy, proportionality, and mutual veto. In Lijphart's typology the key category is the consociational type, as this type entails cooperation by segmental elites in spite of the deep cleavages separating the segments (Lijphart, 1977: 53).

The Sartori and the Lijphart typologies seem to be quite at odds with each other: in several instances where Lijphart predicts stability, Sartori predicts instability, and vice versa. One example is provided by the countries that fall into the category of 'moderate multi-partism'. According to Sartori these countries are likely to be politically unstable because of their fragmented party systems. Lijphart, however, asserts that these countries may be stable democracies if, and only if, the elites are cooperative. As both typologies can hardly (in their original format) be equally valid at the same time, it is interesting to test their predictive and explanatory capacity just by comparing them in this respect.

There are several tests that could be imagined for the purpose of testing the validity of both typologies, i.e. the degree to which the theoretical assumptions underlying the typologies match the empirical characteristics of countries. We use regression analysis to study the interrelation between the party-system scales of Lijphart and Sartori, on the one hand, and a variety of dependent variables that are related to the vote-, office- and policy-seeking behaviour of political parties and to characteristics of party systems, on the other hand. In so doing, we extend the use of typologies from solely explaining stability to a wider range of party-system characteristics.

The first step is to change the original nominal party-system scores into new ordinal ones. Ordinal scoring implies that the two-dimensional typologies are reformatted into a one-dimensional rank ordering of countries. Sartori's rank orders become an indicator of 'multi-partism' (corresponding to the degree of polarization) and Lijphart's dimension can be interpreted as 'degree of coalescent elite behaviour' (which – at least in theory – should linearly correspond to stability). The analysis is based on the multiple R-scores (the square root of R^2) on the basis of regressions of the party-system scales (in dummy format) on variables that are related to votes, policy and office. The highest rank-order scores serve as the reference group in the regression analysis, which can be omitted and to which the other groups are compared. These dependent variables figure prominently in the literature as characteristics related to the functioning of party systems.

In total, 17 hypotheses are tested. For every variable a hypothesis has been formulated on the basis of Lijphart's and Sartori's assumptions. These hypotheses simply express whether we expect no relation or a positive or negative relation between the independent and dependent variables. This is done for both the 1960s and the 1980s, because the predictions may hold better for the 1960s than for the 1980s. The results are reported in Table 8.7. The variables selected cover the features of party government (e.g. colour, duration, reason for termination), party systems (e.g. the type of leadership, the number of parties), the electoral system (e.g. disproportionality), interest group intermediation (e.g. organizational unity) and voter–party relationships (e.g. membership rates). When the real-world relations that are expressed by means of the multiple R-scores match the hypotheses, then we may conclude that the typologies generate reliable predictions. The results are quite promising for both typologies. Three hypotheses that are related to the theory of Sartori are not confirmed (namely CPGDEF, POLARSYS and ELSYS). In the case of Lijphart's theory, one or two hypotheses are not confirmed (CPGDEF and NRPTIES). These results imply that both typologies, although they were devised in the mid-1970s, are still useful tools for designating relevant party-system properties and formulating relevant consequences. Sartori's typology has the disadvantage that the basic hypothesis on polarization (POLARSYS) is not confirmed. Thus, Lijphart's theory is more fully confirmed by the data.

This section focused on the research question of whether the theoretical assumptions underlying party system typologies match the empirical characteristics of countries. The answer to this question resulted from several steps. First, we made the theoretical assumptions explicit and operationalized the relevant empirical characteristics of party systems. Second, we used regression analysis in order to examine to what extent the observed features of party systems correspond with the hypothesized traits. In doing so, this section has illustrated the central importance of hypotheses for doing comparative political research.

Table 8.7 *A test of Sartori's and Lijphart's predictions of party-system properties on the basis of their typologies (multiple R)*

	Sartori			Lijphart		
Typology	hypothesis	1960s	1980s	hypothesis	1960s	1980s
Colour of party government (CPGDEF)	$R = 0$	−0.50	−0.33	$R = 0$	0.35	0.23
Cabinet duration (DUR)	$R < 0$	−0.32	−0.35	$R > 0$	0.28	0.33
Reason for termination (dummy) (RFT_REC)	$R > 0$	0.15	0.35	$R < 0$	−0.20	−0.29
Type of government (TOGORI)	$R > 0$	0.48	0.54	$R > 0$	0.56	0.39
Polarization (POLARSYS)	$R > 0$	−0.41	−0.25	$R < 0$	−0.11	−0.42
Type of leadership (LEADERSH)	$R < 0$	−0.50	−0.50	$R > 0$	0.72	0.72
Number of issue dimensions (ISSUEDIM)	$R > 0$	0.50	0.50	$R > 0$	−0.42	−0.42
Number of parties (NRPTIES)	$R > 0$	0.70	0.49	$R > 0$	−0.43	−0.35
Effective number of parties (EFFNOP)	$R > 0$	0.62	0.55	$R > 0$	0.26	0.38
Fragmentation of votes (FRAGVOT)	$R > 0$	0.70	0.55	$R > 0$	0.17	0.25
Organizational unity (UNITY)	$R < 0$	−0.39	−0.39	$R > 0$	0.73	0.73
Union density (DENSITY)	$R < 0$	−0.60	−0.39	$R > 0$	0.58	0.57
Electoral system (ELSYS)	$R > 0$	0.37	0.37	$R > 0$	0.46	0.46
Total volatility (TOTVOL)	$R > 0$	0.45	0.22	$R < 0$	−0.47	−0.28
Disproportionality (DISPRDEF)	$R < 0$	−0.20	−0.42	$R < 0$	−0.33	−0.35
% Party membership (PERCMEM)	$R < 0$	−0.46	−0.50	$R > 0$	0.21	0.22
% No attachment (NOATTCH)	$R < 0$		−0.36	$R < 0$		−0.31

The scores are multiple R-scores based on regression analysis on the country-by-year data set. The dependent variables are listed in the left-hand column of the table. The independent variables are dummy variables that assign a 0 or a 1 to the countries for each category of the typologies. The sign is added on the basis of separate correlations. $N = 598$: country-by-year format (western Europe). The sources and operationalizations are explained in Appendix 8.1. The hypotheses are implied (not given!) by Sartori's and Lijphart's typologies and assume either no relationship ($R = 0$), a positive relationship ($R > 0$) or a negative relationship ($R < 0$). Adapted from Pennings (1998b).

Without hypotheses it is impossible to explain or even examine variations and trends in party-system characteristics.

8.4 Cabinet Formation and Duration

Coalition theories try to predict what governments will be formed if and when the vote shares of parties and/or their policy stances are known. What coalitions are formed is not totally accidental, as many coalition theories have shown (Laver and Schofield, 1990). Most of these theories are one-dimensional (left–right). Only recently have multi-dimensional theories been tested (Austen-Smith and Banks, 1988; Laver and Budge, 1992; Laver and Shepsle, 1996). Five different types of coalitions are predicted by different one-dimensional theories on the basis of three criteria: the number of parliamentary seats, the policy preferences and the number of (potential) cabinet parties. The combinations among A, B, C, D, E refer to the example in Table 8.8.

- *Minimal winning coalitions* (MWC) or bare majority cabinets are coalitions of two or more parties that are winning and minimal (ABC, ADE, BCD, BE, CE). The term 'minimal' means here that only those parties are included that are necessary to form a majority government. 'Winning' means that the coalition must be based on more than 50 per cent of the parliamentary seats. The underlying assumption of the MWC theory, as first proposed by Riker (1962), is that political parties are power maximizers and solely office-seeking. Power refers here to participation in government with as many portfolios or ministries as possible. One shortcoming of Riker's theory is that his predictions are not very precise, as they predict several simultaneous outcomes.
- *Minimum size coalitions* resemble Riker's definition, but this type of coalition is more precise, as the cabinet should be based on the narrowest possible parliamentary majority (ADE). Parties would prefer this specific type of coalition, as costs of sharing portfolios are minimized.
- *Coalitions with the smallest number of parties* ('bargaining proposition'): this prediction assumes that a coalition is more easily formed with the smallest number of parties bargaining (BE, CE).
- *Minimal range coalitions*: coalitions will form among parties with similar policy preferences (ABC, BCD, CE). This type of coalition differs fundamentally from the first three coalitions in that the element of policy preferences is introduced. The 'range' refers here to the policy distance between parties. A smaller range increases the likelihood of cooperating and forming a government.
- *Minimal connected winning coalitions*, as introduced by Axelrod: coalitions are formed that are connected (adjacent on the policy scale) and devoid of unnecessary partners (ABC, BCD, CDE). The theory is a combination of the minimal range assumption and the Riker principle.

The best predictions are made by the 'policy-based theories' (about 50 per cent of the coalitions are correctly predicted; see Lijphart, 1999). This empirical advantage is also theoretically understandable. Riker's utility-maximizing principle ignores the possibility of minority governments and also the possibility that parties might prefer to join the opposition as this may be electorally more profitable. Hence, we see a trade-off between parsimony and plausibility here: the Riker model is too parsimonious to be plausible.

However, the predictive capabilities of the policy-based theories are also modest. One weakness is that only one dimension, the left–right scale, is used to determine the policy distances between parties. Additionally, most policy-based theories also handle the size principle, but this principle is not always valid. Some pivotal parties, for example, which play a crucial role in coalition building,

Table 8.8   *Overview of the 25 possible coalitions in a situation with five parties*

Party:	A Left	B	C	D	E Right	
Seats:	8	21	26	12	33	
Party	Seats					Total seats
1 A, D	8	12				20
2 A, B	8	21				29
3 B, D	21	12				33
4 A, C	8	26				34
5 C, D	26	12				38
6 A, E	8	33				41
7 A, B, D	8	21	12			41
8 D, E	12	33				45
9 A, C, D	8	26	12			46
10 C, B	26	21				47
11 A, D, E	8	12	33			53
12 B, E	21	33				54
13 A, B, C	8	21	26			55
14 B, C, D	21	26	12			59
15 C, E	26	33				59
16 A, B, E	8	21	33			62
17 B, D, E	21	12	33			66
18 A, C, E	8	26	33			67
19 A, B, C, D	8	21	26	12		67
20 C, D, E	26	12	33			71
21 B, D, E, A	21	12	33	8		74
22 B, C, E	21	26	33			80
23 A, B, C, E	8	21	26	33		88
24 B, C, D, E	21	26	12	33		92
25 A, B, C, D, E	8	21	26	12	33	100

Adapted from Lijphart (1984: 48).

may prefer to form larger coalitions as this increases their potential to impose their preferences on their coalition partners because they are able to govern without one of the partners.

Empirically, minimal winning cabinets (that are based on the size principle) are prevalent in New Zealand, Luxembourg, the UK, Ireland, Iceland, Canada, Austria, Australia, Norway, Japan, Germany, Belgium, Denmark and Sweden. Oversized cabinets (that include more parties than necessary for a bare majority) are prevalent in Switzerland, Israel, France, the Netherlands, Italy and Finland. Of course, these are only major trends as both types may be present in particular countries.

Why does this pattern occur? According to Lijphart there is a strong relationship with the degree of organized pluralism – the number of cleavages in a country. Minimal winning cabinets are a characteristic of the Westminster model of democracy; oversized cabinets are more typical of the consensus model. But, as indicated before, there are exceptions.

Table 8.9 *Prediction set with different assumptions: a hypothetical example*

	Government composition	Seats	Riker	Axelrod	Viability	Median legislator
1	A	20			*	
2	B	20			*	
3	C	20			*	*
4	D	20			*	
5	E	20			*	
6	A, B	40			*	
7	A, C	40				
8	A, D	40				
9	A, E	40				
10	B, C	40			*	*
11	B, D	40			*	
12	B, E	40			*	
13	C, D	40			*	*
14	C, E	40			*	
15	D, E	40			*	
16	A, B, C	60	*	*	*	*
17	A, B, D	60	*			
18	A, B, E	60	*			
19	B, C, D	60	*	*	*	*
20	B, C, E	60	*			
21	C, D, E	60	*	*	*	*
22	C, D, A	60	*			
23	D, E, A	60	*			
24	D, E, B	60	*			
25	E, A, C	60	*			
26	A, B, C, D	80				
27	A, B, C, E	80				
28	B, C, D, E	80				
29	C, D, E, A	80				
30	D, E, A, B	80				
31	A, B, C, D, E	100				
Predicted coalitions			10	3	12	6

Source: Bergman (1995). The Riker, Axelrod, viability and median legislator criteria are explained in the text. An asterisk indicates that such a criterion is met.

Table 8.9 presents an alternative view on coalition theory by showing the 'prediction sets' of two alternative criteria. One is the viability criterion that drops the traditional assumption that cabinet parties need to be represented by at least 50 per cent of the seats in parliament. Instead, the viability criterion calls a cabinet viable if it will survive a vote of confidence. Thus, minority cabinets may also be viable. The other criterion is that the party that controls the median legislator is expected to be a crucial party in the process of cabinet formation. Thus, the assumption is that only cabinets will be formed that include this party. In Table 8.9 the parties are aligned on a left–right dimension in the order of A (furthest to the left) to E (furthest to the right). Four different assumptions are compared:

1 Riker's criterion: only those cabinets are formed that are based on more than 50 per cent of the parliamentary seats ('winning') and that are devoid of unnecessary partners ('minimal') ($n = 10$). One-third of all possible government combinations are included in the prediction set. Fifteen combinations are excluded because they do not form a majority. Another six coalitions are excluded because they are 'oversized'.

2 Axelrod's criterion: coalitions are formed that are connected and devoid of unnecessary partners ($n = 3$).

3 Viability criterion: selects cabinets with adjacent positions on the left–right scales, including the single parties that are capable of running a cabinet ($n = 12$).

4 The median legislator criterion selects the party that controls the median legislator and also all cabinets that include this party, provided that the coalition partners are adjacent on the left–right scale ($n = 6$).

It seems from Table 8.9 that there is a difference between the traditional criteria and the criteria that put the majority threshold aside. When the traditional criterion of winning size is dropped, the prediction set becomes huge. In its original formulation, the viability criterion assumed that a new government must have at least majority support in the parliament. More recently this criterion was reformulated to one of being able to survive a vote of confidence in the parliament (Laver and Schofield, 1990: 66; Budge and Keman, 1990: 34). The viability criterion drops the 'must contain an absolute majority' while keeping the assumptions that we should normally not expect oversized coalitions and that we should expect parties which are adjacent in policy space to form coalitions. The phenomenon that parties sometimes form minority governments can be explained by the 'party goals theory' of Kaare Strøm (see Chapter 7). If a party believes that its voters are going to disapprove of a particular coalition and it might be able to influence policy from its position in parliament, this diminishes the party's desire to get into government. Predictive theories should be as precise as possible. As the viability criterion selects 12 possible coalitions, it is vital to find a way to narrow this prediction set. Bergman suggests one way to do this, namely by predicting that the party that is in control of the median legislator will be decisive for the outcome of the government formation process. The median legislator is found by adding the number of seats that each party controls from the left to the right (or in the reverse order). In the example of Table 8.10 the Social Democrats hold the median legislator after the Danish elections of 1966. In the hypothetical example of Table 8.9 it is assumed that only coalitions will form that include party C (which controls the median legislator), which seems a plausible assumption (Laver and Budge, 1992).

One of the weakest aspects of traditional coalition theories is the (implicit) assumption of the majority threshold, namely that governments are only viable if they control more than 50 per cent of the seats. This assumption does not match with the frequency of minority cabinets. When one wants to drop the 50 per cent threshold for viability, one consequently has to formulate a new conceptualization of what viability means. This is done by Kaare Strøm who formulated a *rational choice* theory on the phenomenon of minority governments. One of his hypotheses

Table 8.10 *One-dimensional view of the Danish party system, 1966*

Left–right	Party	No. of seats
L	Socialist People's Party (SFP)	20
	Social Democrats (SD)	69
	Radical Liberals (RV)	13
	Liberals (V)	34
R	Christian People's Party (KPF)	35
	Others	8
Total		179

Source: Laver and Schofield (1990: 112).

is that political parties are constantly weighting the costs and benefits of being in government. In cases where the costs of governing are higher than the costs of being an opposition party, it is expected that the rise of a minority government is more likely than in other cases. In this way, viability is disconnected from the number of seats and connected to a larger range of factors that relates to the costs and benefits of governing. Strøm (1990b: Chapter 3) selects ten variables that in particular might influence the rise of minority governments:

- *Opposition influence*: a five-point index based on the properties of parliamentary committees. Hypothesis: the greater the potential influence of the opposition, the lower the relative benefits of governing and the higher the probability of minority governments.
- *Electoral salience*: the identifiability of viable government alternatives and the proximity of the formed governments to general elections. Hypothesis: the higher the electoral salience, the better the chance for minority governments.
- *Volatility*: the electoral volatility between successive elections, measured by the Pedersen formula which is similar to Bartolini and Mair's measure of total volatility discussed in Chapter 7. Hypothesis: the greater the volatility, the higher the costs and the greater the chance that minority governments will be formed.
- *Responsiveness*: the proportion of electoral gainers among its constituent parties. Hypothesis: the higher this proportion, the higher the chance of minority governments.
- *Crisis duration*: the duration of the cabinet crisis in days. Hypothesis (based on conventional wisdom): minority governments should be associated with particularly long cabinet crises. (Strøm expects no relationship. Note that it may be theoretically fruitful to incorporate relationships in the model in order to show that they are *not* as important as often thought).
- *Formation attempts*: the total number of formation attempts of every government. Hypothesis: minority governments should be associated with numerous formation attempts (again, this hypothesis is based on conventional wisdom: Strøm expects no relationship).
- *Fractionalization*: measured by Rae's index (which subtracts the sum of the squared seat percentages from 1). Hypothesis: the more fractionalized the

parliamentary system, the more difficult the formation of a winning coalition and the greater the likelihood of an undersized solution.

- *Polarization*: the proportion of all parliamentary seats held by extremist parties. Hypothesis: polarized parliaments should experience frequent minority governments.
- *Government extremism*: the proportional distribution of the opposition along the left–right dimension. Hypothesis: the bargaining advantage of centrist parties makes it easier for them to form minority governments.
- *Investiture*: a dummy variable for constitutional requirements of parliamentary investiture at the time of government formation (1 = existent). Hypothesis: minority governments are more difficult to form if a new government needs an immediate vote of confidence in its first encounter with the national assembly.

The occurrence of minority cabinets may be analysed by both linear and logistic regression. In the case of the latter technique the dependent variable is a dummy variable: either there is a minority cabinet (1) or not (0). In the case of linear regression, the dependent variable is continuous and comprises the percentage of seats. By constructing two different dependent variables we are able to answer the research question by means of two different (but related) techniques. We do this in order to illustrate the differences and similarities between OLS and logistic regression. We hypothesize that the empirical results of these techniques are more or less similar. If so, we would ultimately prefer logistic regression because it is theoretically directly linked to the question: what is the chance of finding minority cabinets given the circumstances which are defined by Strøm's rational choice theory?

The results of both analyses are compared by listing the partial correlation of the linear regression and the R of the logistic regression because these two coefficients can be interpreted in the same way (Table 8.11). Both types of regressions support *all* hypotheses. In both cases the electoral salience is a relatively important factor. The OLS regression also designates the degree of polarization as a meaningful factor. The major theoretical significance of these models is that they confirm the basic predictions based on choice theory. At the same time, it is clear that some (unknown) theoretical factors are missing, as the explained variance of the model is poor. Thus, we have corroborated a rational choice theory on government formation by means of two related statistical techniques. The application of OLS and logistic regression was possible because the dependent variable can be measured with an interval score (i.e. the percentage of cabinet seats needed for OLS regression) and with a dichotomous score (the presence or absence of a minority cabinet) which is needed for logistic regression. Of these two techniques, logistic regression should be preferred because it is most directly linked to the research question: when do minority cabinets occur?

Until now we have discussed the one-dimensional approach to cabinet formation: the policy distances are solely defined by the left–right differences between parties. Laver and Budge (1992) have proposed an innovative

Table 8.11 *OLS and logistic regression on cabinet formation, based on Strøm's data*

		Partial correlation	log *R*
V34	Opposition influence	−0.11	−0.07
V50	Electoral salience	−0.29	−0.18
V27	Decade volatility seats	−0.07	−0.05
V21	Responsiveness	−0.11	0
V05	Crisis	0.13	0.11
V10	Formation attempts	−0.07	−0.06
V25	Fractionalization	−0.09	−0.11
V29	Polarization	−0.23	−0.06
V51	Opposition unipolarity	0.1	0.04
V52	Investiture	0.06	0
	Explained/predicted	0.14	0.706

Source: Strøm (1990b: 77, 83) and Strøm's data file 'clean87.sav'. The operationalization of the variables is explained in the file documentation. (*N* = 326 governments in 15 European countries in the period 1945–85.)

multi-dimensional approach to cabinet formation by applying *cluster analysis* to the party manifesto data which are discussed in Section 4.5. By means of exploratory factor analysis the 54 original issues are rearranged and fused into 20 issue dimensions. These new dimensions represent the main sources of party competition and are therefore more encompassing than the left–right distinction alone.

Laver and Budge's 'modeling of coalition formation in high-dimensional policy spaces' (as they describe it) is based on an inductive kind of modelling, derived from Grofman (1982). Grofman's model assumes that coalitions are formed in a series of stages, in which parties first combine into *protocoalitions*. In the following stages, these protocoalitions combine into larger coalitions (i.e. a protocoalition merges with another protocoalition) until some threshold is reached which makes the coalition large enough to take office (Laver and Budge, 1992: 30). Whether or not the combination is large enough depends on the viability of a government, and not necessarily on its majority. It is assumed that each stage of the government formation process is driven by the desire of political parties to form coalitions with a minimum of ideological diversity, similar to Axelrod's theorem.

Laver and Budge apply *cluster analysis* in order to be able to combine parties into protocoalitions. Cluster analysis approaches coalitions as clusters of parties by taking a set of points (i.e. the 20 dimensional policy positions) and combining them into a cluster. This process of combining continues until there is one single cluster (a grand coalition that comprises all parties). The cluster analysis is based on the matrix of policy distances between all pairs of parties, the so-called *city-block distance matrix* where 'city-block' refers to the metric that measures the policy distance (namely, the distance between two points or parties is the sum of the policy distances between them on each of the 20 issue dimensions). We give an arbitrary example of the Swedish formation process in 1988 in Table 8.12 (Laver and Budge, 1992: 128).

Table 8.12   *City-block dissimilarity coefficient matrix, Sweden 1988*

Case	Ecology	VK	SSA	FP	MS	CP
Ecology	0.0					
VK	50.0	0.0				
SSA	68.0	72.6	0.0			
FP	68.0	59.8	83.0	0.0		
MS	102.9	101.5	105.7	66.9	0.0	
CP	59.8	77.8	65.6	71.6	86.7	0.0

Ecology = The Greens, VK = Communist Party; SSA = Social Democrats; FP = People's Party of the Liberals; MS = Moderate Unity Party, CP = Centre Party. The coefficients are based on the city-block measure.
Source: Laver and Budge (1992: 141).

The clustering technique will group parties on the basis of the distances. The formation of protocoalitions may be visualized by means of a so-called *dendrogram* that indicates not only which clusters are joined but also the distance at which they are joined. Figure 8.2 shows the dendrogram based on the distance matrix for Sweden in 1988.

The cluster analysis, as it is applied here, is based solely on programmatic differences and totally ignores the institutional settings of party behaviour. Therefore, the aim of cluster analysis is not so much to forecast a coalition as to examine the institutional conditions that are at work. When 'obvious' coalitions are not formed, then there must have been additional, often institutional, factors which explain the formation of that particular coalition. In the example of Sweden, we need Strøm's rational choice theory on minority coalitions to understand why the SSA are able to form a single-party government in 1988 when a coalition government was more probable.

Hitherto we have discussed some aspects of cabinet formation. Another widely studied topic is cabinet functioning or cabinet performance (i.e. what cabinets do or produce). There are several ways to measure this, e.g. by means of cabinet duration or socio-economic performance. Here we concentrate on the factors that influence the duration of cabinets.

In the recent literature on cabinet stability there has been a discussion about the relative merits of the attributes of and the events approach towards cabinet duration. Strøm's model concentrates on the attributes, being systemic features of countries that influence the cabinet duration (Strøm, 1985). Frendreis et al. (1986) focus on the so-called events, being unforeseen and unpredictable incidents that lead to the end of cabinets. King et al. (1990) try to combine these two approaches in a so-called unified model.

Let us start with an attributes model and then discuss the pros and cons of such a model. Strøm (1985) proposed a model that explains cabinet duration with the help of a set of attributes – variables that overlap with the previous selection of ten variables that was used to explain government formation. The determinants of cabinet duration may be divided into country attributes, party structure attributes and coalition attributes:

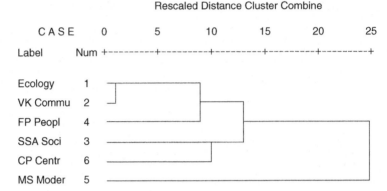

Figure 8.2 *Dendrogram using average linkage (between groups) for Sweden, 1988. The dendrogram is based on the distances that are reported in Table 8.12. One looks for the solution (combination of clusters) just before the distances at which the clusters are combined become too large. In this case, one would expect a VK–FP–SSA or an SSA–CP coalition. In reality a SSA minority cabinet was formed. Source: Laver and Budge (1992)*

1 Country attributes include electoral salience (the salience of general elections for government), opposition influence (a five-point scale based on characteristics of the legislative committee systems), investiture (the (non)existence of legislative investiture requirements), volatility (electoral volatility for parliamentary seats), responsiveness (of government formation to electoral verdicts).

2 Party-system attributes include fractionalization (Rae's index: 1– the sum of the squared percentages of the seats for each party), polarization (extremist party support: Powell's index; see Powell, 1982: 95).

3 Coalition attributes include parliamentary status (the percentage of parliamentary seats held by the governing parties), crisis duration (preceding each government formation), formation attempts (during these crises), opposition concentration (measured as the number of seats held by parties on the numerically largest opposition side as a proportion of all opposition seats).

Note that this combination of variables into one model is the result of a multi-level conceptualization of factors relating to systems, parties and governments. Such a multi-level structure is linked to potential methodological problems, such as the ecological fallacy and problems of inference.

Strøm has applied regression analysis to determine the relative causal effects of the three types of attributes. The regression results are visualized by means of a causal path model (Figure 8.3). Strøm's model has an explained variance of 0.29, being the R^2 of the 'main model' (namely, cabinet duration with parliamentary basis, electoral salience and crisis duration). The strongest beta value is for electoral salience, and the positive sign is no surprise: the more salient elections are for government formation, the longer governments endure. Electoral salience also has several (weak) indirect effects on government durability: through crisis duration, formation attempts and parliamentary basis.

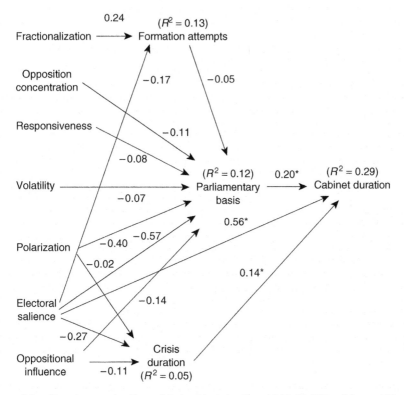

Figure 8.3 *Strøm's causal path model of cabinet duration, 1946–87. DW = 2.3; n = 313. An asterisk implies significance at the 0.01 level. Source: Strøm (1985: 748). Data: Strøm's clean87.sav data file on minority governments*

The low explained variance points to a need for more (and other) factors than the attributes. Whereas the attributes theorists (like Kaare Strøm) seek to explain cabinet duration as a fixed function of measured explanatory variables, the events process theorists model cabinet duration as a product of purely stochastic processes, i.e. generated by a particular 'critical' or 'terminal' event (Browne et al., 1988).[2]

8.5 Interest Intermediation

Corporatism has been much debated since Philippe Schmitter's article 'Still the century of corporatism?' (1974). Since that time many corporatism scales have been developed. Most of them are based on different conceptualizations and operationalizations, so that they are hard to compare. In this section we will compare some of these scales with the help of correlation and regression analysis. These two techniques serve our aim of comparing the degree of correspondence between several scales. The background is set by a discussion between Crepaz and Lijphart, on the one hand, and the authors of this book, on the other. The following examples relate to this discussion (Keman and Pennings, 1995).

Various similar corporatism scales have been developed in order to capture the nature and degree of socio-economic interest intermediation (see Table 8.13). One of the potential problems behind these scales is that their similarity may be highly misleading. Corporatism scales may have strongly similar scores for each of the countries, but more often than not they have a different meaning. Thus, and this is the main lesson of this section, dissimilar indicators sometimes yield the same results. Let us have a look at the following examples of dissimilar corporatism scales:

1 Schmitter, Crouch and Cameron regard the *organizational features* of the actors involved and their *threat potential* (e.g. strike-activities) as vital to their conceptualization.
2 Schmidt and Czada emphasize in their definition of corporatism *social partnership* with state involvement in the bargaining process.
3 Paloheimo and Lehner emphasize 'concertation', i.e. *a general economic consensus* among the main participants which induces a 'logic of accommodation'.

These various definitions indicate that the underlying meaning of the term corporatism is not equivalent. The three groups of indices mentioned here as examples will thus have a different theoretical impact: the scores may more or less match, but that does not imply that they mean the same thing in the different countries. It is striking to observe, for instance, that the indices of Schmidt and Paloheimo statistically almost completely overlap (Tables 8.13 and 8.14), but are at the same time conceptualized quite differently. Although the various indices broadly correspond, quite a few do not show strong intercorrelations. The reason for this is simple: there are some countries that are scored in an opposite fashion. This neatly illustrates the general point made above.

In sum, both the conceptualization and the operationalization of corporatism are strikingly divergent so that the correlations have a very limited value here. It is doubtful whether the method advocated by Lijphart and Crepaz (1991) of combining a number of corporatism indices yields either valid or reliable results. It would have been better if they had selected one (or two) of existing indices for analysis on the basis of the arguments they themselves put forward. The communality is derived from a crucial feature underlying both concepts, namely collective decision-making by means of compromise and cooperation between the relevant actors involved (i.e. political parties in a consensus democracy; socio-economic actors in corporatist arrangements). The assumption is that all actors involved know that if another strategy is pursued the resulting decision-making will more often than not be *sub*optimal. However – and this is an *essential* difference between the concepts – consensus democracy represents a mode of institutionalization of political actors by referring to aspects of parliamentary democracy, whereas corporatist interest intermediation represents the incorporation of societal actors typically by means of non-parliamentary consultation in order to avoid zero-sum outcomes of policy formation.

Table 8.13 A selection of influential corporatism scales

Country	Crouch	Schmitter	Schmidt	Czada (1983)	Czada (1987)	Paloheimo	Lehner	Cameron	Keman	Lehmbruch	Corp. AL	Cons. AL
Australia	0		2	1	2	2	3	40	2	1	-1	-0.9
Austria	1	1	3	3	5	3	4	100	5	4	1.6	-0.4
Belgium	0	7	2	2	4	2	3	77	2	3	0.3	0.6
Canada	0	11	1	1	2	1	1	21.6	1	1	-1.4	-1.5
Denmark	1	4	2	2	4	2	3	91.8	3	3	0.5	0.8
Finland	1	4	2	2	4	2	3	84.6	3	3	0.4	1.5
France	0	13	1	2	1	1	1	16.8	2		-0.7	-0.2
Germany	1	8	2	2	1	2	3	44.8	3	3	0.5	-0.1
Ireland	0	11	1	2	3	1	3	41.6	1	3	-0.5	-0.7
Italy	0	15	1	2	2	1	2	32.8	2	2	-0.9	1
Japan	0		2	1	1	3	5	6.4	3		0.1	0
Netherlands	1	6	3	3	3	2	4	39.2	4	4	1	1.4
New Zealand	0		2	1	3		3		2	1	-1.1	-1.3
Norway	1	2	3	3	5	3	4	117	5	4	1.5	0.2
Sweden	1	4	3	3	5	3	4	126	5	4	1.4	0.1
Switzerland	1	9	3	2	3	3	5	33.6	4	3	0.5	1.7
UK	0	14	1	2	2	1	2	45	2	2	-0.9	-1.3
USA	0	11	1	1	1	1	1	18.9	1	1	-1.3	-1.3

Sources: Crouch (1985), Schmitter (1981), Schmidt (1982), Czada (1983, 1987), Paloheimo (1984), Lehner (1988), Cameron (1984), Keman (1988), Lehmbruch (1984) and Lijphart and Crepaz (1991).

Table 8.14 *Spearman's rho correlations of corporatism indices (n = 18)*

	Crouch	Schmitter	Schmidt	Czada (1983)	Paloheimo
Schmitter	−0.81				
	n = 15				
	Sig 0.00				
Schmidt	−0.78	−0.83			
	n = 18	n = 15			
	Sig 0.00	Sig 0.00			
Czada (1983)	0.70	−0.64	0.58		
	n = 18	n = 15	n = 18		
	Sig = 0.00	Sig 0.01	Sig 0.01		
Paloheimo	0.66	−0.84	0.92	0.43	
	n = 17	n = 15	n = 17	n = 17	
	Sig 0.00	Sig 0.00	Sig 0.00	Sig 0.09	
Lehner	0.59	−0.71	0.87	0.43	0.91
	n = 18	n = 15	n = 18	n = 18	n = 17
	Sig 0.01	Sig 0.00	Sig 0.00	Sig 0.07	Sig 0.00

Source: see Table 8.13. Schmitter's scores are inverted, which explains the negative relations with other indices.

If our line of reasoning is correct, then it follows that both measures are based on the 'logic of accommodation' and may empirically co-vary, but at the same time it does not imply that consensus democracy and corporatism have the same effect on the results of the decision-making process. Hence, there appears to be a structural affinity, but the concepts are not identical, nor can one category be considered as superordinate or subordinate to the other. Assuming a proper measurement of both concepts as comparative variables, we should be able to assess to what extent both dimensions of political decision-making in democracies occur together in reality. To this end we have correlated (using Spearman's rho because we are relating ordinal scales) the various measures of corporatism employed by Lijphart and Crepaz to construct their index of corporatism with the index of consensus democracy (see their Table 1, p. 239). From this exercise it appears that the composite index of corporatism developed by Lijphart and Crepaz (the 'lump sum' measure) is among those that correlate most strongly with their own index of consensus democracy (r_s = 0.569). Only Crouch (r_s = 0.589), Lehmbruch (r_s = 0.577) and Schott (r_s = 0.527) come close to this degree of association. These results demonstrate that the various indices of corporatism differ among each other in at least two respects: firstly, the extent to which countries are considered as being corporatist; and secondly, the way the various authors have placed countries on their respective scales. We must conclude, therefore, given the variation in conceptualization, that the index developed by the authors is meaningless in terms of validity and dubious in terms of reliability. In other words, regardless of the structural affinity between consensus democracy and corporatism, it appears that the empirical relationship is by and large identical. Hence, the lesson here is that additive indices should be based on a univocal conceptualization and operationalization of the constituent elements.

Despite their apparent similarities, corporatism and consensus democracy are different concepts as there seems neither a theoretical nor an empirical reason to subsume corporatism under the characteristics of consensus democracy. They do not have the same meaning and can empirically be distinguished in relation to features of liberal democratic decision-making. In general, it makes sense to inspect the underlying dimensions of a concept and to confront various measures with each other in order to be assured that the chosen indicator is valid and reliable and contributes to a substantially plausible explanation of the dependent variable. Correlation and regression analysis provide the necessary tools to do so.

8.6 Federalism, Centralism and Institutional Autonomy

The constitutional design of the democratic state is a defining element of the room for manoeuvre for government (Lijphart, 1999; Lane and Ersson, 2000). Three variables that are important for the cross-national variation in relation to public policy-making are (Keman, 2000a):

- Federalism versus the unitary state – the degree of territorial autonomy *vis-à-vis* the political centre within the state that often manifests itself, among other things, in the level of taxation and modes of regulation. In unitary states we expect a more direct impact of national governments on decision-making and policy-implementation.
- Centralized versus decentralized governance – the degree to which aspects of policy-making are directed from the central political institutions. Some federal states are centralized in some respects and some unitary states have decentralized features, either functionally or territorially.
- Institutional autonomy – the degree to which subnational governing units, such as local communities or provinces, have powers to control policy-making independently of the centre by means of taxation and regulation (i.e. forms of self-regulation; see Braun, 2000).

These distinctions are necessary in order to understand the variation in forms of state intervention. On the one hand, many democratic states are characterized by institutions that allow for co-decision-making powers by non-central bodies (e.g. by regions; see Urwin, 1985). On the other hand, actual policy implementation is often left to non-central bodies. Hence policy-making is taking place at the other level of the state and therefore less visible in data on policy performance (e.g. housing policy in the Netherlands, or social security in Switzerland; see Keman, 2000b; Armingeon, 2000).

In short, the relationship between state format (unitary versus federal), organization of the state (central versus decentralized), and the levels of decision-making and policy implementation within a polity are not only more complex,

Table 8.15 *Scales of federalism, autonomy and decentralization*

Country	Autonomy	Decentralization	Federalism
Australia	0.89	0.42	0.93
Austria	0.11	−0.12	0.05
Belgium	0.35	0.13	0.41
Canada	0.58	1.29	1.22
Denmark	−0.16	−0.63	−0.25
Finland	−0.96	−0.19	−0.96
France	−0.65	−0.64	−1.23
Germany	1.38	0.89	1.56
Ireland	−1.15	−1.18	−1.02
Italy	−0.13	0.02	0.21
Netherlands	−1.19	−0.82	−0.74
Norway	0.11	−0.76	−0.26
Portugal	−0.91	−0.81	−0.98
Spain	0.39	−0.07	−0.23
Sweden	−1.23	−0.74	−0.89
Switzerland	1.90	2.38	1.72
UK	−0.98	−0.93	−1.00
USA	1.62	1.77	1.44

Autonomy: factor scores based on devolution index (Lane and Ersson, 2000), sovereignty scale (Schmidt, 1996) and veto points (Armingeon et al., 2003); $R^2 = 71.1\%$. *Decentralization*: based on fiscal diffusion (Castles, 2000), autonomy of subnational bodies (Lane and Ersson, 1999) and institutional barriers (Colomer, 1996: 12); $R^2 = 76.6\%$. *Federalism*: composite measure of the indicators of autonomy and decentralization; $R^2 = 66.4\%$. Factor analysis is performed by varimax, one solution. Positive scores indicate more autonomy, decentralization and federalism.

but also crucial in order to understand the procedural and material performance of democratic states (Marks and Hooghe, 2001). In Table 8.15 features of federal and unitary states are shown in terms of three scales developed using factor analysis (Section 4.5.2).

Table 8.15 indicates that most federalist countries are characterized by a high degree of institutional autonomy. Countries with a low degree of federalism, however, are not by definition centralized. Examples of non-federalist but decentralized countries are Spain and Italy. Conversely, Austria and Belgium – both constitutionally federal states – appear rather centralized. These observations are based on rankings published in different literatures (e.g. Lane and Ersson, 1999; Keman, 2000a), which have been transformed by means of factor analysis to reduce complexity, on the one hand, and to enhance the comparability between states, on the other.

Figure 8.4 is a scatterplot of the information that is presented in Table 8.15 (see Chapter8.sps for the SPSS syntax). Federalism is responsible for the vertical spread of the cases, decentralization and autonomy for the horizontal spread. This figure shows that the features of federalism in terms of decentralization and autonomy are variable: although the typical federal states are towards the top of Figure 8.4, these states show considerable differences. The unitary states are at the bottom of the figure, but in the centre of the distribution. One can easily detect a number of 'mixed' cases. For instance, Australia is quite centralist whereas in Canada the institutional autonomy is at the same level as the cluster

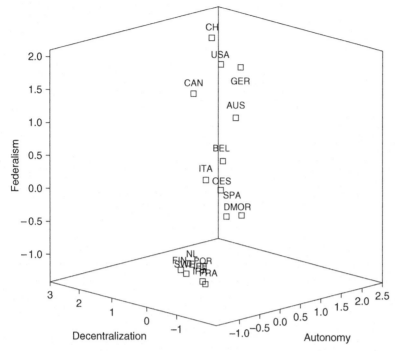

Figure 8.4   *Three-dimensional scatterplot of federalism, centralism and autonomy*

of countries in the centre. The figure shows that these three institutional structures are interrelated, although they are not identical because in that case the distances between the countries would be smaller or even absent. This type of plot is therefore useful for the study of other relationships, such as those between corporatism, consensus democracy and world market integration at the country level (Section 8.5) or those between office-seeking, vote-seeking and policy-seeking behaviour at the party level (Section 7.2.1). The cross-national variation is indeed related to both decision-making (as indicated by budgetary indicators) and policy implementation (in terms of the state's organizational capacity). In general, the literature suggests, however, that the causal impact of state structures is indirect. This is not surprising since we are dealing with formal structure (or set of institutions) where actors (such as party government and bureaucracies) are intervening factors (e.g. Lane, 1997; Castles, 2000; Keman, 2000b).

   The variations in the degree of federalism as expressed in decentralization and institutional autonomy do relate to variations in public policy-making. This can be examined by means of separate bivariate regression analyses in which federalism, decentralization and institutional autonomy are the independent variables and two clusters representing the size of the state and the extent of state intervention are the dependent variables. The first cluster is the issue whether or not federalism and decentralization impact on the level of the public sector (i.e. total expenditures and taxation). The second cluster can be seen as a consequence of this contested issue: if and when federalism, institutional

Table 8.16 *Indicators of the size of the public sector and policy outputs in relation to the constitutional design in 18 OECD countries (1995)*

Dependent variable = Y	Cross-national average public outlays (% of GDP)		Beta weights = X		
	Real	Estimated	Federalism	Decentralism	Autonomy
Public employment	19.3	19.6	−0.28	−0.36	−0.27
Government consumption	18.8	20.7	−0.26	−0.35	−0.36
Size of public sector	45.3	48.9	−0.36	−0.48∗	−0.46∗
Transfer payments	16.4	18.0	−0.35	−0.41∗	−0.36∗
Central taxation	21.1	23.7	−0.62∗	−0.79∗∗	−0.61∗∗

Expenditures sourced from various OECD publications. Estimated averages based on OLS regression; ∗ = significant at 0.05 level; ∗∗ = significant at 0.01 level.

autonomy and decentralization go together with lower levels of 'stateness' and policy intervention then this should be borne out. Table 8.16 demonstrates this by comparing the real levels of state expenditure (levels of state employment and government consumption, i.e. organizational costs; see Lane, 1997) with the estimated levels. In addition, the bivariate relationships with levels of public expenditure and transfer payments are reported.

Table 8.16 shows that there is a negative relationship between higher degrees of federalism, decentralization and autonomy and the variables representing state-related expenditures. This result confirms the idea that unitary and centralist states tend to be 'bigger' in organization and spending. Yet, the caveat here is obviously that this analysis does not imply the organizational costs of public authorities at the sub-national level. In addition, Table 8.16 demonstrates that the level of centralized taxation is crucial for understanding to what extent policy can be decided and made at the non-central level at all (Castles, 2000).

To illustrate this, one can decide to calculate the residual scores of decentralized taxation and transfer payment organized by subnational public authorities. As the modest beta weights indicate that the cross-national variation is relatively high it would signify that the constitutional design influences the actual levels of public expenditures indirectly. In turn this type of analysis shows that the institutional constraints of federalism, institutional autonomy and decentralization affect the policy performance differently.

Although the association between federalism and subnational decision-making and policy implementation is quite strong, Table 8.17 demonstrates equally clearly that the patterns of spending and taxation differ considerably. In fact, the table shows that the 'federal' states (marked in bold) are actually in the middle of the distribution, whereas Denmark and Finland are deviant cases, and Portugal and France are typical unitary and centralized states, considering their below par levels of expenditure (see Braun, 2000; Castles, 2000).

The comparative analysis of the constitutional design of democratic states has shown that:

Table 8.17 *Patterns of spending and taxation in the OECD, 1976–95*

	Federalism and local tax	Autonomy and local tax	Decentralization and local tax	Federalism and transfers	Autonomy and transfers	Decentralization and transfers
Australia	-2.85	-2.62	-1.86	0.04	0.15	-0.46
Austria	1.60	1.49	1.94	-1.84	-1.72	-2.15
Belgium	-6.10	-5.94	-5.56	-0.42	-0.43	-0.75
Canada	3.38	4.74	3.18	-1.94	-2.76	-1.13
Denmark	8.19	8.00	8.98	11.14	11.23	10.24
Finland	4.40	4.24	2.89	2.92	2.74	3.91
France	-0.77	-2.03	-1.90	-7.87	-7.15	-7.38
Germany	1.11	1.70	2.39	-2.26	-2.27	-2.73
Ireland	-3.78	-3.71	-3.40	-0.77	-1.17	-1.67
Italy	-5.81	-5.17	-5.44	6.59	6.09	6.34
Netherlands	-4.43	-3.75	-4.22	5.22	4.37	4.64
Norway	3.12	2.39	4.15	3.72	4.28	2.57
Portugal	-1.77	-2.05	-2.04	-8.01	-8.08	-8.24
Spain	-2.45	-3.61	-2.77	1.17	2.13	1.36
Sweden	9.76	10.24	9.51	-3.38	-4.11	-3.59
Switzerland	1.28	1.25	-0.13	-1.62	-1.02	0.66
UK	-4.33	-4.53	-4.41	-0.34	-0.49	-0.77
USA	-0.55	-0.64	-1.30	-2.33	-1.77	-0.86

N = 18. For explanation, see Table 8.15. Local taxation includes all non-central taxes. Transfer payments are those distributed at the subnational level (source: OECD, Revenue Statistics). A negative score means that the levels of decentralization, taxation and transfer payments are lower than could be expected, and conversely a positive score implies higher levels than expected in relation to the degrees of federalism, autonomy and decentralization. Countries in **bold** are generally considered to be typically federal and decentralized.

1 general indicators of federalism need to be refined conceptually so as to enhance the internal and external validity within comparative analysis;
2 these refined measures allow for a discussion of patterns of variation and widely contested issues in comparative politics such as the impact of federalism on state organization and its public expenditures;
3 assumed relationships are not only complex but also in need of additional explanations.

For, apart from country-specific factors that may account for the cross-national variations, the role of 'politics' and actors is absent in this institutional analysis. Hence, we can now conclude that the relevant actors are crucial to understanding how federalism works as exemplified by the degree of decentralization and levels of institutional autonomy (Wachendorfer-Schmidt, 2000).

8.7 Presidentialism

The distinction between parliamentarism and presidentialism clearly matters for the democratic process and the policy process (Sartori, 1994; Linz, 1994; Pennings, 2003). In this section we will study presidentialism from two comparative perspectives:

- The *most different approach* – are worldwide presidential systems less democratic than parliamentary systems? (Note that the most different approach is only partly applicable, because this question is not based on the causal logic behind this approach: we are only asking for variations and not for explanations.)
- The *comparative case study approach* – how can we account for the exceptionally high democratic and socio-economic performance of the US presidential system?

The second research design is a logical continuation of the first (see Chapter 3). This design confronts the empirical findings of comparative research with one challenging case that does not fit. This case derives its more or less deviant status from comparative research, but its existence can at the same time not be explained by this type of research. For that we need the comparative case study.

In the most different design we may distinguish between several types of executive systems: parliamentary, limited presidential, dual systems, unlimited presidential, communist, military and absolute (Derbyshire and Derbyshire, 1990). The results of this analysis are quite consistent: parliamentary systems are more democratic than other systems. The limited presidential systems are clearly less democratic, as is shown by the one-way analysis of variance on the Gastil index (Table 8.18). The unlimited presidential systems are the least democratic systems, even less than the military and the absolute executive systems.

Another way of looking at the democratic character of the various executive systems is to examine the frequency and character of political protest and

Table 8.18 *One-way analysis of variance of the Gastil democracy index by regime type, 1972–89*

Group	n	Mean	Standard deviation	Standard error	Minimum	Maximum	95% confidence interval for mean
Parliamentary	468	12.18	2.53	0.12	4	14	11.95–12.41
Limited							
presidential	648	6.94	3.46	0.14	2	14	6.68–7.21
Dual	90	10.31	2.88	0.3	5	14	9.71–10.91
Unlimited							
presidential	90	2.81	1.13	0.12	2	6	2.57–3.05
Communist	342	4.22	1.78	0.1	2	9	4.03–4.41
Military	198	4.05	1.86	0.13	2	11	3.79–4.31
Absolute	90	5.42	1.45	0.15	3	9	5.12–5.73
Total	1926	7.33	4.14	0.09	2	14	7.14–7.51

Summary statistics: F-ratio = 461.15; F prob. = 0.0000.

violence. Here we limit the data analysis to the parliamentary systems ($n = 33$) and limited ($n = 53$) and unlimited presidentialism ($n = 7$). Analysis of variance is applied in order to determine to what extent these systems differ in their degree of democracy. For this purpose we utilize the yearly political events data of the *World Handbook of Political and Social Indicators* (Taylor and Jodice, 1977) for 93 countries in the period 1948–82 (although first published in 1977, the period was later extended to 1982). These events were identified by coding the content of the New York Times Index and numerous national newspapers. Table 8.19 shows that there are significant differences between the executive systems. The most important differences are distinguished by their (significant) relevant high F-scores: executive renewal, adjustments and transfers and political execution.

A second approach is *the comparative case study approach*. A comparative case study examines one case in relation to other cases in order to test a series of theoretical assumptions (see also Chapter 3). For example, one might ask why presidentialism in the USA is a highly democratic institution whereas presidential systems in general are not that democratic (i.e. executive powers dominate parliamentary rule, which may frustrate the democratic process). This case study has actually been done by Riggs (1994), and we will follow his reasoning here.

Presidentialism is based on the separation of powers between executive (president) and legislative institutions (Congress) that stems from the fixed term of the president. In parliamentary systems the head of state and the head of government are two different persons with different roles, whereas in presidential regimes the elected head of government always serves concurrently as head of state. Thus, presidentialism is defined by Riggs as representative government in which the head of government is elected for a fixed term of office; that is, he or she cannot be discharged by a no-confidence vote. The fixed term ensures continuity of leadership, but at the same time presidents are hampered in their leadership roles. Their inability to fulfil popular expectations often leads

Table 8.19 *Analysis of variance of political events by regime type, 1948–82*

Event type	Parliamentary	Limited presidential	Unlimited presidential	Mean	F	Sign. F
Protest demonstrations	-0.06	0.16	-0.89	3.51	0.447	0.639
Regime supportive demonstrations	-0.21	0.04	0.73	0.57	13.312	0
Riots	0.16	0.05	-0.12	2.79	2.093	0.124
Armed attack	6.49	-4.94	6.81	17.1	4.528	0.011
Assassination (success)	-0.04	0.02	0.04	0.23	0.612	0.542
Political strikes	0.72	-0.31	-0.104	0.124	16.01	0
Executive renewal	0.24	-0.13	-0.16	0.41	36.673	0
Executive adjustments	-0.3	0.08	0.81	1.17	36.674	0
Unsuc. reg. executive transfer	0.07	-0.04	0.07	0.12	7.107	0.001
Reg. executive transfers	0.02	-0.02	0.02	0.41	1.11	0.329
Unsuc. irreg. executive transfers	-55.97	26.9	60.17	66.36	21.045	0
Irreg. executive transfers	-34.69	16.15	41.26	48.54	15.646	0
Election	59.4	-20.08	-127.98	319.82	13.265	0
Imposition of political sanctions	-1462.2	288.96	4702.63	8732.62	7.66	0
Political execution	-2828.99	-813.13	19540	3357.6	49.654	0
Relaxation of sanction	-411.04	136.55	903.85	1602.65	14.438	0
Death from violence	-6.21	-1.16	38.09	29.81	14.438	0

N = 3255 (35 years for 93 countries).
Source: Taylor and Jodice (1977) [Data file ICPSR I7761].

to crises and regime breakdowns (Riggs, 1994: 81). Because of the fixed term, presidential regimes lack the basic motor of parliamentarism which promotes party discipline.

Riggs (1994: 95) argues that the survival of presidentialism in the USA hinges on, among various factors, the responsiveness of its political parties and the semi-disciplined voting patterns which this engenders. 'Responsiveness' is defined by Riggs as a balanced intra-party distribution of power that combines local autonomy with headquarters guidance. Intra-party groups are permitted to organize informally but not to become oppressively prominent. Because of the 'responsive' two-party system and federalism, the president cannot command the loyalty nor control the actions of local politicians (p. 107). The separation of powers in the federal government also means that presidential power is shared with Congress and a powerful judicial system. Compared with the presidential systems, the governmental powers in the USA are not very extensive. Due to the centripetal (non-ideological) two-party system the actual programmes of the government are never radically reformed (p. 109).

Riggs' case study clearly shows how features of presidentialism, federalism, (non-)corporatism and the party system interact with each other. The functioning and policy effects of one institution cannot therefore be seen as independent of the impact of other institutions. In the USA the institution of presidentialism is democratic because it is counterbalanced by other institutions and decision-making structures, which leads to enduring forms of 'power sharing'. As a consequence, the American president is not the 'winner who takes all' but the 'winner who shares all' (p. 109).

In conclusion, the most different and the case study approach are different, but related, ways to cope with comparative research questions. Presidential systems are generally less democratic systems than parliamentary systems, but there are presidential systems with a high democratic performance. We have illustrated in this section that presidentialism *varies* and clearly *matters* (under certain conditions) for 'how decisions are made'. We have also illustrated in this section that there are several comparative research designs that may be used to study one phenomenon. Which research design is used depends on the research question. In this section the US presidential system has more or less served as an example of both a *contrasting case* (presidential systems versus parliamentary systems), a *similar case* (part of a group of liberal democracies), a *crucial case* (the American system combines institutional arrangements that make it typical) and a *deviant case* (it does not share the presidential dominance of most presidential systems). In all these different cases the US presidential system is examined from a specific comparative perspective. Consequently, given this variety of comparative approaches and options, comparing as such is not 'one' way to look at things but it embodies a whole range of different methodologies. What makes a research design comparable is that it relates cases to each other in a specific manner. The proper way to come to plausible conclusions is to follow the 'comparative logic' by logically integrating the research question, the research design and the research answer.

8.8 Conclusions

The 'chain of democratic control and command' shows how actors and institutions interact in the iterative process of democratic decision-making. In this chapter a selection of significant institutions of liberal democracies have been discussed: types of democracies and their characteristics, party systems, the formation and duration of governments, the institutional determinants of economic and public sector growth, structures of intermediation, forms of institutional autonomy and presidentialism. In most sections the discussion focuses on the policy effects of these institutions in a way that is similar to 'the chain'. All sections also embody (preliminary) research questions, research designs and research answers. These are summarized in Table 8.20.

Table 8.20 and this chapter do not present, of course, a complete overview of all types of comparative research on institutions. This chapter presents a selection of institutions that is more or less derived from or complementary to Lijphart's systematic study of institutional variations in *Patterns of Democracy* (1999). Furthermore, there are other ways to formulate research questions, research designs and research answers. This is illustrated by the discussion between Keman and Pennings (1995) and Crepaz and Lijphart (1995) on the use of corporatism scales. The most important thing, however, is that the art and craft of doing political research on institutions is set out in the sections and the exercises in an accessible and informative way.

One 'unresolved' problem is that the operationalization of institutional variables is still strongly based on non-dynamic scores. For example, all corporatism scales just present one figure per country to cover the whole of the postwar period, whereas we know that the degree and type of corporatism has changed in most liberal democracies. This poses a problem for statistical research, as it implies that the theoretical variance (how we conceptualize institutional variations) and the empirical variance (how we measure institutional variations) do not match. For this reason the previous sections and also the exercises that follow include the analysis of institutional change, such as party-system change and change in the conditions of consensus democracy.

8.9 Endmatter

Topics highlighted

The working, trends and effects of several institutions that are central in the functioning of democracies are analysed comparatively by means of statistical techniques (i.e. regression and factor analysis). The focus is on the following research questions (see also Table 8.20):

Table 8.20 *Overview and examples of the main stages in comparative research on political and socio-economic institutions*

Research question	Research design	Research answer
§8.2. What types of democracies are there?	Conceptualization and operationalization of democratic institutions and the detection of the underlying dimensions by means of factor analysis	Factor analysis suggests two underlying dimensions, albeit that the clustering of the countries on the basis of factor scores does not wholly match the juxtaposition of majoritarian and consensus democracies
§8.3. Do the theoretical assumptions underlying party-system typologies match the empirical characteristics of countries?	Identification of the theoretical assumptions; operationalization of the empirical characteristics; regression analysis of these characteristics on the main party-system dimension	There is a fair match between what the typologies predict and the actual characteristics of countries
§8.4. What factors determine the formation and duration of governments?	The operationalization and modelling of the determinants of government formation and duration. Test of the models by means of regression	The models confirm the direction of the relationships but the explained variance is low: the models are missing crucial attributes or events
§8.5. How similar are corporatism scales and can they be merged as part of a consensus democracy scale?	The comparison of the conceptualization and operationalization of corporatism scales and the analysis of these scales in relation to consensus democracy	Many corporatism scales are highly related but still very different. They cannot be merged into a consensus democracy scale
§8.6. How does the geographical autonomy of state units affect the policy-making process?	Operationalization of federalism, autonomy and centralism and policy variables; regression and residual analysis	Federal and decentralized states are characterized by lower levels of welfare state provision
§8.7. How democratic is presidentialism and how does it matter for the policy-making process?	The question is answered by means of a most different and a case study design which are logically related to each other	In general, presidential systems are less democratic (but this need not be the case) and there is no *direct* relationship with the policy-making process

1 What types of democracies are there?
2 Do the theoretical assumptions underlying party system typologies match the empirical characteristics of countries?
3 What factors determine the formation and duration of governments?
4 How similar are corporatism scales and can they be merged as part of a consensus democracy scale?
5 How does the geographical autonomy of state units affect the policy-making process?
6 How democratic is presidentialism and how does it matter for the policy-making process?

Exercises

The exercises aim to examine: how the functioning of institutions varies cross-sectionally and through time; and how institutions and institutional change affect the room to manoeuvre of actors and the process of policy-making.

- 8.1. Types of democracies

File: lijphart.sav.

Lijphart distinguishes eight features of consensus democracy on the basis of factor analysis. Apply factor analysis to construct a time series variable of the conditions for consensus democracy on the basis of three variables: disproportionality, effective number of parties and the type of government. Also apply regression analysis to the resulting factor score in order to analyse the consequences of these changes.

Suggested steps: 1. Check whether the three selected variables are suited to factor analysis (examine the positive and negative signs, missing values and operationalization). 2. Make the changes that are necessary in order to decrease the number of missing values and to make the variables interpretable (by means of 'recode' and the if statement). 3. Complete the factor analysis. 4. Establish the degree and nature of change in the conditions for consensus democracy by country (by means of 'select if').

Background reading: Lijphart (1999), Pennings (1997).

- 8.2. Party systems

File: nias.sav.

Select two crucial party system characteristics and determine their development in time and in relation to each other: for example 'the effective number of parties' and 'the dynamics of centrifugalism'.

Suggested steps: 1. Select the main party system variables. 2. Formulate the underlying hypotheses (e.g. we expect that the effective number of parties is increasing since the rise of protest parties). 3. Operationalize the key variables (e.g. the Taakso – Taagepera index for the effective number of parties). 4. Reveal some trends by means of the procedure graph.

Background reading: Lane and Ersson (1999), Pennings and Lane (1998).

- 8.3. Cabinet formation and duration

File: clean87.sav.

Strøm constructed a complicated causal path model in order to explain cabinet duration with institutional variables. Now try to construct a similar model with cabinet formation as the dependent variable (=v07; parliamentary basis) – see Table 8.11 for a selection of possible independent variables). You should start by formulating a number of plausible hypotheses and constructing your own causal path model. Consult the codebook that comes with clean87.sav. What objections can be made to Strøm's causal path model?

- Exercise 8.4. interest intermediation

File: corpor.sav.

Examine how corporatism relates to the eight features of consensus democracy. Do the results suggest that corporatism is very much like consensus democracy?
    Examine the residual scores of the countries. What cross-sectional variations are there?
    Suggested steps: 1. Select the relevant variables. 2. Perform a regression analysis that includes the residuals. 3. Examine the residuals. 4. Construct a scatterplot with corporal and consens. 5. Formulate your conclusions.
    Background reading: Lijphart and Crepaz (1991), Keman and Pennings (1995), Crepaz and Lijphart (1995).

- Exercise 8.5. federalism

File: nias.sav.

Examine the degree to which federalism, decentralization, and
institutional autonomy are interrelated.
    Suggested steps: 1. Aggregate the data to the country level. 2. Construct two scatterplots (autonomy with federalism and decentralism with federalism). 3. Interpret the results.
    Background reading: Wachendorfer-Schmidt (2000).

- Exercise 8.6. presidentialism

Files: polsoc.sav, gastil.sav.

Why are some presidential systems more democratic than others? Distinguish between democratic and non-democratic presidential systems and examine their features.
    Suggested steps: 1. Distinguish within the group of restricted presidential systems between more and less democratic systems (apply the if statement). 2. Determine on theoretical grounds which factor is likely to affect the degree of democracy (e.g. the more economic welfare the higher the level of democracy). 3. Apply ANOVA in order to test this hypothesis.
    Background reading: Riggs (1994), Derbyshire and Derbyshire (1999).

Further reading

- *General*: Lijphart (1999), Weaver and Rockman (1993).
- *Specific*: Laver and Schofield (1990), Lane and Ersson (1999), Keman and Pennings (1995), Pennings and Lane (1998), Keman (2002b).

Appendix 8.1: Overview of the indicators used to test the underlying assumptions of Sartori's and Lijphart's party-system typologies (as reported in Table 8.7)

- CPG = colour of party government (range 1–5; high score = left) (Woldendorp et al., 2000).
- DUR = duration of government measured in days (Woldendorp et al., 2000).
- RFT = reason for termination of government (range 0–1; high score = discordant ending) (Woldendorp et al., 2000).
- TOG = type of government (range: 0–1; high score = multi-party government) (Woldendorp et al., 2000).
- POLARSYS = The degree of polarization measured with the Sigelman and Yough (1978) formula.
- LEADERSHIP = The type of political leadership (range: 1–5; high score = coalescent leadership) (Keman, 1988).
- ISSUEDIM = the number of issue dimensions (Lijphart, 1984).
- NRPTIES = the total number of parties (Bartolini and Mair, 1990).
- EFFNOP = the number of effective parties on the basis of the Laakso–Taagepera index (Mackie and Rose, 1991).
- FRAGVOT = the fragmentation of the votes based on Rae's index of fractionalization (Mackie and Rose, 1991).
- UNITY = the degree of organizational unity of trade unions (range: 0–1; a high score means a high degree of unity) (Cameron, 1984).
- DENSITY = trade union density (percentage of non-agrarian employees) (Visser, 1989).
- ELSYS = the type of electoral system (range: 1–2; a high scores means a PR-like system) (Lijphart, 1999).
- TOTVOL = total volatility (Bartolini and Mair, 1990).
- DISPRDEF = the disproportionality of seats and votes (Mackie and Rose, 1991).
- PERCMEM = percentage of adults that are members of a political party (Katz and Mair, 1992).
- NOATTCH = Percentage of voters without attachment to party for which they voted (from cumulative Eurobarometers file, 1970–90).

Notes

1   One problem with Sartori's typology is that the predominant system, where one party has an enduring winning majority of parliamentary seats, fits rather uneasily with Sartori's framework, as this type is not exclusive – since any other type may become predominant (Mair, 1996a).

2   Cases for which the event does not occur during the period of observation are called censored cases. Cox regression models, also known as proportional hazards models, can be used when there are censored observations, namely those cabinets that ended solely because of the end of the so-called 'constitutional interelection period' (CIEP), which is mostly fixed at 3, 4 or 5 years. Censored governments would probably have lasted longer without a CIEP. For a further discussion we refer to King et al. (1990) and Warwick (1994).

How problems are solved

CONTENTS

9.1 Introduction

This chapter deals with the output and performance side of the so-called 'chain of democratic control and command' which was introduced at the beginning of Part III. This chain represents the stages in the democratic decision-making process and focuses on the interactions between political institutions and actors with regard to socio-economic policy formation. The dependent variables are variations in output and performance. Output refers mainly to the decisions that governments make. The main indicator for output is public expenditures as there is precious little policy-making without any costs. Performance refers to the societal effects of implementing decisions. The distinction between output and performance (or outcomes) is crucial. The output only reflects some of the intentions that policy-makers have. Whether they achieve their goal is a totally different question and is measured by performance. We limit ourselves in this chapter mainly (but not exclusively) to the socio-economic realm, as this is a central concern to any government in the OECD world. A glossary of basic terms is given in Box 9.1.

Socio-economic performance refers to the levels of social and economic welfare. In this chapter we link the variations in democratic and socio-economic performance of welfare states to cross-national and institutional contexts (Almond et al., 1993; Keman, 1993a). We examine the role of actors, institutions and the way actors and institutions interact. In most applications we are comparing similar countries which are facing similar problems. And we ask the question why some countries perform better than others and why the types of policy-making differ.

We work with both aggregated files ($n = 18$ OECD countries) and (pooled) time series data in order to be able to illustrate the pros and cons of both 'large n' and 'small n' in most-similar research designs.[1] Sections 9.3 and 9.4 cover the impact of central actors (parties and unions) and crucial institutions (corporatism, style of leadership, consociationalism) on policy formation and socio-economic problem-solving. The data are aggregated on the level of national systems, and the analysis integrates the results of Boolean analysis, regression analysis, factor analysis and analysis of variance in order to be able to show how these different techniques complement each other.

Box 9.1   Glossary of basic terms

- *Output*: decision of governments, known as public regulation and expenditures.
- *Performance or outcomes*: the effects or results of governmental decisions and interventions on society.
- *Style of political leadership*: the way in which conflicts are resolved by political elites (being either more competitive or coalescent, which is expressed on a four-point scale).
- *Political business cycle*: the cyclical trend in socio-economic state intervention that is caused by governments which attempt to influence their re-election prospects by manipulating the state of the economy in ways that are (electorally rewarding in the short run).
- *Social democratic model*: the assumption that parliamentary social democratic policy strategies will produce higher levels of welfare state development and full employment than non-social democratic strategies, especially when accompanied by trade union power.
- *Gastil democracy index*: the ranking of each nation on separate seven-point scales for 'political rights' and 'civil liberties'.
- *Mandate model* (or theory): the assumption that the democratic process is based on a mandate from voters to political parties on the basis of their manifestoes.
- *Democratic performance*: the degree to which democratization (process) and democraticness (level) affect the (outcomes of) decision-making and the quality of life.

The second part of this chapter is less aggregated in measurement (and more complicated) than the first part, yet it also relates to the 'chain of democratic control and command'. It covers time series analysis on output and performance variables that relate to the so-called political business cycle (meaning that governments may attempt to influence the re-election prospects – Section 9.5). In Section 9.7 the mandate model of party accountability (i.e. parties carry out pledges once in government) is tested on data that cover the USA, the UK (representing two-party systems) and the Netherlands (representing a multi-party system). This combination of topics enables us not only to describe variations in policy types and policy regimes (in terms of more or less restrictive policy-making) but also to explain the policy outcomes of these policy types and regimes.

Finally, the chapter also includes some non-economic issues. Democratic performance, meaning the quality of democracy, and the output and performance in the international arena are also important aspects of policy-making that have received considerable attention in comparative analysis (Section 9.6).

Finally, the exercises focus on the empirical validation and explanation of variations in types of policy performance. The main determinants of these variations relate to actors (Chapter 7) and institutions (Chapter 8).

9.2 Welfare-Related Outputs and Performance

The aim of this section is to introduce the main indicators of social and economic welfare. These indicators are linked to the output or outcomes in the socio-economic realm, although it is sometimes hard to distinguish between these. Output refers to all the decisions and interventions in the economy. Performance refers to the intended or unintended effects of these decisions and interventions.

Social welfare means the regulation and provision of social security (i.e. income maintenance), health care, education, etc. Economic welfare means the increase in the national or public income (redistributive justice) and the regulation of the private economy (the enhancement of public welfare). Both components of the welfare state are highly interdependent and can and should be seen as inter-dependent rather than separate (Keman, 1988).

Many indicators have been developed in order to measure socio-economic performance. For the sake of clarity we distinguish between three types:

- social indicators, which refer to levels of social welfare (education, health, transfers, etc.);
- economic indicators, which refer to levels of economic welfare (unemployment, employment, inflation, economic growth);
- indicators that reflect the relationship between social and economic indicators (e.g. when one goal is accomplished at the cost of another goal, known as a trade-off).

Sometimes the distinction between social and economic indicators is somewhat unclear. Unemployment, for example, has both a social and economic side, as it affects and is affected by the level of social and economic welfare in a country. Below, a selection of indicators is shown that are frequently used in comparative socio-economic research.

The following are examples of *economic performance* measures (we are only discussing a small selection of all existing measures):

- unemployment rates – unemployment as a percentage of the total labour force (source: OECD);
- employment – the percentage change, with respect to the previous period, in the total number of employed as a percentage of the total population (source: OECD);
- inflation – private consumption deflator, percentage change from previous period (source: OECD);
- the misery index (percentage unemployed plus inflation divided by 2) is a commonly used measure in policy studies (Castles, 1998).

A useful *economic output* measure is the TEDC scale. TEDC stands for 'Tax-related Extraction–Distribution Cycle' (Keman, 1993a), meaning that it measures the degree to which governments extract money from society and redistribute it to society in order to (re)direct the economic welfare of a country. The scale therefore represents the degree of economic interventionism. This scale is based on factor analysis on a selection of variables. Factor analysis is used (instead of scalability analysis) because we want to extract one dimension from a variety of indicators:

- deficit spending (variable name def) – general government financial balances, surplus (+) or deficit (–), as a percentage of nominal GDP;
- total taxation (variable name tax) – total tax receipts as a percentage of GDP;
- public expenditure (variable name pe) – general government total outlays as percentage of GDP;
- the total of social security contributions as a percentage of GDP (variable name ssc).

Examples of *social performance* measures are (and again we select a few measures) infant mortality, school enrolment, income inequality and poverty (Ravallion, 1994). Social performance clearly is the most difficult to measure because these measures are heavily based on individual circumstances and therefore rely on survey research, such as is employed by the Luxembourg Income Study (Atkinson et al., 1995). These measures are examples of bottom-up aggregates: the data are country means of scores on individuals (persons or families).

Social output measures are easier to construct than social performance measures because the former are based on official data, mostly on public expenditures, such as social expenditures on health, education and transfers. One summarizing measure is complementary to the TEDC scale, namely the WEDC scale, which stands for the 'Welfare-related Extraction–Distribution Cycle' (Keman, 1993a). This scale measures the degree of social state intervention. It is based on factor analysis on the variables direction taxation (variable name dtax), social security contributions by employers (variable name sscap), social security contributions by employees (variable name sscwo), education expenditures (variable name ed), health care expenditures (variable name he) and transfer payments to households (variable name trans). All expenditures data are taken as a percentage of gross domestic product as this is the standard measure of the OECD and enhances the comparability of the data.

All the variables underlying the TEDC and WEDC indicators are derived from OECD data (see the list of references). Most of the social and economic indicators mentioned will be discussed and applied further in the following sections when they are related to research questions and research designs. Let us summarize the rationale underlying the research design on the basis of the information in Chapters 1–3. The basic steps are as follows. First we explain *what*, *how* and *why* we are comparing:

1 *What* we compare are systemic variations in the 'chain of democratic control and command'; this chain designates what kind of variations in actors and institutions are important in relation to policy-making. Hence the main research question is how different democratic institutional environments affect socio-economic policy formation.
2 *How* we compare is defined by the research question, which relates the relevant independent variables (i.e. political institutions and actors) to the dependent variable which is often one of the output and performance indicators that are discussed in this section.
3 *Why* we are comparing originates from the need to explain variations in policy output and policy performance cross-temporally and cross-nationally. It is impossible to explain without comparing variations in the dependent and independent variables.

Hence, the research design results from a series of explicit choices:

1 the choice of cases and periods, being the 'universe of discourse';
2 the choice of data and transformations, being the operationalizations on the dependent and independent variables;
3 the choice of statistical techniques enabling the analysis of the relationships between the dependent and independent variables in such a way that we can detect patterned variations and causal relationships.

In short, the research question defines *what* we want to know, and the research design expresses *how* we want to produce this knowledge. By following all the necessary steps in the right order (e.g. first the question, then the hypotheses, then the analyses) we can draw sound, plausible and well-founded conclusions about reality (= positive science), refuting existing knowledge or dispelling existing myths. The following sections will present examples of this scientific approach.

9.3 Actors and Socio-economic Problem-Solving

In this section we shall analyse the role of actors *vis-à-vis* socio-economic policy outputs and outcomes, in particular those of social democratic parties (Pennings, 1995; Keeman, 2003). We will apply three techniques – regression, discriminant analysis and Boolean analysis – in order to analyse the relationships between the dependent and independent variables. These techniques are chosen because they are part of the examples that are derived from two well-known explanations of variations in welfare state development:

1 the development of social insurance schemes around 1900 (Alber, 1982);
2 the so-called social democratic model (Korpi, 1983).

The first investigation relates variations in the degree and extension of social insurance to systemic features of (pre-)democratic polities in their earliest phase of development. Some important determinants are the degree of industrialization, urbanization, the level of socio-economic development, the level of enfranchisement, the share of votes of labour parties ('left votes'), the degree of unionization, the degree and type of religiousness and the regime type. Alber chose to keep the data analysis descriptive, so he did not apply advanced statistics to analyse the relationships between the dependent and independent variables.

Berg-Schlosser and Quenter (1996) used Alber's (1992) data and operationalizations in order to discuss the application of several statistical techniques (see Table 9.1). They applied macro-quantitative and macro-qualitative methods to Alber's data on the variation and development of social insurance schemes. They argued that these two different methodological outlooks are complementary, as the quantitative techniques are designed to analyse relationships between *variables* whereas the qualitative techniques are better equipped to study variations between *cases* (see also the discussion of Ragin's comparative methodology in Section 6.3).

The quantitative approach (represented by regression and discriminant analysis) and the qualitative approach (represented by Boolean analysis) are applied on one single data set which is partly shown in Table 9.1.

When examining relationships between dependent and independent variables it is crucial to be critical about the results because of excluded exogeneous factors that may be influencing the results. This is demonstrated by the first part of Berg-Schlosser and Quenter's analysis, which is macro-quantitative. Bivariate regression analysis is used to examine the relationship between the share of left votes (X) and extension of social insurance (Y). The scatterplot of the relationship shows that the (moderately strong) explained variance ($R^2 = 0.4$) is mainly caused by the outlier Germany, which has relatively high scores on both variables (see also Section 6.7). After deleting this case, the explained variance reduces to near zero! In this sense, regression analysis is more or less 'case-blind', and a proper use of it assumes that the assumptions on the distribution of cases are not violated (see Chapter 6).

Table 9.1 *A selection of Jens Alber's data on (determinants of) social welfare around 1990*

Country	Socio-economic development[a]		Share of enfranchised men		Share of votes for labour parties		The reach of social insurance schemes[b]	
	Real figure	Boolean score	Real figure	Boolean score	Real figure	Boolean score	Real figure	Boolean score
Austria	38	0	85	1	0	0	9	1
Belgium	70	1	90	1	21	1	3.8	0
Denmark	49	0	87	1	14.3	1	10.5	1
Germany	69	1	94	1	27.2	1	40.8	1
Finland	18	0	19	0	0	0	1.8	0
France	54	1	88	1	11.3	1	6.8	1
Italy	48	0	25	0	13	1	2.8	0
Netherlands	68	1	51	0	3	0	0	0
Norway	45	0	90	1	3	0	3.3	0
Sweden	41	0	25	0	0.4	0	3.3	0
Switzerland	65	1	79	0	9.7	1	4	1
UK	111	1	62	0	1.3	0	9.8	1
Median	51.5	–	82	–	6.4	–	3.9	–

If the 'real figures' are higher than the median score the Boolean score is 1. Otherwise the Boolean score is 0. Thus, the Boolean score can be interpreted as high/low or present/absent.

[a]Socio-economic development in 1900 is the sum of the share of the working population in the industrial sector plus the urban population.

[b]The reach of social insurance schemes is operationalized as the share of the working population that is included in these schemes (accidents, sickness, rent and unemployment insurances).

Source: Berg-Schlosser and Quenter (1996: 107) as adapted from Alber (1982).

A different quantitative technique is discriminant analysis, which groups the cases around the two poles of the dichotomized dependent variable. The dichotomization is based on the median because this measure of central tendency is not influenced by cases with extreme values. The aim of discriminant analysis is to predict whether the cases belong to the group with a high level of social insurance or to the group with a low level. The independent variables are interval variables, whereas the dependent variable is dichotomous. In Section 6.5 it has been explained that the distance between the poles should be as large as possible and the distances between the cases and the poles should be as small as possible. The simultaneous inclusion of the most important variables (industrialization, urbanization, enfranchisement and left votes) has led to a correct grouping of 9 of the 12 cases. Only Belgium, Norway and the Netherlands were not grouped correctly: they were predicted to be in the group with a high level, whereas the observed level was low. Chapter9.sps gives all the technical details of this analysis.

Berg-Schlosser and Quenter argued that discriminant analysis as a quantitative technique differs from regression in that it is more case-oriented, but it is in their view still not as well equipped to discriminate between groups of cases as Boolean analysis (or qualitative comparative analysis).[2] Qualitative comparative analysis is highly (but not exclusively) variable-oriented, whereas qualitative comparative analysis is more oriented towards the analysis of cases (Ragin, 1987). This difference is illustrated by applying Boolean analysis to Alber's data. An initial simple quantitative comparative analysis is based on three of the most significant variables of Jens Alber's work on the historical development of social insurance schemes (the dependent variable) in western Europe (Alber, 1982):

- socio-economic development (E);
- mass enfranchisement of new voters (W);
- the left votes as a percentage of all votes (L).

These three Boolean variables make 2 = 8 possible combinations, namely from not present to all conditions available: 000, 100, 110, 010, 011, 001, 101, 111. The quantitative comparative analysis suggests the following minimization for situations where the dependent variable is 0 (the character '·' stands for 'and', and the plus sign stands for 'or', i.e. high levels of E, W, L often coincide with low levels of social insurance):

$$0 = E + W + L.$$

Table 9.2 shows the minimized functions that summarize the six cases with a low social insurance level into one single function,

$$0 = w \cdot e,$$

meaning a low degree of enfranchisement and a low level of socio-economic development (lower case indicates the low level). This function is only valid for three of the six cases: Finland and Sweden (0,0,0) and Italy (0,0,1).

The two positive outcome cases Denmark (0,1,1) and Switzerland (1,0,1) are indicated by the formula:

$$1 = e \cdot W \cdot L + E \cdot w \cdot l.$$

The formula signifies that a highly developed social insurance scheme is prevalent in the case of *either* low socio-economic development (e), mass enfranchisement (W) and a high share of the left votes (L), *or* a high level of socio-economic development (E), a low level of enfranchisement (w) and a low share of left votes (l); see Table 9.3.

The seven 'unexplained' cases are so-called contradictory cases that cannot be explained by the three selected independent variables. Note that these kinds of and/or statements are also part of regression analyses except that they figure at the basis of the analysis (all regression starts with conjunctive and disjunctive modelling) whereas the reported statements emerge as the *results* of Boolean analysis.

Table 9.2 *The QCA minimized function summary for the model: Social Insurance (0) = E + W + L*

	0 Configs		Cases		1 Configs		Cases	
	n	%	*n*	%	*n*	%	*n*	%
ew–[a]	2	40	3	50	0	0	0	0
Checked	2	40	3	50	0	0	0	0
Total	5	100	6	100	5	100	0	0

The table is derived from the QCA output. E = socio-economic development; W = enfranchisement; L = left votes.

[a]ew – refers to countries with a low score on socio-economic development and enfranchisement.

Table 9.3 *The QCA minimized function summary for the model: Social Insurance (1) = E + W + L*

	0 Configs		Cases		1 Configs		Cases	
	n	%	*n*	%	*n*	%	*n*	%
eWL[a]	0	0	0	0	1	20	1	17
Ewl[b]	0	0	0	0	1	20	1	17
Checked	0	0	0	0	2	40	2	33
Total	5	100	6	100	5	100	6	100

The table is derived from the QCA output. E = socio-economic development; W = enfranchisement; L = left votes.

[a]eWL refers to a low score on socio-economic development, a high score on enfranchisement and a high score on left votes.

[b]Ewl refers to a high score on socio-economic development, a low score on enfranchisement and a low score on left votes.

The statement of Berg-Schlosser and Quenter that quantitative and qualitative comparative methods are complementary is certainly true. The quantitative method requires a theoretical insight into the (assumed) interrelationships between variables, whereas the qualitative approach requires insights into the peculiarities and characteristics of particular cases. The less well qualitative comparative analysis is able to minimize functions, the more important the role of theory and interpretation becomes. For example, if qualitative comparative analysis does not minimize a set of constellations at all (meaning that there are as many functions as cases), then theory (i.e. hypotheses that discriminate between cases) is the only device left to group the functions into additive formulae. When there are many cases, this grouping on the basis of theoretical considerations becomes nearly impossible. Another problem with Boolean analysis is the data reduction. The dichotomization places quite different cases in the same categories. As a consequence, because quite different situations lead to the same results, the explanatory capacities of qualitative comparative analysis are often limited. For a further overview and evaluation of the method, see Ragin et al. (1996).

Two recent advancements have been made in configurational analysis which are both accompanied by new software tools. First, there is *Tosmana*, which implements classical Boolean algebra, but in addition seeks to tackle one of the main limitations of qualitative comparative analysis, namely its restriction to Boolean sets (Cronqvist, 2004). Tosmana introduces *multi-value minimization* as an additional feature of *Boolean minimization*. We will not discuss this further here since it is well documented and publicly accessible (http://www.tosmana.net).

Secondly, Ragin (2000) has introduced fuzzy sets which can be used to study social and political phenomena as a matter of degree instead of fixed types. A fuzzy set is a set with elements whose membership grades can have any real value between 0 and 1. This 'grading capacity' of fuzzy sets is a major advancement on its predecessor Boolean analysis (also denoted as 'crisp sets') which is confined to binary scores that are too unrefined to capture the diversity of most social and political phenomena. Fuzzy sets enable researchers to model complex and diverse constellations in such a way that patterns and variations are revealed which remain invisible when the dominant qualitative and quantitative techniques are used.

The argument based on the fuzzy-set logic is that it is much more appropriate to conceptualize social and political phenomena as 'sets' with imprecise boundaries that facilitate gradual transitions from membership to non-membership and vice versa (Klir and Yuan, 1995: 4). The fuzzy-set approach allows partial membership of a case in a given configuration. The cases' membership scores reflect the degree to which cases belong in sets or not, where 0 is fully out, 1 is fully in, and 0.5 is the cross-over point, being neither more in nor more out. By allowing for *partial membership*, sets become 'fuzzy' in contrast to 'crisp'.

It is here that the fuzzy-set *logic* steps in. Fuzzy sets enable the identification of necessary and sufficient conditions by means of the so-called subset principle:

- A condition is necessary when its score is consistently higher than the outcome (the outcome is a subset of the condition).
- A condition is sufficient when its score is consistently lower than the outcome (the condition is a subset of the outcome).

In social reality strictly necessary and sufficient conditions are exceptional. Ragin (2000) has introduced the concepts of quasi-necessity and quasi-sufficiency in order to enlarge the applicability of the fuzzy-set logic. This was also motivated by the fact that the measurement of membership scores is often imprecise, especially in the middle range. These imprecisions are taken into account by incorporating an 'adjustment factor' of, for example, 0.17. In this case, in order to constitute a violation, a case's membership in the outcome must exceed its membership in the causal condition by more than 0.17 fuzzy-membership points.

Fuzzy sets will be used here in order to demonstrate how welfare states can be studied empirically as a matter of degree instead of fixed types with the help of so-called fuzzy-sets (for a detailed discussion, see Kvist, 1999; Pennings, 2005; Ragin and Pennings, 2005). Binary scores are too unrefined to capture the diversity of welfare state programmes. The majority of welfare states, for example, may neither qualify to be fully out of particular welfare state programmes nor to be fully in. They are somewhere in-between.

The diversity of welfare statism is examined in the period 1980–97 in the OECD. Welfare statism is operationalized on the basis of a selection of variables in the OECD's Social Expenditures Database (Castles, 2004). These data are used to illustrate how the diversity of welfare programmes and their performance are poorly captured by simple dichotomies. In addition, it is shown that fuzzy sets offer a parsimonious way to trace causal patterns behind these variations. This is a crucial asset of fuzzy sets since it is not enough to signal diversity (which often leads to idiosyncrasy). Diversities should be explained, compared and validated.

The fuzzy membership degrees are used to study the conditions for the rise and cutbacks in social expenditures. Are cutbacks mainly occurring in neo-liberal or Anglo-Saxon contexts, are they to be expected in countries with overloaded welfare states, or are they a general phenomenon? These are contradicting hypotheses and there is still no consensus in the literature on which of them is correct (Pierson, 1994; Scarbrough, 2000; Huber and Stephens, 2001).

The existing literature on welfare states discusses a large number of conditions which enhance or hamper their development (e.g. Huber and Stephens, 2001). Especially important are the following social, economical, political and demographical conditions and accompanying hypotheses (Castles, 2004):

- *Societal conditions* – the type and degree of interest intermediation (variable name corporatism): the sum of the standardized scores of centralization and coordination of wage bargaining, union density and the collective coverage rate (Vergunst, 2004). The higher the degree of interest intermediation, the higher the chance of positive sum outcomes which boost the level of expenditures.
- *Political context* – the colour of party government (CPG) (variable name leftgov) according to the Schmidt index (Schmidt, 1992). The larger the share of left government seats in subsequent governments, the higher the level of welfare statism (Armingeon et al., 2003).
- *Economic openness* – the degree of economic openness (variable name openness: the sum of imports and exports as a percentage of gross domestic product). The more open a country is, the higher the level of welfare statism (Katzenstein, 1985; Armingeon et al., 2003).
- *Demography* – the number of elderly people (variable 'elderly': the percentage of people older than 65). The higher the number, the higher the levels of welfare state expenditures are expected to be (Armingeon et al., 2003).

We expect that the level of social expenditures is a function of the colour of party government, corporatism, openness of the economy and the number of elderly people. In all cases, positive relations are expected: high levels of the independent variables are expected to correspond with high levels of the dependent variable. In short,

Social expenditures = leftgov + corporatism + openness + elderly.

Table 9.4 *The causation of social expenditures in three time periods (based on minimization of the causal chains in the FS/QCA-output)*

1980–85	1986–91	1992–7
openness (left + elderly)	openness (left + ~corporatism + elderly)	openness (left + elderly)
~left • corporatism		~left • elderly

~ = not; • = and; + = or
Source: Pennings 2005: 327

The fuzzy-set analysis is conducted with a fuzzy-adjustment score of 0.17, a test proportion of 0.80 and a *p*-score of 0.05. The following analysis is limited to sufficient conditions because none of the conditions turns out to be necessary.

The output of the fuzzy-set analysis presents combinations of conditions that are to be minimized. This minimization is based on this fundamental rule: if two expressions (i.e. combinations of causal conditions) produce the same outcome (i.e. level of social spending) and differ in only one causal condition, then the condition that distinguishes the two expressions can be considered irrelevant and can be removed to create a simple, combined expression (Ragin, 1987: 93).

The computer program FS/QCA (which can be located via http://www. compasss.org) is used to identify the causal combinations that affect the degree of welfare programmes. First, the conditions for high or rising levels of social welfare expenditures are examined. The results are listed in Table 9.4. The expression 'openness (left + elderly)', for example, means that economic openness is a prerequisite for social spending in combination with left governments or a high number of elderly people. The overall results in Table 9.4 indicate that social expenditures are high in the case of an open economy in combination with leftist governments and/or an aged population. But high levels of social expenditures may also coincide with non-left governments in combination with corporatism or a high percentage of elderly people. In this respect fuzzy-set analysis incorporates both the capacity to generalize – common to the variable-oriented approach – and the capacity to detect uncommon or unexpected combinations of elements – more in line with the case oriented approach (Ragin, 2000).

The next logical step is to examine whether the 'exceptions to the rule' make any sense. As is explained in Ragin (2000), cases can be plotted by taking the lowest scores when examining sufficient conditions (which follows from the subset principle). In the case of sufficiency the outcome should be higher than the cause. Figure 9.1 shows that in several cases the cause is equal to or even higher than the outcome (Note that the number of cases in the plot is fewer than 20 because several cases are overlapping – they have identical scores). These are the cases on or below the diagonal of the plot. In these instances, the level of social expenditures is lower than expected on the basis of the openness of the economy, the number of elderly, the colour of party government and corporatism.

The cause is equal to the outcome for Belgium, Portugal, the USA, Canada and Australia. The cause is lower than the outcome in case of Ireland. This example shows that the low level of social expenditures most of the Anglo-Saxon world

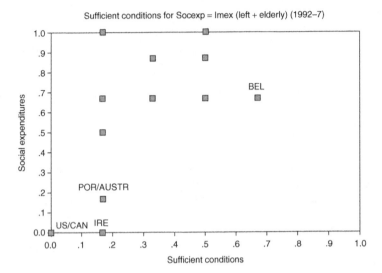

Sufficient conditions for Socexp = Imex (left + elderly) (1992–7)

Figure 9.1 *Plot of sufficient conditions for social expenditures. Source: Pennings, 2005: 330*

cannot be explained by the four conditions (Myles, 1996). This is just a simple example to illustrate that fuzzy logic may provide a parsimonious way to identify the cases that travel non-typical trajectories.

However, there are a number of limitations of this new approach to configurational analysis. First, more detailed analyses and comparisons between mainstream approaches and the fuzzy-set approach should be established in order to understand the added value of this new approach in the social sciences. Second, fuzzy-set logic cannot fully replace the other comparative approaches. Qualitative case studies remain necessary, for example, to account for deviant cases, including those found in this section. Quantitative studies are needed in order to arrive at generalizations and to formulate hypotheses. Third, fuzzy-set logic may not always prove to be the best way to study causal conditions since it is only applicable to a not-so-large number of countries for which only a small number of causal conditions are relevant. As a consequence, for certain complex research designs, the fuzzy-set approach may prove to be too limited (Pennings, 2003). However, potentially, fuzzy sets offer opportunities to combine the best of the two worlds of case- and variable-oriented research (see also Part I).

9.4 Institutions and Socio-Economic Problem-Solving

In order to examine how the institutional environment matters for the type and degree of social and economic problem-solving (and management) it is important to define the institutional impact in relative terms, i.e. in relation to actors and economic conditions. Institutions do not take decisions by themselves, of course, but they do shape the conditions under which actors are involved in decision-making. That is why it makes sense to study institutions within a wider (relational, interactive) context of reference. This is done in this section.

Our starting point is the most similar research design. Since the 1970s the OECD world has been confronted with severe economic crises (i.e. the oil shocks in 1973 and 1979). The reactions of the OECD countries to these crises differed significantly. Our purpose here is to explain these different reactions with special reference to the political-institutional environment in which actors operate (and make decisions).

We have already stressed the importance of the difference between the concepts of output and outcomes. Here we have opted for two interval scales which are derived from Armingeon et al. (2003).

- *Policy output* (pop) refers to government policies and is measured as public expenditure as a percentage of gross domestic product (i.e. total outlays of government excluding consumption of fixed capital).
- *Policy outcomes* (poc) are the effects of government policy-making (equivalent to performance). This time we use an additive index that includes indicators of economic performance (unemployment plus inflation), the so-called misery index.

Thus far we have been describing variations: exploring the Y-variable. This is a necessary step in most quantitative research. Before the explanatory stage is reached, one has to be aware of the type and degree of variation of the dependent variable. During the explanatory stage of the research the variations in the dependent variable must be explained by independent variables which are selected on the basis of theoretical assumptions. This selection is directed by the research design. In case of a most similar design countries are selected that are most alike so that the number of explanatory variables is and should be, by definition, limited.

Given what we have said about the interactive institutional approach (meaning that institutions have an interactive relationship with actors) it makes sense to select three types of factors (Keman, 2003):

1 Economic factors:

- economic growth;
- world market dependency.

2 Structural factors (institutions):

- consensus-generating traditions;
- left–right complexion of government.

3 Actors:

- political parties;
- voters;
- employers and employees.

Table 9.5 *The relationships between economic factors and policy types and policy outcomes (Pearson's r)*

	1965–73		1974–80		1981–90		1991–2000	
	POP	POC	POP	POC	POP	POC	POP	POC
WM	0.29	−0.18	0.56	0.17	0.59	0.00	0.18	−0.17
	(0.25)	(0.95)	(0.02)	(0.50)	(0.01)	(0.99)	(0.50)	(0.95)
EG	−0.011	0.89	−0.08	0.18	−0.46	0.55	−0.363	0.24
	(0.68)	(0.73)	(0.76)	(0.50)	(0.07)	(0.02)	(0.15)	(0.36)

POP = Policy Output, POC = Policy Outcomes, WM = world market dependence

EG = economic growth. Significance levels in parentheses. $n = 17$.

In the case of an exclusive saliency of the economic factors ('economics matters') we would expect a high explained variance. If such a strong relationship were to be found, we could subsequently forget about other factors. This is the main reason why the first step in the analysis starts with the economic factors. The division into the time periods corresponds to the phases of affluence, crisis and recovery.

Table 9.5 justifies the following observations:

- The economic factors are not decisive (the Pearson's *r* scores show low or no association).
- It makes sense to distinguish between national factors (i.e. economic growth) and international factors (i.e. WM) as their influence is different, especially between 1974 and 1990.

The table also illustrates the relevance of the distinction between output and outcomes. This is apparent in case of the variable world market dependence, being the additive index of imports and exports as a percentage of gross domestic product. In periods of deterioration the world market dependence relates quite strongly to interventionistic policy-making. This is understandable as open economies with high scores on world market dependence are vulnerable to outside influences (i.e. fluctuations on the world market). These countries need an extensive social infrastructure in order to guarantee everybody's material well-being if (part of) the economy is negatively affected by fluctuations on the world market. At the same time the world market dependence has had no significant impact on the policy outcomes. This is also understandable as there is no reason why open economies should perform better or worse than closed economies.

The generally low correlations between the economic variables and the policy variables enable us to introduce the institutional factors and the role of actors as mentioned above. Two institutional structures may influence the way political and socio-economic actors handle conflicting views on socio-economic policy making. Remember that, in particular, the socio-economic area is often one of the most crucial battlefields in politics, especially in times of recession. Chapter 7 illustrated

Table 9.6 *The relationships between institutions, output and outcomes (Pearson's r)*

	1965–73		1974–80		1981–90		1991–2000	
	POP	POC	POP	POC	POP	POC	POP	POC
Leadership	0.06	−0.25	0.30	−0.21	0.50	−0.25	0.55	0.10
	(0.81)	(0.33)	(0.24)	(0.42)	(0.04)	(0.34)	(0.02)	(0.70)
Corporatism	0.26	−0.53	0.43	−0.64	−0.33	−0.70	0.56	−0.40
	(0.32)	(0.03)	(0.08)	(0.00)	(0.20)	(0.00)	(0.21)	(0.11)

POP = Policy Output, POC = Policy Outcomes. Significance levels in parentheses. $n = 17$.

this point by showing that the left–right division is one of the most important structuring forces of political systems and the relationships between parties.

We distinguish between two arenas of conflict resolution: those in the political and in the socio-economic realm:

- In the political arena the style of leadership refers to the way conflicts are resolved by the political elites (namely, either more competitive or more coalescent), and is measured as the additive standardized scores of the effective number of parties, the type of electoral system ('plurality' versus 'modified pr' and 'pr') and the type of government (i.e. single-party and MWC and surplus coalition) (Armingeon et al., 2003).
- In the socio-economic arena the degree of corporatism refers to modes of conflict resolution by means of frequent interactions between governments and the main organized economic groups (also called tripartism or interest intermediation or industrial relation systems). This variable is measured on a five-point scale where 5 indicates greatest integration of the economy and 1 least integration of the economy. This index should be considered as a proxy for corporatism (Armingeon et al., 2003; Siaroff, 1999).

Both the concepts 'style of leadership' and 'corporatism' have been discussed in the previous chapter and we shall therefore not go into further detail.

Table 9.6 shows two interesting results:

- The style of leadership only coincides with state intervention in the periods after 1980.
- Corporatism affects the policy performance, but this effect has weakened in the latest period.

These patterns suggest that the relations between institutions, output and outcomes are strongly time-dependent. Since the relationships are far from perfect, there must be exceptions, meaning countries where these institutional structures do not coincide with the expected outcomes. Regression analysis can be used as a tool to determine to what degree this is the case.

Table 9.7 *Residual scores of the regression of policy types (Y) on the style of leadership (X)*

Switzerland	−2.73
Australia	−1.31
USA	−0.85
Finland	−0.63
Italy	−0.22
Ireland	−0.13
Canada	0.19
Germany	0.21
Norway	0.22
France	0.28
UK	0.39
Belgium	0.42
New Zealand	0.44
Denmark	0.56
Austria	0.72
Netherlands	0.97

Residual analysis (see Section 5.4.2) tells you whether countries have a higher (positive residual) or a lower (negative residual) Y-score than you would expect on the basis of the independent variable(s). One problem with residual analysis is how to determine an adequate threshold for residual scores: what score makes an outlier? There are no general rules for answering this question. As in our analysis the distribution of cases is not too dispersed and, consequently, the outlier scores are moderate, we have chosen not too high a threshold, namely a standardized residual score of ±1. Given this threshold, Switzerland is a clear example of an outlier (see Table 9.7). This country combines a restrictive style of policy-making with a coalescent leadership. (However, one should be aware that the data on public expenditures in Switzerland probably underestimate the level of public expenditures, see Castles, 2004.) The graphical juxtaposition of the Netherlands and Switzerland makes clear what the positive and negative residual scores mean: these outliers indicate that cooperation in politics (coalescence) is not always a necessary or a sufficient condition for active state intervention.

Factor analysis can be used in order to see whether the degree of coalescent leadership, corporatism, world market integration and interventionistic policy types can be summarized in one dimension. Factor analysis means in this case the amalgamation of four variables into one new variable, as has been done before in case of the factors TEDC and WEDC. This is done in Table 9.8.

The countries are ordered on the factor scores, which leads to an interesting result. It seems that the size of the country dominates the results. Small countries are characterized by a relatively high degree of coalescent leadership, corporatism, and interventionism in the economy. One major cause for this can be found in the high degree of small countries' world market integration, which is assumed to increase their vulnerability or their need to adapt to fluctuations in the world market. Corporatism and coalescent leadership can be seen as institutional devices to cope with this problem. These institutions direct the

Table 9.8 *Factor analysis on four variables: style of leadership, corporatism, world market dependence and policy types*

USA	−1.95
Australia	−1.20
UK	−1.11
Canada	−1.11
New Zealand	−1.00
France	−.39
Italy	−.17
Switzerland	0.04
Germany	0.14
Ireland	0.14
Finland	0.43
Austria	0.52
Norway	0.96
Denmark	1.01
Sweden	1.09
Netherlands	1.15
Belgium	1.44

Positive factor scores are most likely in the case of small countries with coalescent styles of leadership. High factor scores are more likely with larger countries with competitive cultures. Eigenvalue = 2.46; explained variance = 61.6%.

negotiating process towards pay-off (the equal distribution of economic distress) and avoid a zero-sum outcome (where one actor absorbs the welfare of another).

Coalescent leadership and corporatism are institutions with a more or less constant or structural impact on the policy-making process. The behaviour of actors is less structural in character. The latter is measured by proxies for the behaviour of parties and governments, interest groups and citizens (voters) (the source is in all cases – Armingeon et al., 2003):

- Complexion of government and parliament (CPG) – a five-point scale constructed by Schmidt (1992) in which 5 = left wing, 3 = balance, 1 = right wing.
- Strike activity (socio-economic unrest) – working days lost per 1000 workers (the natural log was taken).
- Electoral strength of left parties (LEFTV) – the additive electoral results of social democratic, left socialist and communist parties.

Correlating these non-structural variables – which may change from election to election – with more structural variables may shed some light on the interactive relationship between actors and institutions.

Table 9.9 shows one crucial aspect of the interrelationships between institutions and actors. The institutions (corporatism and the style of political leadership) shape the room to manoeuvre of political and socio-economic actors. The stability of the relationship is an indicator of the working of institutions. The stable negative signs indicate that corporatism has a tempering effect on strike activities,

Table 9.9 *The relationship between the behaviour of actors and the political-institutional room to manoeuvre (Pearson product-moment correlations)*

	1965–73		1974–80		1981–90		1991–2000	
	LS	CO	LS	CO	LS	CO	LS	CO
CPG	0.32	0.56	0.24	0.67	0.15	0.39	0.54	0.60
	(0.22)	(0.02)	(0.35)	(0.00)	(0.58)	(0.12)	(0.25)	(0.01)
Strikes	−0.54	−0.81	−0.32	−0.72	−0.35	−0.62	−0.19	−0.49
	(0.03)	(0.00)	(0.21)	(0.00)	(0.17)	(0.00)	(0.47)	(0.05)
Leftv	0.30	0.41	0.39	0.50	0.33	0.44	0.28	0.53
	(0.24)	(0.10)	(0.12)	(0.04)	(0.19)	(0.07)	(0.28)	(0.03)

Notes: LS = leadership CO = corporatism CPG = political complexion of government and parliament, Strikes = working days lost, Leftv = left votes. $n = 17$.

whereas for the style of leadership this relationship is non-significant. Overall, there are important differences between the time periods so that one should be cautious in assigning one uniform effect of institutions on the behaviour of actors.

It has become clear from the above analysis that we should be very careful with an all too deterministic reasoning or jumping to causal conclusions. Additionally, it is also clear now how 'critical cases' are selected (see also Part I). They emerge as particular cases from the analysis because of their specific combination of values which turns them into non-representative exceptional cases that do not corroborate the theory. Comparative cases, on the other hand, emerge as common and therefore representative cases.

Finally, we should be aware that, since we are merely discussing correlations here, causality is first and foremost a theoretical assumption which we try to make plausible, but which will be difficult (or even impossible) to prove empirically. Thus, the plausibility of an assumed causal relationship depends on the adequacy of the steps taken in the research design. Here we see the interaction between method (the way to approach a research question) and statistics (the devices used to answer the research question in quantitative terms). This interaction must be seen in relation to the cyclical character of the research process: theory is often needed to approach reality in a comparative manner and the results of this research often lead to adapted theories, which are again the basis for new research designs.

9.5 Electoral Cycles and Macro-Economic Policy

Politico-economic models of the macro-economy and political process can be developed by assuming that the government maximizes its own utility subject to various constraints (Schneider and Frey, 1988: 240). The most important constraint is political: a government only stays in power if it is re-elected. For that it needs the electoral support of voters. The electorate's voting decision is supposed to depend on the state of the economy, and the government may attempt to influence its re-election prospects by altering the state of the economy. This is one of the basic assumptions of the so-called *political business cycle.*

Schneider and Frey's overview of empirical studies which have tested for systematic business fluctuations coinciding with election periods has found mixed results at best. In this section we will focus on the empirical study of Sabine Lessmann (1987) because it presents an interesting integration of three techniques that are used to test the political business cycle: regression analysis, discriminant analysis and analysis of variance. Lessmann has chosen these three statistical techniques for the identification and specification of the assumed synchronization of expenditure in electorally appealing areas with the timing of general elections. The focus here is primarily on the research design: assuming that the political business cycle exists, how can we determine how it works? It is clear from the beginning that the research design must possess specific characteristics in order to enable a fruitful analysis. Most importantly, the data must have a time series format in order to be able to detect the pattern that suggests a business cycle, since it is change that matters.

In Lessmann's analysis, a regression analysis is run with three dummy variables as independent variables, denoting the pre-election, election and first post-election year. The expenditure variables are then regressed on the different years. The intercept or constant is in this case equal to the mean of the second post-election years which are assigned 0s throughout. The values of a and b will tell us which independent variable leads to what kind of allocation. R^2 quantifies the proportion of variance in the expenditure data, accounted for by the different years of the election period. The F-ratio associated with R^2 determines whether the groups differ significantly. The results of the regression analysis will tell us whether the different years of the election period can account for much of the variance encountered in the expenditure series. Secondly, the results will indicate if it is the pre-election year or the election year which is actually more important as an explanatory factor. Thirdly, and most importantly, we will see if there is any systematic synchronization at all.

In order to determine which groups of years actually differ from each other, Lessmann took one of the 'multiple comparisons between means' approaches in the framework of an analysis of variance (ANOVA; see Section 6.6). Important comparisons are the allocations in pre-election and election years versus post-election allocations. Other values such as the sum of squares, the mean squares and F are the same as those obtained with regression analysis.

Finally, discriminant analysis is also a regression technique which aims to distinguish statistically between two or more groups of cases on the basis of a number of interval variables. This enables us to compare, for example, expenditures in election years with expenditures in the first post-election year in order to see whether they are statistically different or not. If they are different, then there is some empirical ground for a political business cycle.

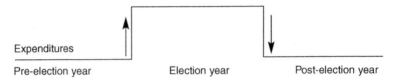

Figure 9.2 *Schematic example of a political business cycle*

Lessmann's various analyses are carried out as follows: firstly, the expenditures in election years were statistically compared with the expenditures in the first post-election year. According to the literature on political business cycles, the two groups should be different, and the expenditures in the election year group should be systematically higher than those in the post-election year group. Secondly, the expenditures in election years were compared with the second post-election years. Thirdly, the two analysed groups consisted of the pre-election and the election year itself. According to some suggestions in the literature, the expenditures of the election years should be statistically different but also higher. Fourthly and finally, the expenditures of the pre-election year were tested against the expenditures of the first post-election year. In this case the pre-election years were assumed to be higher. In its most simple form this can be visualized as in Figure 9.2.

Lessmann's analysis is limited to Germany. A similar research design can also be applied to our selection of 18 OECD countries with the help of the country–year data set (1965–90). We can test the assumption that parties will lower the taxes in the year before an election year in order to gain votes. Further, we add two extra variables into the models – social transfers and the complexion of government and parliament – which offer the *alternative hypotheses* that the level of taxes relates more to the type of welfare state and/or the government complexion than to the occurrence of election years.

First of all we have to distinguish between three types of years: pre-election (variable name preelyr), election year (variable name elyr) and post-election years (variable name postelyr). Next we construct a dummy variable that divides the years into election and non-election years (variable name prior). The three statistical techniques are applied in order to test the initial hypothesis. These steps are taken in the file Chapter9.sps, under Section 9.5. The results of the analysis are presented in Table 9.10.

In the ANOVA and regression analysis the relative weight of trans, prior and CPG are measured. The results of both analyses show that the dummy variable Prior is not able to explain variation in the dependent variable taxes (given the low F and beta scores which are also not significant). The discriminant analysis tests if the level of the taxes and transfers corresponds to two groups: the pre-election years and the non-pre-election years. The discriminant analysis clearly shows that such a grouping cannot be made on the basis of these variables. The values of the eigenvalue, canonical correlation and chi-square are very low, and the overall model is not significant (see Section 6.5 for an explanation of these

Table 9.10 *The application of three statistical techniques on political business cycles*

	ANOVA		Regression		Discriminant functions[a]	
	F	Sign. F	Beta	Sign. t	Wilk's lambda	Sign.
Transfers	480.6	0.0	0.71	0.0	0.9996	0.7249
Prior	0.010	0.919	0.0	0.97	0.9994	0.9168
CPG	23.5	0.0	0.23	0.0	0.9994	0.9817
Explained/predicted	57.8		0.56		51.04	
n	335		335		444	

[a]The variables in the discriminant function do not add significantly to the distinction between the categories of the dependent variable.

terms). The overall conclusions confirm the results of Lessmann and many others, namely that the evidence for a political business cycle is extremely poor. Other factors, such as the type of the welfare state and the colour of government, appear to be more important.

9.6 Democratic Performance

The term democratic performance refers to the quality of democracy as indicated by, for example, freedom, equality, rates of participation and political stability (See Lane and Ersson, 1994). If we are looking for variations in the degree of democracy we mostly cannot apply the most similar research design, since the similarity of, for example, OECD countries is partly derived from the fact that these countries have the same level of democracy (but not equality). Hence, the first half of this section demonstrates a most different research design which is based on a comparison of the research of Burkhart and Lewis-Beck (1994) on the relationship between democracy and economic welfare and the research of Vanhanen (1990, 1997) on democratization.

The Burkhart–Lewis-Beck data set is an adapted and extended version of the well-known Gastil/Freedom House democracy indicators (for an overview, see Lane and Ersson, 1997: 93). Gastil ranks each nation on separate seven-point scales for 'political rights' and 'civil liberties'. Burkhart and Lewis-Beck added to these data dummies for the position of countries, $c = $ core, $m = $ semiperiphery, $p = $ periphery). They also employ the energy consumption per capita (logged) as an economic development measure (which has a correlation of 0.9 with gross national product per capita). Burkhart and Lewis-Beck test the 'economic development thesis' with the model

$$D_t = a + bD_{t-1} + cE_t + d(M \times E_t) + e(P \times E_t) + u,$$

where D_t is the democracy index at time t, D_{t-1} is the democracy index from the year before, E_t is energy consumption per capita (logged to base 10) at time t, $M \times E_t$ is the dummy variable for semiperiphery status multiplied by E_t, and P is a dummy for periphery status.

The Burkhart and Lewis-Beck model is an autoregressive model having the lagged dependent variable at the right-hand sight of the equation (as in: $Y_t = Y_{t-1} + X_t$). This type of modelling is not without complications as it may well boost the R^2 and beta weight. D_{t-1} acts to control for omitted independent variables: as the other forces acting on democracy are uncertain, they will be essentially summarized in the democratic performance of the nation during its previous year. Their estimation procedure is GLS-ARMA (a pooled time series cross-sectional technique based on Generalized Least Squares), as this procedure avoids first-order autocorrelation and cross-sectional heteroscedasticity. Their model throws up a pseudo-R^2 of 0.71 and the b-scores are 2.49 (for E_t), -1.33 (for $M \times E_t$) and -1.54 (for $P \times E_t$). Their conclusion is that economic development matters most for nations in the core; it still matters, but about half as much, in the semiperiphery. For nations on the periphery, the economic effect is just a little less. Taken together, economic factors, both international and domestic, appear decisive in shaping a nation's democratic future.

We will replicate the analysis in a simpler format, with OLS regression on a 1988 cross-section (Table 9.11). The results of our analysis match with those of Burkhart and Lewis-Beck, albeit that our estimates indicate moderate effects (see the SPSS set-up in Chapter9.sps). This outcome confirms our suspicion that the autoregressive model might not throw up a reliable R^2. A theoretical, rather than statistical, explanation of the moderate performance of the Burkhart and Lewis-Beck model is provided by Vanhanen (1990, 1997). He proposed an alternative for the socio-economic hypothesis of democratization, by hypothesizing that 'democratization takes place under conditions in which power resources have become so widely distributed that no group is any longer able to suppress its competitors or to maintain its hegemony' (Vanhanen, 1990: 66). Vanhanen's dependent variable is an index of democratization (ID) which multiplies the following two variables and divides the outcome by 100:

1 The degree of legal competition (in a democracy there will be at least two equal groups which are free to compete for power) which is operationalized as 100 minus the percentage of the votes won by the largest party (a high score indicates a high degree of competition).
2 The degree of participation, which is operationalized as the number of voters as a percentage of the total population (a high score indicates a high degree of participation).

Vanhanen's independent variable is the index of power resources (IPR) which is operationalized by means of six indicators:

- (1) Urban and (2) non-agricultural population indicate the degree of occupational diversification and the level of socio-economic development.

Table 9.11 *Two models on democratization (1988)*

Variable	Burkhart and Lewis-Beck (1994) model, $n = 131$			Vanhanen (1990) model, $n = 147$	
	beta	Sign. *t*		beta	Sign. *t*
LG10ecpc	0.57	0	IPR	0.84	0.00
Met	−0.52	0			
Pet	−0.43	0			
Constant		0.06			
R^2_{adj}	0.36			0.71	

LG10ecpc = energy consumption per capita (logged to base 10); Met = the dummy variable for semiperiphery status multiplied by E_i; Pet = the dummy variable for periphery status multiplied by E_i; IPR = index of power resources.

Sources: Burkhart and Lewis-Beck (1994) and Vanhanen (1990).

- (3) Students and (4) literates indicate the distribution of knowledge and intellectual power resources.
- (5) Family farms and (6) the degree of decentralization of non-agricultural economic resources are intended to measure the degree of resource distribution.

The main difference with Burkhart and Lewis-Beck is that Vanhanen looks not only at the level of welfare but also, and more importantly, at the distribution of a wider range of power resources. Vanhanen's conceptualization and operationalization of the index of power resources indeed results in a much higher explained variance of 0.709.

This example shows us that a high explained variance is only to be trusted when *both* the theoretical and statistical specifications of the model are correct. The Burkhart and Lewis-Beck model is far more complicated than our replication. But by reducing its complexity and by comparing its results with other research outcomes, it becomes clear what the weaknesses of this model are.

Hitherto, we have focused on the bivariate relationship between democracy and economic development. But there is also a large body of literature discussing a variety of possible determinants of democratizion. Below we will discuss both the concept of democratization and the conditions for it and, in doing so, follow the presentation and argumentation by Keman (2002). Various ways of conceptualizing, measuring and transforming democracy into a valid and reliable cross-national variable are explored. The analysis shows that the main components of democracy are:

- pluralism – representing the possibilities of organizing as a group on the societal level free of the state;
- polyarchy – indicating the positive conditions for the population to participate in national decision-making;
- democraticness – a combined measure of both these variables and thus presenting the degree of democraticness in a society from a comparative perspective.

Keman's study is based on 172 countries in the world (40 per cent non-democracies; 10 per cent old democracies; 50 per cent recent (established after 1945) or new (after 1988) democracies). The starting point is the well-known conceptualization of democracy by Dahl as polyarchal democracy, being a political system with the following six institutions:

- universal suffrage and the right to run for public office;
- free and fairly conducted elections;
- availability and observance of the right to free speech and protection to do so;
- the existence of and free access to alternative (and often competing) information (not controlled by government);
- the undisputed right to form and to join relatively autonomous organizations, in particular political parties (and, crucially, parties in opposition);
- the responsiveness of government (and parties) to voters and accountability of government (and parties) to election outcomes and parliament.

It is this set of institutions taken together that distinguish polyarchic regimes from other regime types. The coming about of these institutions can then be seen as the process towards democratization. The endured existence and observance of the whole set is the hallmark of an established democracy (see also: Schmidt, 2000: 393–5; Keman, 2000b).

Among many comparativists, Tatu Vanhanen is a prime example of someone who has attempted to describe and analyse the process of democratization (Vanhanen, 1990, 1997). As explained earlier, his index of polyarchy is based on two measures representing 'participation' and 'competition' that together form an index of democratization (ID). From his analysis it appears that countries on average score higher today than in the 1980s (1980 = 8.96; 1990 = 13.9) on the index of democratization. Indeed, the world has changed towards more democratization and now contains a growing number of countries that have taken the road to greater polyarchy.

Coppedge and Reinicke (1990) have developed a scale that examines the available institutions that promote a pluralist organization of society. In addition to examining the requirements for free and fair elections, they have developed indicators to measure the degree of freedom of organization, of speech and information, and of access to government sources of information. This operationalization is quite close to Dahl's idea of polyarchy (see Dahl, 1984, 1998: 85). Hence, Coppedge and Reinicke measure the extent to which groups in society can organize themselves and are capable of conducting a viable opposition. Yet, as Schmidt (2000: 402) rightly observes, this kind of operationalization tends to ignore the formal institutions (i.e. rule of law) that restrict the powers of government and the state. To some extent this defect has been solved by Jaggers and Gurr (1995), who have collected data across most nation-states on:

- those institutions that facilitate and promote political choice by citizens;
- the availability of basic civil and political rights for all citizens;
- the existence of constitutional requirements that limit the executive powers.

Jaggers and Gurr have developed a scale that enables them not only to differentiate between 'autocracy' and 'democracy', but also the level of democracy available. What do these cross-national variables tell us about the level of democratization?

First of all, it appears that the method employed leads to different results. The number of non-democratic countries is proportionally twice as high according to Coppedge and Reinicke as according to Jagger and Gurr (the difference is 30 cases). Yet, Keman has found that the differences are less if one controls the results for regime types such as the ones developed by Alvarez et al. (1996): presidentialism, parliamentarism, dictatorships and autocracies. It should be noted that on the level of individual cases the differences are – again – not great, but certain cases appear to be odd or out of place (partly due to the fact that the data used are more often than not supplied by public authorities or derived from constitutional documents).

Contrary to the indicators and scales discussed here, there is also research which focuses explicitly on the execution of individual rights not interfered with by the state (and its agencies). An example is the Freedom House index of political and civil rights (Freedom House, 2005) which has been established since 1971. These scales run from 1 to 7, where a low value implies actual availability and observation for these rights. Taken together, these two scales provide information on the extent to which a nation not only is formally democratic, but also can be considered as truly liberal democratic in practice and therefore as close as can be to Dahl's polyarchy.

As can be seen in Table 9.12 the prevalence and observance of political and civil rights do make a difference. What is striking is the marked difference between parliamentarism and presidentialism in this respect. The latter regime type consistently shows a worse record in observing civil and political rights, notwithstanding its rule of law.

Table 9.12   *Distribution of political and civil rights worldwide, 1999*

	Civil rights	Political rights
Polyarchies		
Parliamentary	2.03 (11.9%)	1.39 (8.5%)
Presidential	2.87 (23.9%)	2.26 (19.7%)
Non-democracies		
Dictatorial	4.48 (39.6%)	4.80 (44.5%)
Autocratic	5.15 (24.6%)	5.44 (27.3%)
Total mean	3.60 (100%)	3.43 (100%)
N	157	157
Correlations		
Civil rights	1.00	0.90
Polyarchy scale	−0.66	−0.70
Vanhanen index	−0.70	−0.68
Jaggers and Gurr	−0.76	−0.83
Coppedge and Reinicke	0.69	0.67

Note: The lower the score the better the performance.

Source: Schmidt (2000).

Table 9.13   *Factor analysis of democracy scales and indexes*

	Pluralism		Polyarchy	
Variables used	• Political rights • Civil rights • Coppedge and Reinicke		• Vanhanen • Jaggers and Gurr	
Loadings	PCA	PAF	PCA	PAF
	0.946	0.502	0.926	0.585
	0.949	0.817	0.926	0.585
	0.856	0.821		
% of variance	84.28%	84.15%	85.79%	88.26%

PCA = principal component analysis; PAF = principal axis factoring.

Although various dimensions of democracy are measured as a system and its performance as a procedure, it is not yet satisfactory as a truly comparative variable. According to Bollen and Paxton (2000), this is mainly due to the (ab)use of 'subjective' measures (such as those of Coppedge and Reinicke) or to the unreliability of the findings by Freedom House (1999) or Gastil (1990). An alternative line of inquiry could be to return to Dahl's original ideas and to combine the various measures (Bollen and Paxton, 2000: 78–9). Keman's approach is to combine objective measures with subjective ones and to distinguish between conditions for pluralism and institutions of polyarchy. To this end he collected a number of scales and indexes (see Bollen, 1993; Bollen and Paxton, 2000; Schmidt, 2000) that have been developed both subjectively and objectively, and grouped these variables as being productive for creating pluralistic conditions or promoting polyarchic institutions (see Keman, 2002b, for the variables used). By combining subjective and objective measures the *reliability* of the data in use might be improved. By ex ante dividing the measures into more pluralistic and polyarchic the *validity* of the variables in use is affected. The statistical procedure to carry this out is factor analysis (Table 9.13) – with one factor solution, principal axis factoring (PAF) aiming at high levels of explained variance (see Part II). The results are two valid and reliable variables indicating the extent of democracy and degree of democraticness across the world.

Table 9.14 reports the distribution of the level of pluralism and polyarchy and the related democraticness. Of the 127 nations that have positive scores on both dimensions – pluralism and polyarchy – about one-third ($N = 43$) of can be considered – according to this operationalization – as genuinely democratic (i.e. the score is > 1.0). This is a relatively high number of countries.

Of course, what can be noticed from Table 9.14 is that the 'older' and 'richer' the countries are, the stronger their democraticness appears to be. In addition, the parliamentary types of democracy score consistently higher than any other type of regime, including presidentialism. Finally, it should be noticed that Latin American countries do fare better than post-communist ones. This supports the idea that 'ageing' is an important factor in developing higher levels of democraticness.

Table 9.14 *Average scores of indicators of the level of democracy for type of countries, duration and regime type*

	Pluralism (N = 161)		Polyarchy (N = 145)		Democraticness (N = 127)	
Type of countries	1.06	(17.4%)	1.25	(20.0%)	2.29	(22.0%)
OECD members (N = 28)						
Post-communist (N = 23)	−0.67	(3.7%)	0.04	(15.9%)	−0.55	(4.7%)
Latin American (N = 22)	0.59	(19.9%)	0.32	(15.2%)	0.73	(17.3%)
Other countries (N = 72)	−0.48	(59.6%)	−0.62	(49.7%)	−1.19	(56.7%)
Duration						
Old	1.23	(19.2%)	1.40	(18.6%)	2.66	(21.3%)
Recent	0.81	(46.5%)	0.75	(37.2%)	1.48	(42.7%)
New	−0.11	(34.3%)	0.20	(44.2%)	−0.04	(36%)
Regime type						
Presidential	0.45	(27.1%)	0.48	(34.1%)	0.89	(31.4%)
Parliamentary	0.94	(22.1%)	1.23	(20.5%)	2.16	(21.5%)
Dictatorial	−0.56	(32.9%)	−0.65	(30.3%)	−1.22	(32.2%)
Autocratic	−0.82	(17.9%)	−1.25	(15.2%)	−2.48	(14.9%)

NB: N = number of cases included for each indicator; percentages in parentheses are of total N (see headings). Recent = after 1945; new = after 1988.

In the rest of this section we shall employ these three indexes of democracy to (re)consider a number of associations with the other variables that can be seen as explaining the cross-national variation in democraticness as well as possibly accounting for certain societal performances. We shall employ the 'variable-oriented' approach for a worldwide universe of discourse because this type of analysis with a high number of cases and few variables is crucial for the development of a 'middle-range' theory regarding the democraticness of political systems (see Lane and Ersson, 1999).

Surveying the literature on democracy as a system and its development (i.e. the process) the following answers have been offered:

- Economic development and socio-economic circumstances influence both its development and working (e.g. Berg-Schlosser and de Meur, 1996).
- Modernization of society and the extension of public welfare are conducive to (further) democratization of the nation-state (e.g. Dahl, 1998).
- Institutionalization of democracy as a regime in relation to its viability, which over time enhances the level of democraticness (e.g. Diamond and Plattner, 1994).
- Organized political action in terms of participation and opposition, which 'makes democracy work' (in whatever way), is an important and often neglected facet of democratic politics (e.g. Norris, 1999).

To what extent do these factors account for the cross-national variation regarding the extent of pluralism, polyarchy and democraticness (as empirically developed in the previous paragraphs)? Table 9.15 reports four regression models

Table 9.15 *Regression analysis of factors explaining democracy*

Independent variables		Pluralism		Polyarchy		Democraticness	
		Dependent variables					
Economics	α	−14.1		−25.8		−3.6	
Gnppc[†]	β	0.45	(3.95)	0.42	(3.91)	0.51	(4.80)
Govexppc[‡]	β	0.12*	(1.08)	0.25	(2.33)	0.17*	(1.59)
	R^2	25.5%		33.1%		35.8%	
Society	α	−17.7		−18.6		−3.7	
Urbanization	β	−0.12*	(−1.13*)	0.07*	(0.70)	0.01*	(0.09)
HDI	β	0.66	(6.49)	0.56	(5.64)	0.61	(5.71)
	R^2	32.4%		36.9%		36.8%	
Institutions	α	−7.3		−7.2		−1.5	
Presidentialism	β	0.34	(4.48)	0.34	(4.51)	0.37	(4.79)
Parliamentarism	β	0.74	(10.49)	0.73	(9.76)	0.76	(9.78)
	R^2	40.3%		39.3%		42.6%	
Politics	α	−16.5		−19.44		−3.9	
Electoral turnout	β	0.35	(3.37)	0.38	(3.84)	0.38	(3.79)
Central gov. exp.	β	0.19	(1.81)	0.24	(2.39)	0.25	(2.54)
	R^2	16.8%		22.9%		23.5%	

Note: OLS procedure has been employed; number of cases is 82 and 110; *t*-values are in parentheses; non-significant results are flagged:*
[†]Gnppc – GNP per capita [‡]Govexppc – Government expenditures per capita.

representing four equations that reflect the main answers to the question: how do we explain the occurrence and viability of democracy? The four models are all, but for two factors, statistically significant (the rate of urbanization and the size of the public sector appear irrelevant in this context) and thus all help to explain why democracies only develop and sustain if certain conditions are met. Most of the results are unsurprising and underwrite existing knowledge (Landman, 2003). Yet, it is also clear that none of the models is superior to the others, either in terms of explained variance (adjusted R^2), or in the magnitude of influence.

The first model, depicting the working of the market as well as the state, demonstrates that the 'wealth of a nation' is certainly an incentive for democratization. However, this is not the case for the size of the public sector. Yet, at the same time it is also clear that this is an insufficient condition *per se*. There are many outliers that prove the contrary. For example, many non-democratic nations also have considerable levels of public expenditure. Likewise, a number of states with aggregated economic riches spring to mind that are close to dictatorship or autocracy (e.g. some of the Arabian countries). In short, we hold the view that economic wealth certainly can help to foster democracy and is more often than not associated with higher level of democraticness, but is not the driving force as many political scientists and economists in the period directly after the Second World War claimed (Castles, 1998).

The same can be said of the societal forces (the second model). Although much of the literature claims that the composition of society and its consequences for inter-class rivalry are important for understanding the process of democratization as well as the stability of a democratic' regime, this hypothesis is not supported by our analysis. From our analysis it transpires that urbanization – used as a proxy for modernization – is unrelated to the indicators for democracy. Hence, it is either an invalid proxy indicator or the modernization thesis is not valid. We think both explanations are plausible (and this is supported in much of the literature; see Rueschmeyer et al., 1992; Landman, 2003). Conversely, the quality of life as expressed by the Human Development Index is an important asset for developing and sustaining democracy. Yet, again as with economic factors, we can only go along with this claim as far as it implies a necessary condition; but – judging by an explained variance of approximately 36.8 per cent – it is an insufficient condition for improving the level of democraticness of a nation. In addition, it should be noted that both explanations – the economy and society – tend to become functional ones. If so, and we think this is correct, the causality of the argument is weak if not absent. Rather, we would go along with those who advocate a more 'case-oriented' approach that enables researchers to disentangle the subtle variations within a society and to develop 'path-dependent' explanations (e.g. Putnam, 1993).

The third model concerns the impact on the level of democraticness of the organization of the democratic polity. Too often the institutional fabric of democracy has been considered as the end-result of democratization. We think this view is biased if not wrong because institutions are not static, but are continuously modified by actors. The reason is that, both in 'old' and 'new' democracies, the struggle for more or better democracy is mainly fought out over institutions, which explains why they are not constants.

The last model reported in Table 9.15 concerns the active use of designated powers by the people and by the state. On the one hand, we examined the use of the ballot box, and on the other hand, we scrutinized the idea that central government is strongly associated with democraticness: a democratic state will be conducive to greater state intervention (by popular demand). Both contentions are only weakly supported, and – as was the case with economics and society – we can only repeat our observation that, although there is a relationship, it is not convincing and cannot be considered as a major factor for democratization and democraticness as such (Keman, 2002).

In summary, the cross-national analysis of factors promoting pluralism, polyarchy and democraticness demonstrates (*ceteris paribus*) that favourable economic conditions and high(er) levels of human development are incentives for achieving higher levels of democraticness. However, like political factors, they are not crucial *per se*, nor functional under all circumstances. It appears rather that the interplay of these factors benefits further democratization and may well enhance the level of democraticness of a nation. Hence, there is not a definitive set of factors, conditions or prerequisites (although their absence may certainly harm the level of democraticness attained!) that allows for a successful development and extension of democracy.

A largely neglected, but very relevant aspect of democraticness is its performance. Do democracies perform better than non-democracies? It is widely accepted that high levels of democraticness are associated with the period for which a country has had a constitution and experienced a democratic polity. Conversely, this is expressed in the absence of high levels of protest and violence. In short, the more enduring a democracy is, the more 'ordered' society appears to be. However, cyclical effects of economic misery (such as inflation and unemployment) do not directly affect democratic governance. It appears to be rather a matter of a structural deficiency, i.e. a poor nation not only is associated with less democraticness, but also (apparently) has less 'room for manoeuvre' to remedy such a situation and thence develop democratic governance.

This conclusion is in accordance with a large part of the literature that focuses on the determinant of democratization and democratic development (see Landman, 2003): economic developments are important conditions for democratic governance. Yet, as Manfred Schmidt (1989, 2000) has demonstrated, there is more to it than that. Although 'economics' matters, it does not and cannot explain satisfactorily the cross-national variation in the political performance of nations across the world. This can easily be demonstrated by replicating the so-called 'Zöllner model' to our universe of discourse ($n = 52$ democracies).

The Zöllner model assumes that both demographic factors (such as the level of the dependent population) and economic affluence (e.g. the level of gross national product per capita) determine the provision of public welfare by governments. In other words, governments, democratic and non-democratic alike, will produce social policies depending on 'objective' developments of the society they rule. Yet, so it is argued, this may be true to a certain extent, but it does not fully account for the cross-national variation in social policy provision, nor – and that is our main point – for what other factors are relevant as well and to what degree (see Schmidt, 1989, 2000).

In Table 9.16 we examine to what extent the Zöllner model explains the policy outputs of democratic government. The results demonstrate that indeed the demographic situation and economic circumstances are relevant for understanding the cross-national variations of policy outputs. At the same time it is also obvious that there is ample room for further explanation, as the explained variance (adjusted R^2) never exceeds 66.1 per cent (for social policy expenditures).

Second, it should be noted that the level of public expenditure is hardly the result of the central variables of the Zöllner model. Conversely, we observe that the policy choices made show a certain degree of priority: social welfare and health care are predominant, whereas this is less the case with education. Hence, there are other factors at work that direct the level and functional allocations of public expenditure.

Thirdly, the parameter which is significant in all equations in Table 9.16 is the previous level of expenditures (in the 1970s), and this accounts for most of the explained variance. This does not support the Zöllner model, but rather demonstrates that the original choices made also determine the present levels of policy output by governments. This implies two additional explanations: one, that political decisions made and put into effect have a strong tendency to be 'path-dependent' (Putnam, 1993), or that policy-making tends to be influenced by incrementalism (Keman, 1993b). Whatever way one looks at this, it is apparent

Table 9.16 *Application of the Zöllner model (N = 52)*

Dependent variables	Independent variables			
	Population	Level of affluence	Original level	Explained variance
Central government expenditures	−0.07	0.04	0.46*	18.0%
Social policy	0.10	0.40*	0.57*	66.1%
Health care	−0.04	0.57*	0.052*	51.5%
Education	0.21	0.24	0.43*	25.1%
Defence	−0.06	−0.17	0.87*	65.0%

Note: All models are OLS regressions; the significant results are flagged (*); the coefficients are expressed as standardized values.

that factors other than 'objective' developments alone do account for policy-making in democratic systems. For it is an accepted point of view in the literature on 'new' institutionalism and public policy analysis that the institutional design of political systems by and large produces effects such as incrementalism, inertia and path dependency, which in turn affect the policy outcomes, i.e. political performance (see, for example, Keman, 1997; Castles, 1998). For this reason, institutional factors should be taken into account in order to explain the political and procedurial performance of representative government.

9.7 Parties and Accountability

Responsiveness and accountability are two important aspects of the process of democratic decision-making and therefore central mechanisms in the chain of democratic control and command. In Chapter 7 we discussed and analysed party responsiveness in relation to the median voter. In this section we will focus on party accountability, which is strongly linked to the *mandate theory*. This theory states that voters mandate parties to fulfil their promises once they are in office. The way parties use this mandate depends on the type of party system (two-party system vs. multi-party system) and the constitutional features of the system (presidentialism or not). This section applies the mandate theory to a multi-party system (the Netherlands) and two-party systems (the USA and UK).

Budge and Hofferbert have presented a range of regression equations that model the linkages between party programme emphases, on the one hand, and expenditures in several policy areas, on the other, for the American political parties. These models are based on different hypotheses about factors that might influence the impact of parties. In general, we distinguish between three types of modelling:

- additive or conjunctive modelling (for 'or–or' relationships);
- multiplicative modelling (for 'and–and' relationships);
- a combination of the above types (for more complex and elaborate models).

Table 9.17 *Regression equations that model the impact of American parties on the level of social expenditures*

Label	Equation	Type	Hypothesis
Competitive model	$\gamma = \alpha + \beta R + \beta D$	Additive	Expenditure will rise if the Democrats or the Republicans focus on it, and they will rise even more if both parties emphasize it
Complementary model	$\gamma = \alpha + \beta(R + D)$	Additive	The Democrats and Republicans have an equal influence on the level of expenditure
Consensus model	$\gamma = \alpha + \beta(R \times D)$	Multiplicative	Expenditure will only rise when there is consensus (or when $R \times D > 0$)
Control model	$\gamma = \alpha + \beta(R \times P_R)$ $+ \beta(D \times P_D)$	Both additive and multiplicative	Both the Republicans and the Democrats may have influence as long as they have the president (P = the presidency)
General programme model	$\gamma = \alpha - \beta R - \beta D$ $+ \beta(R \times P_R)$ $+ \beta(D \times P_D)$	Both additive and multiplicative	When in office, both parties take the opposite position to that of the parties not in office (thereby undoing each others' influence)
General partisan influence model	$\gamma = \alpha - \beta R - \beta D$ $+ \beta(R \times P_R)$ $+ \beta(D \times P_D) + R$	Both additive and multiplicative	The same as the general programme model, but this time a constant extra influence is given to the Republicans

Source: Budge and Hofferbert (1990).

Table 9.17 summarizes the models. They can be applied to any category of expenditures and corresponding programme emphases. Here we will not replicate their analysis, but ask to what extent their models are applicable to other political systems. Here we take the example of the Dutch system, but any other multi-party system could have been chosen. We limit the analysis to the three main Dutch parties: the CDA (Christian Democrats), the PvdA (Labour Party) and the VVD (Liberals).

Following van Wijck's (1991) operationalization, the degree of income inequality is measured by the old age pension as a proportion of the average monthly income. We also followed van Wijck's method to cope with two major adjustments to the old age pension in 1965 and 1985. To be sure that these policy shifts do not influence the results, two dummies are added to all regression equations (named D65 and D85). We refer to the file Chapter 9.sps for all the details.

Table 9.18 gives an overview of the mandate models applied to the Netherlands. These models are adjusted to the multi-party system by assuming that the CDA, PvdA and VVD are the three major parties (either in the role of cabinet party or opposition party). The results show that the CDA plays an important role as a 'pivotal party'. In the competitive model the CDA appears to be the only party that matters. This pivotal role can be explained by the fact that this party was present in all postwar cabinets (until 1994). As a consequence, it did not matter much for policy outcomes whether either the PvdA or the VVD joined the CDA-dominated cabinet. The two dummy variables D65 and D85, both representing policy shifts, have stronger causal effects than the party variables.

The Budge and Hofferbert test of the mandate theory has recently been compared with other mandate theory approaches. Royed (1996) gives an overview of the major tests of mandate models. She criticizes the Budge and Hofferbert approach by stating that the relationship between policy statements and spending is not direct, that the percentage of sentences is a very imprecise indicator of party intentions and that the spending categories are too broad and aggregated. Given these limitations, the results of the Budge–Hofferbert approach are at best a very rough estimate of the relationship between party programmatic commitments and policy actions due to a trade-off between a large cross-sectional comparability and a low degree of specificity of the dependent and independent variables. Hence, Royed reverses this trade-off by making the dependent and independent variables more specific and by consequently reducing the universe of discourse.

In doing so, Royed is seeking an alternative to the mechanical relationships that are assumed by Budge and Hofferbert. She focuses more on 'real' specific promises that are made and compares them with the 'real' accomplishments related to that specific pledge. Royed compares the effectiveness of the 'Conservative revolutions' in the USA (Reagan) and the UK (Thatcher). Royed's primary finding is that more Conservative Party pledges were fulfilled, compared to those of the Republican and Democratic parties in the USA. Royed's basic data are summarized in Table 9.19. Whereas Budge and Hofferbert find that both the USA and the UK confirm the mandate model equally, Royed argues that the institutional differences between the two countries make the UK more effective (i.e. the mandate model is more fully confirmed) than the USA. The most basic difference is the presidential/parliamentary distinction. The USA is characterized by a system with separation of powers, low party cohesion and multiple centres of power – a combination that may invoke *deadlock*. In both countries the decision-making environment may vary. In the USA there may be *divided or united government*, and the UK may have a large, small or even no majority. Even when there is united government in the USA (meaning that the president is of the same party as 'controls' both houses), there are still incohesive parties, and an independent legislature and a strong committee system.

Royed opts for a firmer connection between party programmatic commitments ('pledge') and policy action ('pledge fulfilment') by examining, for different policy areas, to what degree *specific* pledges are fulfilled. The results in Table 9.19 show that the Thatcher administration was indeed more effective in achieving its

Table 9.18 *The mandate models applied to the Netherlands, 1948–91 (n = 40)*

Label	Hypothesis	Equation	Result	R^2_{adj}	DW	Interpretation
Competitive model	The sum of all parties' emphases is positive $(\beta_1 + \beta_2 + \beta_3 > 0)$	$DVT = \alpha + \beta_1 D65_t + \beta_2 D85_t + \beta_3 CDAP_t + \beta_4 VVDP_t + \beta_5 PVDAP_t + e_t$	$DVT = -0.011 + 0.081\ D65_t - 0.122\ D85_t + 0.003\ CDAP_t + e$	0.6	2.9	The CDA party beta is the only one that is significant. The other parties do not matter
Complementary model	The total positive emphases of all parties leads to less income inequality $(\beta_3 > 0)$	$DVT = \alpha + \beta_1 D65_t + \beta_2 D85_t + \beta_3 TOT_t + e_t$	$DVT = -0.008 + -0.081\ D65_t + -0.111\ D85_t + 0.001\ TOT_t$	0.6	2.8	Both governmental and opposition favoured income equality
Consensus model	Only when there is a consensus between government and opposition do we expect an increase in income equality $(\beta_3 > 0)$	$DVT = \alpha + \beta_1 D65_t + \beta_2 D85_t + \beta_3 CON_t + e_t$	$DVT = -0.005 + 0.081\ D65_t + -0.115\ D85_t + 0.00002\ CON_t + e$	0.6	2.8	The degree of consensus is very moderate
Control model	Only parties in government matter	$DVT = \alpha + \beta_1 D65_t + \beta_2 D85_t + \beta_3 GVT_t + e_t$	$DVT = -0.003 + 0.086\ D65 + -0.111\ D85 + 0.002\ GVT + e$	0.6	2.9	Only the ideology of the government has a significant beta score
General programme model	The objectives of government and opposition parties are opposed	$DVT = \alpha + \beta_1 D65_t + \beta_2 D85_t + \beta_3 GVT_t + \beta_4 OPP_t + e_t$	Ditto	0.6	2.9	Ditto

DVT = the degree of income inequality; TOT$_t$ = sum of positive and negative emphases of the parties in year *t*; CON = the product of the party emphases; GVT = positive minus negative emphases of the government; OPP = same for opposition parties.

Sources: CBS (1994), *Vijfennegentig jaren statistiek in tijdreeksen*. 's Gravenhage: SDU en CBS; Klingemann et al. (1994).

Table 9.19   *Rate of fulfilment of party pledges by policy area in the USA and UK under the Reagan and Thatcher administrations*

| | USA: Republicans | | | | UK: Conservatives | | | |
| | 1980 | | 1984 | | 1979 | | 1983 | |
	Fulfilled %	*n*	Fulfilled %	*n*	Fulfilled %	*n*	Fulfilled %	*n*
Social welfare	66.7	30	53.8	13	88.2	17	84.2	19
Economic	64.6	48	55.9	34	84.4	32	86.1	36
Civil rights/liberties	36.4	11	63.6	11	50	8	100	1
Natural resources	55	20	70	10	57.1	7	88.9	9
Education	33.3	6	16.7	6	100	4	66.6	3
Crime	50	4	77.8	9	83.3	6	100	6
Other	90	10	66.7	6	100	4	100	7
Total	61.2	129	58.4	89	80.8	78	87.6	81

Source: Royed (1996). *n* = the total number of pledges.

goals than the Reagan administration. Royed argues that the high performance in the Thatcher era is *not* borne out by leadership qualities or economic circumstances (these factors were similar in both countries) but by the decision-making environment.

The fact that Royed reaches a different conclusion than Budge and Hofferbert is based on their different conceptualization, operationalization, theoretical assumptions and data gathering. Although their research questions are the same, the differences in research design result in a different research answer. Instead of correlating platform pledges to spending data (as Budge and Hofferbert did), Royed examines relationships between 'real' pledges and 'real' fulfilments. This alternative approach leads to the plausible outcome that the effectiveness of the decision-making system is higher in the UK than in the USA.

9.8 Conclusions

In this chapter we have illustrated several research designs related to output and/or performance in the socio-economic, democratic and international domains. Most designs have in common that they are looking for the variations in performance given different sets of actors, institutions and conditions. In this chapter we have used several designs, among them a most similar design (*n* = 12) based on one time point (the year 1900) in Section 9.3; a most similar design (*n* = 18) for three aggregated time periods in Section 9.4; a pooled time series analysis on 18 countries and 26 time points and a most different design in Section 9.6; a time series analysis based on one country in Section 9.7.

The ways in which the sections are summarized in Table 9.20 are, of course, simplifications of the research question, the research design and the research

Table 9.20 Overview and examples of the main stages in comparative research on types of policy outputs and performance

Research question	Research design	Research answer
§9.3 To what extent do actors (parties, unions) affect socio-economic policy-making?	Conceptualization and operationalization of (in)dependent variables and selection of cases, time period and techniques (i.e. Boolean analysis and fuzzy-set methodology)	The influence of parties and unions depends on the time period and the institutional environment
§9.4 What role do institutions play in socio-economic problem-solving?	Ditto. A special problem is the discrepancy between the theoretical and empirical variance of many institutional variables	Institutions affect the type and degree of socio-economic interventionism, but the 'fit' is moderate
§9.5 Do governments affect their re-election prospects by means of incidental or strategic policy-making?	Design of a cross-national and longitudinal test of public expenditures before and after elections	There is no cross-national generalizable evidence on the manipulation of the re-election results
§9.6 How do democratization and democraticness relate to welfare indicators?	Statistical tests on model's is that include democracy, welfare indicators and institutional variables	The tests show some correspondence between democracy and welfare, but they are neither necessary nor sufficient conditions
§9.7 Under which political-institutional conditions do we find a firm connection between 'party pledges' and 'pledge fulfilment'?	Conceptualization and operationalization of the 'mandate model'	Majoritarian democracies offer better conditions for 'pledge fulfilment'. All forms of power-sharing (also within majoritarian democracies) hamper 'pledge fulfilment'

answer. Yet, in general, it is important to be able to summarize in one or two sentences the main steps that are taken in any research.

The importance of the research design for the results of the research has several implications:

1 Two researchers, asking the same question, may obtain different results because of a different research design.
2 The research design leads one to the answer, and by manipulating the design one may direct the research to one particular answer, mostly the one that confirms the research question.

The first implication is rather common and even crucial for making progress in political science, as it stimulates discussion and critical evaluation. In Section 9.7 we have seen an example which relates to the mandate theory. The second implication is more problematic. To solve this problem, there are several rules which have to be followed in order to make the research plausible and reliable:

1 The model should be correctly specified, and the assumptions of statistical analysis should not be violated.
2 Alternative insights, results and explanations should be discussed during all the steps taken during the research.
3 All the steps should be presented in such a way that others can replicate the research as it is done.

These three conditions for scientific research also form a checklist which can be used to check the overall validity and reliability of the results which are reported in papers and publications.

9.9 Endmatter

Topics highlighted

The effects of the interactions between political institutions and actors on socio-economic policy formation are explored by means of the following research questions (the prevailing techniques are Boolean analysis, regression analysis, factor analysis, ANOVA and discriminant analysis):

1 To what extent do actors (parties, unions) affect socio-economic policy-making?
2 What role do institutions play in socio-economic problem-solving?
3 Do governments affect their re-election prospects by means of incidental or strategic policy-making?
4 To what extent does the degree of democracy depend on economic welfare?
5 Under which political-institutional conditions do we find a firm connection between 'party pledges' and 'pledge fulfilment'?

Exercises

The purpose of the following exercises is to get acquainted with the empirical and technical aspects of data-analysis on socio-economic policy output and performance. The exercises correspond with the preceding sections. The rough working may help you through a possible impasse, but first come up with your own solution before looking at the working.

- 9.1. Welfare related output and outcomes

File: nias.sav.

1   Compute the WEDC scale with the help of factor analysis on the variables dtax, sscap, sscwo, ed, he, trans.
2   Compute the TEDC scale with the help of factor analysis on the variables def, tax, pe, ssc.
3   Both examine and correct for autocorrelation in a model that tries to explain the variations in the WEDC and TEDC variables. Split the model into cross-time and cross-sectional components and report the results.
4   Also determine what difference it makes whether the WEDC and TEDC scales are measured on the basis of time series or on the basis of separate years. How do you explain this difference?

Suggested steps: 1. Calculate the two scales both for each year and on the basis of the pooled time series data. 2. Construct a model that includes cross-sectional variables such as corporatism and leadership and with time series variables (the openness of the economy, trade union density, the share of left votes). 3. Perform a PCSE and an OLS regression on WEDC. 4. Split the country and year variables into dummy variables and incorporate them into two separate models. 5. Report on the results.
Background reading: Keman (1993b).

- 9.2. Actors and socio-economic problem-solving (using Boolean analysis and fuzzy sets)

Examine the material on the working papers section of the Compass website, http://www.compasss.org. There you will find a number of recent applications of the fuzzy set logic. Select one paper and argue to what extent the fuzzy set theory offers a new comparative methodology that is able to overcome problems which are claimed to be typical of the traditional quantitative and qualitative approaches.
Background reading: Ragin (2000).

- 9.3. Institutions and socio-economic problem-solving

File: poL4.sav.

In general we may predict that corporatism, consociationalism and a cooperative style of political leadership enhance state interventionism in the socio-economic realm. Apply residual analysis in order to examine the exceptions to this 'rule'. What are the theoretical implications of this test?

Suggested steps: 1. Study the relevant dependent and independent variables and their intercorrelation. 2. Perform the regression analysis. 3. Study (plot) the residuals. 4. Interpret the results.

Background reading: Iversen (1999), Swank (2002).

• 9.4. Electoral cycles and macro-economic policy

File: nias.sav.

Design a test for the Lessmann model in which you incorporate alternative explanations for variations in tax levels and expenditures.

Suggested steps: 1. Determine the alternative explanatory variable for both the tax levels and public expenditure. 2. Integrate this new variable into the Lessmann model. 3. Test the model with the help of regression and report on the results.

Background reading: Lessmann (1987).

• 9.5a. Democratic performance (1)

File: vanhanen.sav.

Perform a regression of the Index of Democracy on the Index of Power Resources as included in the Vanhanen data set and include the residuals and the ID estimates. Report on how well the regression equation estimates the ID values for single countries and which countries are the most deviant cases.

Suggested steps: 1. Perform a regression analysis that includes the residual scores. 2. Study and discuss the results – see also Vanhanen's (1990: 97–9) discussion of these residuals.

Background reading: Vanhanen (1990, 1997).

• 9.5b. Democratic performance (2)

File: keman2002.sav.

This exercise will examine performance in policy areas that represent the development of *public welfare:* social policy, education and health care. These areas represent the core of the 'welfare state' (see also Keman 2002; Castles, 2004). The research question we wish to answer is: to what extent do 'age' and 'type of government' influence the policy choices made, as reflected in the allocated levels of expenditure? In other words: does it make a difference whether a democratic regime exists longer or not, and whether it is a presidential, parliamentary or a dual power system? Also give a theoretical explanation for the differences between these systems.

Background reading: Keman (2002).

• 9.6. Parties and accountability

Budge and Hofferbert have applied several models, such as the competitive, the consensus, the complementary and the control model, in order to uncover the influence of parties on the policy-making process. Test the Budge and Hofferbert mandate models for any country for which you have relevant data. Note that a test of the mandate model is also possible without any Manifesto data. You may have a look at the Dutch data in the file elfrso.sav.

Suggested steps: 1. Write an overview of the Budge and Hofferbert models and specify the underlying hypotheses. 2. Specify the models for a particular country (given the party systems and the presence/absence of a president). In the case of a multi-party system, simplify the models. 3. Specify the models for that particular country. 4. Use regression analysis to test the models. 5. Compare the results with Budge and Hofferbert's results.

Background reading: Budge and Hofferbert (1990), Royed (1996).

Further reading

- *General*: Keman (2002), Lane and Ersson (2002).
- *Specific*: Ragin (2000).

Notes

1 One rule of thumb is that one needs more than five cases per variable. Thus, in strict statistical terms, a number of 18 cases is not just 'small', but too small!
2 In our view this is not fully correct. Regression with a dichotomous variable is strictly equivalent, statistically speaking, to discriminant analysis.

Appendix

Statistical tables

Statistical probabilities for Tables A.1–A.4 have been calculated using PCalc 2.1.

Table A.1 *Cumulative standard normal distribution*

z	0.00	0.01	0.02	0.03	0.04	0.05	0.06	0.07	0.08	0.09
0.0	0.5000	0.5040	0.5080	0.5120	0.5160	0.5199	0.5239	0.5279	0.5319	0.5359
0.1	0.5398	0.5438	0.5478	0.5517	0.5557	0.5596	0.5636	0.5675	0.5714	0.5753
0.2	0.5793	0.5832	0.5871	0.5910	0.5948	0.5987	0.6026	0.6064	0.6103	0.6141
0.3	0.6179	0.6217	0.6255	0.6293	0.6331	0.6368	0.6406	0.6443	0.6480	0.6517
0.4	0.6554	0.6591	0.6628	0.6664	0.6700	0.6736	0.6772	0.6808	0.6844	0.6879
0.5	0.6915	0.6950	0.6985	0.7019	0.7054	0.7088	0.7123	0.7157	0.7190	0.7224
0.6	0.7257	0.7291	0.7324	0.7357	0.7389	0.7422	0.7454	0.7486	0.7517	0.7549
0.7	0.7580	0.7611	0.7642	0.7673	0.7704	0.7734	0.7764	0.7794	0.7823	0.7852
0.8	0.7881	0.7910	0.7939	0.7967	0.7995	0.8023	0.8051	0.8078	0.8106	0.8133
0.9	0.8159	0.8186	0.8212	0.8238	0.8264	0.8289	0.8315	0.8340	0.8365	0.8389
1.0	0.8413	0.8438	0.8461	0.8485	0.8508	0.8531	0.8554	0.8577	0.8599	0.8621
1.1	0.8643	0.8665	0.8686	0.8708	0.8729	0.8749	0.8770	0.8790	0.8810	0.8830
1.2	0.8849	0.8869	0.8888	0.8907	0.8925	0.8944	0.8962	0.8980	0.8997	0.9015
1.3	0.9032	0.9049	0.9066	0.9082	0.9099	0.9115	0.9131	0.9147	0.9162	0.9177
1.4	0.9192	0.9207	0.9222	0.9236	0.9251	0.9265	0.9279	0.9292	0.9306	0.9319
1.5	0.9332	0.9345	0.9357	0.9370	0.9382	0.9394	0.9406	0.9418	0.9429	0.9441
1.6	0.9452	0.9463	0.9474	0.9484	0.9495	0.9505	0.9515	0.9525	0.9535	0.9545
1.7	0.9554	0.9564	0.9573	0.9582	0.9591	0.9599	0.9608	0.9616	0.9625	0.9633
1.8	0.9641	0.9649	0.9656	0.9664	0.9671	0.9678	0.9686	0.9693	0.9699	0.9706
1.9	0.9713	0.9719	0.9726	0.9732	0.9738	0.9744	0.9750	0.9756	0.9761	0.9767
2.0	0.9772	0.9778	0.9783	0.9788	0.9793	0.9798	0.9803	0.9808	0.9812	0.9817
2.1	0.9821	0.9826	0.9830	0.9834	0.9838	0.9842	0.9846	0.9850	0.9854	0.9857
2.2	0.9861	0.9864	0.9868	0.9871	0.9875	0.9878	0.9881	0.9884	0.9887	0.9890
2.3	0.9893	0.9896	0.9898	0.9901	0.9904	0.9906	0.9909	0.9911	0.9913	0.9916
2.4	0.9918	0.9920	0.9922	0.9925	0.9927	0.9929	0.9931	0.9932	0.9934	0.9936
2.5	0.9938	0.9940	0.9941	0.9943	0.9945	0.9946	0.9948	0.9949	0.9951	0.9952
2.6	0.9953	0.9955	0.9956	0.9957	0.9959	0.9960	0.9961	0.9962	0.9963	0.9964
2.7	0.9965	0.9966	0.9967	0.9968	0.9969	0.9970	0.9971	0.9972	0.9973	0.9974
2.8	0.9974	0.9975	0.9976	0.9977	0.9977	0.9978	0.9979	0.9979	0.9980	0.9981
2.9	0.9981	0.9982	0.9982	0.9983	0.9984	0.9984	0.9985	0.9985	0.9986	0.9986
3.0	0.9987	0.9987	0.9987	0.9988	0.9988	0.9989	0.9989	0.9989	0.9990	0.9990
3.1	0.9990	0.9991	0.9991	0.9991	0.9992	0.9992	0.9992	0.9992	0.9993	0.9993
3.2	0.9993	0.9993	0.9994	0.9994	0.9994	0.9994	0.9994	0.9995	0.9995	0.9995
3.3	0.9995	0.9995	0.9995	0.9996	0.9996	0.9996	0.9996	0.9996	0.9996	0.9997
3.4	0.9997	0.9997	0.9997	0.9997	0.9997	0.9997	0.9997	0.9997	0.9997	0.9998

Table A.2 *Values of χ^2 corresponding to p*

df	$\chi^2_{0.005}$	$\chi^2_{0.01}$	$\chi^2_{0.025}$	$\chi^2_{0.05}$	$\chi^2_{0.10}$	$\chi^2_{0.90}$	$\chi^2_{0.95}$	$\chi^2_{0.975}$	$\chi^2_{0.99}$	$\chi^2_{0.995}$
1	0.000039	0.00016	0.00098	0.0039	0.0158	2.71	3.84	5.02	6.63	7.88
2	0.0100	0.0201	0.0506	0.1026	0.2107	4.61	5.99	7.38	9.21	10.60
3	0.0717	0.115	0.216	0.352	0.584	6.25	7.81	9.35	11.34	12.84
4	0.207	0.297	0.484	0.711	1.064	7.78	9.49	11.14	13.28	14.86
5	0.412	0.554	0.831	1.15	1.61	9.24	11.07	12.83	15.09	16.75
6	0.676	0.872	1.24	1.64	2.20	10.64	12.59	14.45	16.81	18.55
7	0.989	1.24	1.69	2.17	2.83	12.02	14.07	16.01	18.48	20.28
8	1.34	1.65	2.18	2.73	3.49	13.36	15.51	17.53	20.09	21.95
9	1.73	2.09	2.70	3.33	4.17	14.68	16.92	19.02	21.67	23.59
10	2.16	2.56	3.25	3.94	4.87	15.99	18.31	20.48	23.21	25.19
11	2.60	3.05	3.82	4.57	5.58	17.28	19.68	21.92	24.72	26.76
12	3.07	3.57	4.40	5.23	6.30	18.55	21.03	23.34	26.22	28.30
13	3.57	4.11	5.01	5.89	7.04	19.81	22.36	24.74	27.69	29.82
14	4.07	4.66	5.63	6.57	7.79	21.06	23.68	26.12	29.14	31.32
15	4.60	5.23	6.26	7.26	8.55	22.31	25.00	27.49	30.58	32.80
16	5.14	5.81	6.91	7.96	9.31	23.54	26.30	28.85	32.00	34.27
18	6.26	7.01	8.23	9.39	10.86	25.99	28.87	31.53	34.81	37.16
20	7.43	8.26	9.59	10.85	12.44	28.41	31.41	34.17	37.57	40.00
24	9.89	10.86	12.40	13.85	15.66	33.20	36.42	39.36	42.98	45.56
30	13.79	14.95	16.79	18.49	20.60	40.26	43.77	46.98	50.89	53.67
40	20.71	22.16	24.43	26.51	29.05	51.81	55.76	59.34	63.69	66.77
60	35.53	37.48	40.48	43.19	46.46	74.40	79.08	83.30	88.38	91.95
120	83.85	86.92	91.57	95.70	100.62	140.23	146.57	152.21	158.95	63.65

Table A.3 *Values of t for v degrees of freedom and p = 1 − α*

v \ 1 − α	0.75	0.90	0.95	0.975	0.99	0.995	0.9995
1	1.000	3.078	6.314	12.706	31.821	63.657	636.619
2	0.816	1.886	2.920	4.303	6.965	9.925	31.599
3	0.765	1.638	2.353	3.182	4.541	5.841	12.924
4	0.741	1.533	2.132	2.776	3.747	4.604	8.610
5	0.727	1.476	2.015	2.571	3.365	4.032	6.869
6	0.718	1.440	1.943	2.447	3.143	3.707	5.959
7	0.711	1.415	1.895	2.365	2.998	3.499	5.408
8	0.706	1.397	1.860	2.306	2.896	3.355	5.041
9	0.703	1.383	1.833	2.262	2.821	3.250	4.781
10	0.700	1.372	1.812	2.228	2.764	3.169	4.587
11	0.697	1.363	1.796	2.201	2.718	3.106	4.437
12	0.695	1.356	1.782	2.179	2.681	3.055	4.318
13	0.694	1.350	1.771	2.160	2.650	3.012	4.221
14	0.692	1.345	1.761	2.145	2.624	2.977	4.140
15	0.691	1.341	1.753	2.131	2.602	2.947	4.073
16	0.690	1.337	1.746	2.120	2.583	2.921	4.015
17	0.689	1.333	1.740	2.110	2.567	2.898	3.965
18	0.688	1.330	1.734	2.101	2.552	2.878	3.922
19	0.688	1.328	1.729	2.093	2.539	2.861	3.883
20	0.687	1.325	1.725	2.086	2.528	2.845	3.850
21	0.686	1.323	1.721	2.080	2.518	2.831	3.819
22	0.686	1.321	1.717	2.074	2.508	2.819	3.792
23	0.685	1.319	1.714	2.069	2.500	2.807	3.768
24	0.685	1.318	1.711	2.064	2.492	2.797	3.745
25	0.684	1.316	1.708	2.060	2.485	2.787	3.725
26	0.684	1.315	1.706	2.056	2.479	2.779	3.707
27	0.684	1.314	1.703	2.052	2.473	2.771	3.690
28	0.683	1.313	1.701	2.048	2.467	2.763	3.674
29	0.683	1.311	1.699	2.045	2.462	2.756	3.659
30	0.683	1.310	1.697	2.042	2.457	2.750	3.646
40	0.681	1.303	1.684	2.021	2.423	2.704	3.551
60	0.679	1.296	1.671	2.000	2.390	2.660	3.460
120	0.677	1.289	1.658	1.980	2.358	2.617	3.373
∞	0.674	1.282	1.645	1.960	2.326	2.576	3.291

Table A.4 Values of F for $\alpha = 0.05$ and v_1 and v_2 degrees of freedom for numerator and denominator

v_2 \ v_1	1	2	3	4	5	6	7	8	9	10	12	15	20	24	30	40	60	120	∞
1	161.4	199.5	215.7	224.6	230.2	234.0	236.8	238.9	240.5	241.9	243.9	245.9	248.0	249.1	250.1	251.1	252.2	253.3	254.3
2	18.51	19.00	19.16	19.25	19.30	19.33	19.35	19.37	19.38	19.40	19.41	19.43	19.45	19.45	19.46	19.47	19.48	19.49	19.50
3	10.13	9.55	9.28	9.12	9.01	8.94	8.89	8.85	8.81	8.79	8.74	8.70	8.66	8.64	8.62	8.59	8.57	8.55	8.53
4	7.71	6.94	6.59	6.39	6.26	6.16	6.09	6.04	6.00	5.96	5.91	5.86	5.80	5.77	5.75	5.72	5.69	5.66	5.63
5	6.61	5.79	5.41	5.19	5.05	4.95	4.88	4.82	4.77	4.74	4.68	4.62	4.56	4.53	4.50	4.46	4.43	4.40	4.36
6	5.99	5.14	4.76	4.53	4.39	4.28	4.21	4.15	4.10	4.06	4.00	3.94	3.87	3.84	3.81	3.77	3.74	3.70	3.67
7	5.59	4.74	4.35	4.12	3.97	3.87	3.79	3.73	3.68	3.64	3.57	3.51	3.44	3.41	3.38	3.34	3.30	3.27	3.23
8	5.32	4.46	4.07	3.84	3.69	3.58	3.50	3.44	3.39	3.35	3.28	3.22	3.15	3.12	3.08	3.04	3.01	2.97	2.93
9	5.12	4.26	3.86	3.63	3.48	3.37	3.29	3.23	3.18	3.14	3.07	3.01	2.94	2.90	2.86	2.83	2.79	2.75	2.71
10	4.96	4.10	3.71	3.48	3.33	3.22	3.14	3.07	3.02	2.98	2.91	2.85	2.77	2.74	2.70	2.66	2.62	2.58	2.54
11	4.84	3.98	3.59	3.36	3.20	3.09	3.01	2.95	2.90	2.85	2.79	2.72	2.65	2.61	2.57	2.53	2.49	2.45	2.40
12	4.75	3.89	3.49	3.26	3.11	3.00	2.91	2.85	2.80	2.75	2.69	2.62	2.54	2.51	2.47	2.43	2.38	2.34	2.30
13	4.67	3.81	3.41	3.18	3.03	2.92	2.83	2.77	2.71	2.67	2.60	2.53	2.46	2.42	2.38	2.34	2.30	2.25	2.21
14	4.60	3.74	3.34	3.11	2.96	2.85	2.76	2.70	2.65	2.60	2.53	2.46	2.39	2.35	2.31	2.27	2.22	2.18	2.13
15	4.54	3.68	3.29	3.06	2.90	2.79	2.71	2.64	2.59	2.54	2.48	2.40	2.33	2.29	2.25	2.20	2.16	2.11	2.07
16	4.49	3.63	3.24	3.01	2.85	2.74	2.66	2.59	2.54	2.49	2.42	2.35	2.28	2.24	2.19	2.15	2.11	2.06	2.01
17	4.45	3.59	3.20	2.96	2.81	2.70	2.61	2.55	2.49	2.45	2.38	2.31	2.23	2.19	2.15	2.10	2.06	2.01	1.96
18	4.41	3.55	3.16	2.93	2.77	2.66	2.58	2.51	2.46	2.41	2.34	2.27	2.19	2.15	2.11	2.06	2.02	1.97	1.92
19	4.38	3.52	3.13	2.90	2.74	2.63	2.54	2.48	2.42	2.38	2.31	2.23	2.16	2.11	2.07	2.03	1.98	1.93	1.88
20	4.35	3.49	3.10	2.87	2.71	2.60	2.51	2.45	2.39	2.35	2.28	2.20	2.12	2.08	2.04	1.99	1.95	1.90	1.84
21	4.32	3.47	3.07	2.84	2.68	2.57	2.49	2.42	2.37	2.32	2.25	2.18	2.10	2.05	2.01	1.96	1.92	1.87	1.81
22	4.30	3.44	3.05	2.82	2.66	2.55	2.46	2.40	2.34	2.30	2.23	2.15	2.07	2.03	1.98	1.94	1.89	1.84	1.78
23	4.28	3.42	3.03	2.80	2.64	2.53	2.44	2.37	2.32	2.27	2.20	2.13	2.05	2.01	1.96	1.91	1.86	1.81	1.76
24	4.26	3.40	3.01	2.78	2.62	2.51	2.42	2.36	2.30	2.25	2.18	2.11	2.03	1.98	1.94	1.89	1.84	1.79	1.73
25	4.24	3.39	2.99	2.76	2.60	2.49	2.40	2.34	2.28	2.24	2.16	2.09	2.01	1.96	1.92	1.87	1.82	1.77	1.71
26	4.23	3.37	2.98	2.74	2.59	2.47	2.39	2.32	2.27	2.22	2.15	2.07	1.99	1.95	1.90	1.85	1.80	1.75	1.69
27	4.21	3.35	2.96	2.73	2.57	2.46	2.37	2.31	2.25	2.20	2.13	2.06	1.97	1.93	1.88	1.84	1.79	1.73	1.67
28	4.20	3.34	2.95	2.71	2.56	2.45	2.36	2.29	2.24	2.19	2.12	2.04	1.96	1.91	1.87	1.82	1.77	1.71	1.65
29	4.18	3.33	2.96	2.70	2.55	2.43	2.35	2.28	2.22	2.18	2.10	2.03	1.94	1.90	1.85	1.81	1.75	1.70	1.64
30	4.17	3.32	2.92	2.69	2.53	2.42	2.33	2.27	2.21	2.16	2.09	2.01	1.93	1.89	1.84	1.79	1.74	1.68	1.62
40	4.08	3.23	2.84	2.61	2.45	2.34	2.25	2.18	2.12	2.08	2.00	1.92	1.84	1.79	1.74	1.69	1.64	1.58	1.51
60	4.00	3.15	2.76	2.53	2.37	2.25	2.17	2.10	2.04	1.99	1.92	1.84	1.75	1.70	1.65	1.59	1.53	1.47	1.39
120	3.92	3.07	2.68	2.45	2.29	2.18	2.09	2.02	1.96	1.91	1.83	1.75	1.66	1.61	1.55	1.50	1.43	1.35	1.25
∞	3.84	3.00	2.60	2.37	2.21	2.10	2.01	1.94	1.88	1.83	1.75	1.67	1.57	1.52	1.46	1.39	1.32	1.22	1.00

Table A.5   *Critical values of Kolmogorov–Smirnov test (two-sided test)*

Sample size n	$p = 0.10$	$p = 0.05$
1	0.950	0.975
2	0.776	0.842
3	0.636	0.708
4	0.565	0.624
5	0.509	0.563
6	0.468	0.519
7	0.436	0.483
8	0.410	0.454
9	0.388	0.430
10	0.369	0.409
11	0.352	0.391
12	0.338	0.375
13	0.325	0.361
14	0.314	0.349
15	0.304	0.338
16	0.295	0.328
17	0.286	0.318
18	0.278	0.309
19	0.272	0.301
20	0.265	0.294
25	0.24	0.26
30	0.22	0.24
35	0.20	0.22
> 35	$\dfrac{1.22}{\sqrt{n}}$	$\dfrac{1.36}{\sqrt{n}}$

Source: Adapted from Zijp (1974: 247)

Table A.6 *Durbin–Watson statistic (upper (d_U) and lower (d_L) critical values for a test at the 5% level of significance)*

	Number of explanatory variables									
	1		2		3		4		5	
T	d_L	d_U	d_L	d_U	d_L	d_U	d_L	d_U	d_L	d_U
15	1.08	1.36	0.95	1.54	0.82	1.75	0.69	1.97	0.56	2.21
16	1.10	1.37	0.98	1.54	0.86	1.73	0.74	1.93	0.62	2.15
17	1.13	1.38	1.02	1.54	0.90	1.71	0.78	1.90	0.67	2.10
18	1.16	1.39	1.05	1.53	0.93	1.69	0.82	1.87	0.71	2.06
19	1.18	1.40	1.08	1.53	0.97	1.68	0.86	1.85	0.75	2.02
20	1.20	1.41	1.10	1.54	1.00	1.68	0.90	1.83	0.79	1.99
25	1.29	1.45	1.21	1.55	1.12	1.66	1.04	1.77	0.95	1.89
30	1.35	1.49	1.28	1.57	1.21	1.65	1.14	1.74	1.07	1.83
40	1.44	1.54	1.39	1.60	1.34	1.66	1.29	1.72	1.23	1.79
50	1.50	1.59	1.46	1.63	1.42	1.67	1.38	1.72	1.34	1.77
75	1.60	1.65	1.57	1.68	1.54	1.71	1.51	1.74	1.49	1.77
100	1.65	1.69	1.63	1.72	1.61	1.74	1.59	1.76	1.57	1.78

Source: Adapted from R.S. Pindyck and D.L. Rubinfeld (1991) Econometric Models and Economic Forecasts. New York: McGraw-Hill, p. 568.

Bibliography

Abrams, P. (1982) *Historical Sociology*, Ithaca, NY: Cornell University Press.

Alber, J. (1982) *Vom Armenhaus zum Wohlfahrtsstaat: Analysen zur Entwicklung der Sozialversicherung in Westeuropa*. Frankfurt a.m. Main/New York: Campus Verlag.

Almond, G.A. and Verba, S. (1965) *The Civic Society: Political Attitudes and Democracy in Five Nations*. Beverley Hills: Sage.

Almond, G.A., Powell, B.G. and Mundt, R.J. (1993) *Comparative Politics. A Theoretical Framework*. New York: Harper Collins College Publishers.

Alvarez, M., Cheibub, J.A., Limongi, F. and Przeworski, A. (1996) Classifying political regimes. Unpublished manuscript, University of Chicago.

Armingeon, K. (2000) 'Swiss federalism in comparative perspective', in U. Wachendorfer-Schmidt (ed.), *Federalism and Political Performance*. London: Routledge.

Armingeon, K. (2002) 'Interest intermediation: the cases of consociational democracy and corporatism', in H. Keman (ed.) *Comparative Democratic Politics. A Guide to Contemporary Theory and Research*. London: Sage, pp. 143–66.

Armingeon, K. and Sciarini, P. (eds) (1996) 'Deutschland, Österreich und die Schweiz im Vergleich', *Sonderheft der Revue Suisse de Science Politique*, 2 (4): 277–303.

Armingeon, K., Beyeler, M. and Menegale, S. (2003) *Comparative Political Data Set 1960–2001*. Institute of Political Science, University of Berne. http://www.ipw.unibe.ch/mitarbeiter/ru_armingeon/CPD_Set_en.asp (accessed 24 September 2004).

Apter, D.E. and Andrain, Ch.F. (1972) *Contemporary Analytical Theory*. Engelwood Cliffs, NJ: Prentice Hall.

Atkinson, A.B., Rainwater, L. and Schmeeding, T.M. (1995) *Income Distribution in OECD Countries: Evidence from the Luxembourg Income Study*. Paris: OECD.

Austen-Smith, D. and Banks, J. (1988) 'Elections, coalitions, and legislative outcomes', *American Political Science Review*, 82: 405–22.

Axelrod, R. (1970) *Conflict of Interest: A Theory of Divergent Goals with Applications to Politics*. Chicago: Markham.

Babbie, E. (2004). *The Practice of Social Research* (10th edn). Belmont, CA: Thomson and Wadsworth.

Barry, B.M. (1978) *Sociologists, Economists and Democracy*. Chicago: University of Chicago Press.

Bartolini, S. (1993) 'On time and comparative research', *Journal of Theoretical Politics*, 5: 131–67.

Bartolini, S. (1995) *Electoral Competition: Analytical Dimensions and Empirical Problems*. San Domenico, Italy: European University Institute.

Bartolini, S. and Mair, P. (1990) *Identity, Competition and Electoral Availability. The Stabilisation of European Electorates, 1885–1985*. Cambridge: Cambridge University Press.

Beck, N. and Katz, J. (1995) 'What to do – and not to do – with time-series-cross-section data in comparative politics', *American Political Science Review*, 89: 634–47.

Beck, N. and Katz, J. (2004) Time series cross section issues: dynamics. Paper presented at the RC33 conference on Social Science Methodology in Amsterdam, August. Available from http://www.nyu.edu/gsas/dept/politics/faculty/beck/beck_home.html

Bendix, R. (1977 [1959]) *Weber: An Intellectual Portrait*. London: Allen & Unwin.

Berg-Schlosser, D. and de Meur, G. (1994) 'Conditions of inter-war Europe. A Boolean test of major hypotheses', *Comparative Politics*, 26: 253–79.

Berg-Schlosser, D. and de Meur, G. (1996) 'Conditions of authoritarianism, fascism, and democracy in interwar Europe: systematic matching and contrasting of cases for "small *N*" analysis', *Comparative Political Studies*, 29 (4): 423–68.

Berg-Schlosser, D. and Mitchell, J. (eds) (2002) *Authoritarianism and Democracy in Europe (1919–39)*. London: Palgrave-Macmillan.

Berg-Schlosser, D. and Quenter, S. (1996) 'Makro-quantitative vs. makro-qualitative methoden in der Politikwissenschaft – Vorzüge und Mängel komparativer Verfahrensweisen am Beispiel der Sozialstaatstheorie', *Politisches Vierteljahresschrift*, 37: 100–18.

Bergman, T. (1995) *Constitutional Rules and Party Goals in Coalition Formation. An Analysis of Winning Minority Governments in Sweden*. Umeå: Umeå University.

Berndt, E.R. (1996) *The Practice of Econometrics: Classic and Contemporary*. Reading, MA: Addison-Wesley.

Berry, W.D. (1993) *Understanding Regression Assumptions*. Quantitative Applications in the Social Sciences, 92. London: Sage.

Blalock, H.M. Jr (ed.) (1972) *Causal Models in the Social Sciences*. London: Macmillan.

Blalock, H.M Jr (1979) *Social Statistics*, second edition. Tokyo: McGraw-Hill.

Bohrnstedt, G.W. and Knoke, D. (1982) *Statistics for Social Data Analysis*. Ithaca, NY: F.E. Peacock Publishers.

Bollen, K.A. (1993) 'Liberal democracy: validity and method factors in cross-national measures', *American Journal of Political Science*, 37 (4): 1207–30.

Bollen, K.A. (1994) *Structural Equations with Latent Variables* (6th edn). New York: Wiley.

Bollen, K.A. and Paxton, P. (2000) 'Subjective measures of liberal democracy', *Comparative Political Studies*, 33 (1): 58–86.

Braun, D. (1995) 'Handlungstheoretische Grundlagen in der empirisch-analytischen Politikwissenschaft. Eine kritische Übersicht', in A. Benz and W. Seibel (eds), *Beiträge zur Theorieentwicklung in der Politik- und Verwaltungswissenschaft*. Baden Baden: Nomos.

Braun, D. (ed.) (2000) *Public Policy and Federalism*. Aldershot: Ashgate.

Browne, E.C., Frendreis, J.P. and Gleiber, D.W. (1988) 'Contending models of cabinet stability: a rejoinder', *American Political Science Review*, 82: 930–41.

Bryce, J. (1921) *Modern Democracies*, 2 vols. London: Macmillan & Co.

Bryk, A.S. and Raudenbush, S.W. (1995) *Hierarchical Linear Models: Applications and Data-analysis Methods*. Newbury Park, CA: Sage.

Budge, I. (1993) 'Rational choice as comparative theory: beyond economic self interest', in H. Keman (ed.), *Comparative Politics: New Directions in Theory and Method*, Amsterdam: VU University Press.

Budge, I. and Farlie, D.J. (1983) *Explaining and Predicting Elections: Issue Effects and Party Strategies in 23 Democracies*. London: Allen & Unwin.

Budge, I. and Hofferbert, R.I. (1990) 'Mandates and policy outputs: US party platforms and federal expenditures', *American Political Science Review*, 84: 111–31.

Budge, I. and Keman, H. (1990) *Parties and Democracy: Coalition Formation and Government Functioning in Twenty States*. Oxford: Oxford University Press.

Budge, I., Robertson, D. and Hearl, D. (eds) (1987) *Ideology, Strategy and Party Change: Spatial Analyses of Post-War Election Programmes in 19 Democracies*. Cambridge: Cambridge University Press.

Budge, I., Klingemann, H.-D., Volkens, A., Bara, J. and Tanenbaum, E. (2001) *Mapping Policy Preferences. Estimates for Parties, Electors, and Governments*, Oxford: Oxford University Press.

Burkhart, R.E. and Lewis-Beck, M.S. (1994) 'Comparative democracy: the economic development thesis', *Political Science Review*, 88: 903–10.

Burnham, P., Gilland, K., Grant, W. and Layton-Henry, Z. (2004) *Research Methods in Politics*. London: Palgrave-Macmillan.

Cameron, D.R. (1984) 'Social democracy, corporatism, labour quiescence and the representation of economic interest in advanced capitalist society', in J.H. Goldthorpe (ed.), *Order and Conflict in Contemporary Capitalism*. Oxford: Clarendon Press, pp. 143–78.

Castles, F.G. (1978) *The Social Democratic Image of Society*. London: Routledge & Kegan Paul.

Castles, F.G. (ed.) (1982) *The Impact of Parties. Politics and Policies in Democratic Capitalist States*. London: Sage.

Castles, F.G. (1985) *The Working Class and Welfare in Australia and New Zealand*. Wellington: Allen and Unwin.

Castles, F.G. (1987) 'Comparative public policy analysis: problems, progress and prospects', in F.G. Castles, F. Lehner and M.G. Schmidt (eds), *Managing Mixed Economies*. Berlin and New York: Walter de Gruyter, pp. 197–224.

Castles, F.G. (ed.) (1989) *The Comparative History of Public Policy*. Oxford: Polity Press.

Castles, F.G. (ed.) (1993) *Families of Nations: Patterns of Public Policy in Western Democracies*. Aldershot: Dartmouth.

Castles, F.G. (1998) *Comparative Public Policy. Patterns of Post-War Transformation*. Cheltenham: Edward Elgar.

Castles, F.G. (2000) 'Federalism, fiscal decentralization and economic performance', in U. Wachendorfer-Schmidt (ed.), *Federalism and Political Performance*. London: Routledge.

Castles, F.G. (2004) *The Future of the Welfare State. Crisis Myths and Crisis Realities*. Oxford: Oxford University Press.

Castles, F.G. and Mair, P. (1984) 'Left–right political scales: some expert judgements', *European Journal of Political Science*, 12: 73–88.

Castles, F.G. and McKinlay, R.D. (1979) 'Does politics matter? An analysis of the public welfare commitment in advanced democratic states', *European Journal of Political Research*, 7 (2): 169–86.

Castles, F.G. and Pierson, P. (2000) *The Welfare State Reader*. Oxford: Blackwell Publishers.

Collier, D. (1993) 'The comparative method', in A.W. Finifter (ed.) *Political Science: The State of the Discipline II*. Washington, DC: APSA, pp. 105–19.

Collier, D. and Mahon, J.E. (1993) 'Conceptual stretching revisited: adapting categories in comparative analysis', *American Political Science Review*, 87 (4): 845–55.

Colomer, J.M. (1996) (ed.) *Political Institutions in Europe*. 1st edn. London: Routledge.

Coppedge, M. and Reinicke, W.H. (1990) 'Measuring polyarchy', *Studies in Comparative International Development*, 25 (1): 51–72.

Crepaz, M.M.L. and Lijphart, A. (1995) 'Linking and integrating corporatism and consensus democracy: theory, concepts and evidence', *British Journal of Political Science*, 15 (2): 281–8.

Cronqvist, L. (2004) Tosmana – Tool for Small-N Analysis [SE Version 1.102]. Marburg.

Crouch, C. (1985) 'Conditions for trade union restraint', in L. Lindberg and C.S. Maier (eds), *The Politics of Inflation and Economic Stagnation*. Washington D.C.: Brookings Institution, pp. 115–99.

Czada, R. (1983) 'Kondensbedingungen und Auswirkungen neokorporatistischer Politikentwicklung', *Journal für Sozialforschung*, 23: 421–40.

Czada, R. (1987) 'The impact of interest politics on flexible adjustment policies', in H. Keman, H. Paloheimo and P.F. Whiteley (eds), *Coping with the Economic Crisis. Alternative Responses to Economic Recession in Advanced Industrial Societies*. London: Sage, pp. 20–53.

Czada, R. Heritier, A. and Keman, H. (eds) (1998) *Institutions and Political Choice: On the Limits of Rationality* (revised edition). Amsterdam: VU Press.

Daalder, H. (1974) 'The consociational democracy theme', *World Politics*, 26: 604–21.

Dahl, R.A. (1971) *Polyarchy. Participation and Opposition*. New Haven, CT: Yale University Press.

Dahl, R.A. (1984) 'Polyarchy, pluralism, and scale,' *Scandinavian Political Studies*, 7 (4): 225–40.

Dahl, R.A. (1998) *On Democracy*. New Haven, CT and London: Yale University.

Dalton, R.J. (1991) 'Comparative politics of the industrial democracies', in W.J. Crotty (ed.), *Political Science*. Evanston, IL: Northwestern University Press, pp. 5–43.

De Meur, G. and Berg-Schlosser, D. (1994) 'Comparing political systems: Establishing similarities and dissimilarities', *European Journal of Political Research*, 26 (2): 193–219.

de Swaan, A. (1973) *Coalition Theories and Cabinet Formation*. Amsterdam: Elsevier.

Derbyshire, J.D. and Derbyshire, I. (1990) *Political Systems of The World*. Edinburgh: Chambers.

Derbyshire, J.D. and Derbyshire, I. (1999) *Political Systems of the world* (3rd edn). Oxford: Helicon.

Diamond, L. and Plattner, M.F. (eds) (1994) *Nationalism, Ethnic Conflict, and Democracy*. Baltimore, MD: Johns Hopkins University Press.

Dierkes, M., Weiler, H. and Antal, A.B. (eds) (1987) *Comparative Policy Research: Learning from Experience*. Aldershot: Gower.

Dogan, M. and Pelassy, D. (1990) *How To Compare Nations: Strategies in Comparative Politics* (2nd edn). Chatham, NJ: Chatham House.

Downs, A. (1957) *An Economic Theory of Democracy*. New York: Harper & Row.

Dunleavy, P. and Margetts, H. (1995) 'Understanding the dynamics of electoral reform', *International Political Science Review*, 16 (1): 9–29.

Duverger, M. (1968) *The Study of Politics*. London: Routledge.

Easton, D. (1965) *A Systems Analysis of Political Life*. New York: Wiley.

Ersson, S. and Lane, J.E. (1998) 'Electoral instability and party system change in western Europe', in P. Pennings and J.-E. Lane (eds), *Comparing Party System Change*. London: Routledge, pp. 23–39.

Esping-Andersen, G. (1990) *The Three Worlds of Capitalism*. Cambridge: Polity Press.

Esping-Andersen, G. (1999) *Social Foundations of Post-Industrial Economies*. Oxford: Oxford University Press.

Everitt, B.S. (1993) *Cluster Analysis (3rd edn)*. London: Heinemann.

Farr, J., Dryzek, J.S. and Leonard, S.T. (1995) *Political Science in History, Research Programs and Political Traditions*, Cambridge: Cambridge University Press.

Finer, S. E. (1970) *Comparative Government*. Harmondsworth: Penguin.

Flora, P. (1974) *Modernisierungsforschung: Zur empirischen Analyse der gesellschaftlichen Entwicklung*. Opladen: Westdeutscher Verlag.

Fox, J. (1991) *Regression Diagnostics*. Quantitative Applications in the Social Sciences, 79 Newbury Park, CA: Sage.

Fox, J. (1997) *Applied Regression Analysis*. London: Sage.

Freedom House (2005) *Freedom in the World 2004. The Annual Survey of Political Rights and Civic Liberties*. www.freedomhouse.org Accessed 16 June 2005.

Frendreis, J.P. (1983) 'Explanation of variation and detection of covariation: the purpose and logic of comparative analysis', *Comparative Political Studies*, 16: 255–72.

Frendreis, J.P., Gleiber, D. and Browne, E. (1986) 'The study of cabinet dissolutions in parliamentary democracies', *Legislative Studies Quarterly*, 11.

Gallagher, M., Laver, M. and Mair, P. (2001) *Understanding Comparative Politics. A Framework for Analysis*. London and New York: Routledge.

Gastil, R.D. (1990) 'The comparative survey of freedom: experiences and suggestions', *Studies in Comparative International Development*, 25: 25–50.

Gerth, H.H. and Wright, M.C. (eds) (1968) *From Max Weber*. London: Macmillan Press.

Giddens, A. (1971) *Capitalism and Modern Theory: An Analysis of the Writings of Marx, Durkheim and Weber*. Cambridge: Cambridge University Press.

Goodin, R.E. and Klingemann, H.-D. (1996) *A New Handbook of Political Science*. Oxford: Oxford University Press.

Greene, W.H. (2003) *Econometric Analysis* (5th edn). London: Prentice Hall.

Grofman, B. (1982) 'A dynamic model of protocoalition formation in ideological N-Space', *Behavioural Science*, 27: 77–90.

Gurr, T.R. (1970) *Why Men Rebel*. Princeton, NJ: Princeton University Press.

Hague, R. and Harrop, M. (2004) *Comparative Government and Politics: An Introduction* (6th edn). London: Palgrave-Macmillan.

Héritier, A. (1993) 'Policy network analysis: a tool for comparative research', in H. Keman (ed.), *Comparitive Politics. New Directions in Theory and Method*, Amsterdam: VU University Press.

Heywood, P. (1997) *Politics*. Basingstoke: Macmillan.

Hibbs, D.R. (1987) *The Political Economy of Industrial Democracies*. Harvard, Harvard University Press.

Hix, S. (1999) *The Political System of the European Union*. London: Macmillan.

Holsti, O.R. (1969) *Content Analysis for the Social Sciences and Humanities*. Reading, MA: Addison-Wesley.

Holt, R.T. and Turner, J.E. (eds) (1970) *The Methodology of Comparative Research*. New York: Free Press.

Huber, J. and Inglehart, R. (1995) 'Expert interpretations of party space and party locations in 42 societies', *Party Politics*, 1 (1): 73–111.

Huber, E. and Stephens, J.D. (2001) *Development and Crisis of the Welfare State: Parties and Policies in World Markets*. Chicago: University of Chicago Press.

Inglehart, R. (1990) *Culture Shift in Advanced Industrial Society.* Princeton, NJ: Princeton University Press.

Inglehart, R. (1997) *Modernization and Postmodernization: Cultural, Economic, and Political Change in 43 Societies.* Princeton, NJ: Princeton University Press.

Iversen, T. (1999) *Contested Economic Institutions. The Politics of Macroeconomics and Wage Bargaining in Advanced Democracies.* Cambridge: Cambridge University Press.

Iversen, T. (2002) *Contested Economic Institutions. The Politics of Macroeconomics and Wage Bargaining in Advanced Democracies.* Cambridge: Cambridge University Press.

Jaccard, J., Turrisi, R. and Wan, C.K. (1990) *Interaction Effects in Multiple Regression.* Quantitative Applications in the Social Sciences, 72. London: Sage.

Jaggers, K. and Gurr, T.R. (1995) 'Tracking democracy's third wave with the Polity III data', *Journal of Peace Research,* 32 (4): 469–82.

Janoski, T. and Hicks, A.M. (1994) *The Comparative Political Economy of the Welfare State.* Cambridge: Cambridge University Press.

Kamrava, M. (1996) *Understanding Comparative Politics. A Framework for Analysis.* London: Routledge.

Kanji, G.P. (1999) *100 Statistical Tests.* London: Sage.

Kaplan, D. (ed.) (2002) *The Sage Handbook of Quantitative Methodology for the Social Sciences.* Newbury Park, CA and London: Sage.

Katz, R.S. and Mair, P. (1992) *Party Organizations: A Data Handbook on Party Organizations in Western Democracies, 1960–1990.* London: Sage.

Katzenstein, P. (1985) *Small States in World Markets: Industrial Policy in Europe.* Ithaca, NY: Cornell University Press.

Katznelson, I. and Milner, H. (eds) (2002) *Political Science: The State of the Discipline.* New York: Norton.

Keman, H. (1988) *The Development Towards Surplus Welfare: Social Democratic Politics and Policies in Advanced Capitalist Democracies, 1965–84.* Amsterdam: CT Press.

Keman, H. (1990) 'Social democracy and welfare statism', *Netherlands Journal of Social Sciences,* 26 (1): 17–34.

Keman, H. (1993a) 'Proliferation of the welfare state. Comparative profiles of public sector management, 1965–90', in K.A. Eliassen and J. Kooiman (eds), *Managing Public Organizations.* London: Sage, pp. 13–33.

Keman, H. (1993b) 'The politics of managing the mixed economy', in H. Keman (ed.), *Comparative Politics. New Directions in Theory and Method.* Amsterdam: VU University Press, pp. 161–89.

Keman, H. (1993c) 'Comparative Politics: a distinctive approach to political science?', in H. Keman (ed.), *Comparative Politics. New Directions in Theory and Method.* Amsterdam: VU University Press, pp. 31–57.

Keman, H. (ed.) (1993d) *Comparative Politics. New Directions in Theory and Method.* Amsterdam: VU University Press.

Keman, H. (1995) 'The Low Countries: confrontation and coalition in segmented societies', in J. Colomer (ed.), *Political Institutions in Europe.* London: Routledge, pp. 211–53.

Keman, H. (ed.) (1997) *The Politics of Problem-Solving in Postwar Democracies.* Basingstoke: Macmillan.

Keman, H. (1998) 'Political institutions and public governance', in R. Czada, A. Héritier and H. Keman (eds), *Institutions and Political Choice. On the Limits of Rationality.* Amsterdam: VU University, pp. 109–33.

Keman, H. (2000a) 'Federalism and policy performance. A conceptual and empirical inquiry', in U. Wachendorfer-Schmidt (ed.), *Federalism and Political Performance.* London: Routledge.

Keman, H. (2000b) 'The structure of government', in M. Sekuchi (ed.) *Encyclopedia of Life Support Systems.* Oxford: Oxford University Press (www.eolss.co.uk).

Keman, H. (ed.) (2002a) *Comparative Democratic Politics. A Guide to Contemporary Theory and Research.* London: Sage.

Keman, H. (2002b) 'Policy-making capacities of European party government', in K.R. Luther and F. Müller-Rommel (eds) *Political Parties in the New Europe.* Oxford: Oxford University Press, pp. 207–45.

Keman, H. (2002c) 'Political institutions in the "low countries": Confrontation and coalescence in segmented societies', in J. Colomer (ed.) *Political Institutions in Europe*. London: Routledge, pp. 207–44.

Keman, H. (2003) 'Explaining miracles: third ways and work and welfare', *West European Politics*, 26 (2), 115–35.

Keman, H. and McDonald, M. (1996) 'Accountable and responsible policy-making through democratic party-government. An explorative analysis of 16 OECD nations (1972–1991)'. Paper presented at the Joint Sessions of the ECPR, Oslo.

Keman, H. and Pennings, P. (1995) 'Managing political and societal conflict in democracies: do consensus and corporatism matter?', *British Journal of Political Science*, 25 (2): 271–81.

Kim, H. and Fording, R.C. (1998) 'Voter ideology in Western democracies, 1946–1989', *European Journal of Political Research*, 33 (1): 73–97.

Kim, J.-O. and Mueller, C.W. (1978) *Factor Analysis*. Quantitative Applications in the Social Sciences, 14. Thousand Oaks, CA: Sage.

King, G., Alt, J.E., Burns, N.E. and Laver, M. (1990) 'A unified model of cabinet dissolution in parliamentary democracies', *American Journal of Political Science*, 34 (3): 846–71.

King, G., Keohane, R.D. and Verba, S. (1994) *Designing Social Inquiry*. Princeton, NJ: Princeton University Press.

Kitschelt, H. (2002) 'Popular dissatisfaction with democracy: populism and party systems', in Y. Mény and Y. Surel (eds) *Democracies and the Populist Challenge*. New York: Palgrave, pp. 179–96.

Kleinnijenhuis, J. and Pennings, P. (2001). 'Measurement of party positions on the basis of party programmes, media coverage and voter perceptions', in M. Laver (ed.), *Estimating the Policy Position of Political Actors*. London/New York: Routledge, pp. 162–82.

Klingemann, H.-D., Hofferbert, R.I., Budge, I. et al. (1994) *Parties, Policies and Democracy*. Boulder, CO: Westview Press.

Klir, G. and Yuan, B. (1995). *Fuzzy Sets and Fuzzy Logic*. Upper Saddle River, NJ: Prentice Hall.

Korpi, W. (1983) *The Democratic Class Struggle*. London: Routledge & Kegan Paul.

Krämer, J. and Rattinger, H. (1997) 'The proximity and the directional theories of issue voting: comparative results for the USA and Germany', *European Journal of Political Research*, 32: 1–29.

Kriesi, H.-P. and Koopmans, R. (1995) *New Social Movements in Western Europe: A Comparative Analysis*. London: UCL Press.

Krippendorff, K. (2004) *Content Analysis. An Introduction to its Methodology*. London: Sage.

Kromrey, J.D. and Foster-Johnson, L. (1998) 'Mean centering in moderated multiple regression: Much ado about nothing', *Educational and Psychological Measurement*, 58: 42–68.

Krouwel, A. (1999) *The catch-all Party in Western Europe 1945–1990: A Study in Arrested Development*. Doctoral dissertation, Vrije Universiteit Amsterdam.

Kvist, J. (1999) 'Welfare reform in the Nordic countries in the 1990s: using fuzzy-set theory to assess conformity to ideal types', *Journal of European Social Policy*, 9 (3): 231–52.

Landman, T. (2003) *Issues and Methods in Comparative Politics. An Introduction* (2nd edn). Oxford: Oxford University Press.

Lane, J.E. and Ersson, S. (1994) *Comparative Politics: A Theory and Approach*. Cambridge: Polity.

Lane, J.E. and Ersson, S. (1997) *Comparative Political Economy. A Developmental Approach (2nd edn)*. London: Pinter.

Lane, J.E. and Ersson, S. (1999) *Politics and Society in Western Europe*. London: Sage.

Lane, J.E. and Ersson, S. (2000) *The New Institutional Politics. Performance and Outcomes*. London: Routledge.

Lane, J.E. and Ersson, S. (2002) *Government and the Economy. A Global Perspective*. London: Continuum.

Lane, R. (1997): *The Art of Comparative Politics*. Boston: Allyn & Bacon.

Lange, P. and Meadwell, H. (1991) 'Typologies of democratic systems: From political inputs to political economy', in H.J. Wiarda, *New Directions in Comparative Politics*. Boulder, CO: Westview Press, pp. 82–117.

Laver, M. (1983) *Invitation to Politics*. Oxford: Robertson.

Laver, M. (1995) 'Party policy and cabinet portfolios in the Netherlands', *Acta Politica*, 1: 3–28.

Laver, M. (ed.) (2001), *Estimating the Policy Position of Political Actors*. London and New York: Routledge/ECPR Studies in European Political Science.

Laver, M. and Budge, I. (1992) *Party Policy and Government Coalitions*. Basingstoke: Macmillan.

Laver, M. and Hunt, W.B. (1992) *Policy and Party Competition*. London: Routledge.

Laver, M. and Schofield, N. (1990) *Multiparty Government. The Politics of Coalition in Europe*. Oxford: Oxford University Press.

Laver, M. and Shepsle, K.A. (1996) *Making and Breaking of Governments. Cabinets and Legislatures in Parliamentary Democracies*. Cambridge: Cambridge University Press.

Lehmbruch, G. (1984) 'Concertation and the structure of corporatist networks', in J.H. Goldthorpe (ed.), *Order and Conflict in Contemporary Capitalism*. Oxford: Clarendon Press, pp. 60–80.

Lehner, F. (1988) 'The political economy of distributive conflict' in F.G. Castles, F. Lehner and M.G. Schmidt (eds), *Managing Mixed Economies*. Berlin: de Gruyter, pp. 54–96.

Lessmann, S. (1987) *Budgetary Politics and Elections: An Investigation of Public Expenditures in West Germany*. Berlin/New York: Walter de Gruyter.

Lewis, P.G., Potter, D.C. and Castles, F.G. (eds) (1978) *The Practice of Comparative Politics: A Reader*. London: Longman.

Lichbach, M.I. and Zuckerman, A.S. (1997) *Comparative Politics. Rationality, Culture and Structure*. Cambridge: Cambridge University Press.

Lijphart, A. (1968) *The Politics of Accommodation: Pluralism and Democracy in the Netherlands*. Berkeley: University of California Press.

Lijphart, A. (1971) 'Comparative politics and the comparative method', *American Political Science Review*, 65: 682–93.

Lijphart, A. (1975) 'The comparable cases strategy in comparative research', *Comparative Studies*, 8 (2): 158–77.

Lijphart, A. (1977) *Democracy in Plural Societies: A Comparative Exploration*. New Haven, CT and London: Yale University Press.

Lijphart, A. (1984) *Democracies. Patterns of Majoritarian and Consensus Government in Twenty-One Democracies*. New Haven, CT and London: Yale University Press.

Lijphart, A. (1994) 'Democracies: forms, performance, and constitutional engineering', *European Journal of Political Research*, 25 (1): 1–17.

Lijphart, A. (1997) 'Dimensions of democracy', *European Journal of Political Research*, 31 (1–2): 195–204.

Lijphart, A. (1999) *Patterns of Democracy. Government Forms and Performance in Thirty-six Countries*. New haven, CT and London: Yale University Press.

Lijphart, A. and Crépaz, M. (1991) 'Corporatism and consensus democracy in eighteen countries', *British Journal of Political Science*, 21: 235–46.

Linz, J.J. (1994) 'Presidential or parliamentary democracy: does it make a difference?' in J.J. Linz and A. Valenzuela (eds), *The Failure of Presidential Democracy. Vol. 1: Comparative Perspectives*. Baltimore, MD: Johns Hopkins University Press, pp. 3–87.

Lipset, S.M. (1963) *Political Man: The Social Bases of Politics*. New York: Doubleday Anchor Books.

Lipset, S.M. and Rokkan, S. (1967) 'Cleavage structures, party systems, and voter alignments: An introduction', in S.M. Lipset and S. Rokkan (eds) *Party Systems and Voter Alignments: Cross-national Perspectives*. New York: Free Press, pp. 1–64.

Long, J.S. (1983) *Confirmatory Factor Analysis. Quantitative Applications in the Social Sciences*, 33. London: Sage.

Mackie, T.T. and Rose, R. (1991) *The International Almanac of Electoral History*. London/Basingstoke: Macmillan Press.

Macridis, R.C. and Burg, S.L. (1991) *Introduction to Comparative Politics: Regimes and Change*. (2nd edn) New York, Harper Collins.

Mair, P. (1996a) 'Party systems and structures of competition', in L. LeDuc, R.G. Niemi and P. Norris (eds), *Comparative Democratic Elections*. Beverly Hills, CA: Sage, pp. 83–106.

Mair, P. (1996b) 'Comparative politics: an overview', in R.E. Goodin and H.-D. Klingemann (eds), *A New Handbook of Political Science*. Oxford: Oxford University Press, pp. 309–35.

Mair, P. (2002) 'In the aggregate: mass electoral behaviour in western Europe, 1950–2000', in H. Keman (ed.), *Comparative Democratic Politics. A Guide to Contemporary Theory and Research*. London: Sage, pp. 122–42.

Manheim, J.B., Rich, R.C., Wilnat, L. (2002) *Empirical Political Analysis: Research Methods in Political Science.* New York: Longman.

Marks, G. and Hooghe, L. (2001) *Multi-level Governance and European Integration,* Lanham, MD: Rowman & Littlefield.

Marsh, D. and Stoker, G. (1999) *Theory and Methods in Political Science.* London: Macmillan.

Mayer, L.R. (1972) *Comparative Political Inquiry.* Homewood, IL: Dorsey Press.

Mayer, L.R. (1989) *Redefining Comparative Politics: Promise versus Performance,* Beverley Hills, CA and London: Sage.

McDonald, M.D., Budge, I. and Pennings, P. (2004) 'Choice versus sensitivity: party reactions to public concerns', *European Journal of Political Research,* 43 (6): 845–68.

McKeown, B.F. and Thomas, D.B. (1988) *Q Methodology.* Newbury Park, CA: Sage.

Mény, Y. and Surel, Y. (eds) (2002) *Democracies and the Populist Challenge.* New York: Palgrave.

Mill, J.S. (1872) *System of Logic,* reprinted in *John Stuart Mill on Politics and Society.* London: Fontana, 1976, pp. 55–89.

Mokken, R.J. (1971) *A Theory and Procedure of Scale Analysis.* The Hague: Mouton.

Moore, B. Jr. (1966) *Social Origins of Dictatorship and Democracy.* Boston: Beacon Press.

Myles, J. (1996) 'When markets fail: social welfare in Canada and the United States', in G. Esping-Andersen (ed.) *Welfare States in Transition. National Adaptations in Global Economies.* London: Sage.

Norris, P. (ed.) (1999) *Critical Citizens: Global Support for Democratic Government.* New York: Oxford University Press.

O'Donnell, G.A. (1979) *Modernization and Bureaucratic Authoritarianism: Studies in South American Politics.* Berkeley: Institute of Internationals Studies/UCLA.

Olson, M. (1982) *The Rise and Decline of Nations: Economic Growth, Stagflation and Social Rigidities.* New Haven, CT: Yale University Press.

Paloheimo, H. (ed.) (1984) *Politics in the Era of Corporatism and Planning.* Helsinki: Finish Political Science Association.

Pennings, P. (1995) 'The impact of parties and unions on welfare statism', *West European Politics,* 18 (4): 1–17.

Pennings, P. (1997) 'Consensus democracy and institutional change', in H. Keman (ed.), *The Politics of Problem-Solving in Postwar Democracies.* Basingstoke: Macmillan, pp. 21–42.

Pennings, P. (1998a) 'Party responsiveness and socio-economic problem-solving in western democracies', *Party Politics,* 4 (3): 119–130.

Pennings, P. (1998b) 'The triad of party system change: votes, office and policy', in P. Pennings and J.-E. Lane (eds), *Comparing Party System Change.* London: Routledge, 1 pp. 79–100.

Pennings, P. (1999) 'Explaining variations in public employment', *International Journal of Comparative Sociology,* 40 (3): 332–50.

Pennings, P. (2002a). 'The dimensionality of the EU policy space: the European elections of 1999', *European Union Politics,* 3 (1): 59–80.

Pennings, P. (2002b) 'Voters, elections and ideology in European democracies', in H. Keman (ed.), *Comparative Democratic Politics: A Guide to Contemporary Theory and Research.* London: Sage, pp. 99–121.

Pennings, P. (2003a) 'Beyond dichotomous explanations: Explaining constitutional control of the executive with fuzzy-sets', *European Journal of Political Research,* 42 (4): 541–68.

Pennings, P. (2003b) 'The methodology of the fuzzy-set logic', in S. Pickel, G. Pickel, H.J. Lauth and D. Jahn, *Vergleichende politikwissenschaftliche Methoden – Neue Entwicklungen und Diskussionen.* Wiesbaden: Westdeutscher Verlag, pp. 87–104.

Pennings, P. (2005) 'Analysing the diversity and causality of welfare state reforms with fuzzy sets', *Quality and Quantity,* 39 (3): 317–339.

Pennings, P. and Keman, J.E. (2002). 'Towards a new methodology of estimating party policy positions', *Quality & Quantity,* 36 (1): 55–79.

Pennings, P. and Keman, H. (2003) 'The Dutch parliamentary elections in 2002 and 2003: The rise and decline of the Fortuyn movement', *Acta Politica,* 38 (1): 51–68.

Pennings, P. and Lane, J.-E. (eds) (1998) *Comparing Party System Change.* London: Routledge.

Peters, B.G. (1998) *Comparative Politics: Theory and Methods.* Basingstoke: Macmillan.

Petrocik, J.R. (1996) 'Issue ownership in Presidential elections, with a 1980 case study', *American Journal of Political Science*, 40: 825–50.

Powell, G.B. (1982) *Contemporary Democracies. Participation, Stability and Violence*. Cambridge, MA: Harvard University Press.

Pierson, P. (1994) *Dismantling the Welfare State? Reagan, Thatcher, and the Politics of Retrenchment*. Cambridge: Cambridge University Press.

Popping, R. (2000) *Computer-Assisted Text Analysis*. London and Newbury Park, CA: Sage.

Przeworski, A. (1987) Methods of cross-national research, 1970–1983 in A.B. Anthal, M. Dierkes and H. Weiler (eds), *Comparative Policy Research: Learning from Experience*. Aldershot: Gower.

Przeworski, A. and Teune, H. (1970) *The Logic of Comparative Social Inquiry*. New York: Wiley Interscience.

Przeworski, A., Alvarez, M.E., Cheibub, J.A. and Limongi, F. (2000) *Democracy and Development. Political Institutions and Well-Being in the World, 1950–1990*. Cambridge: Cambridge University Press.

Putnam, R.D. (1993) *Making Democracy Work*. Princeton: Princeton University Press.

Rabinowitz, G. and Macdonald, S.E. (1989) 'A directional theory of issue voting', *American Political Science Review*, 89: 93–121.

Ragin, Ch.C. (1987) *The Comparative Method. Moving beyond Qualitative and Quantitative Strategies*. Berkeley: University of California Press.

Ragin, Ch.C. (ed.) (1991) *Issues and Alternatives in Comparative Social Research*. Leiden: Brill.

Ragin, Ch.C. (2000) *Fuzzy-Set Social Science*. Chicago: University of Chicago Press.

Ragin, Ch.C. and Becker, H.S. (eds) (1992) *What Is a Case? Exploring the Foundations of Social Inquiry*. Cambridge: Cambridge University Press.

Ragin, Ch.C. and Pennings, P. (eds) (2005) 'Fuzzy sets and social research', *Sociological Methods and Research*, (special issue), 33 (4): 423–577.

Ragin, Ch.C, Berg-Schlosser, C.D. and de Meur, G. (1996) 'Political methodology: qualitative methods', in R.E. Goodin and H.-D. Klingemann, *A New Handbook of Political Science*. Oxford: Oxford University Press, pp. 749–68.

Ravallion, M. (1994) *Poverty Comparisons*. Chur: Harwood Academic Publishers.

Riggs, F.W. (1994) 'Conceptual homogenization of a heterogeneous field. Presidentialism in comparative perspective', in M. Dogan and A. Kazancigil (eds), *Comparing Nations. Concepts, Strategies, Substance*. Oxford and Cambridge: Basil Blackwell, pp. 72–152.

Riker, W.H. (1962) *The Theory of Political Coalitions*. New Haven, CT: Yale University Press.

Roberts, C.W. (1997) *Text Analysis for the Social Sciences: Methods for Drawing Statistical Inferences from Texts and Transcripts*. New York: Erlbaum.

Roberts, B. (1978) 'The explanations of politics: Comparison, strategy, and theory', in P.G. Lewis, D. Potter and F.G. Castles (eds), *The Practice of Comparative Politics*. London: Longman, pp. 287–305.

Rokkan, S. (1970) *Citizens, Elections, Parties: Approaches to the Comparative Study of the Processes of Development*. Oslo: Universitetsforlaget.

Royed, T.J. (1996) 'Testing the mandate model in Britain and the United States: Evidence from the Reagan and Thatcher eras', *British Journal of Political Science*, 26 (1): 45–80.

Rueschemeyer, D., Huber, E. and Stephens, J.D. (1992) *Capitalist Development and Democracy*. Cambridge: Polity Press.

Sartori, G. (1970) 'Concept misformation in comparative politics', *American Political Science Review*, 64: 1033–53.

Sartori, G. (1976) *Parties and Party Systems: A Framework for Analysis*. Cambridge: Cambridge University Press.

Sartori, G. (1991) 'Comparing and miscomparing', *Journal of Theoretical Politics*, 3: 243–57.

Sartori, G. (1994) *Comparative Constitutional Engineering: An Inquiry into Structures, Incentives and Outcomes*. New York: New York University Press.

Sayrs, L.W. (1989) *Pooled Time Series Analysis*. Quantitative Applications in the Social Sciences, 70. London: Sage.

Scarbrough, E. (2000) 'West European welfare states: the old politics of retrenchment', *European Journal of Political Research*, 38 (2): 225–59.

Scharpf, F.W. (1998) 'Political institutions, decision styles and policy choices', in R.M. Czada, A. Windhoff-Héritier and H. Keman (eds), *Political Choice. Institutions, Rules and the Limits of Rationality*. Amsterdam: VU Press, pp. 53–86.

Scharpf, F.W. and Schmidt, V.A. (eds). (2000) *Welfare and Work in the Open Economy*. Oxford: Oxford University Press.

Schmidt, M.G. (1982) 'Does corporatism matter? Economic crisis, politics and rates of unemployment in capitalist democracies in the 1970s', in G. Lehmbruch and P.C. Schmitter (eds), *Patterns of Corporatist Policy-Making*. London: Sage, pp. 237–58.

Schmidt, M.G. (1987) 'The politics of labour market policy', in F.G. Castles, F. Lehner and M.G. Schmidt. (eds), *Managing Mixed Economies*. Berlin and New York: Walter de Gruyter, pp. 4–53.

Schmidt, M.G. (1989) 'Social policy in rich and poor countries: socio-economic trend and political-institutional determinants', *European Journal of Political Research*, 17: 41–59.

Schmidt, M.G. (1992) 'Regierungen: Parteipolitische Zusammensetzung', in D. Nohlen (ed.) *Lexikon der Politik*. Munich: Beck, pp. 393–400.

Schmidt, M.G. (1995) 'Germany: The Grand Coalition state', in J. Colomer (ed.), *Political Institutions in Europe*. London: Routledge, pp. 62–98.

Schmidt, M.G. (1996) 'When parties matter: A review of the possibilites and limits of partisan influence on public policy', *European Journal of Political Research*, 30 (2): 155–83.

Schmidt, M.G. (1998) *Sozialpolitik in Deutschland. Historische Entwicklung und internationaler Vergleich* (3rd edn). Opladen: Leske und Budrich.

Schmidt, M.G. (2000) *Demokratietheorien* (3rd edn). Opladen: Leske und Budrich.

Schmidt, M.G. (2002) 'Germany: the grand coalition state', in J.M. Colomer (ed.) *Political Institutions in Europe*. 2nd edn. London: Routledge, pp. 57–94.

Schmitter, Ph.C. (1974) 'Still the century of corporatism?' *Review of Politics*, 26 (1): 85–131.

Schmitter, Ph.C. (1981) 'Interest intermediation and regime governability in contemporary western Europe and North America', in S. Berger (ed.) *Organizing Interests in Western Europe: Pluralism, Corporatism and the Transformation of Politics*. Cambridge: Cambridge University Press, pp. 285–327.

Schmitter, Ph.C. (1993) 'Comparative politics', in *The Oxford Companion to Politics of the World*. Oxford: Oxford University Press.

Schneider, F. and Frey, B.S. (1988) 'Politico-economic models of macroeconomic policy: a review of the empirical evidence', in Th.D. Willett (ed.), *Political Business Cycles. The Political Economy of Money, Inflation, and Unemployment*. Durham, NC and London: Duke University Press, pp. 240–75.

Shively, W.P. (2001) *Craft of Political Research*. New York: Prentice Hall.

Siaroff, A. (1999) 'Corporatism in 24 industrial democracies: meaning and measurement', *European Journal of Political Research*, 36: 175–205.

Siaroff, A. (2000) *Comparative European Party Systems. An Analysis of Parliamentary Elections since 1945*. New York and London: Garland Publishing.

Sigelman, L. and Yough, S.N. (1978) 'Left–right polarization in national party systems: a cross-national analysis', *Comparative Political Studies*, 11 (3): 355–79.

Skocpol, T. (1979) *State and Social Revolution: A Comparative Analysis of France, Russia and China*. Cambridge: Cambridge University Press.

Skocpol, T. (1985) 'Bringing the state back. Strategies of analysis in current research', in P. Evans, D. Rueschemeyer, and T. Skocpol (eds) *Bringing the State Back In*. Cambridge: Cambridge University Press, pp. 1–45.

Skocpol, T. and Somers, M. (1980) 'The use of comparative history in macrosocial inquiry', *Comparative Studies of Society and History*, 22: 174–97.

Skrondal, A. and Rabe-Hesketh, S. (2004) *Generalized Latent Variable Modeling: Multilevel, Longitudinal and Structural Equation Models*. Boca Raton, FL: Chapman & Hall/CRC.

Smelser, N.J. (1976) *Comparative Methods in the Social Sciences*. Englewood Cliffs, NJ: Prentice Hall.

Snijders, T.A.B. (2003) 'Multilevel analysis', in M. Lewis-Beck, A.E. Bryman, and T.F. Liao (eds), *The SAGE Encyclopedia of Social Science Research Methods, Volume II*. London and Newbury Park, CA: Sage, pp. 673–7.

Snijders, T.A.B. and Bosker, R. (1999) *Multilevel Analysis: An Introduction to Basic and Advanced Multilevel Modeling*. London and Newbury Park, CA: Sage.

Spector, P.E. (1992) *Summated Rating Scale Construction. Quantitative Applications in the Social Sciences*, 82. London: Sage.

Stepan, A. (2001) *Arguing Comparative Politics*. Oxford: Oxford University Press.

Stimson, J.A. (1985) 'Regression in space and time: a statistical essay', *American Journal of Political Science*, 29 (4): 891–913.

Strøm, K. (1985) 'Party goals and government performance in parliamentary democracies', *American Political Science Review*, 79: 738–54.

Strøm, K. (1990a) 'A behavioural theory of competitive political parties', *American Journal of Political Science*, 34 (2): 565–98.

Strøm, K. (1990b) *Minority Government and Majority Rule*. Cambridge: Cambridge University Press.

Swank, D. (2002) *Global Capital, Political Institutions, and Policy Change in Developed Welfare States*. Cambridge: Cambridge University Press.

Tabachnik, T. and Fidell, L. (2001) *Using Multivariate Statistics* (4th edn). Upper Saddle River, NJ: Pearson.

Tacq, J. (1997) *Multivariate Analysis Techniques in Social Science Research*. London and Thousand Oaks, CA: Sage.

Taylor, C.L. and Jodice, D.A. (1977) *World Handbook of Political and Social Indicators* (3rd edn). New Haven, CT and London: Yale University Press.

Tilly, C. (1984) *Big Structures, Large Processes, Huge Comparisons*. New York: Russel Sage Foundation.

Urwin, D.W. (1985) 'The price of a kingdom: territory, identity and the centre-periphery dimension in Western Europe', in Y. Meny and V. Wright (eds) *Centre-Periphery Relations in Western Europe*. London: George Allen & Unwin, pp. 151–70.

van de Geer, J.P. (1986) *Introduction to Linear Multivariate Data Analysis*. Leiden: DSWO Press.

van der Brug, W. (2001) 'Analysing party dynamics by taking partially overlapping snapshots', in M. Laver (ed.), *Estimating the Policy Position of Political Actors*, London and New York: Routledge/ECPR, pp. 115–32.

van der Brug, W. (2004) 'Issue ownership and party choice', *Electoral Studies*, 23: 209–33.

van Kersbergen, K. (1995) *Social Capitalism: A Study of Christian Democracy and the Welfare State*. London: Routledge.

van Schuur, W.H. (1984) *Structure in Political Beliefs. A New Model for Stochastic Unfolding with an Application to European Party Activists*. Amsterdam: CT Press.

van Schuur, W.H. (1993) 'Nonparametric unidimensional unfolding for multicategory data', *Political Analysis* (4): 41–74.

van Schuur, W.H. (1995). 'Problems and prospects of measurement in the social sciences', in J.J. Hox and W. Jansen (eds), *Measurement Problems in Social and Behavioral Research*. Amsterdam: Stichting Centrum voor Onderwijsonderzoek (SCO), pp. 23–50.

van Wijck, P. (1991) *Inkomensverdelingsbeleid in Nederland: over Individuele Voorkeuren en Distributieve Effecten* (Income distribution in the Netherlands: on individual preferences and distributive effects). Tilberg: Tinbergen Institute Research Series, 19.

Vanhanen, T. (1990) *The Process of Democratization. A Comparative Study of 147 States, 1980–1988*. New York: Crane Russak.

Vanhanen, T. (1997) *Prospects of Democracy: A Study of 172 Countries*. London: Routledge.

Vanhanen, T. (2004) 'Struggle for democracy in Sub-Saharan Africa', *Acta Politica*, 39: 207–47.

Vergunst, N.P. (2004) *The Institutional Dynamics of Consensus and Conflict*. Doctoral dissertation,: Department of Political Science, Vrije University of Amsterdam.

Visser, J. (1989) *European Trade Unions in Figures*. Deventer: Kluwer.

Volkens, A. (1994) *Programmatic Profiles of Political Parties in 27 Countries, 1945–92: Dataset CMP94*. Berlin: WZB.

Von Beyme, K. (1985) *Political Parties in Western Democracies*. Aldershot: Gower.

Wachendorfer-Schmidt, U. (ed.) (2000) *Federalism and Political Performance*. London: Routledge.

Wallerstein, I. (1974–89) *The Modern World System* (3 vols). New York: Academic Press.

Warwick, P. (1994) *Government Survival in Parliamentary Democracies*. Cambridge: Cambridge University Press.

Weaver, R.K. and Rockman, B.A. (eds) (1993) *Do Institutions Matter? Government Capabilities in the United States and Abroad*. Washington, DC: Brookings Institution.

Weber, M. (1972, [1918]) *Wirtschaft und Gesellschaft: Grundriss der verstehenden Soziologie* (5th edn). Tübingen: Mohr-Siebeck.

White, L.G. (1994) *Political Analysis: Technique and Practice*. Belmont, CA: Wadsworth.

Wilensky, H. (1975) *The Welfare State and Equality: Structural and Ideological Roots of Public Expenditures*. Berkeley: University of California Press.

Woldendorp, J., Keman, H. and Budge, I. (1993) 'Political data 1945–90: Party government in 20 democracies', *European Journal of Political Research*, 1 (24): 1–120.

Woldendorp, J., Keman, H. and Budge, I. (2000) *Party Government in 45 Democracies. Composition, Duration, Personnel*. Dordrecht: Kluwer.

Yin, R.K. (1996) *Case Study Research. Design and Methods*. Thousand Oaks, CA: Sage.

Zyp, W.L. (1974) *Handleiding voor Statistische Toetsen*. Groningen: Tjeenk Willink.

Index

CPSIA information can be obtained at www.ICGtesting.com
Printed in the USA
BVOW09s2003200516

448961BV00006B/19/P